The Great Wall of Confinement

The Great Wall of Confinement

The Chinese Prison Camp
through Contemporary Fiction
and Reportage

Philip F. Williams
and Yenna Wu

UNIVERSITY OF CALIFORNIA PRESS
Berkeley / Los Angeles / London

University of California Press
Berkeley and Los Angeles, California

University of California Press, Ltd.
London, England

© 2004 by the Regents of the University of California

Library of Congress Cataloging-in-Publication Data

Williams, Philip F.
    The great wall of confinement : The Chinese prison camp through
contemporary fiction and reportage / Philip F. Williams and Yenna Wu.
        p.   cm.
    Includes bibliographical references and index.
    ISBN 0-520-22779-4 (cloth : alk. paper)
    1. Concentration camps—China.   2. Forced labor—China.
3. Political prisoners—China.   I. Wu, Yenna.   II. Title.
HV8964.C5C62   2004
365'.45'0951—dc22   2003024223

Manufactured in the United States of America
13   12   11   10   09   08   07   06   05   04
10   9   8   7   6   5   4   3   2   1

The paper used in this publication meets the minimum requirements
of ANSI/NISO Z39.48–1992 (R 1997) (*Permanence of Paper*).

To Patrick Hanan
and to the memory
of Helmut Martin

Contents

Illustrations

Acknowledgments

The authors gratefully acknowledge financial assistance through grants from the following organizations: Harvard University's John K. Fairbank Center for East Asian Research (postdoctoral fellowship); the University of California Pacific Rim Research Program (two-year research grant); the Chiang Ching-Kuo Foundation for International Scholarly Exchange (Walter Judd Research Grant); the Academic Senate and the Center for Ideas and Society at the University of California, Riverside; and the Pacific Cultural Foundation. Sabbatical leaves from Arizona State University and the University of California at Riverside also contributed to the completion of this project.

Internal and external reviews of this book by the University of California Press helped the authors rectify various omissions. We are most grateful for this, and especially for the editorial expertise of Randy Heyman, Mary Severance, and Sheila Levine.

The authors would like to thank the following individuals for their valuable suggestions about research materials or otherwise assisting with this project: Bu Naifu (Wumingshi), Gao Xin, Howard Goodman, C. T. Hsia, Jeffrey C. Kinkley, Perry Link, Roderick MacFarquhar, James D. Seymour, David Der-wei Wang, Harry Wu, and Ming Yang. The responsibility for any errors in the book naturally remains with the authors.

We would not have been able to obtain final approval of the revised manuscript in October 2002 without the assistance of various friends and relatives during a decade of work on this book. We particularly wish to thank Ming-Teh Hsieh and Tsun-Hsi Wu Hsieh, Kwing-Wah Chan and Grace Chan, Wen-Li Chen, Jeff Williams, Kit Williams, and Nigel.

Introduction

Claims that the twentieth century was "the American century" or that the twenty-first century is "the Chinese century" smack of great-power chauvinism and cultural provincialism. Rather than advancing the absurd notion that any one country in the modern world can dominate an entire century, Alain Besançon has aptly characterized the twentieth century as the "century of concentration camps."[1] This phenomenon of massive government restrictions and control over "undesirable" but legally innocent citizens has spanned the globe. It includes turn-of-the-century British camps to intern Boer women and children in South Africa; Japanese camps to imprison enemy civilians in its World War II Southeast Asian empire; U.S. camps to incarcerate West Coast Japanese American families during those same years; and deadly camps throughout the Eurasian land mass under the totalitarian regimes of Stalin, Hitler, and Pol Pot, to name but a few.[2] Primo Levi has warned that no nationality should imagine itself too peaceful or refined ever to institute concentration camps: "It can happen, and it can happen everywhere."[3]

1. Alain Besançon, "Why Is the Twentieth Century the Century of Concentration Camps?" International Conference on Human Rights in North Korea, 1–3 December 1999, Seoul, Korea.

2. Wolfgang Sofsky discusses the cross-cultural comparison of concentration camp systems in *The Order of Terror: The Concentration Camp,* trans. William Templer (Princeton: Princeton Univ. Press, 1997), p. 11. The internment of West Coast Japanese Americans in 1942–45 was a gross violation of their constitutional rights, but was not recognized as such by the U.S. Supreme Court until the 1980s.

3. Primo Levi, *The Drowned and the Saved,* trans. Raymond Rosenthal (New York: Simon & Schuster, 1988), p. 199.

Concentration camps intern political prisoners or others defined as undesirable, and do so outside the normal channels of a legal system. By this definition, China endured more than its share of concentration camps during the twentieth century. Moreover, China is the only major world power to have entered the twenty-first century with a thriving concentration camp system, which has been most commonly known as "the laogai system" [*laodong gaizao zhidu*] since May 1951.[4] Within a few years of the regime's founding in 1949, the government of the People's Republic of China (PRC) and its utterly dominant Chinese Communist Party (CCP, *Zhongguo gongchandang*) institutionalized two crucial components of the laogai system, "remolding through labor" [*laodong gaizao*, or *laogai*] (26 August 1954) and "reeducation through labor" [*laodong jiaoyang*, or *laojiao*] (3 August 1957).[5]

In the ad hoc system of reeducation through labor, a prisoner can be sentenced to renewable terms of up to three years in the PRC prison camp system without any sort of court hearing or legal procedure, but merely an administrative order that the "troublemaker" be sent to a camp for hard forced labor. There is no appeal process in laojiao administrative detention, which may be mandated by the Public Security Bureau, the detainee's "work unit" [*gongzuo danwei*], or even the local government's civil affairs department.[6] During the Mao Era (1949–76), laojiao inmates commonly spent two decades in forced labor camps, and during the Deng Era (1978–92), inmates had their sentences extended for as long as a decade—all without appearing before a judge or being allowed to contest the charges against them. Novelist Cong Weixi (b. 1933) and human rights campaigner Harry Wu (b. 1937) spent two decades in labor camps as a result of Mao Era laojiao administrative sentencing, and human rights stalwart Liu Qing (b. 1946) spent ten years in the camps during the Deng Era.

The other major type of PRC forced labor, remolding through labor,

4. Yang Diansheng & Zhang Jinsang, eds., *Zhongguo tese jianyu zhidu yanjiu* [Research on the Prison System with Chinese Characteristics] (Beijing: Falü chubanshe, 1999), p. 30.

5. Wu Hongda (a.k.a. Harry Wu, Hongda Harry Wu), *Zhongguo de Gulage—dalu laogai dui ji nugong chanpin zhenxiang* [The Chinese Gulag: The True Story of the Mainland's Remolding-through-Labor Brigades and Slave Labor Products] (Taipei: Shibao wenhua, 1992), p. 14. This is the Chinese-language version of Wu's *Laogai: The Chinese Gulag* (Boulder, CO: Westview Press, 1992). The PRC is a classic example of a single-party Leninist regime, in which there is hardly any separation between the government and the ruling party. We use the term "party-state" for this political amalgamation.

6. W. J. F. Jenner, *The Tyranny of History: The Roots of China's Crisis* (London: Penguin, 1992), p. 136. The Public Security Bureau is the PRC's nationwide police organ. Practically every citizen who works for a state enterprise or some other state entity belongs to a work unit with a vertical command structure.

involves some kind of conviction and sentencing, but these are hardly more than formalities. Conviction is virtually assured, and sentencing is nearly always foreordained.[7]

The capriciousness of the forced labor system derives in large part from the retarded development of the PRC legal system. The PRC's first code of criminal law was not approved and promulgated until 1979—three decades after the party-state's founding. Before 1979, judges and procurators had to make do with various draft statutes and quasi-legal "decisions" ratified by the National People's Congress, the State Council, or some other governmental body.[8] Prior to the Deng Era, PRC criminal justice thus had a pronounced ad hoc quality that made even the laogai convicts often seem more like "social undesirables" than bona fide convicted criminals.[9] This was especially true during the 1950s, when the camps housed a large percentage of political prisoners, as is typical in concentration camp systems. Laogai and laojiao prisoners were often held in the same prison camp, where the harshness of living and working conditions accentuated the "feel" of a concentration camp from the inmate's perspective.

On 29 December 1994, the watershed PRC Prison Law [*Zhonghua renmin gongheguo jianyu fa*] formally placed all the various types of prison institutions such as laogai under the umbrella term of "the prison system" [*jianyu zhidu*].[10] Yet in popular parlance and even in novels and many academic writings that have appeared since that time, the word "laogai" still thrives much as before. After all, the phenomenon it represents remains very much alive—both in the memories of former inmates and in the daily

7. Detailed background information about reeducation through labor, remolding through labor, and retained ex-inmate worker status [*liuchang jiuye*] will be provided in Chapter 2, along with a discussion of why the authors have used a more precise and China-specific translation for *laogai* than "labor reform," a term often used in Western-language scholarship. Among other shortcomings, the term "labor reform" carries the overly mild connotations of Western reform schools, which while unpleasant are simply not in the same league with laogai camps. The term also has positive connotations related to a shorter workday and prohibitions against child labor. One first-generation Western researcher of Chinese Communist rule who promulgated the term "Labor Reform" (his capitalization) while downplaying the human costs of modern Chinese forced labor was A. Doak Barnett. See *Communist China: The Early Years, 1949–55* (New York: Praeger, 1964), pp. 203–204.

8. The procurator is a type of state prosecutor, the duties of which will be explained further in Chapter 2. The National People's Congress is the PRC's major legislative organ, whose Standing Committee is under the tight control of the CCP.

9. In the Deng Era (1978–92) and Jiang Zemin Era (1992–2002), PRC criminal law continued to have an ad hoc flavor by international standards, but there was more respect for rules and procedure than during the Mao Era. Hu Jintao succeeded Jiang Zemin as the paramount leader in 2002.

10. Yang Diansheng & Zhang Jinsang, eds., *Zhongguo tese jianyu zhidu yanjiu*, pp. 3, 30.

life of convicts still serving time in labor camps. Moreover, PRC officials have accurately noted that the contrasting functions and characteristics of these various types of prisons have not changed. Scholars Yang Diansheng and Zhang Jinsang insist that the "remolding" of inmates through manual labor "still brings into play an extremely important function" of PRC corrections — even in the wake of the 1994 Prison Law.[11] Moreover, in an 8 February 1995 "Notice" issued by the State Council, "reeducation through labor" is repeatedly mentioned, as is the necessity to both "remold" and "punish" *[chengfa]* prisoners while further "developing prison enterprise production."[12]

The term "concentration camp" cannot be legally used in PRC publications with reference to that regime's prison camps, which have typically been termed "remolding-through-labor brigades" *[laogai dui]* and "reeducation-through-labor facilities" *[laojiao suo]*.[13] Nor are PRC publications allowed to contain any reference to a PRC camp as a "remolding-through-labor camp" *[laogai ying]*, a term that has been reserved since the early 1990s for the old gulag camps of the former Soviet Union.[14] However, PRC publications have regularly referred to Chiang Kai-shek's Guomindang (GMD) prison camp founded in 1941 at Shangrao in Jiangxi province as a "concentration camp" *[jizhongying]*, for it contained a sizable number of political prisoners and had a demanding forced-labor regimen.[15] According to the logic of *tifa* — PRC terms that are officially sanctioned and publishable — concentration camps cannot be said to exist in the PRC. They have supposedly appeared only in other countries or else under China's former GMD regime.

The PRC writer Wang Ruowang (1918–2001), who was incarcerated in prisons under both Chiang Kai-shek and Mao Zedong, found the conditions in Mao's prisons considerably harsher. It thus seems far-fetched

11. Ibid., pp. 195–196. Since 1994, PRC prison camps have remained laogai brigades in everything but name.

12. Ibid., p. 35. This 1995 State Council resolution is entitled "Guanyu jinyibu jiaqiang jianyu guanli he laodong jiaoyang gongzuo de tongzhi" [Notice concerning the Further Strengthening of Prison Management and of Work in Reeducation-through-Labor].

13. Although the literal meaning of *laojiao suo*, or *laodong jiaoyang suo*, is "reeducation through labor facility," it is more accurately termed a "camp" *[ying]* rather than a "facility."

14. For more on the stringency with which the party-state regulates the acceptability of written formulations *[tifa]* in the PRC's state-controlled publications (which include literature and memoirs), see Michael Schoenhals, *Doing Things with Words in Chinese Politics: Five Studies* (Berkeley: Institute of East Asian Studies, Univ. of California, 1992).

15. Xue Meiqing et al., eds., *Zhongguo jianyu shi* [A History of Chinese Prisons] (Beijing: Qunzhong chubanshe, 1986), pp. 300–303. Shangrao and other GMD prisons will be discussed further in Chapter 1. The GMD is also known as the Kuomintang or KMT.

for the PRC government to have claimed that Chiang Kai-shek enjoyed a monopoly on concentration camps in twentieth-century China.[16] Moreover, a number of laojiao inmates who emigrated from the PRC and published their memoirs abroad have commonly referred to the labor camps as "concentration camps."[17] Jeffrey C. Kinkley, the leading Western scholar on twentieth-century Chinese literature about crime and law, has also found the term "concentration camp" applicable to many of the PRC's prison camps.[18] While considerable variability among the camps is naturally present in a country as large and diverse as China, the living and working conditions in their camps have often evoked the harshness associated with concentration camps, particularly during spikes in the death rate such as the record-breaking famine of 1959–62.

There has been one major exception to the general rule of harsh conditions in PRC prison camps. A special kind of prison has been reserved for certain high-ranking or famous convicts, including the last Manchu emperor, Puyi; high-ranking prisoners of war such as the former GMD military officer Shen Zui; and well-connected PRC intellectuals like Dai Qing.

Concentration camps and other instruments of informal and quasi-legal incarceration have been a natural outgrowth of the protracted cycles of state violence in Mao Era China, where "administrative violence . . . [was a] legitimate normal policy."[19] Particularly during the Cultural Revolution, pervasive state repression joined with party-instigated mob violence to create an atmosphere of "endemic injustice" reminiscent of that which David Der-wei Wang analyzes in Li Baojia's late Qing novel *A Living Hell* [Huo diyu] (1906).[20]

---

16. Wang Ruowang's autobiographical novella "Ji'e sanbuqu" [A Hunger Trilogy] offers a stark comparison of GMD and CCP prisons. See Wang's *Yanbuzhu de guangmang* [Glory That Cannot Be Concealed] (Beijing: Renmin wenxue chubanshe, 1983), pp. 78–222. For the English translation, see *Hunger Trilogy*, trans. Kyna Rubin with Ira Kasoff (Armonk, NY: M. E. Sharpe, 1991).

17. See, for example, Peng Yinhan, *Dalu jizhongying* [The Mainland Concentration Camp] (Taipei: Shibao wenhua chuban, 1984); and Wumingshi (pseud. of Bu Naifu, alias Bu Ning), *Hai de chengfa: Xiashaxiang jizhongying shilu* [Punishment of the Sea: A True Account of the Xiashaxiang Concentration Camp] (Taipei: Xinwen tiandi she, 1985). These books will be discussed further in Chapters 3 and 4. Both authors were informally detained "undesirables," not legally convicted criminals.

18. Jeffrey C. Kinkley, "A Bettelheimian Interpretation of Chang Hsien-liang's Concentration Camp Novels," *Asia Major* 4.2 (1991): 83–113.

19. Lynn T. White III, *Policies of Chaos: The Organizational Causes of Violence in China's Cultural Revolution* (Princeton: Princeton Univ. Press, 1989), p. 13.

20. David Der-wei Wang, *Fin-de-Siècle Splendor: Repressed Modernities of Late Qing Fiction, 1849–1911* (Stanford: Stanford Univ. Press, 1997), p. 179.

Forms of extralegal incarceration and state violence are also more likely to exist in what Gregory J. Kasza calls a "conscription society" characterized by "administered mass organizations" (AMOs).[21] A single-party Leninist regime like the PRC increases its citizenry's extreme dependency and powerlessness vis-à-vis the party-state by outlawing autonomous interest groups in favor of vertically structured, party-controlled AMOs such as the PRC's national workers' federation.[22] Unquestioning and energetic obedience to commands from the higher-ups is what the party-state and its representatives expect from members of AMOs. AMO members who fail to act in concert with the leaders or who express reservations about the party line not only jeopardize their standing with the AMO, but can easily incur suspicion as passive resisters or "unreliable elements" *[bu ke xinren fenzi]*. A coercive tool like laojiao administration detention has assisted local party bureaucrats in purging the AMOs' ranks of real and imagined skeptics and passive resisters who have committed no crime but who threaten to spread a contagion of doubt and noncompliance within a work unit or an AMO. However, while laojiao and related "weapons of the mighty" have effectively disrupted the lives of millions of ordinary Chinese people, such institutional juggernauts have sometimes failed to overcome determined passive resistance and other "weapons of the weak."[23] Because of the individual acts of passive resistance by tens of millions of farmers and other ordinary PRC citizens, recklessly experimental Maoist policies such as the Great Leap Forward and forced agricultural communization proved unsustainable and eventually had to be scrapped.[24]

Although PRC laogai and laojiao prison camps formed but a part of the global century of concentration camps and conscription societies, they also bear the special imprint of Chinese culture. The corvée system of mandatory, unremunerated labor service to the state is deeply rooted in

21. Gregory J. Kasza, *The Conscription Society: Administered Mass Organizations* (New Haven: Yale Univ. Press, 1995).

22. The national workers' federation enjoys the party-state's support while accepting its heavy-handed control, usually signaled by the specious term "leadership" *[lingdao]*. On the other hand, any workers who have tried to organize labor unions that are independent of control by the CCP have been imprisoned and often treated with special brutality, as will be discussed in connection with Han Dongfang's case in Chapter 4.

23. For the theory and practice of passive resistance, see James C. Scott, *Weapons of the Weak: Everyday Forms of Peasant Resistance* (New Haven: Yale Univ. Press, 1985). The concept of "weapons of the mighty" such as laojiao that have been used in response to passive resistance and other behavior that falls outside of AMO norms is the authors'.

24. Edward Friedman, Paul G. Pickowicz, & Mark Selden, *Chinese Village, Socialist State* (New Haven: Yale Univ. Press, 1991), pp. 241–243.

Chinese civilization, as is the sentencing of convicts to forced labor in camps, mines, and military posts.[25] Furthermore, Chinese criminal law has traditionally been conceptualized more as a tool of the state than as a means of protecting individual prerogatives or rights from the encroachment of the state. We do not claim that the PRC's sprawling network of prison camps was somehow inevitable, but rather that the Chinese cultural climate proved conducive to the establishment of what Jean-Luc Domenach has called "the forgotten archipelago" of the PRC prison system.[26]

Years before Mao Zedong moved into the Zhongnanhai imperial palace in Beijing, he compared himself favorably with many of China's most famous and influential emperors.[27] Though in many ways an admiring disciple of Stalin, Mao felt even more akin to those emperors who had ordered millions of forced laborers to construct the "Great Wall" and the Grand Canal—engineering feats that often garner giddy praise from officials and tourists, but different sentiments from people such as folk song writers, who are mindful of their toll in individual lives. Perhaps the most famous folktale along these lines is "Meng-Jiang nü," which tells of a corvée laborer's wife who discovers to her horror that her husband has died under the harsh working conditions at one of the many tenuously connected frontier fortifications popularly referred to in modern times as "The Great Wall."[28]

Mao would not merely follow Stalin's lead in building a larger and more economically ambitious prison camp system than the Russian czars or the Chinese emperors had ever contemplated attempting. He went on

25. A contemporary form of month-long corvée labor service has persisted in rural areas within the PRC. See Jasper Becker, *The Chinese: An Insider's Look at the Issues Which Affect and Shape China Today* (New York: Oxford Univ. Press, 2002), p. 41.

26. Jean-Luc Domenach, *Chine: l'archipel oublié* [China: The Forgotten Archipelago] (Paris: Librairie Arthème Fayard, 1992).

27. Mao Zedong's 1945 poem "Snow" is a well-known example of such self-aggrandizing writing.

28. Actually, there was no single border fortification identifiable as the "Great Wall," a term that is more mythic than historic in its modern usage. While the Grand Canal at least served important functions in trade and transportation, the "Great Wall" frontier fortifications proved even less effective against foreign invasion than France's Maginot Line, but were erected at much greater cost in human suffering and popular resentment. According to Arthur Waldron, "In both high and popular culture, the message [about Qin Shihuang Huangdi and his frontier wall building] was usually the same: the Wall was the work of a tyrant, and had no military utility. Only rarely in the corpus of traditional literature about the border and border fortifications does one find anything positive." See *The Great Wall of China: From History to Myth* (Cambridge: Cambridge Univ. Press, 1990), pp. 27–28, 101, 203.

to declare in June 1949 that he would also "remold" [gaizao] Chinese re-actionaries through "forced labor" [qiangpo laodong] and "propaganda" [xuanchuan] into "new men" [xinren].[29]

Mao's conviction that he could successfully and permanently reconfigure the subjective world of the prisoner to become that of an avidly obedient tool of the party was certainly more ambitious than Stalin's expectations for the gulag zek, or what Mao's successors in the Deng-Jiang Era have expected from their prisoners.[30] Instead, the Deng-Jiang Era leaders seem to be pursuing their desire for monumentality with record-breaking engineering projects such as the Three Gorges Dam over the Yangzi River.[31] In contrast, Mao wished to "remold" all Chinese persons into "new socialist men" as part of a grandiose "responsibility to remold the world" [gaizao shijie de zeren].[32] Mao Era prisoners discovered that the dictator really meant what he said here, for the indoctrination and denunciation rituals in prisons known as "struggle sessions" were usually very intense, seeking to reprogram prisoners' thinking in various ways while forcing them to become adept at play-acting and rhetorical jousts. This emphasis on indoctrination and the remolding of thought in the Mao Era laogai differed sharply from what Solzhenitsyn and most other zeks experienced in the Soviet gulag, where fulfilling one's work quotas and obeying the rules were practically all that mattered to the typical warden.

Yet one cannot simply point to traditional Chinese thought as the source of the differences between Stalinist and Maoist ideas about remolding people's thinking. Originally, the Chinese term gaizao functioned as a verb that would take an inanimate thing rather than a human as its object. In describing programmatic transformations of the populace, pre-modern Chinese thinkers resorted to quite different formulations, such as "renovating the people" [xin min] or "civilizing the masses through education" [jiaohua], neither of which carried gaizao's connotations of blunt

29. Mao Zedong, "Lun renmin minzhu zhuanzheng: jinian Zhongguo gongchandang ershiba zhounian" [On the People's Democratic Dictatorship: In Commemoration of the Twenty-Eighth Anniversary of the Founding of the Chinese Communist Party], Mao Zedong xuanji [Selected Works of Mao Zedong], vol. 4 (Beijing: Renmin chubanshe, 1991), pp. 1468–1482, esp. 1476–1477.

30. Zek is an informal Russian term for a prison camp inmate.

31. The Three Gorges Dam project has been spearheaded by former premier Li Peng, whose 1997 tour of a "Potemkin resettlement village built especially for his visit" was reminiscent of the elaborately deceptive preparations made for Mao Zedong's grandiose tours of factories and farms during the Great Leap Forward. See Becker, The Chinese, p. 356.

32. Mao Zedong, "Shijian lun" [On Practice], Mao Zedong xuanji, vol. 1 (Beijing: Renmin chubanshe, 1991), pp. 282–298, esp. 296. This essay is dated July 1937.

instrumentality. Legal scholar David Finkelstein notes that *gaizao* connotes "a more thoroughgoing overhaul" than the Chinese Nationalists' terms for criminal rehabilitation, such as *jiaohua*.[33]

Because Confucius refused to consider himself a mere tool of the powerful, and since he deemed it a cardinal transgression to treat others in a manner that he himself would not wish to be treated, it stands to reason that he and his philosophical descendants would have avoided conceptual formulations in which people were to be treated as things and not as human beings.[34] Confucianism has emphasized positively transforming a person through such means as providing him a moral example to follow or finding him a proper place in a structured hierarchy—not by tempering him like a "pliant tool of the Party" through punitive hard labor.[35]

PRC notions about imprisoning and rehabilitating ("remolding") malleable offenders into conformity with state norms of conduct stem in significant part from Western thought, particularly a common zeal for new approaches to punishing deviant behavior in the Reformation, the Enlightenment, and the twentieth-century welfare state. Reformation thinkers' horror of idleness and their apotheosis of what J. M. Coetzee calls "the discipline of continual work" spread widely throughout Europe and its colonial possessions, where nineteenth-century roundups of beggars and other vagrants led to what Michel Foucault has called "the great confinement."[36] Foucault's concept of the "great confinement" is basically sound, but he errs in claiming that it peaked from 1650 to 1789; it actually peaked

33. David Finkelstein, "The Language of Communist China's Criminal Law," in *Contemporary Chinese Law: Research Problems and Perspectives,* ed. Jerome Alan Cohen (Cambridge: Harvard Univ. Press, 1970), p. 193. See also Liang Qichao, *Xin min lun* [On Renovating the People] (Taipei: Zhonghua shuju, 1978).

34. The two relevant sayings from *The Analects,* attributed to Confucius, are 2:12, *Junzi bu qi* [The noble-minded person will not be a tool], and 12:2, *Ji suo bu yu wu shi yu ren* [Do not treat others in a way you would not want to be treated yourself]. For more on the cultural and historical contexts of these sayings, see E. Bruce Brooks & A. Taeko Brooks, *The Original Analects: Sayings of Confucius and His Successors* (New York: Columbia Univ. Press, 1998), pp. 90, 111, 252.

35. The relatively low position of law and punishment in the traditional Chinese scheme of social control is discussed in Stanley B. Lubman, *Bird in a Cage: Legal Reform in China after Mao* (Stanford: Stanford Univ. Press, 1999), p. 14. Liu Binyan quotes the "pliant tool" phrase from an editorial in the late-1950s *Beijing Daily,* adding that the phrase applies to ordinary citizens and convicts as well as party members. See Liu Binyan, *A Higher Kind of Loyalty,* trans. Zhu Hong (New York: Random House, 1990), p. 96.

36. J. M. Coetzee, "Idleness in South Africa," in *The Violence of Representation: Literature and the History of Violence,* eds. Nancy Armstrong & Leonard Tennenhouse (Routledge: London, 1989), pp. 119–139, esp. 125. See also Max Weber, *The Protestant Ethic and the Spirit of Capitalism,* trans. Talcott Parsons (London: Allen & Unwin, 1976).

from 1815 to 1914.[37] According to Patricia O'Brien, "Foucault's account of the . . . [Enlightenment Era] herding together of the poor and homeless into newly created hospitals and beggars' prisons was more an intentional than an implemented policy."[38]

Among the Europeans who embraced the apotheosis of labor and greatly influenced PRC corrections was Karl Marx, who claimed in 1875 that forced labor is "criminals' sole means of betterment."[39] In similar fashion, Lenin insisted in 1920 that compulsory prison labor be imposed without delay on the proletariat's enemies.[40] The right wing of state socialism also apotheosized work; in a 30 November 1933 speech glorifying Nazism, Martin Heidegger proclaimed, "All human behavior is work . . . The essence of work determines the existence of Germans and, no doubt, the general existence of humans on earth."[41] It is little wonder that laogai prison manuals for cadres and guards have inveighed against nonlaboring prisoners as "parasites" [jishengchong] upon the party-state.[42]

Enlightenment jurists of the late eighteenth century such as Jeremy Bentham (1748–1832) and Cesare Becceria successfully argued for the reduction or elimination of corporal and capital punishment in favor of imprisonment, which in both China and the West had previously functioned largely as a mode of pre-trial detention. Foucault correctly emphasizes the important legacy of greater control and surveillance of convicts through expanded imprisonment, but he fails to perceive the yawning gap that often separates theory from practice. O'Brien has noted that the architecture of most prisons in France bears little resemblance to Bentham's Panopticon—and even the relatively high degree of visual surveillance possible in the few Panopticon-like jails is of little use when the distant war-

37. Keith Windschuttle, *The Killing of History* (New York: Free Press, 1997), pp. 145–146.

38. Patricia O'Brien, *The Promise of Punishment: Prisons in Nineteenth-Century France* (Princeton: Princeton Univ. Press, 1982), p. 19.

39. Karl Marx & Friedrich Engels, "Critique of the Gotha Program," in *Basic Writings on Politics and Philosophy,* ed. Lewis S. Feuer (Garden City, NY: Anchor Books, 1959), pp. 112–132, esp. 131–132.

40. James Bunyan, *The Origins of Forced Labor in the Soviet State, 1917–1921: Documents and Materials* (Baltimore: Johns Hopkins Univ. Press, 1967), p. 119. Lenin's speech of 29 March 1920 was directed to the Ninth Party Congress, which gave its formal seal of approval to forced convict labor in April 1920.

41. Quoted in Victor Farías, *Heidegger and Nazism,* ed. Joseph Margolis & Tom Rockmore (Philadelphia: Temple Univ. Press, 1989), p. 145. *Arbeit macht frei* was a prominent slogan in Nazi prison camps.

42. *Laogai gongzuo* [The Work of Remolding through Labor] (Beijing: Qunzhong chubanshe, 1983), p. 13.

dens and guards can neither hear what the prisoners are saying nor make out their facial expressions.[43]

Bentham greatly overestimates the efficacy of putting prisoners under surveillance, claiming that it would not only deter wrongdoing by the convicts but even make it impossible for them to *think* about engaging in wrongdoing.[44] As Dorrit Cohn has observed, Foucault similarly "overstates the absolute power of the one-way gaze he derives from Bentham's penitentiary design. Modern institutions that supposedly transfix their charges in this manner are not, after all, known to produce uniformly obedient and submissive prisoners, students, workers, or sons and daughters."[45] Within the context of what Borge Bakken calls the "exemplary society," "the Foucauldian approach is insufficient by not seeing clearly enough the importance of resistance and the strategies of bending exemplary rules and evading power and control."[46] Finally, Foucault's presentation of premodern corporal punishment and modern surveillance-based incarceration as mutually exclusive ideal types does not tally with their widespread coexistence and intermingling in societies as different as nineteenth-century America and twentieth-century China. Even Jiang Zemin–Era PRC officials saw no conflict between keeping most prisoners out of public sight under "modern" jailhouse surveillance and parading death row inmates through crowded marketplaces with "premodern" placards of denunciation around their necks.

Foucault's insistence that all present-day prisons and related modern institutions can trace their genealogy directly back to Enlightenment thought and social practice obscures some crucial contributions of a third variety of influential Western thought, the proponents of the socially interventionist welfare state since 1895, such as Beatrice and Sidney Webb.[47] These theorists' influence on contemporary correctional practices in both China and the West has been stronger and yet more diffuse than their Enlightenment counterparts, both reiterating the Reformation's emphasis

---

43. According to O'Brien, "Few new [prison] structures were actually built" in France during the period Foucault claims to have been dominated by "Panopticism." See *The Promise of Punishment,* p. 14.

44. Jeremy Bentham, *The Panopticon Writings,* ed. Miran Bozovic (London: Verso, 1995), p. 105.

45. Dorrit Cohn, "Optics and Power in the Novel," *New Literary History* 26.1 (1995): 3–20, esp. 3–4.

46. Borge Bakken, *The Exemplary Society: Human Improvement, Social Control, and the Dangers of Modernity in China* (Oxford: Oxford Univ. Press, 2000), p. 2.

47. David Garland, *Punishment and Welfare: A History of Penal Strategies* (Aldershot, U.K.: Gower, 1985).

on rehabilitation and guiding legal codes and judicial practice in the direction of differentiated sentencing and graded treatment of prisoners. Unlike the Enlightenment jurists, who tailored the punishment to fit the crime but not the particular circumstances of the individual offender, welfare-state thinkers have insisted that decisions about punishment must take into consideration such factors as the convict's age, character, possible mental retardation, psychological defects, and socioeconomic status. The "surveillance"-based institutional data collection about inmates by psychologists and others in the helping professions stems from new welfare-state developments in the late nineteenth and twentieth centuries that stand in sharp contrast with Enlightenment-era uniformity in sentencing and laissez-faire skepticism about the state's role in actively rehabilitating prisoners. In contrast, Foucault inaccurately traces the helping professions' intervention in the criminal justice system to the Enlightenment, instead of to the actual period of approximately a century afterward, when prevailing ideas about the state's intervention in society were very different. Foucault keeps tracing everything back to the Enlightenment in order to bolster his dramatic but overreaching hypothesis that all of society's key modern institutions are the inexorable outcome of impersonal power relations and certain ideas that were all circulating at "one moment" in the late eighteenth century.[48]

In sum, Enlightenment thought seems to have made less of an impact on the social ideas undergirding the contemporary Chinese prison camp than either the modern welfare state or the Reformation. Like Foucauldian discourse itself, the laogai has not been very receptive to what J. G. Merquior has called the "emancipatory and humanitarian direction" in Enlightenment thought and culture.[49] In a gesture characteristic of Enlightenment thought, Bentham specifically banishes forced labor from his Panopticon prison: "As forced labour is punishment, labour must not here be forced."[50]

In terms of Chinese influences on the PRC labor camp system, the late Qing period (c. 1897–1911) is a crucial stage in the genealogy of "remolding" as a disciplinary practice aimed at individuals and groups. Influential Western doctrines such as Herbert Spencer's Social Darwinism combined with traditional Chinese ideas about exemplary norms' transformative power over human behavior to lay the groundwork for

---

48. Windschuttle, *The Killing of History*, pp. 151–153.
49. J. G. Merquior, *Foucault* (London: Fontana Press/Collins, 1985), p. 103.
50. Bentham, *The Panopticon Writings*, p. 78.

Mao Zedong's massive remolding schemes. Liang Qichao (1873–1929) argued in 1906 that China's successful entry into the competitive modern world would depend upon the popular masses' remaking their flawed cultural habits through a "mind cleansing" *[xinli xidi]*. In a similar vein some years later, Sun Yat-sen (1866–1925) advocated the institution of "psychological reconstruction" *[xinli jianshe]* for revamping what he saw as the hopelessly atomized Chinese citizen, a mere grain of incohesive sand in a shifting social dune.[51] According to Huang Jinlin, both Liang Qichao and Sun Yat-sen believed this transformative process would contribute not only to the "wealth and power" *[fu qiang]* of China, but more importantly would advance the broad masses to the level of full-fledged citizen-subjects and "masters of their country" *[guojia de zhuren]*.[52] Mao Zedong also viewed the transformative process as necessary for national wealth and power, but envisioned a violent class-based struggle among the citizenry, large segments of which would become what Hu Ping has called "tamed" *[xunhua]* objects of the party-state's avowed dictatorship *[zhuanzheng]*.[53]

As early as 1915, leftist thinkers such as Chen Duxiu had already written about "remolding the thought of youth" *[gaizao qingnian zhi sixiang]*, but they viewed this as a voluntaristic practice within society, not a task for the state's coercive power.[54] By the 1930s, various CCP functionaries had begun to discuss remolding individual humans instead of groups or abstract entities (see Chapter 2), though they had not yet applied the concept of "remolding" to their prison regimes in the Jiangxi and northern Shaanxi guerrilla base regions.[55] The first surviving published records of the CCP's avowed "remolding" of inmates through forced labor emerged from camps in the Shanxi-Inner Mongolian Border Region

51. The citations of Liang Qichao and Sun Yat-sen come from James Pusey, *China and Charles Darwin* (Cambridge: Harvard Univ. Press, 1983), p. 455.

52. Huang Jinlin, *Lishi, shenti, guojia: jindai Zhongguo de shenti xingcheng (1895–1937)* [History, Body, and Nation: The Formation of the Modern Chinese Body (1895–1937)] (Taipei: Lianjing, 2000), pp. 83–84.

53. Hu Ping (b. 1947), *Ren de xunhua, duobi, yu fanpan* [Taming of the Human, and the Responses of Evasion and Rebellion] (Hong Kong: Yazhou kexue chubanshe, 1999), p. 2. The political theorist and New York–based editor of the monthly journal *Beijing zhi chun* [Beijing Spring], Dr. Hu Ping (b. 1947), should be distinguished from the PRC-based reportage writer Hu Ping (b. 1948), author of such full-length narratives as *Zhongguo de mouzi* [China's Eyes Unpeeled] (Hong Kong: Tiandi tushu, 1990).

54. Chen Duxiu, "Tongxin" [Editorial Correspondence], *Xin qingnian* [La Jeunesse] 1.1 (September 1915): 2.

55. The Jiangxi and northern Shaanxi guerrilla bases were headquartered in Ruijin and Yan'an, respectively.

[Jin-Sui bianqu] in July 1944.[56] During the mid- to late 1940s, this nascent laogai prison camp system developed most thoroughly within various CCP-controlled regions of Dongbei (Manchuria). The system rapidly spread throughout the rest of China beginning in 1949, when Mao Zedong's essay "On the People's Democratic Dictatorship" revealed his intention to remold Chinese prisoners nationwide through "forced" *[qiangpo]* labor and indoctrination.[57]

Nearly every ex-inmate novelist and memoir writer discussed in this book bore the searing consequences of this essay's words, often for years at a stretch. Across China, these words would keep demanding new prison walls, very often built by the prisoners themselves. These walls attracted no foreign tourists and few patriotic apostrophes to China's majesty, but participated in the greatest confinement China had ever seen.

Chapter 1 probes the cultural foundations of China's prison camp system, from ancient times to the Republican Era dominated by Chiang Kai-shek's Guomindang. Chapter 2 traces the development of the Chinese Communist prison camp system from the Jiangxi Soviet in the 1930s to the PRC's Deng-Jiang Era. Chapters 3 and 4 draw mainly upon inmate memoirs and prison fiction to examine the cycle of incarceration in a PRC prison camp, spanning from arrest and initial detention to death or release. Chapter 5 explores ex-prisoners' motivations for writing and analyzes several types of prison writings, including specific literary texts.

As with any literary work or testimonial text, no simplistic mirroring of reality is involved; each of the narratives analyzed in this study has been generated by a fallible human consciousness that necessarily *filters* reality during the processes of thought and representation.[58] Shoshana Felman and Dori Laub are right that neither testimony nor literature simply "reflects" or "mirrors" reality. Yet their poststructuralist assumptions about the "impossibility of representation" lead them to the absurd conclusion that the Nazi Holocaust is *"historically impossible, an event without a referent"* (original italics, p. 102). In fact, Hitler's *Mein Kampf* cites the Turkish government's violent obliteration of that country's Armenian minority of nearly 2 million people in 1915 as a general blueprint for his plans to destroy European Jewry without encountering unmanageable "inter-

---

56. Xue Meiqing et al., *Zhongguo jianyu shi*, p. 338.

57. The severe connotations of "remolding" are discussed in J. Y. Fyfield, *Re-educating Chinese Anti-Communists* (New York: St. Martin's Press, 1982), p. 73.

58. Shoshana Felman & Dori Laub, *Testimony: Crises of Witnessing in Literature, Psychoanalysis, and History* (New York: Routledge, 1992), pp. xiv–xv.

ference" from the international community.[59] A cursory acquaintance with the literature of testimony from early twentieth-century Armenian survivors might have saved Felman and Laub from jumping to the self-defeating conclusion that the Nazi Holocaust "does not enter, and cannot be framed by, any existing frame of reference (be it of knowledge or belief)."[60] The mere fact that the coinage of the term "genocide" coincided with the Nazi Holocaust could not lead anyone but a hard-core nominalist to the Eurocentric conclusion that earlier genocides simply did not happen or can be responsibly ignored—including genocides of non-Western provenance.

Here we argue that both mimetic and symbolic representation remain key functions of most testimony and literature, and that notions of "reflection" and "mirroring" are vulgar distortions of the concept of mimesis, which refers to the approximate *imitation* of reality rather than the supposed duplication or "replacement" of reality.[61] The inability of any work of narration to mirror or reflect reality in its vast complexity does not imply that prison camp narratives are mimetically insignificant, for intersubjective agreement among sources does lead to a degree of objectivity, though certainly not to an *absolute* objectivity.[62] In general, mimesis in representation tends to be denser in nonfictional testimonial narratives and reportage than it is in prison camp fiction, which is often

59. A classic account of the Armenian genocide is Arnold J. Toynbee, *Armenian Atrocities: The Murder of a Nation* (London: Hodder & Stoughton, 1915). Toynbee also exposes the "internal affair" excuse for inaction in the face of flagrant human rights abuses as an evasion of responsibility. "The American ambassador at Constantinople, after asking the Turkish Government in vain to stop the massacres [of Armenians], proceeded to address himself to the German Ambassador; but Herr Wangenheim declared that he could not interfere in any way with Turkey's internal 'affairs'"(p. 110).

60. Felman & Laub, *Testimony*, pp. 102–103.

61. Though Marston Anderson reasonably assumes that twentieth-century Chinese fiction can "focus on psychological and emotional realities," he later turns around and makes an unproven poststructuralist pronouncement about the supposed failure of "the mimetic undertaking" due to "realism's hidden agenda" to "truly replace reality" as a "substitution" for it. See *The Limits of Realism: Chinese Fiction in the Revolutionary Period* (Berkeley: Univ. of California Press, 1990), pp. 96, 200. Even purveyors of "socialist realism" (more accurately, revolutionary romanticism) who have parroted the party line about how literature directly "reflects" reality have not gone so far as to make the still more untenable claim that writing is a "true replacement" for reality, placing the two on an equal plane.

62. On the continuing relevance of mimesis to literary representation, see Robert Storey, *Mimesis and the Human Animal: On the Biogenetic Foundations of Literary Representation* (Evanston, IL: Northwestern Univ. Press, 1996); Philip F. Williams, "Can We Paradigm? Re-examining the Mimetic Heresy and Some Other Imbroglios in Recent Western-Language Academic Studies of Modern Chinese Literature," *Tamkang Review: A Quarterly of Comparative Studies of Chinese and Foreign Literatures* 30.3 (2000): 111–148, esp. 117–121.

colored by romantic or symbolic motifs, and is sometimes downright idealized.

Specialists in literature and other readers who are particularly interested in the literary aspects of prison camp writings may wish to skip ahead to Chapter 5 before turning back to read the first four chapters. Historians and social scientists may be better off reading the chapters in order.

Although a broad variety of literary texts contribute to the discussion that follows, this book does not aim at an exhaustive treatment of any particular writer or literary narrative within the subgenre of prison fiction and reportage. Instead, *The Great Wall of Confinement* provides an interdisciplinary overview that hopefully will stimulate further research in this area.

CHAPTER I

The Cultural Foundations of China's Prison Camp System

Several conditions have contributed to the endurance of the PRC's prison camp system. For approximately two and a half millennia, traditional Chinese political and legal culture has countenanced and institutionalized forced labor for both public works civilian conscripts (corvée labor) and prisoners. Of particularly ancient provenance, conscript labor *[yi, yaoyi]* has a history of over three millennia in China. On the other hand, no solid evidence points to Chinese convict labor *[tuxing* or *tuyi]* earlier than the Spring and Autumn period (722–468 B.C.E.) of the mid- to late Zhou dynasty.[1]

China's traditional political culture also placed very little in the way of legal or religious restraints on the ruler's power to mobilize forced laborers, often on a large scale.[2] Michael Loewe notes that "no sanctions existed which could limit the power of the ruler" in the legacy of legal thought and practice that was passed down to the imperial dynasties from their pre-Qin predecessors. This was the case even among the relatively secularized kingdoms and dukedoms of the Warring States period (481–

---

1. Li Jiafu, *Zhongguo fazhi shi* [A History of China's Legal System] (Taipei: Lianjing chuban shiye gongsi, 1988), p. 175. Forced labor on public projects began at least as early as Roman times in the West; see Norman Johnston, *The Human Cage: A Brief History of Prison Architecture* (New York: Walker & Co., 1973), p. 5. The ancient Greeks' practice of private slavery obviously predates this Roman practice and has also existed to a far more modest degree throughout the bulk of Chinese history. However, the subject of private slavery falls outside the scope of this book, which focuses instead on state-managed forced labor.

2. See Michael Loewe, "The Heritage Left to the Empires," in *The Cambridge History of Ancient China: From the Origins of Civilization to 221 B.C.,* ed. Michael Loewe & Edward L. Shaughnessy (Cambridge: Cambridge Univ. Press, 1999), p. 1009.

221 B.C.E.), when no ruler could reasonably claim to have an exclusive mandate from Heaven or some other supernatural entity. "But if they could not point to a source of power to which they could ascribe the prime origin of their own commands," adds Loewe, "neither were they inhibited by the need to obey such an authority or godhead; there was no concept of law that could override a monarch's own decisions."[3] R. P. Peerenboom makes a similar point: even if dressed up in Confucian morality, "the all-powerful Legalist sovereign remained above the law," which was "whatever the ruler declared it to be." Peerenboom also compares the twentieth-century leadership of the Chinese Communist Party with the imperial monarch: both were positioned high above a very malleable sort of law.[4]

Another factor favoring forced labor has been that the officials who actually drafted or sentenced forced laborers were thereby enabling the revenue-strapped traditional government to perform various beneficial tasks. According to Brian E. McKnight and James T. C. Liu, "Traditional Chinese governments did not collect sufficient revenues to permit them to pay for a great many necessary local functions," and thus had to draft local residents "to perform these functions."[5]

Furthermore, Chinese officials' decrees of forced labor have not been limited by a concept of the individual Chinese subject's autonomy or rights. This strongly hierarchical society has severely subordinated the individual's discretion and prerogatives to collective entities such as the family, the clan, the village, the guild, and the state. The Chinese discourse on individual rights emerged only in the wake of ideas selectively imported since the nineteenth century from the West and Japan, and has tended to treat rights as mere creations of the state or "legislative enactments" that the government can restrict or invalidate at its own discretion.[6] To the extent that rights could be argued to have implicitly existed in premodern Chinese legal thought, they were greatly overshadowed by duties and heavily dependent upon "the relationship of individuals to each other"

3. Ibid., p. 1004.

4. R. P. Peerenboom, *Law and Morality in Ancient China: The Silk Manuscripts of Huang-Lao* (Albany: State Univ. of New York Press, 1993), p. 269.

5. Brian E. McKnight & James T. C. Liu, trans., *The Enlightened Judgments, Ch'ing-ming Chi: The Sung Dynasty Collection* (Albany: State Univ. of New York Press, 1999), p. 123. These collected accounts of legal cases from the Southern Song (1127–1279) include a number dealing with corvée labor draftees (pp. 123–127) and convicts sentenced to forced labor or "registered control" (pp. 419–494).

6. Andrew J. Nathan, *Chinese Democracy* (Berkeley: Univ. of California Press, 1985), p. 116.

within a hierarchy that provided a context for their articulation.[7] According to Philip C. C. Huang, the Qing dynasty legal code "never conceded anything like inviolable rights guaranteed by a law that rose above the will of a sovereign and that could be asserted against arbitrary interference by the state."[8]

All these factors provided fertile soil for one of China's great modern experiments—or "grand failures,"[9] in retrospect: the Marxist-Leninist top-down ideological imperative to "remold" [gaizao] allegedly backsliding citizens through forced labor into socialist "new men."[10] By most accounts from people subjected to remolding, the great experiment did not work, although some inmate accounts, particularly those published in China, maintain that the remolding was successful. The Guomindang "war criminal" Shen Zui (b. 1913), for example, claims to have become a "new person" [xinren] due to socialist labor remolding. The majority of accounts published outside of China, however, such as those by Lai Ying and Jean Pasqualini (Bao Ruowang), describe their prison experience as humiliatingly punitive rather than rehabilitative.[11] And by the 1980s, approximately half of the PRC's camp inmates were openly denying that they had committed any crime, the confession of which had long been viewed as a key starting point for successful remolding. By the 1990s, camp authorities paid considerably more attention to economic production than to the remolding of the prisoners' thought.[12]

The ratio of political prisoners to total inmates in the labor camps has

7. Lubman, *Bird in a Cage,* p. 19.

8. Philip C. C. Huang, *Code, Custom, and Legal Practice in China: The Qing and the Republic Compared* (Stanford: Stanford Univ. Press, 2001), p. 26.

9. Zbigniew Brzezinski, *The Grand Failure: The Birth and Death of Communism in the Twentieth Century* (New York: Scribner's, 1989).

10. Twentieth-century Chinese establishment intellectuals have rarely expressed much concern about the way Marxian materialism denies "any fundamental explanatory role to juridical notions" such as rights and justice. Such liberalist concepts barely enter into either Marx's combative critique of capitalism or his utopian vision of future communist society. See Allen E. Buchanan, *Marx and Justice: The Radical Critique of Liberalism* (Totowa, NJ: Rowman & Allanheld, 1982), p. 75.

11. Shen Zui, *Zhanfan gaizao suo jianwen* [Matters Seen and Heard in the War Criminals' Remolding Facility], 2 vols. (Hong Kong: Baixing wenhua, 1987), esp. vol. 2, p. 331; Lai Ying, *The Thirty-Sixth Way,* trans. Edward Behr & Sidney Liu (Garden City, NY: Doubleday, 1969); and Bao Ruo-wang & Rudolph Chelminski, *Prisoner of Mao* (1973; rpt. Harmondsworth: Penguin, 1976).

12. Harold M. Tanner, *Strike Hard! Anti-crime Campaigns and Chinese Criminal Justice, 1979–1985* (Ithaca: Cornell Univ. East Asian Series, 1999), pp. 149, 158; James D. Seymour & Richard Anderson, *New Ghosts, Old Ghosts: Prisons and Labor Reform Camps in China* (Armonk, NY: M. E. Sharpe, 1998), pp. 206–207.

shrunk to fewer than one in ten, but in the face of a rapid rise in serious crime during the Deng-Jiang Era, central authorities have not moved decisively to overhaul the system.[13] As the PRC's prison camp system has outlasted the largely defunct ideology that was instrumental in establishing it under the 1950s tutelage of the Stalinist "Soviet big brother" *[Sulian dage]*, the origins of this system deserve close scrutiny.

Premodern China's Legacy of Nonpunitive Forced Labor

States around the world have routinely drafted persons into the army during wartime, but China is notable for its long-standing tradition of peacetime conscription of forced laborers to toil on public construction projects.[14] Most Chinese dynasties drafted large numbers of their subjects to perform occasional unremunerated labor service, or corvée labor, an institution that goes back three millennia to the Zhou dynasty.[15]

According to David Keightley, forced labor was "the natural obligation of all" except the ruler himself during the oldest historically verifiable Chinese dynasty, the Shang (1200?–1045 B.C.E.).[16] As Keightley defines it, forced labor is "work performed for another person (not related by kinship ties) without control over the nature or extent of one's effort."[17] Keightley's characterization of the Shang's "fictive kinship relationships"

---

13. A tone of alarm over the Deng-Jiang Era's "fourth high tide" of spikes in serious crime comes across in an internal 1993 report from the Ministry of Public Security and serves as a harbinger of mid-1990s "strike hard" *[yan da]* crackdowns on crime that would mirror similar efforts under Deng beginning in the early 1980s. The earlier three "high tides" of crime in the PRC's history were connected with "counterrevolutionary" opposition to the 1949 Communist takeover; desperation from three years of deadly famine in the wake of the disastrous Great Leap Forward of 1958–59; and violence after the Cultural Revolution began in 1966. See Michael Dutton, trans., "The Basic Character of Crime in Contemporary China," *China Quarterly* 149 (1997): 160–177, esp. 163.

14. Ray Huang points to the continuity between ancient and modern mobilizations of labor conscripts for public works in *China, a Macro History: Turn of the Century Edition* (Armonk, NY: M. E. Sharpe, 1997), pp. 99–100, 292–293.

15. Lü Simian, *Zhongguo tong shi* [A General History of China] (Shanghai: Kaiming shudian, n.d.), pp. 140, 146–147; Cho-yun Hsu, "The Spring and Autumn Period," in *The Cambridge History of Ancient China*, p. 580.

16. David N. Keightley, "Public Works in Ancient China: A Study of Forced Labor in the Shang and Western Chou" (Ph.D. dissertation, Columbia Univ., 1972), p. 379.

17. Ibid., p. 2. The Erlitou archaeological site in Henan provides some support for the existence of the seemingly legendary Xia dynasty, but most scholars still consider the Shang the earliest historical Chinese dynasty. Keightley has also referred to Shang forced labor as "dependent labor" in "The Shang: China's First Historical Dynasty," *The Cambridge History of Ancient China*, pp. 282–283.

between lord and dependent undercuts the view of Communist ideologue Guo Moruo, who classified the Shang dynasty as a "slave society."[18] Guo's parroting of Stalin's periodization scheme of slave society–feudalism–capitalism–communism has grossly distorted and oversimplified Chinese cultural history. But the CCP's top commissars of theory resisted attempts during the early 1980s to debunk this scheme, leaving intact Mao Zedong's sacrosanct notion that China's imperial period of two millennia was a stagnant "feudal" age.[19] Scholars such as Li Jiafu, however, have convincingly demonstrated that neither the Shang dynasty nor its Zhou successor was a "slave society."[20] According to Keightley, as dependent laborers in a "forced-labor society," "all groups owed varying amounts of service to the group above."[21] Admittedly, Chinese society has changed considerably since the Shang period, but one can still find modern-day manifestations of that dynasty's heritage of "large-scale mobilization of labor" by the patrimonial state's elite.[22]

Contemporary writer and social critic Bo Yang (b. 1920) laments that the Chinese people have come to "excel at lining up by the million . . . and being whipped into submission to complete huge engineering projects like the Great Wall of China or the Grand Canal."[23] This state-

18. Keightley, "Public Works," pp. 36, 95; Guo Moruo, *Nuli zhi shidai* [The Era of the Slave System] (Beijing: Renmin chubanshe, 1974). The Shang dependent laborers' lack of attachment to the soil also prevents their classification as serfs.

19. Laszlo Ladany, *The Communist Party of China and Marxism, 1921–1985: A Self-Portrait* (Stanford: Hoover Institution Press, 1988), p. 452.

20. Li Jiafu, *Zhongguo fazhi shi*, pp. 341–346.

21. Keightley, "Public Works," p. 378. On pp. 125 and 414–415, Keightley adds that the Shang public works had virtually nothing to do with hydraulic projects such as canal construction and maintenance, thereby disputing the famous hypothesis of hydraulic despotism advanced in Karl A. Wittfogel, *Oriental Despotism: A Comparative Study of Total Power* (New Haven: Yale Univ. Press, 1957).

22. Keightley, "The Shang," pp. 290–291.

23. Bo Yang (pseud. of Guo Yidong), "The Wonderful Chinaman," in *"The Ugly Chinaman" and the Crisis of Chinese Culture*, trans. and ed. Don J. Cohn & Jing Qing (St. Leonards, Australia: Allen & Unwin, 1992), p. 155. See also *"Choulou de Zhongguoren" fengbo* [The "Ugly Chinaman" Controversy] (Beijing: Zhongguo Huaqiao chuban gongsi, 1989). Corvée laborers' tendency to fatalistically accept their often harsh lot finds expression in *Sui Yangdi yanshi* [Merry Adventures of Emperor Yang of the Sui], ed. Wang Yizhao (1631 preface; rpt. Taipei: Tianyi chubanshe, 1974), p. 193. C. Martin Wilbur argues that the Confucian imperative of filial devotion *[xiao]* "may have encouraged docility to *corvée* labor"; see *Slavery in the Former Han Dynasty, 206 B.C.–25 A.D.* (Chicago: Field Museum of Natural History Anthropological Series no. 34, 1943), p. 247. Yet this was not always the case, as pointed out by David L. McMullen, "The Real Judge Dee," lecture, Harvard University, 11 March 1991. The late seventh- and early eighth-century scholar-official Di Renjie advised the court not to draft corvée labor for the construction of a mausoleum on account of popular unrest over a similar public works project early in the Tang dynasty.

ment might seem hyperbolic at first glance, but some historians have estimated that there were a million or more fatalities among forced laborers conscripted to work on the "Great Wall" *[Changcheng]* in the third century B.C.E.[24] As a well-published cultural historian, Bo Yang is almost surely aware that the official history of the Sui dynasty conservatively estimates the number of corvée laborers drafted to construct the Grand Canal during 608–611 at over a million.[25]

A literary source that offers more specifics about the conscription of laborers for the Grand Canal project claims that over 5 million people participated, including 50,000 soldiers who were ordered to guard and supervise the laborers and support personnel.[26] Reports of a high mortality rate among the Grand Canal laborers and the draconian punishments of conscripts caught in the act of escaping or hiding from corvée service resonate with accounts of Qin Shi Huangdi's construction of the original Great Wall in the third century B.C.E.[27] According to "A Record of Opening Up the Canal" [Kai he ji], nearly half of the laborers conscripted for the Grand Canal project died, and an upright official who warned the ambitious Sui Yangdi about the likely dire consequences of embarking on yet another mammoth public works project was put under house arrest and pressured into committing suicide. As part of the Qin dynasty term for forced or convict laborer, *chengdan,* the word *cheng* [city wall] had developed negative connotations of harsh and hazardous working conditions. Thus in referring to the "Great Wall" of their own age, the Ming period (1368–1644) authorities were careful in using the term for ordinary walls, *qiang,* instead of the historically tainted term for "the Great Wall," *Changcheng.*[28]

24. Reports of a million fatalities from Qin Shi Huangdi's Great Wall construction project appear in Charles O. Hucker, *China's Imperial Past* (Stanford: Stanford Univ. Press, 1975), pp. 44–45.

25. "Di ji" [Imperial Chronicles], in *Sui shu* [Official History of the Sui Dynasty], in *Ershiwu shi* [The Twenty-Five Histories], 2nd ed. (Taipei: Kaiming shudian, 1965), p. 12. Arthur F. Wright notes that for the first time in Chinese history, women were also conscripted for the Grand Canal's construction, as there were not enough men available to handle the various tasks; see *The Sui Dynasty* (New York: Knopf, 1978), p. 179.

26. "Kai he ji" [A Record of Opening Up the Canal], in *Tang-Song chuanqi ji* [A Collection of Tang-Song *chuanqi*], in *Lu Xun sanshi nian ji* [The Thirty-Year Collection of Lu Xun], vol. 5 (Hong Kong: Xin yi chubanshe, 1967), p. 215. This is a work of historical fiction rather than history proper, but it is safe to assume that at least several hundred thousand corvée laborers toiled at constructing the Grand Canal—and probably many more.

27. Ibid., p. 221.

28. See the definition of the term *chengdan* in Sima Qian's (ca. 145 B.C.E. to ca. 86 B.C.E.) "Qin Shi Huang benji" [Basic Annals of Qin Shi Huang] in his *Shi ji* [The Historical Records], in *Ershiwu shi,* p. 25. See also *Zhongwen da cidian* (Taipei: Zhongguo Wenhua Daxue chubanbu, 1982), vol. 2, p. 1190. For a different interpretation of *chengdan,* see Cai

The Chinese state's predilection for mobilizing vast amounts of forced labor continued in modern times, though it had eased significantly by the final quarter of the twentieth century. During the 1930s and 1940s, the Guomindang (GMD, Nationalist) military under Chiang Kai-shek pressed millions of unwilling villagers and townsfolk into the ranks of its armed services and forced labor brigades. Although the GMD government did not use forced labor as much as Mao Zedong's Communists later would, the GMD did utilize it in such areas as military recruitment, road building, and railroad construction.[29]

During the following decade and a half, the Communist party-state of Mao Zedong's PRC had around "2.5 million people working full-time per year at *corvée* labor," according to one cautious estimate.[30] Hardened by long experience with bitter internecine conflict and intermittent foreign invasion, both of these rulers conscripted a vast amount of forced labor and deployed it in conditions that were often perilously harsh. These actions played a significant role in a demographer's ranking of both the Mao Zedong and Chiang Kai-shek regimes among the world's four most lethal governments of the twentieth century (in terms of total deaths resulting from government actions).[31]

Shuheng, *Zhongguo xingfa shi* (Nanning: Guangxi renmin chubanshe, 1983), pp. 87–88, 92. For more information on *chengdan,* see Li Jiafu, *Zhongguo fazhi shi,* pp. 67, 72, 78–80, 176. The sections of the "Great Wall" still standing today are mostly of Ming provenance.

29. See R. J. Rummel, *China's Bloody Century: Genocide and Mass Murder since 1900* (New Brunswick, NJ: Transaction, 1991), pp. 81, 114–116. Rummel agrees with Ho Ping-ti's estimate of 3 million deaths of GMD military conscripts who were not yet involved in combat but gathered together under perilously harsh conditions. This number is equivalent to the official GMD figure for the total number of Chinese soldiers killed or wounded in battle during the eight-year War of Resistance to Japan (1937–45). See Ho Ping-ti, *Studies on the Population of China, 1368–1953* (Cambridge: Harvard Univ. Press, 1957), pp. 250–251. One short story that portrays the high desertion rate of GMD military conscripts in the 1940s is Gao Xiaosheng, "Li Shunda zao wu," in *1979 nian quanguo youxiu duanpian xiaoshuo pingxuan huojiang zuopin ji* [The Anthology of National Prize-Winning Short Stories of 1979] (Shanghai: Shanghai wenyi chubanshe, 1980), pp. 125–146. This was translated into English as "Li Shunda Builds a House" by Ellen Klempner in *The New Realism: Writings from China after the Cultural Revolution,* ed. Lee Yee (New York: Hippocrene Books, 1983), pp. 31–55.

30. Steven Rosskam Shalom, *Deaths in China due to Communism: Propaganda versus Reality* (Tempe: Arizona State Univ. Center for Asian Studies Monograph Series, 1984), p. 102. Shalom argues that Richard Walker's estimate of the number of deaths due to Chinese Communist actions and policies is too high and needs to be adjusted downward. Shalom's estimate of 2.5 million corvée laborers does not include the millions of PRC prisoners then doing forced labor either in camps or "under the supervision of the masses."

31. R. J. Rummel, *Death by Government* (New Brunswick, NY: Transaction, 1994), p. xv. The two other most lethal regimes of the century were Stalin's and Hitler's.

Imperial China's Heritage
of Forced Labor and Exile for Convicts

As in many other ancient civilizations, the various governments in pre-Qin China mostly resorted to varieties of corporal punishment in meting out justice to criminal offenders.[32] These retributive measures, first mentioned over 2,500 years ago in the *Shu jing* [The History Classic] as the *wu xing*, or "Five Punishments," ranged in severity from a set number of strokes with the bamboo bastinado all the way to execution.[33] The pattern of dividing all the punishments into five major types and placing each one along a spectrum from lightest to heaviest lasted for some two and a half millennia, all the way up to the early twentieth century.

What gradually fell into disfavor during the formative Han period (206 B.C.E.–220 C.E.) were the ancient mutilating punishments in the intermediate range of the scale between caning and execution, such as chopping off the offender's nose, feet, or testicles—brutal punishments of the type that were still occasionally practiced in various "advanced" Western countries as recently as the eighteenth century.[34] Therefore, the Han dynasty reforms substituting one- to three-year terms of forced labor *[tu]* or internal lifelong exile *[liu* or *liufang]* for the archaic mutilating punishments marked a humane advance in the Chinese criminal justice system.[35] Though commonly three years in duration, terms of premodern penal servitude could occasionally be as short as one year or,

32. Lü Simian, *Zhongguo tong shi*, p. 183. According to *The History Classic*, the Chinese borrowed their most ancient code of punishments, the *wu xing*, from a neighboring nationality, the Miao. See more discussion in Cai Shuheng, *Zhongguo xingfa shi*, pp. 58–64, and Li Jiafu, *Zhongguo fazhi shi*, pp. 163–165. See also Derk Bodde & Clarence Morris, *Law in Imperial China Exemplified by 190 Ch'ing Dynasty Cases* (Cambridge: Harvard Univ. Press, 1967), p. 11.

33. The *wu xing* continued to undergo minor revisions until its demise early in the twentieth century, but its basic template was established by the Sui Code of 581–583. See *Zhongwen da cidian*, vol. 1, pp. 631–632; Li Jiafu, *Zhongguo fazhi shi*, pp. 163–187; and Bodde & Morris, *Law in Imperial China*, pp. 77–78.

34. Laszlo Ladany, *Law and Legality in China: The Testament of a China-Watcher*, ed. Marie-Luise Näth (Honolulu: Univ. of Hawaii Press, 1992), p. 2. A. Roger Ekirch argues that forced indentured servitude and exile to a colony was Great Britain's preferred punishment for serious crime in the eighteenth century, in "Great Britain's Secret Convict Trade to America, 1783–1784," *The American Historical Review* 89.5 (1984): 1285–1291.

35. Bodde & Morris, *Law in Imperial China*, p. 76. This is considered *internal* exile because it almost always takes place within China's boundaries. The increasingly common contemporary PRC practice of getting rid of especially "dangerous" dissidents by exiling them abroad resonates far more with Brezhnevian Russia than with either premodern or Maoist China.

more rarely, as long as four or five years for especially serious offenses. Needless to say, this compares favorably with the two-decade stints that were common among political prisoners during the Mao Era—not to mention the ten- to fifteen-year terms often given to such prisoners during the Deng-Jiang Era. As for the imperial "Five Punishments," caning with the bamboo bastinado and execution remained at the two ends of the spectrum of punishments, and the archaic term *wu xing* continued in use. Several degrees existed within each type of punishment: a relatively light form of lifelong exile would be to a place several hundred kilometers from one's home, and the most severe types of exile were approximately 2,000 kilometers—to the farthest frontier or to a malarial region.[36]

The Han reforms of the intermediate punishments triggered greater revenue outlays for the state, which had to pay for most or all of the traveling expenses incurred by armed guards escorting the prisoners to labor camps or exile in a distant province—along with related expenses incurred by the prisoners themselves.[37] From a strictly bottom-line perspective, it would have been cheaper for the state to continue mutilating its intermediate-range convicts and leaving them to cope on their own with their injuries. Still, since the prisoners' unremunerated labor helped defray part of the expenses required for their upkeep, labor camps presented fewer fiscal burdens to the state than did confinement in jails, which were traditionally viewed as holding pens for prisoners awaiting trial or sentencing.[38] For example, an unusual early twelfth-century Chinese experiment with using the jail stay itself as a mode of punishment was soon discarded as fiscally unsustainable, because the modest government revenues of

36. See Li Jiafu, *Zhongguo fazhi shi,* pp. 175–181.

37. Forcing the inmate to make a long journey on foot to a distant site of hard labor added punitive sting to the traditional punishment of penal servitude, as suggested by Bodde & Morris, *Law in Imperial China,* p. 81. Local officials posted en route to the labor camp could sometimes be persuaded to contribute to the guard convoy's traveling expenses—as could the prisoner himself, in return for more lenient treatment.

38. Traditional Chinese jails also regularly held key witnesses along with suspects and convicts awaiting sentencing, which made confinement within them especially inappropriate as a means of punishment. The fact that no Song dynasty official was ever recorded as having reduced the duration of a convict sentence by the length of time the inmate had stayed in jail is a strong argument for the idea that imprisonment itself was typically not viewed as a means of punishment. According to McKnight, the authorities usually tried "to make life in jail bearable and the stay there brief"; see *Law and Order in Sung China* (Cambridge: Cambridge Univ. Press, 1992), p. 355. Sybille Van der Sprenkel notes that the same view of jail confinement prevailed during the Qing dynasty; see *Legal Institutions in Manchu China: A Sociological Analysis,* p. 62.

imperial times could ill afford such heavy expenditures in the area of punishment.[39]

Convict labor also provided other potential benefits. In performing socially useful work, convicts could redeem themselves in accord with the ancient Confucian imperative of "correcting one's faults and renewing oneself" *[gaiguo zixin]*.[40] Moreover, in a far-flung continental empire like China, exiles and forced laborers could play especially valuable roles as settlers or soldiers in sparsely populated border regions. On a modest scale, the government could thereby alleviate imbalances in the geographical distribution of China's population at the same time it was punishing wrongdoing. According to Joanna Waley-Cohen, the Qianlong emperor's "purpose of sending convicts to Xinjiang [during a phase of rapid population growth in the eighteenth century] was to clear the crowded heartland, to settle the new frontier, and, through punishment, to offer criminals a means of redeeming themselves."[41]

Until 1725, forced labor terms typically had to be served outside of the convict's home province, thereby amounting to a sort of temporary internal exile.[42] Common inmate tasks included salt mining, iron smelting, farming, construction, and general manual labor at a prison camp *[laocheng ying]*.[43] Many labor camps had a military function, especially if they were located in a border region; and many a convict sent to such a camp remained in the military after the completion of his penal term.

The fate of military camp inmate *[peijun* or *chongjun]* befell such prominent martial characters as Lin Chong and Wu Song in the classic sixteenth-century novel *Shuihu zhuan [Water Margin]*.[44] In one of this novel's many

39. McKnight, *Law and Order in Sung China*, p. 356.

40. Geoffrey MacCormack argues that the intent behind traditional Chinese punishments was reformation of the criminal, deterrence of potential criminals, retribution or requital for harm done, or some combination of these motivations. See *The Spirit of Traditional Chinese Law* (Athens: Univ. of Georgia Press, 1996), pp. 209–211.

41. This is Joanna Waley-Cohen's paraphrase of the Qianlong emperor's view in Cohen, *Exile in Mid-Qing China: Banishment to Xinjiang, 1758–1820* (New Haven: Yale Univ. Press, 1991), p. 64.

42. Bodde & Morris, *Law in Imperial China*, p. 82. This practice continued after 1725 but was no longer a requirement. A man in Hebei received such a sentence around 1825; he had resisted arrest on the charge of mining unlicensed salt. And in 1793, a woman in Fujian was sentenced to penal servitude because she knew of a certain man's murderous intentions but failed to report him either before or after the murder was committed. See also pp. 260–261, 453–454.

43. For more on the term *laocheng ying*, see *Shuihu quanzhuan* [The Complete *Water Margin*], vol. 1, attributed to Shi Nai'an and Luo Guanzhong (Shanghai: Shanghai renmin chubanshe, 1975), pp. 113–119, 342.

44. Ibid., chaps. 9 & 27.

satirical portraits of corrupt officialdom, Lin Chong receives the cushiest job in the entire prison camp and escapes a prescribed beating only after presenting bribes and a special letter of introduction to the two top prison officials there.[45]

Matters did not necessarily turn out so well for the inmate in actuality, however. The journey to the site of punitive exile in late imperial times was often so arduous that the convicts' safe arrival there would have been a stroke of good fortune.[46] The renowned Qing literatus Liu E (1857–1909) endured such a harsh journey on the way to his punitive exile in faraway Xinjiang that he died barely a year after his arrest.[47] On the other hand, imperial Chinese governments had an interest in preventing the wanton mistreatment of prisoners; there are a number of cases on record of jailers and guards receiving severe punishment for such abuses of their power.[48]

During the seventeenth and eighteenth centuries, lifelong exile and forced labor were often combined, not only in Xinjiang and elsewhere in the far west, but also at such frigid northeastern sites as Shangyangbao in Liaoning province (present-day Kaiyuan County). Many scholar-official families from the lower Yangzi region around Suzhou who fell afoul of the Qing dynasty's Literary Inquisition [wenzi yu] made the long trek to punitive exile in Shangyangbao, where they had to engage in hard labor such as wall construction and farm work.[49] According to a contemporary observer, the combination of a poor diet, the harsh environ-

45. Ibid., pp. 113–115. This episode has been translated into English by Sidney Shapiro in *Outlaws of the Marsh* (Bloomington: Indiana Univ. Press, 1981), pp. 153–156. Lin Chong's unusually light job duties amounted to little more than sweeping the floor at a temple twice a day. On the other hand, the risks of being placed in a dependent status like that of prison camp inmate come across through the episode in which one of Lin Chong's powerful enemies plots to have him killed shortly after his arrival at the labor camp. Fortunately for Lin, the plot fails.

46. Bao Jialin (Chia-lin Pao Tao), "Ming mo Qing chu de Suzhou cainü Xu Can" [The Late-Ming to Early-Qing Talented Suzhou Woman Xu Can], in *Ming-Qing wenhua xinlun* [New Theories of Ming-Qing Culture], ed. Wang Chengmian (Taipei: Wenjin chubanshe, 2000), pp. 455–475, esp. 459–461.

47. Harold Shadick, translator's introduction to Liu E, *The Travels of Lao Ts'an* (Ithaca: Cornell Univ. Press, 1952), p. xv. The original novel is Liu E, *Lao Can youji* (1907; rpt. Taipei: Xing Tai wenhua chubanshe, 1980).

48. After a Hebei prisoner who had been chained in an unlawful manner and subjected to extortionate demands committed suicide around 1820, both the prison guard and the government underling who were responsible for this received the severe sentence of life exile and one hundred blows from a heavy bamboo cane. See Bodde & Morris, *Law in Imperial China*, pp. 450–451.

49. Bao Jialin, "Suzhou cainü Xu Can," p. 460.

ment, and daily coolie labor made almost all the exiles there so thin and bony that their limbs resembled kindling.[50]

Compared with a number of twentieth-century novels and stories, premodern Chinese fictional accounts of penal exile almost never describe the day-to-day life of prisoners in detail.[51] Moreover, the premodern storytellers' strong preference for urban settings in China proper impelled some of them to conjure up such unlikely scenarios as a prisoner being exiled to a highly desirable urban locale.[52] For example, the protagonist Xu Xuan is exiled from scenic Hangzhou to the sightseer's mecca of Suzhou in the Ming story "Bai Niangzi yong zhen Leifeng Ta" [Madam White's Eternal Imprisonment in Thunder Peak Pagoda].[53]

Clearly, the modern-day use of forced labor and prison camps has an ancient pedigree in China and cannot be accurately portrayed as merely a Soviet grafting onto a Chinese rootstock, with perhaps a few local Chinese features added on.[54] To be sure, the nature of China's prison camp system and the terminology surrounding it underwent numerous major changes during the twentieth century. However, the system rests upon ancient cultural assumptions that forced labor and exile are normal parts

50. Xu Can's (1628–81?) contemporary Wu Zhaoqian is cited in Bao Jialin, "Suzhou cainü Xu Can," p. 460.

51. Later chapters, especially Chapter 5, deal at length with twentieth-century fiction and reportage involving a prison camp setting.

52. Patrick Hanan has argued that the premodern Chinese vernacular story "is vastly unrepresentative, with its concentration on cities and towns." See *The Chinese Vernacular Story* (Cambridge: Harvard Univ. Press, 1981), p. 127.

53. The protagonist Xu Xuan is forced to wear a "traveling cangue" around his neck while marching under escort to a *laocheng ying* in "Bai Niangzi yong zhen Leifeng Ta," in *Jing shi tongyan* [Tales to Warn the World], vol. 2, ed. Feng Menglong (1624; rpt. Beijing: Renmin wenxue chubanshe, 1981), pp. 420–448, esp. p. 428. A traveling cangue is a yoke that allows its wearer mobility; some other cangues keep their wearers immobile. This story has been translated as "Eternal Prisoner under the Thunder Peak Pagoda" by Diana Yu in *Traditional Chinese Stories: Themes and Variations*, ed. Y. W. Ma & Joseph S. M. Lau (1986; rpt. Boston: Cheng & Tsui, 1996), pp. 355–378, esp. 363.

54. Perhaps the most extreme expression of the view that the PRC camp system is wholly a Soviet import may be found in Liu Qingbo, *Zhonggong laodong gaizao de pipan* [A Critique of the Chinese Communists' Remolding through Labor] (Taipei: Zhengzhong shuju, 1975), p. 14. Hongda Harry Wu is less categorical in his views on this subject, but he mentions only the Soviet gulag and the Nazi concentration camps in his discussion of the Chinese laogai system's origins in *Laogai: The Chinese Gulag*, pp. xi–xii, 3–5. In contrast, a number of scholars have argued for the existence of continuity between the imperial and modern Chinese systems of punishment. See, for example, Seymour & Anderson, *New Ghosts, Old Ghosts*, pp. 12–15; Jean-Louis Rocca, *L'empire et son milieu: la criminalité en Chine populaire* [The Empire and Its Milieu: Criminality in China] (Paris: Plon, 1991), pp. 41–44; and Michael R. Dutton, *Policing and Punishment in China: From Patriarchy to "the People"* (Cambridge: Cambridge Univ. Press, 1992), pp. 350–351.

of the state's criminal justice system, which has strictly defined the individual's "duty to obey authority," but not the limit of that authority.[55]

Late Qing and Early Republican Era Legal Reforms

In the wake of the officially endorsed Boxer Uprising of 1900 and its harsh suppression by the eight-nation army of occupation in Beijing, the chastened Qing court veered sharply from its disastrous course of reflexive xenophobia to embrace internationally inspired reforms.[56] The major ensuing development in the realm of law and punishment was Empress Dowager Cixi's 1901 appointment of expert scholar-officials such as Shen Jiaben to reform the Qing Legal Code.[57] Although these Chinese reformers emphasized the Japanese legal system as a model, that nation had in turn borrowed many of its modern statutes from the German Code of 1889, especially in the area of civil law.[58] This westernization of China's legal system pivoted upon the creation of a judiciary that would be an independent branch of government and thereby remove the foreign maritime powers' major justification for maintaining their extraterritorial privileges in China.[59] Like their successors in the Republican Era, legal reformers in the late Qing shared the long-term goal of eliminating those unfair extraterritorial privileges.[60]

55. Marinus Johan Meijer, "Abuse of Power and Coercion," in *State and Law in East Asia: Festschrift Karl Brüger,* ed. Dieter Eikemeier & Herbert Franke (Wiesbaden: Otto Harrassowitz, 1981), p. 203.

56. See Edward J. M. Rhoads, *Manchus and Han: Ethnic Relations and Political Power in Late Qing and Early Republican China, 1861–1928* (Seattle: Univ. of Washington Press, 2000), pp. 71–74. The subsequent Republican Era (1912–49) witnessed an increasing pace in the internationalization and effectiveness of China's legal system. For an examination of how this phenomenon played out in the area of international relations, see William C. Kirby, "The Internationalization of China: Foreign Relations at Home and Abroad in the Republican Era," in *Reappraising Republican China,* ed. Frederic Wakeman Jr. & Richard Louis Edmonds (Oxford: Oxford Univ. Press, 2000), pp. 179–204. China's cooperative movement in agricultural economics also had its roots in the late Qing but expanded rapidly during the Republican Era, according to Charles W. Hayford, *To the People: James Yen and Village China* (New York: Columbia Univ. Press, 1990), p. 170.

57. Xu Xiaoqun, "The Fate of Judicial Independence in Republican China, 1912–37," *China Quarterly* 149 (1997): 1–28, esp. 2–3. See also Ladany, *Law and Legality in China,* p. 45; and Li Jiafu, *Zhongguo fazhi shi,* pp. 387–388.

58. The civil codes of both the post-Mao PRC and the contemporary Republic of China (ROC) on Taiwan still bear a significant resemblance to their German model.

59. Xu Xiaoqun, "The Fate of Judicial Independence," pp. 2, 4, 7, 17; and Huang Jinlin, *Lishi, shenti, guojia,* pp. 125–127.

60. Douglas R. Reynolds, *China, 1898–1912: The Xinzheng Revolution and Japan* (Cambridge: Harvard Univ. Press, 1993), p. 181.

Some of the more ambitious changes in the first draft of the Qing Revised Code had to be watered down in the face of conservative criticism, but the final version that was approved in 1910 marked a significant advance. For instance, the Revised Code of 1910 outlawed the state's time-honored use of torture to induce confession and substituted fines and imprisonment for various harsh traditional punishments such as lifelong internal exile and court-ordered caning with the bastinado.[61] To be sure, some premodern Chinese intellectuals took a dim view of judicial torture. The seventeenth-century writer and playwright Li Yu notes that an accused person will confess to practically anything just to avoid further torture from the ankle-press [jiazu], suggesting that only murder or armed robbery suspects be subjected to that instrument of torture.[62]

Even though the Qing dynasty did not last long enough for the Revised Code of 1910 to be adequately tested in practice, it marked a general shift away from sentences of exile and penal labor—until the inauguration of Maoist governance revived their widespread utilization four decades later. To be sure, the fall of the Qing dynasty in 1911—and with it the imperial system itself—presaged a decade and a half of chaotic disunity among regional "warlord" governments during the early Republican Era. However, an intensification of progressive legal codification occurred during the more settled times of the late 1920s. Against the background of the authoritarian and often repressive rule of the GMD leader Chiang Kai-shek, relatively liberal jurists and legal experts completed China's new Criminal Code of 1928 and Civil Code of 1929.[63] Inspired by the late Qing Revised Code along with Japanese and Western models, the new law codes further separated the judicial and executive arms of the government, reducing the gap between China's criminal justice system and that of the West.[64] Admittedly, the GMD government's

61. Ladany, Law and Legality in China, p. 46; and Li Jiafu, Zhongguo fazhi shi, p. 388.

62. See the fourth story of Li Yu's Lian cheng bi [Priceless Jade] (Hangzhou: Zhejiang guji chubanshe, 1986), pp. 82, 86. For an English translation, see Patrick Hanan, ed., Silent Operas (Hong Kong: Chinese Univ. of Hong Kong Press, 1990), pp. 66, 74.

63. Ladany, Law and Legality in China, p. 50. China's 1928 Criminal Code was revised in 1935.

64. Much of the rationale for the foreign powers' extraterritorial privileges in China had been based on the incompatibility of their legal systems with those of China, and the greatly increased conformance of China's new law codes with Japanese and Western models was a significant factor in the final cessation of extraterritoriality in 1943. Kirby notes that the Nationalist Chinese regime "regained judiciary control over Chinese residents in foreign concessions" prior to their retrocession in 1943; see "The Internationalization of China," p. 187.

harsh struggle with both internal rebellion and foreign invasion during the 1930s and 1940s set the stage for the ruling party's frequent interference in judicial affairs.[65] Spotty enforcement of many of these new laws and chronic government underfunding of the judiciary led many observers to see these laws more as laudable expressions of future goals than as binding statutes of the day.[66] However flawed and imperfectly administered the revamped GMD legal system was during the Republican Era, it nevertheless represents "measurable progress" and helped lay the groundwork for the genuinely democratic, multiparty system that eventually developed in Taiwan during the 1980s and 1990s.[67]

Prison and Conscript Labor under the Guomindang

In the Republican Era, incarceration in county jails or relatively "modern" urban prisons replaced the premodern internal exile in prison camps as the typical intermediate punishment on a scale ranging from minor fines to execution. Aside from a small number of large and relatively new urban detention facilities, such as Beijing's model prison, which opened in 1912, Republican Era facilities were typically spartan county jails that had major funding problems. As with many cultural phenomena, the disappearance of exile as a punishment in the Republican Era was not absolute. Yuan Shikai temporarily reinstated exile and caning in the mid-1910s, and the 1933 GMD scheme of rural "wasteland reclamation" [yiken] through forced labor lasted nearly a decade before the authorities abandoned it.[68] Prison labor certainly continued to exist on a modest scale under the GMD, but never dominated the correctional system as it later would under Communist rule.

65. Xu Xiaoqun, "The Fate of Judicial Independence," pp. 16–17.

66. For instance, the new laws against corruption, while "admirable expressions of intent," tended to lack "administrative follow-through." Moreover, though the Press Law of 1930 was considerably less restrictive than the CCP-administered press controls after 1949, it remained vague enough in places to allow for too much discretion on the part of its enforcers. See Lloyd E. Eastman, *The Abortive Revolution: China under Nationalist Rule, 1927–1937* (Cambridge: Harvard Univ. Press, 1974), pp. 18, 25–26; and Eastman, *Seeds of Destruction: Nationalist China in War and Revolution, 1937–1949* (Stanford: Stanford Univ. Press, 1984), p. 59.

67. Xu Xiaoqun, "The Fate of Judicial Independence," pp. 26, 28.

68. Dutton, *Policing and Punishment in China,* pp. 178–181. For the most complete and updated study of imprisonment during the Republican period, see Frank Dikötter, *Crime, Punishment, and the Prison in Modern China* (New York: Columbia Univ. Press, 2002).

A number of political prisoners under the GMD have indicated that forced labor was not part of their routine. Imprisoned by the GMD in 1942–43, Ho Chi-minh just had to cook his own rice and soup and boil his own tea; each prisoner had his own stove.[69] Writer and political commentator Li Ao notes that when he was a political prisoner under martial law in Taipei County, about half of his fellow prisoners participated in voluntary manual labor simply as a way to relieve the boredom of confinement; he preferred to read in his cell.[70]

There were around 1,000 inmates at Shangrao Prison (established 1941), what one former prisoner called the largest of the GMD "fascist concentration camps" [faxisi jizhongying]. Shangrao prisoners' complaints about being shut up indoors too often and having insufficient time for daily exercise outdoors suggest that their forced labor on public works projects was considerably less prolonged and exhausting than what their later counterparts would experience in the Mao Era camps.[71] Nonetheless, Shangrao's combination of forced labor and a poor diet could be seen as a minor harbinger of the convict labor regimen's mid-twentieth-century revival in China. This is somewhat analogous to Shen Dingyi's 1920s design for a new institution he called a fanxing yuan [Self-examination Reformatory], which "prefigures the re-education schemes adopted by Mao and the Communists in Yan'an."[72]

Imprisonment that amounted to exile was rare under Chiang Kai-shek

69. See David G. Marr, ed., *Reflections from Captivity: Phan Boi Chau's "Prison Notes" and Ho Chi-minh's "Prison Diary,"* trans. Christopher Jenkins, Tran Khanh Tuyet, & Huynh Sanh Thong (Athens: Ohio Univ. Press, 1978), pp. 78, 89.

70. Li Ao, "Jianyu xue Tucheng" [Leaning from the Tucheng Prison], in *Dalu Taiwan zuo lao ji* [Accounts of Imprisonment in the Mainland and Taiwan], ed. Liu Qing et al. (Hong Kong: Baixing banyuekan, 1983), pp. 95–158, esp. 100–101.

71. Bao Ziyan & Yuan Shaofa, eds., *Huiyi Xuefeng* [Remembering Feng Xuefeng] (Beijing: Zhongguo wenshi chubanshe, 1986), pp. 134, 135, 137. Confinement at Shangrao was certainly unpleasant, but the leftist essayist inmate Feng Xuefeng had the time and freedom to "write a lot" as well as often reread his favorite Chinese novel *A Dream of Red Mansions* (pp. 137, 140)—a far milder regimen than his counterparts in the PRC prison camps of the 1950s and 1960s would encounter. For a more doctrinaire PRC account of the Shangrao camp complex, see the anonymously authored *Shangrao jizhongying* [Shangrao Concentration Camp] (Shanghai: Shanghai renmin chubanshe, 1981). For information on other GMD prison camps, see Xue Meiqing et al., eds., *Zhongguo jianyu shi*, pp. 296–306. Such GMD camps for political prisoners were often infiltrated by secret agents of CCP security chief Kang Sheng, thereby presenting an intelligence liability to the GMD party-state, according to Richard Deacon (pseud. of Donald McCormick), *A History of the Chinese Secret Service* (London: Frederick Muller, Ltd., 1974), p. 290.

72. R. Keith Schoppa, *Blood Road: The Mystery of Shen Dingyi in Revolutionary China* (Berkeley: Univ. of California Press, 1995), p. 199.

and his successor Chiang Ching-kuo. However, it did not actually stop in the Republic of China (ROC) until the notorious lockup for political prisoners on Green Island [Lü dao] was finally closed after Taiwan ended martial law in 1987. In *Shan lu* [Mountain Path], novelist Chen Yingzhen, who was imprisoned on Green Island, has artfully evoked the emotional despair of exile—the ex-inmate's sense of having been totally forgotten for years or even decades by a society preoccupied with banquets and weddings.[73]

Conscript labor was quite a different story, however; Chiang Kai-shek often made massive use of it during his reign on the mainland. In the wake of failed attempts to implement a lottery for the military draft, and as fewer willing recruits to Chiang's army could be found by 1941, military press-gangs fanned out over the countryside to abduct able-bodied men, tie their hands behind their backs, and march them to the nearest induction camp.[74] Extreme and often callous security measures taken to stem desertions further endangered the health and safety of the abducted military recruits, who also faced the overall 23% casualty rate of the GMD army during the eight-year war against Japan.[75]

The GMD conscription of forced civilian laborers also expanded dramatically during wartime, with the party-state regularly drafting as many as half a million laborers to work on a single project, such as the Hunan-Jiangxi railway or a series of runways large enough to accommodate B-29 bombers.[76] These laborers' working conditions were harsh, their shelter and sanitary facilities rudimentary at best, and their mortality rate was high, with several thousand dying from work on the Burma Road project alone.[77] Many Chinese villagers understandably came to fear the govern-

73. Chen Yingzhen, *Shan lu* (Taipei: Yuanjing, 1984), p. 39. Translated into English by Nicholas Koss as "Mountain Path" in *"Death in a Cornfield" and other Stories from Contemporary Taiwan*, ed. Ching-Hsi Perng and Chiu-kuei Wang (Hong Kong: Oxford Univ. Press, 1994), p. 21.

74. Lloyd E. Eastman, *Seeds of Destruction*, p. 148. The poor felt the brunt of this forced conscription, since the wealthy could usually bribe their way out if abducted.

75. Ibid., pp. 146, 149–151. An estimated 3 million Chinese wartime conscripts died, according to Rummel, *China's Bloody Century*, p. 116.

76. Chiang Kai-shek, leader of the Republic of China (ROC) during the Nanjing Decade (1927–37) and the war years that followed, seemed to view labor conscription as part of the proper militarization of his society's structure and spirit. In 1933, Chiang exhorted all fellow GMD members to "have the army's organization and discipline, . . . obey, . . . and sacrifice everything for the collectivity, for the party, for the nation." Quoted in Frederic Wakeman Jr., "A Revisionist View of the Nanjing Decade: Confucian Fascism," in *Reappraising Republican China*, pp. 141–178, esp. 171.

77. Eastman, *Seeds of Destruction*, pp. 57–58.

ment's order for labor service even more than the tax collector or the military press-gangs.[78]

Conclusion

The use of forced labor in Chinese public works has a virtually unbroken history of over three millennia, going back all the way to the dawn of China's recorded history. Though unambiguous evidence of Chinese penal labor is less ancient, it has nonetheless occurred more or less continuously for at least the past twenty-two centuries.

After approximately a century and a half of revolution and reform, forced labor in China has declined only in recent decades.[79] However, the most powerful political force in the Chinese cultural scene for the past half century, the CCP party-state, has been reluctant to distance itself from this ancient cultural pattern, even during the relatively peaceful 1980s and 1990s. The next chapter will examine how the CCP reformulated this long tradition of forced labor to suit its own aims and interests.

78. Ibid., p. 58.
79. Specifically, forced labor remained quite widespread from the late 1930s to the late 1970s, particularly during the Mao Era. Its declining trajectory during the 1980s and 1990s occurred in part due to the radical reduction in the PRC government's forced retention of ex-inmate workers in the vicinity of labor camps. Released camp inmates were increasingly allowed to leave the prison environs and work as *getihu* [individual proprietors] or in other capacities within the mixed economy. For more on the rise and decline of the system known as *liuchang jiuye* [retention of ex-inmate workers on the camp site], see the end of Chapter 2 and Seymour & Anderson, *New Ghosts, Old Ghosts,* pp. 189–198.

The Development of the Chinese Communist Prison Camp

The Jiangxi Soviet's Inaugural CCP Camp System, 1931–34

The Russian Bolshevik theory championing revolutionary urban putsches turned out to be a disaster when put into practice during the late 1920s and 1930s by Chinese Communists in several cities, including Guangzhou, Changsha, and Nanchang. Regrouping in various upland rural redoubts that bordered on two or more southern provinces, many of the chastened CCP revolutionaries decided to build up their strength among the huge population of disaffected villagers rather than to continue clinging dogmatically to China's tiny urban proletariat.[1] The first Chinese Communist governments thereby arose in southeastern rural guerrilla strongholds that lay at a relatively safe distance from the GMD central government's power base in the lower Yangzi Valley.

The unrestrained mob butchery of rural landlords soon backfired in northern Guangdong's Hai-Lu-Feng Soviet under the leadership of Peng Pai, who was shot in 1931. However, the Jiangxi Soviet in the eastern portion of that landlocked province fared better under the less extreme leadership of Mao Zedong and Zhu De.[2] Within a month after founding the

---

1. See William Wei, *Counterrevolution in China: The Nationalists in Jiangxi during the Soviet Period* (Ann Arbor: Univ. of Michigan Press, 1985), p. 155.

2. See Domenach, *L'archipel oublié,* p. 44. For more on the treatment of counterrevolutionaries up to the Communist victory in the civil war, see Patricia E. Griffin, *The Chinese Communist Treatment of Counterrevolutionaries: 1924–1949* (Princeton: Princeton Univ. Press, 1976), pp. 13–14. See also Jean-Louis Margolin, "China: A Long Journey into Night," in *The Black Book of Communism: Crimes, Terror, Repression,* ed. Stéphane Courtois et al., trans. Jonathan Murphy & Mark Kramer (Cambridge: Harvard Univ. Press, 1999), pp. 463–546, esp. 470–471.

Chinese Soviet Republic in southeastern Jiangxi province on 7 November 1931, Mao Zedong and the other top leaders in this Chinese Red Army base area initiated a long-enduring pattern of sweepingly rejecting the legal codes developed in the late Qing and the Republican Era.[3] Mao and his confreres cavalierly threw out these legal codes with the same sort of contempt that the Comintern had long expressed for "bourgeois law."[4]

In their place, the Jiangxi Soviet Central Executive Committee issued decrees and policy statements such as the December 1931 "Instruction No. 6," which sets out key rules for punishing the real and imagined opponents of their rebel state, "counterrevolutionaries"—using the jargon that would hold sway under the CCP until the mid-1990s.[5] This was the first of several Jiangxi Soviet government decrees on trial and sentencing guidelines, which culminated in the Central People's Commissariat of Justice's December 1933 "Draft Statute of the Chinese Soviet Republic Governing Punishment of Counterrevolutionaries."[6]

Beginning in the late 1920s, true believers and official propagandists from both the CCP and the GMD would regularly vilify one another as "counterrevolutionaries" [fan'geming] and as a "bandit gang" [feibang]. This extreme variety of mutual vilification was not really put to rest until well after the deaths of both Chiang Kai-shek and Mao Zedong in the mid-1970s. The label of counterrevolutionary amounts to a pronouncement of political criminality in the eyes of a one-party police state, though sometimes it can also refer to ordinary property-related offenses such as vandalism that would be routinely punishable under a less repressive legal system.[7] The mere presence of opposition to CCP rule, or "counterrevolution," justifies state terror, according to Mao Zedong: "Every village should be in a state of terror for a brief period; otherwise, counterrevolutionary activities in the villages cannot be suppressed . . . To correct wrongs one must go to the other extreme."[8]

---

3. In rebuilding the PRC's legal system during the 1980s and 1990s, Mao Zedong's more pragmatic successors had to reinvent much of the legal wheel that the late Qing and Republican Era had bequeathed to Mao's party-state.

4. See Stéphane Courtois & Jean-Louis Panné, "The Comintern in Action," in *The Black Book of Communism*, pp. 271–332, esp. 275–276.

5. Griffin, *Treatment of Counterrevolutionaries*, p. 33.

6. Ibid., pp. 155–160.

7. In the mid-1990s, the various decrees and statutes against counterrevolution in the PRC were finally changed to laws against "endangering state security" [weihai guojia anquan], while that government's long tradition of cracking down hard on real and imagined political opposition remained unchanged.

8. Mao Zedong, "Report on an Investigation of the Peasant Movement in Hunan, March 1927," *Selected Works of Mao Zedong*, vol. 1 (Beijing: Foreign Languages Press, 1965), p. 28.

Justification of large-scale political arrests, as well as other features of the aforementioned December 1931 "instruction" and similar decrees in the Jiangxi Soviet, would recur in the legal policies and criminal law instituted by successive Chinese Communist regimes throughout the twentieth century. This general pattern was much the same for Leninist regimes throughout Eurasia, especially during the phase of consolidation. According to Richard K. Carlton, "Every Communist assumption of power—in Poland, Czechoslovakia, Hungary, Romania, Bulgaria, Yugoslavia, and Albania—was accompanied by mass arrests aimed primarily at the elimination of the opposition. Some prisoners were interned and others were assigned to forced labor."[9]

The CCP authorities strongly opposed the widely recognized principle of every citizen's equality before the law, in their polemics as well as in their laws and ordinary practices. The Jiangxi government's strongly hierarchical approach to enforcing its laws undoubtedly encountered some opposition. Otherwise, why would Luo Mai (pseud. of Li Weihan, an important CCP official) have bothered writing a fiery polemic in favor of "smashing" the idea of equality before the law?[10] The enduring popular appeal of equality before the law may be sensed from Perry Link's report on a PRC audience's response to an early 1980s theatrical performance: "The longest applause in a broadcast of Xing Yixun's 'Power and Law' was for the line, 'All people are equal before the law.'"[11]

Ordinarily, CCP members who stand accused of a crime initially go before a secret hearing held by a party committee, and can be tried by a court only after having first been stripped of their party membership. This partial screening from criminal prosecution among CCP members has long persisted, and is the modern counterpart to the traditional *Ba yi* [The Eight Considerations], "the system of milder sanctions for the educated classes" that late Qing legal reformers had abolished as anachronistic and elitist. In its formal recognition of the unequal status before the law of CCP members vis-à-vis the general public, the partial screening of party

9. See Richard K. Carlton, ed., *Forced Labor in the "People's Democracies"* (New York: Mid-European Studies Center, 1955), p. 8.

10. Luo Mai's polemic, originally published in *Douzheng* [Struggle] 61 (May 1934), may be consulted in *Shisou ziliaoshi gongfei ziliao* [Materials on the Chinese Communists from the Shisou Archive] (Stanford: Hoover Institution, 1960), no. 008.2105, 7720, vol. 6, 1134, reel 18.

11. See Perry Link, *The Uses of Literature: Life in the Socialist Chinese Literary System* (Princeton: Princeton Univ. Press, 2000), p. 270.

members from prosecution represents another step backward from the legal reforms of the late Qing and Republican Era.[12]

Indeed, for a government that was so violently opposed to inequalities in socioeconomic class, the Jiangxi Soviet adopted a strikingly hierarchical treatment of criminal suspects on the basis of such factors as their formal ranking within both the party and society, along with their willingness to confess and implicate other alleged wrongdoers. While explicitly militating against a "class society" *[jieji shehui]*, Mao Zedong and his confreres were from the very beginning establishing an intensely hierarchical "ranked society" *[dengji shehui]*, as suggested by Fox Butterfield.[13] Admittedly, the legal systems in countries that embrace the principle of all citizens' equality before the law cannot always live up to it in practice. However, legal systems that aspire to this ideal come much closer to achieving it in practice than do legal systems that treat the principle of equality before the law with indifference or contempt.

A pronounced ambiguity in wording and numerous escape clauses in the legal policies ensured that CCP judicial cadres enjoyed broad discretion in sentencing a prisoner. Griffin notes that the Jiangxi Soviet leaders pursued the "maximum degree of flexibility" at the expense of "stability" in their legal system.[14] The phrase "under less serious circumstances" *[qingxing jiao qing]* repeatedly introduces various punishments less severe than

12. The *Ba yi* date from at least the Tang Code *[Tang lü]*, according to Li Jiafu, *Zhongguo fazhi shi*, p. 125. See also Ladany, *Law and Legality in China*, p. 46; Bodde & Morris, *Law in Imperial China*, pp. 34–35; and Harold M. Tanner, "Policing, Punishment, and the Individual: Criminal Justice in China," *Law and Social Inquiry: Journal of the American Bar Foundation* 20.1 (1995): 277–303, esp. 287. For a literary representation of the continuing secrecy surrounding CCP members' alleged criminal activity, see Liu Binyan, "Diwuge chuan dayi de ren" [The Fifth Person to Wear the Overcoat], *Beijing wenyi* 11 (1979): 28–35, esp. 35. Translated as "The Fifth Man in the Overcoat" by John S. Rohsenow with Perry Link in Liu Binyan, *"People or Monsters?" and Other Stories and Reportage from China after Mao*, ed. Perry Link (Bloomington: Indiana Univ. Press, 1983), pp. 79–97. Of course, if a party member is the target of a purge by the higher-ups, such as in Mao Zedong's purge of Liu Shaoqi, the internal party decision about whether to strip the target of his party membership can be made very swiftly in order to expedite the miscreant's punishment. Liu Shaoqi could not have been locked up in an unheated Kaifeng prison cell to die lying in his own excrement until he had first been formally ejected from the party.

13. Fox Butterfield, *Alive in the Bitter Sea* (New York: Times Books, 1982).

14. Griffin, *Treatment of Counterrevolutionaries*, pp. 143, 147, 149. Writing from a late-1960s perspective, John Hazard notes that both Mao Zedong and Kim Il-song infused their legal systems with even more flexibility than was the case in other state socialist nations, and wonders if this might represent a permanent "hostility toward formality and complexity in the maintenance of the social order." See *Communists and Their Law* (Chicago: Univ. of Chicago Press, 1969), p. 143.

the oft-stipulated penalty of execution, but these circumstances are nowhere specified, nor is the responsibility or methodology for arriving at these extenuating circumstances explained.

The ad hoc and arbitrary aspects of the legal system were also enhanced by regular recourse to the principle of analogy, whereby "undesignated crimes were to receive the same degree of punishment as similar crimes listed." An example of this is in Article 30 of the 1933 Draft Statute of the Chinese Soviet Republic Governing Punishment of Counterrevolutionaries: "Any counterrevolutionary criminal behavior not included in this statute may be punished according to an article in this statute dealing with similar crimes."[15] As Richard Carlton notes in regard to the various people's republics and people's democracies in central and eastern Europe after World War II, anything constituting a threat to "the system of government and the social order" can be considered a criminal offense, even if no prohibition of that perceived threat is on the books.[16] CCP procurators [jiancha guan], who combined the functions of prosecutor and administrative supervisor within the criminal justice system, thus enjoyed an immense flexibility that allowed them to order the arrest and trial of a suspect for performing an activity that had not been specifically prohibited in any statute or decree.[17] It would not be until the promulgation of the PRC Criminal Law of 1979 that a new restriction on the principle of analogy (Article 79) finally lowered the frequency of its use: case-by-case approval from the Supreme People's Court would thenceforth be required.[18]

Severe punishments such as execution[19] or multi-year terms of "hard labor" [kugong] in "redemption-through-labor reformatories" [laodong ganhua yuan] would be meted out to most "counterrevolutionary elements" [fan'geming fenzi] from such ideologically reprehensible social backgrounds as landlord, rich farmer, and capitalist.[20] Formally instituted

15. Griffin, *Treatment of Counterrevolutionaries*, pp. 51, 155, 160.

16. The principle of analogy violates the time-honored legal principle of *nullum crimen sine lege, nulla poena sine lege penale.* See Carlton, *Forced Labor in the "People's Democracies,"* p. 10.

17. Tanner notes the Soviet Russian precursor of the Chinese Communist procurator in *Strike Hard!,* pp. 42–43.

18. Ibid., pp. 16–17.

19. One of most striking official directives on executions was sent down by the Chinese Workers' and Peasants' Red Army Third Army Corps in 1932. According to the directive, if a landlord refused to hand over an assessed fine and meet with rebel officials, both he and his family members would be executed, and the graves of his ancestors would be dug up and desecrated. See Griffin, *Treatment of Counterrevolutionaries*, p. 34.

20. Ibid.; Wu Hongda, *Zhongguo de Gulage*, p. 73. The term "farmer" is preferred to the inappropriately pejorative "peasant" for *nongmin* or *zhuangjiaren*, with the understanding

in 1932, the redemption-through-labor reformatories had the dual mission of "redeeming" *[ganhua]* inmates through persuasion and forcing prisoners to engage in economic production *[shengchan]*.[21] The *laodong ganhua yuan* thus emerged as the forerunner of the modern laogai, with its emphasis on remolding and production.

Ganhua, a phrase that the Communists borrowed from GMD penology, is a Mencian concept akin to "guided redemption" that refers to a positive change of errant behavior through someone else's persuasion or good example. In less than two decades, "retutelage through labor" *[laodong ganhua]* would give way to "remolding through labor" *[laodong gaizao* or *laogai]*, which would remain the standard term throughout the latter half of the twentieth century. *Laodong gaizao* has often been translated as "labor reform," but this is problematic for a number of reasons. *Gaizao* has long been officially translated in the PRC as "remolding," for the term connotes a more thoroughgoing transformation than mere "reform," which is usually translated as *gaige*. Deng Xiaoping utilizes the term *gaizao* when referring to the early-1950s "movement of ideological remolding among intellectuals," having urged the CCP to "continue breaking up the intellectuals' ranks and remolding them."[22]

Lighter penalties for exactly the same counterrevolutionary offense would typically be handed down to offenders from the relatively impoverished and thus automatically "oppressed" social classes such as poor and middle farmers and hired laborers.[23] Offenders in these less serious cases

---

that Chinese farmers often moonlight at occupations other than the raising of crops and livestock. See, for example, David Zweig, *Freeing China's Farmers: Rural Restructuring in the Reform Era* (Armonk, NY: M. E. Sharpe, 1997). According to Chinese Communist class analysis during Mao's lifetime, benevolence was effectively inversely proportional to wealth, making landlords and capitalists the most evil, or "black," and hired laborers and poor farmers the most benevolent, or "red." "Middle farmers" *[zhong nong]*, who till their own land but neither hire laborers nor hire themselves out, were almost always considered "red," while "rich farmers" *[fu nong]*, who both hire laborers and work their own land, were usually considered "black." In the largely rural Jiangxi Soviet, rich farmers and landlords were the most common targets of punishment, which all too often was execution. The fanaticism that was partly to blame for the high death toll above and beyond battle casualties in Jiangxi resonates with that of the nineteenth-century Taiping rebels, who were notorious for executing large numbers of people for such relatively minor offenses as opium smoking and adultery. See Jonathan D. Spence, *God's Chinese Son: The Taiping Heavenly Kingdom of Hong Xiuquan* (New York: Norton, 1996), p. 194.

21. Xue Meiqing et al., eds., *Zhongguo jianyu shi*, p. 327.

22. Deng Xiaoping, *Report on the Rectification Campaign* (Beijing: Foreign Languages Press, 1957), pp. 16, 21. See also Trygve Lötveit, *Chinese Communism, 1931–1934: Experience in Civil Government*, 2nd ed. (London: Curzon Press, 1979), p. 114.

23. Shao-chuan Leng, *Justice in Communist China: A Survey of the Judicial System of the Chinese People's Republic* (Dobbs Ferry, NY: Oceana Publications, 1967), p. 7. Carlton dis-

could be administratively sentenced to a "hard labor brigade" *[kugong dui* or *laoyi dui]* without going through the formality of even a makeshift trial.[24] Because of their bad class background and the government's need for cheap labor, able-bodied rich farmers and landlords who were charged with no crime at all were also often conscripted for corvée service in the hard labor brigades.[25]

Whether a redemption-through-labor reformatory or a hard labor brigade, each prison camp would theoretically pursue its dual mission: to guide inmates to "make themselves anew" *[zixin]* in terms of ideology and work habits and to force them to engage in production to help defray government expenditures on prison maintenance. In representing the supposed ideological transformation of the inmate, the Jiangxi Soviet's "making oneself anew" would later give way to the PRC's "remolding" *[gaizao].*[26] Yet the *laogai* system's theoretical commitment to remolding has often been lacking in practice; a 1991–92 survey of the high illiteracy rate in Qinghai's relatively prosperous Fifth Laogai Brigade reveals that "teaching prisoners *[fanren]* is not something that is considered a priority of the management."[27]

This dual mission would remain much the same in CCP-controlled regions for the rest of the twentieth century and into the twenty-first, along with the rarely proclaimed but easily perceived punitive mission.[28] Over

---

cusses a similar double standard in the Warsaw Pact regimes for "the people" versus enemies such as "bourgeois exploiters" in terms of legal and constitutional protections. See *Forced Labor in the "People's Democracies,"* p. 10.

24. Lötveit, *Chinese Communism, 1931–1934,* p. 115. This practice of administrative detention and sentencing to forced labor would become formally institutionalized in the PRC during the 1950s as "reeducation through labor" *[laodong jiaoyang* or *laojiao]* and would be reaffirmed and maintained during the Deng-Jiang Era. Regarding the least serious types of offenses, many civil cases and the most minor criminal cases were remanded to conciliation committees for settlement, as would mostly remain the norm after 1949.

25. Theoretically, rich farmers were supposed to be drafted for labor brigade service only during the slack agricultural season, while landlords were supposed to serve "permanently," or throughout the year and for as many years as their labor was required. Because the Jiangxi Soviet perished through GMD military conquest in 1934, it is hard to say how many years the landlord-class laborers might have been forced to toil in camps before being released from labor servitude. See Lötveit, *Chinese Communism, 1931–1934,* pp. 154, 181.

26. Ibid., pp. 114–115.

27. Seymour & Anderson, *New Ghosts, Old Ghosts,* p. 168.

28. Were forced labor not partly punitive in nature, it would be hard to explain why so many PRC prisoners have mutilated themselves or swallowed foreign objects in order to get a rest from work in the infirmary. One 1990s Xinjiang prison administrator admitted off the record that conditions inside the camps had to be harsher and more painful than life on the outside for the system to work properly; he seemed to be referring to the deterrent effect that a punitive prison regime would have. See Seymour & Anderson, *New Ghosts, Old Ghosts,* p. 176.

several decades, the range of prison labor products would expand from the straw sandals and coarse paper of the Jiangxi Soviet to everything from farm produce to motor vehicles in the Deng-Jiang Era.[29] Both the laogai system's insider apologists and its most outspoken critics, such as Harry Wu, have tended to overestimate the overall profitability and efficiency of prison enterprises. For example, Wu has claimed that Chinese prison enterprises "constitute a large proportion of the PRC's national economy."[30] James Seymour and Richard Anderson indicate that while some laogai and laojiao enterprises are profitable, many more are not, when the overhead costs of the system are factored in. A 1990 PRC study conceded that the production output of these prison enterprises in 1988 covered no more than 85% of the costs required to maintain the system.[31] As Jean-Luc Domenach has pointed out, the PRC prison system was not organized along the lines of economic rationality, but was originally "conceived for political objectives and on a military model."[32]

Chinese prison enterprises sometimes compared favorably with civilian state enterprises during the guerrilla base period and the Mao Era, but not during the 1980s and 1990s, with the increasing efficiency and adaptability of the PRC's mixed economy. As Seymour and Anderson have noted, the fact that the Qinghai provincial authorities have significantly downsized their laogai and transferred significant land holdings to civilian enterprises during the Deng-Jiang Era suggests that modern economic rationality does not favor a large prison sector in the economy.[33]

Other national prison systems such as that in the U.S. have also encountered major problems in making prison enterprises economically rational, as discussed by James B. Jacobs. He lists seven typical shortcomings of U.S. prison enterprises, including backward infrastructure, inconvenient location, insufficient capital, an unmotivated and poorly educated workforce, security-related delays, restrictions on the marketing of prison-made goods, and unpredictable inflows and outflows of the prison workforce.[34]

29. Wu, *Laogai: The Chinese Gulag,* p. 45.

30. Ibid., p. 41.

31. In 1988, the national prison production total of 4 billion yuan amounted to merely 0.2% of the PRC's agricultural and industrial output, according to Seymour & Anderson, *New Ghosts, Old Ghosts,* p. 209.

32. Domenach, *L'archipel oublié,* p. 414.

33. Seymour & Anderson, *New Ghosts, Old Ghosts,* p. 174.

34. James B. Jacobs, "United States of America: Prison Labour, a Tale of Two Penologies," in *Prison Labour: Salvation or Slavery?,* ed. Dirk van Zyl Smit & Frieder Dünkel, Oñati International Series in Law and Society (Aldershot, U.K.: Ashgate, 1999), pp. 269–280, esp. 275–278.

To a large degree, most of these problems also afflict prison enterprises in the PRC and virtually every other country that utilizes a similar system. The PRC's frequent use of highly exploitative practices can somewhat mitigate these problems within the prison enterprises, but cannot overcome them.

The dearth of procedural safeguards for individual suspects and prisoners that characterized the Jiangxi Soviet would continue to contribute to regular miscarriages of justice under subsequent CCP regimes.[35] A CCP document from 1931 indicates that their Jiangxi legal officials were being "misled by false confessions that they had themselves extracted by the use of torture."[36] Although various prohibitions against torture and corporal punishment had been formalized in 1931 and 1933, "the traditional practice of using force to extract a confession continued in widespread use."[37] This pattern would continue after the establishment of the PRC, whose prison officials were naturally inclined to exert strong pressure on inmates to confess—as can be seen in the get-tough language and threatening tone of the ubiquitous prison slogan *Tanbai cong kuan, kangju cong yan* [Lenient treatment for those who confess, and severity for those who resist].[38]

Records of Jiangxi Soviet criminal trial proceedings make no mention whatsoever of the defense attorney, who would remain at best a marginal figure in nearly all criminal trials in CCP regimes throughout the twentieth century.[39] Writing from an early-1990s perspective, former political prisoner Gao Xin notes that practically all PRC criminal defense attorneys are submissive party members who do little more than meekly argue for mitigating circumstances in the judge's sentencing of their clients—along with serving as an informal conduit for letters between the inmates and their families.[40] If a defendant pleaded his own case with too much vigor or too little contrition, the court would often extend his sentence or add another type of punishment for the defendant's having dared

35. Seymour & Anderson note that what continued to be most sorely lacking in the laogai of the 1990s was "a system of procedures which would protect the generally agreed-upon rights" of each camp prisoner *[laogai fan]* (*New Ghosts, Old Ghosts*, p. 217).

36. Lötveit, *Chinese Communism, 1931–1934*, p. 142.

37. Griffin, *Treatment of Counterrevolutionaries*, p. 41.

38. Leng, *Justice in Communist China*, p. 162. Various PRC constitutions and laws have included prohibitions against torture, and manuals for prison cadres and guards have joined in criticizing torture; see *Laogai gongzuo*, p. 17. Yet this practice has continued in many labor camps [*laogai ying*, in non-PRC parlance] all the way into the twenty-first century.

39. Lötveit, *Chinese Communism, 1931–1934*, p. 117.

40. Gao Xin, *Beiwei yu huihuang: yige "Liu si" shounanzhe de yu zhong zhaji* [Disgrace and Glory: Prison Jottings of a Victim of "June Fourth"] (Taipei: Lianjing, 1991), pp. 132–133.

to question the basis of what was nearly always a preordained guilty verdict.[41] The largely ceremonial function of a typical criminal trial under the CCP tallies with the cynical view of law among many of the leaders in charge of administering it, as can be seen in an excerpt from a 1934 article by Commissar of Justice Liang Botai: "Whatever is to the advantage of the revolution is the law. Whenever it is to the advantage of the revolution, the legal procedure [falü de shouxu] can at any time be adapted. One ought not to hinder the interests of the revolution because of legal procedure."[42]

Such official CCP scorn for legal procedure abetted the widespread use of state terror and mob violence not only in the Jiangxi Soviet, but also during PRC witch-hunts against landlords and counterrevolutionaries (early 1950s), capitalist roaders (who "take the road to capitalism") and "reactionaries" of all kinds (late 1960s), and nonviolent protesters and union organizers (1989–90). What Gregor Benton aptly calls the "purge mania" that spread widely from the Jiangxi Soviet would also reverberate through CCP culture and politics for many decades.[43] In 1949, Mao Zedong laid crucial groundwork for such future chaos and injustice by insisting that his newly founded national government (PRC) cast aside all previous legal codes from the Republican Era and late Qing, and cobble together a minimalist new legal system from the ground up.[44]

Dong Biwu and some other relatively moderate CCP officials argued for greater use of legal procedure and constitutional restraints during the 1950s, but hard-line decision makers such as Mao Zedong and Peng Zhen

41. Lötveit, *Chinese Communism, 1931–1934*, p. 118. On the common practice of lengthening the prison term for a convict who unrepentantly appealed his guilty verdict during the Mao Era, see Jerome Alan Cohen, *The Criminal Process in the People's Republic of China, 1949–1963: An Introduction* (Cambridge: Harvard Univ. Press, 1968), pp. 38–40. The typical pattern of a trial in the CCP-dominated criminal justice system has been accurately summarized by the phrase *xian pan hou shen* [verdict first, trial second]. The conviction rate in the PRC criminal justice system was more than 99% of all cases brought to trial as of the early 1980s, and it is doubtful that it has declined more than a couple of percentage points since then.

42. Quoted from the journal *Hongse Zhonghua* [Red China] and cited in Lötveit, *Chinese Communism, 1931–1934*, p. 140. The authors have modified Lötveit's translation somewhat for style and clarity.

43. Gregor Benton, *Mountain Fires: The Red Army's Three-Year War in South China, 1934–1938* (Berkeley: Univ. of California Press, 1992), p. 282. According to Harold Tanner, Liang Botai's informal "societal" model of socialist legality would be a descendant of the nihilistic view of law during the USSR's War Communism period (1918–21), and contrasts with the procedurally oriented "jural" model of socialist legality that achieved ascendancy under post-Stalin and post-Mao regimes. See *Strike Hard!*, pp. 26–27.

44. Leng, *Justice in Communist China*, p. 27.

saw to it that the PRC's laws remained an extremely flexible adjunct to party policies and political movements.[45] Occasional liberalizing calls for reducing party control of the legal system would typically be trumped by mainstream appeals to the overarching principle of the party's "absolute leadership" (i.e., control), and judges would commonly consult with and defer to relevant party committees in matters such as sentencing.[46]

Proximate Influences: The CCP Guerrilla Bases and the USSR

Having summarily discarded all the "reactionary" legal codes and judicial structure of the Republican Era in early 1949, Mao Zedong turned to two sources in his improvisation of the state's new legal machinery: the law codes and judicial organs of both the USSR and the old CCP guerrilla bases—mainly the Jiangxi Soviet and the arid northwestern region headquartered at Yan'an in northern Shaanxi province (1936–47).[47] There has been much discussion of the degree to which the Soviet gulag influenced the PRC system; basically, the Soviet system can be seen as a proximate influence on the Chinese Communist system. China had a long history of forced labor; the USSR provided a twentieth-century model, along with advice from Soviet correctional officers during the 1950s. Among the many contributions of the CCP guerrilla camps to be discussed below is the emphasis on "making oneself anew" [zixin] through labor, a notion that by 1949 would have evolved into the more objectifying "remolding" [gaizao]. Though Sun Xiaoli criticizes and questions the motives of such commentators as Harry Wu for arguing that the Soviet gulag was a highly significant influence on the Chinese laogai, he offers mainly nativist sentiments and little but vague generalizations and hearsay comments about the supposedly negligible Soviet influence. For instance, he places much emphasis upon the prison camp systems in the CCP guerrilla bases of the 1930s and 1940s, as if their mere existence were sufficient proof to dismiss the significance of Soviet influence during the 1950s. Yet

45. Ibid., p. 164. For more on Dong Biwu's well-meaning but unrealistic prediction that governance by disruptive movements would soon be replaced by the rule of law in the 1950s, see Chow Ching-wen, *Ten Years of Storm: The True Story of the Communist Regime in China* (New York: Holt, Rinehart, & Winston, 1960), pp. 92–93.

46. Leng, *Justice in Communist China*, pp. 62–65.

47. Ibid., p. 28. Wu Hongda refers to a model Soviet Russian 1933 "Remolding-through-labor Legal Code" *[Laodong gaizao fadian]* in *Zhongguo de Gulage*, p. 17.

to Sun's credit, he does acknowledge the pervasive 1950s CCP slogan of "learn from the Soviet big brother," and indicates the names and specialties of some of the Soviet advisors then working closely with the PRC's security and legal apparatus.[48]

With regard to the CCP guerrilla bases, the laws and practices relating to trials and imprisonment in the Yan'an area tended to be more moderate than those of the Jiangxi Soviet, as indicated by fewer executions and less mob-style vigilante justice.[49] However, the two systems resembled each other in several ways, including the large plurality of convicts sentenced to forced labor as well as the terminology used to describe the forced labor and its supposedly corrective influence on prisoners. Of sentences meted out to Jiangxi Soviet counterrevolutionaries in 1932, the most common type was forced labor.[50] A 1939 report from the CCP Shaan-Gan-Ning Border Region in the northwest indicated much the same pattern of sentencing and used basically the same terminology, including "guided redemption" [ganhua] and "making oneself anew" [zixin] for the affective aspect of behavioral correction, as well as laoyi for conscripted or convict labor.[51] Domenach suggests that the Jiangxi Soviet labor camp tradition combined with the Yan'an spirit of coercive "reeducation" to generate Mao Zedong's animating concept of the PRC prison camp system, remolding through labor.[52]

During the Yan'an zhengfeng [rectification] movement of 1942–44, the intelligentsia and even many officials encountered a high-pressure atmosphere of ideological indoctrination, but the verb "remold" had as yet only been occasionally used with an individual human object or point of reference.[53] In 1942, Yan'an journalists received an order from the Central

48. See Sun Xiaoli, Zhongguo laodong gaizao zhidu de lilun yu shijian—lishi yu xianshi [Theory and Practice of the Chinese Remolding through Labor System—History and Actuality] (Sanhe: Zhongguo Zhengfa Daxue chubanshe, 1994), pp. 18–20.

49. After all, this CCP-governed border region was under the nominal authority of the wartime GMD regime from 1937 to 1945, and Mao Zedong had other practical reasons for pursuing more tolerant policies than was the case in the Jiangxi Soviet.

50. Griffin, Treatment of Counterrevolutionaries, pp. 38–39.

51. Qi Li, ed., Shaan-Gan-Ning bianqu shilu [True Accounts from the Shaanxi-Gansu-Ningxia Border Region] (Yan'an?: Jiefang she, 1939), p. 35.

52. Domenach, L'archipel oublié, p. 56.

53. In 1937, Mao Zedong's essay "On Practice" [Shijian lun] underlined the necessity of "remolding" persons and their thought, but did not place this idea in the context of prison management. See Mao Zedong xuanji, vol. 1, pp. 282–298. According to Peter J. Seybolt, by 1943 "disagreement with any particular [CCP] policy had become tantamount to disloyalty, not only to the Party but to the nation." See "Terror and Conformity: Counterespionage Campaigns, Rectification, and Mass Movements of 1942–43," Modern China 12.1 (1986): 39–73, esp. 41.

Propaganda Department to "remold" their newspapers; however, this directive was not aimed at themselves as individuals, as would often be the case from the 1950s through the 1970s.[54] Instead, the more traditional and less foreign sounding, or technocratic, concept of "making oneself anew" [zixin] appeared regularly during the Yan'an period in everything from rice-sprout song drama [yangge] to politico-legal discourse.[55]

The important concept of "remolding" [gaizao] appeared quite frequently from the first decade of the Republic through the 1930s within Chinese political and social-science discourse that referred to a deficient collective object that needed major overhauling, such as a government agency or social group.[56] As early as 1915, Chen Duxiu was advocating the "remolding" of youth as a collective entity.[57] By 1934, "remolding" was being increasingly used with a deficient individual person as its object, such as disgraced or purged party members who were punished through assignment to menial jobs like sweeping floors or carrying water buckets.[58] By 1944, CCP prison authorities in the wartime guerrilla bases were already writing about "remolding prisoners" [gaizao fanren] and "remolding [inmates'] thought" [gaizao sixiang].[59] However, the concept of "remolding" does not seem to have become entrenched in the terminology of China's prison system until around 1950, the year after the term began to appear with increasing frequency in the speeches and writings of Mao Zedong such as "On the People's Democratic Dictatorship" (1949).[60] Key evidence that the idea of remolding had not yet been ap-

54. Brantly Womack, "Media and the Chinese Public: A Survey of the Beijing Media Audience," *Chinese Sociology and Anthropology* 18.3–4 (1986): 162–163.

55. The collectively authored 1943 *yangge* play "Zhao Fugui Makes Himself Anew" [*Zhao Fugui zixin*] is discussed in David Holm, *Art and Ideology in Revolutionary China* (Oxford: Clarendon Press, 1991), pp. 278–279. In *Treatment of Counterrevolutionaries,* p. 105, Patricia Griffin analyzes a type of *zixin* meeting held in 1946 to urge wartime collaborators to make themselves anew.

56. The concept of "remolding" appeared in both the academic debates of armchair reformers and the rancorous calls to do a makeover of the Jiangxi Soviet's government organs and party branches by ferreting out and purging all their hidden counterrevolutionaries. The latter event occurred in 1931 and is one of a long series of CCP political witch-hunts to "eliminate counterrevolutionaries" [*suqing fan'geming* or *su fan*], often from within the party's own ranks. See Wen Yu, *Zhongguo zuo huo* [China's Leftist Calamities] (Hong Kong: Tiandi tushu, 1994), p. 85.

57. Chen Duxiu, "Tongxin," 2.

58. Wen Yu, *Zhongguo zuo huo,* p. 111. This occurred during the Jiangxi Soviet's fourth *su fan* political witch-hunt.

59. Xue Meiqing et al., eds., *Zhongguo jianyu shi,* pp. 338, 360.

60. Translated in Conrad Brandt, Benjamin Schwartz, & John K. Fairbank, *A Documentary History of Chinese Communism* (Cambridge: Harvard Univ. Press, 1952), pp. 449–

plied in a systematic way to prison camps under the CCP in 1949 comes from Qinghe Camp in Hebei, which was formally founded by the Beijing Public Security Bureau in February 1949. Of the two names assigned to this labor camp at that time, neither contains the concept of remolding: the Qinghe Training Brigade *[Qinghe xunlian da dui]* and the Qinghe Discipline and Training Brigade *[Qinghe guan xun dui]*.[61]

Mao's watershed 1949 speech stipulates that his new government will handle most of its reactionary enemies with "remolding through labor" *[laodong gaizao]*, and will force such reactionaries to labor if they are unwilling to do so.[62] Like the new PRC regime's initial imitation of Soviet central planning for the economy, this new mid-century focus on "remolding" individual enemies through hard labor seems to be a Soviet Russian borrowing, most likely from the official 1920s term "reforging" *[perekovka]*.[63] The Soviet Russian penal theorist A. A. Bogdanov claimed in the 1920s that great moral benefit would be achieved through a system of hard convict labor—a notion to which CCP leaders were culturally receptive, according to Seymour and Anderson.[64]

In 1950s draft versions of the PRC Criminal Law, which was not finally promulgated until 1979, "China drew freely upon Soviet penal law theories, while Soviet law and the Soviet legal system were taken as models."[65]

46[1]. The original version of this speech, "Lun renmin minzhu zhuanzheng," can be found in *Mao Zedong xuanji*, vol. 4, pp. 1468–1482. Lenin and Stalin had already conceived of the proletarian dictatorship being wielded against the enemy classes, while the masses would enjoy the tightly circumscribed sort of "democracy" known as "democratic centralism." Mao's innovation, if it can be called such, was to proclaim the absolute identity of the interests of "the people" with those of the CCP; he thus constantly refers to party-controlled organizations as "the people's this" and "the people's that." Mao's speech was delivered on 1 July 1949 to commemorate the twenty-eighth anniversary of the CCP's founding; exactly three months later, the PRC would be formally founded in Beijing.

61. Sun Xiaoli, *Zhongguo laodong gaizao zhidu de lilun yu shijian*, p. 24.

62. Brandt, Schwartz, & Fairbank, *A Documentary History*, p. 457. The authors have modified the translation slightly in order to preserve the important distinction between "remolding through labor" *[laodong gaizao]* and "reeducation through labor" *[laodong jiaoyang]*. See also Mao Tse-tung, "On the People's Democratic Dictatorship," *Selected Works of Mao Tse-tung*, vol. 4 (Beijing: Foreign Languages Press, 1961), p. 419.

63. Jacques Rossi, *The Gulag Handbook: An Encyclopedia Dictionary of Soviet Penitentiary Institutions and Terms Related to the Forced Labor Camps*, trans. William A. Burhans (New York: Paragon House, 1989), p. 298. See also Aleksandr I. Solzhenitsyn, *The Gulag Archipelago, 1918–1956: An Experiment in Literary Investigation*, vol. 2, trans. Thomas P. Whitney (New York: Harper & Row, 1975), p. 67. The Russian term for "reforging" convicts through forced labor was introduced to the northern Solovetsky Island prison camp network no later than 1929.

64. Seymour & Anderson, *New Ghosts, Old Ghosts*, p. 17.

65. Tanner, *Strike Hard!*, p. 9.

Many Russian experts in penology and law went to China shortly after Mao's accession to power to help PRC authorities work on the new legal code, which resembles the USSR Code of 1928 in terms of both its structure and its underlying philosophy. According to Harold Tanner, structural similarities between the Russian and PRC codes include the division into "General and Special Provisions," an opening statement summarizing the functions of the law, and the prioritizing of counterrevolution as the primary and most serious offense of all. Both legal codes were explicitly based on an "instrumentalist philosophy in which law was regarded as a weapon of class struggle," a tool of "social engineering," and a device for "the engineering of human souls."[66]

The founding Minister of Public Security Luo Ruiqing even saw himself as following in the footsteps of the inaugural Soviet Cheka head and security chief, Felix Dzerzhinsky, whose portrait hung prominently on the wall of Luo's office. Luo, who had studied the USSR security apparatus very carefully and admiringly in the USSR in the late 1920s, greatly resembled his model and mentor. According to Roger Faligot and Rémi Kauffer, both security chiefs "were very able and disinterested, without feelings, but without personal ambition; servants of the Revolution, implacable, inflexible, convinced that repression was only the first stage towards a better society, hence the exceptional vigor with which they implemented its tortures, too, but without any personal sadism."[67]

To be sure, PRC penal practice and theory also have indigenous, non-Soviet characteristics, particularly the heavy emphasis on remolding prisoners' inner thoughts.[68] At the same time, the PRC's borrowings from the USSR at the formative stage of laogai development loom large by any standard, and provide a reasonable basis for comparing the two systems.[69]

66. Ibid.

67. Roger Faligot & Rémi Kauffer, *The Chinese Secret Service*, trans. Christine Donougher (London: Headline Books, 1989), pp. 133, 345.

68. Domenach, *L'archipel oublié*, p. 57.

69. Prison camps during the Mao Era were strikingly similar to the USSR gulag, though of course the PRC incarcerated a smaller percentage of its population than did the USSR, and Mao's camps were generally less deadly than Stalin's. While Seymour & Anderson are understandably skeptical about characterizations of the 1990s PRC prison camps as a "gulag," their apparent dismissal of the relevance of the gulag to the laogai seems inappropriately categorical, especially in terms of the Mao Era laogai and its historical impact (*New Ghosts, Old Ghosts*, p. 17). Domenach, for example, shows how instructive comparisons between the laogai and the gulag can be, noting that the percentage of the overall population incarcerated in the prison system was always lower in the PRC than it was in the USSR. See *L'archipel oublié*, pp. 491–492.

Establishment of the PRC Laogai Camps

Key divisions in the CCP's People's Liberation Army (PLA) swept south-
ward from their strongholds throughout the Northeast (Dongbei, or
Manchuria) to conquer practically all of mainland China by the end of
1949. Of course, the PLA divisions in the Northeast received much assistance from PLA forces and Communist guerrilla forces elsewhere in
China. Nonetheless, it was the Northeast, not the Yan'an region in the
northwest, that served as the CCP's key base area and springboard for the
conquest of all of mainland China during the civil war. Though Stalin's
army had pilfered a huge amount of the Northeast's industrial machinery before turning the region over to informal CCP control in the wake
of Japan's surrender in 1945, enough of the Northeast's industrial infrastructure remained to make it the ideal location for pilot enterprises and
industrial reconstruction.

From 1947 to 1949, the CCP took advantage of its early victories over
the GMD in the Northeast and that region's relatively developed industrial economy to establish several prison camps, whose productive facilities far outclassed their forerunners in Jiangxi and Yan'an.[70] Instead of
limiting their purview to basic economic activities such as farming, simple textile production, road construction, and military porterage, the
Northeast camps branched into relatively high-tech areas such as mining
and artillery shell manufacturing.[71]

One of the largest early laogai camps was Shenyang's Gongchangling
laogai dui, which was established in September 1949.[72] Another significant
step in the development of the CCP prison camp took place in Lingshou,
Hebei, from 1946 to 1949. Prison cadres directed inmates to work at opening up new farmland and building roads in underdeveloped regions.[73]

The Northeast camps also pioneered the explicitly military organization of camp inmates into partially self-supervising units such as "brigades"
[dui], "squads"*[ban]*, and "groups" *[zu]*, thereby requiring fewer guards

70. The Northeast is unusually rich in natural resources and benefited economically from
large inputs of Japanese capital and industrial construction — especially from 1932 to 1945 —
in spite of suffering the injustice and indignity of foreign control through the puppet
Manchukuo regime.

71. Wu, *Laogai: The Chinese Gulag,* p. 59. Laszlo Ladany notes that "many new reforms
were introduced in the Northeast before being adopted for the whole country by the Central Government" in Beijing; see *The Communist Party of China and Marxism,* p. 197.

72. Xue Meiqing et al., eds., *Zhongguo jianyu shi,* p. 383.

73. Ibid., pp. 380–381.

and cadres to supervise the swollen ranks of prisoners. In the original design, a "group" consisted of several inmates, several groups belonged to a "squad," and several squads made up a "small brigade" *[xiao dui]*.[74] According to An Sinan, an inmate from 1968 to 1979, the "large brigade" *[da dui]* has been the largest grouping of prisoners, numbering from 600 to 1,000; the "medium brigade" *[zhong dui]* would contain from 150 to 200 inmates; the "small brigade" *[xiao dui]* or "brigade division" *[fen dui]* would number about 50 prisoners; and the "small group" *[xiao zu]* would have from 10 to 20 inmates. At the medium brigade level and above, cadres would lead as "brigade heads" *[duizhang]* or "political instructors" *[zhidaoyuan]*, while prisoners themselves would be in charge at the lowest levels of the hierarchy as "small-group heads" *[xiao zuzhang]* and occasionally "small-brigade heads" *[xiao duizhang]*. Top camp officials typically include the "commissar" *[zhengwei]*, the "branch brigade head" *[zhiduizhang]*, and the "commandant" *[changzhang]*.[75] Prisoners normally address their guards with the honorific "squad leader" *[banzhang]*, even though a guard might be assigned to a larger or smaller administrative unit than the squad.[76] Because much regional and historical variation continues to exist among Chinese prisons, however, not all prison camps make use of all the above categories and terms, and some camps use other terms. This militarily structured organization based on brigades became a defining trademark of the PRC laogai, the full title of which is Remolding-through-Labor Discipline and Production Brigades *[laodong gaizao guanjiao shengchan dui]*.[77]

From the beginning, the PRC laogai has had a dual character as both a national and a local entity. National governmental organs such as the

74. Ibid., p. 382.

75. Wu, *Laogai: The Chinese Gulag*, p. 59; Xue Meiqing et al., eds., *Zhongguo jianyu shi*, p. 382; and An Sinan, *Lian yu sanbuqu* [The Purgatory Trilogy] (Taipei: Zhongguo dalu zazhishe, 1985), p. 199.

76. Prisoners address their guards as *banzhang* [squad leader] in Zhang Xianliang, *Tu lao qinghua* [Passionate Words from a Village Prison], in *Zhang Xianliang xuanji* [An Anthology of Zhang Xianliang], vol. 2 (Tianjin: Baihua wenyi chubanshe, 1985), p. 27. Harry Wu generally renders *banzhang* by the honorific of "captain" in Wu & Wakeman, *Bitter Winds*, pp. 59, 63, 230–231.

77. Writing about Mao Era China, the social theorist Stanislav Andreski notes that "the present [Maoist] regime aims at the full military utilization of manpower, and is more totalitarian than any system which existed [in China] since the times of Shang Yang [in the state of Qin during the third century B.C.E.]." See Andreski's *Military Organization and Society* (Berkeley: Univ. of California Press, 1971), p. 114. The long appellation for "laogai" is often shortened to Labor-through-Remolding Brigades *[laogai dui]*. See Wu Hongda, *Zhongguo de Gulage*, p. 24.

Ministry of Public Security *[Gong'an bu]* and especially the Ministry of Justice *[Sifa bu]* exert varying degrees of supervision over the laogai, but its camps are mostly under the direct administrative purview of county, municipal, or provincial governments.[78] Under the Department of Justice at the provincial level *[Sifa ting]*, most provinces have a laogai bureau *[laogai ju]* in charge of administering prison camps; Hubei is an example of a province that delegates relatively little of its laogai administrative duties to local governments.[79] On the whole, considerable variety in the administration of PRC prison camps exists from one region to another, with the military-run Xinjiang Production and Construction Corps *[Xinjiang shengchan jianshe bingtuan]* in the far northwest standing out as probably the most unusual variant. Instead of reporting to a civilian organ such as a laogai bureau, the Xinjiang bingtuan prison camps have been under the Xinjiang Military District's authority since the early 1950s.[80]

Extrapolating from various provincial statistics and accounts, Domenach concludes that prison camps held from 4 to 6 million inmates during the PRC's Founding Terror of 1949–52, during which time at least 2 million counterrevolutionaries and other real and imagined enemies were killed.[81] Domenach estimates that prison camps housed 3 million inmates in the mid- to late 1980s; and Seymour and Anderson estimate 2 million in the late 1990s.[82] During the consolidation of the new regime and its

78. Wu, *Laogai: The Chinese Gulag*, pp. 9–10. The laogai came entirely under the supervision of the Ministry of Justice in 1983. As Harry Wu explains, there has all along been a nationwide standard of dual nomenclature of the prison camps, with one name referring to a prison's location or administrative unit within a province or city, and another name indicating what sort of goods it produces. For instance, the Hunan Province No. 2 Prison is also known as the Hunan Heavy Truck Factory. Yet because of regional variations in prison camp administration, some prison administrators do not adhere to this nationwide standard, so it has been impossible for researchers to assemble a definitively comprehensive listing of PRC prison camps. The dearth of truly reliable PRC government figures on its prisoner population has also left researchers little choice but to make round estimates for the number of camp inmates at any given time.

79. Seymour & Anderson, *New Ghosts, Old Ghosts*, p. 27; Wu, *Laogai: The Chinese Gulag*, p. 10.

80. Seymour & Anderson, *New Ghosts, Old Ghosts*, p. 45. Even as prison camps in Qinghai and Gansu increasingly refused to allow incoming transfers of prisoners from other provinces during the Deng-Jiang Era, the Xinjiang bingtuan was still accepting prisoners from other provinces during the late 1990s.

81. Domenach, *L'archipel oublié*, pp. 71–72. Sentences to prison camps were two to four times more frequent than executions, according to information Domenach culled from Guangdong province in 1951.

82. Ibid., p. 487; Seymour & Anderson, *New Ghosts, Old Ghosts*, p. 206. Seymour and Anderson add that it is not the number of prisoners in the contemporary laogai that is alarming, "but what goes on in its worst prisons."

campaigns to suppress counterrevolutionaries in the early 1950s, as many as 90% of the inmates were counterrevolutionaries and only about 10% common criminals, according to Harold Tanner.[83] By the Deng-Jiang Era, quite the opposite would be true, with well over 90% of prison inmates being common criminals, and considerably younger on average than their imprisoned counterparts from the early 1950s.[84] Political repression would remain a significant function of the prison camps all along, but the influx of ordinary criminals *[xingshi fan]* into the camps during the Deng-Jiang Era greatly exceeded that of political prisoners.

Some of the prison facilities that the newly founded PRC inherited from previous regimes in China were capacious, up-to-date, and ready for immediate occupancy, such as Shanghai's famous Tilanqiao Prison. Tilanqiao Prison, a giant Panopticon-like jail built by the British in Shanghai shortly after the turn of the twentieth century, could accommodate over 30,000 prisoners.[85] Some Foucauldians might view Tilanqiao as an early transplant of insidious Euro-American modes of discipline and surveillance to China, where it would take root and grow with a vengeance under the Western-influenced CCP regime.[86] Yet pragmatic skeptics of Foucault's

83. Harold M. Tanner, "China's 'Gulag' Reconsidered: Labor Reform in the 1980s and 1990s," *China Information: A Quarterly on Contemporary Chinese Studies* 9.2/3 (1994–95): 40–71, esp. 43. On the basis of an analysis of a rare 1959 prison registry, Frank Dikötter suggests that political prisoners and other counterrevolutionaries may by then have constituted well under half of all urban prisoners; "the regime did not hesitate to put poor peasants, soldiers and workers behind bars for the slightest misdemeanor." See Dikötter, "Crime and Punishment in Post-Liberation China: The Prisoners of a Beijing Gaol in the 1950s," *China Quarterly* 149 (1997): 147–159, esp. 150, 159.

84. Wu, *Laogai: The Chinese Gulag*, p. 144.

85. For a semi-autobiographical description of Tilanqiao by a former inmate, see Wumingshi (pseud. of Bu Naifu, alias Bu Ning), *Hong sha* [Red Sharks] (Taipei: Liming wenhua shiye, 1989), pp. 135–136. See also Wang Fei, ed., *Shanghai jianyu renquan jilu* [The Human Rights Record of Shanghai's Prisons] (Shanghai: Shanghai renmin chubanshe, 1992), p. 4.

86. In his characteristically speculative and rhetorical approach, Michel Foucault leaps from a novelistic description of the quarantining and observation of seventeenth-century bubonic plague victims to a highly abstract discussion of the utilitarian philosopher Jeremy Bentham's Panopticon prison blueprint. (It is idealized due to the impossibility of observing every single prisoner at all moments from a lone focal point in the observation tower. Peepholes for individual guards to observe individual prison cells have remained a common fixture in Chinese prisons.) Foucault mentions only the similarities between the quarantined plague victims and the prisoners in Bentham's Panopticon beginning on p. 201, yet turns around and emphasizes only the contrasts starting on p. 206. See the chapter "Le panoptisme" in *Surveiller et punir: naissance de la prison* (Paris: Éditions Gallimard, 1975), pp. 197–229. Foucault concludes this chapter by tautologically conflating a number of highly distinctive social units: "What would be surprising if the prison were to resemble factories, schools, barracks, [and] hospitals—which all resemble prisons?" (229). In fact, only

relevance to the study of Chinese prisons could counter that Tilanqiao Prison did not actually become a model for subsequent Chinese prisons; during the decades of PRC rule, Tilanqiao has functioned largely as a holding pen for inmates undergoing interrogation and awaiting long-term sentences to labor camps.[87] Frank Dikötter has pointed out that unlike the atypical Tilanqiao, model prisons in modern China have been "not so much a foreign transplant as the microcosm of an exemplary society in which the emulation of models . . . was seen as a mission of educative transformation, a project for social discipline, and a strategy for national power."[88]

At any rate, China had far too small a supply of prisons, model or otherwise, for the heavy demand they were facing in the early 1950s. The rapid influx of inmates was immense due to the arrest of so many personnel associated with the GMD army and government, along with the CCP's vigorous campaigns to "suppress counterrevolutionaries" [zhenya fan'geming] and other perceived enemies of the vigilant party-state. As a result of the prison shortage, many groups of convicts were sent to undeveloped areas to live in tents or makeshift huts while constructing permanent barracks and other buildings in the new prison camp.[89]

Other prisoners found themselves confined in or around an existing detention facility that was being expanded into a full-size camp, such as Chadian, some 30 kilometers northeast of Tianjin, and on the railway line connecting Beijing with Shenyang. Originally built by the Japanese and later taken over by the GMD to house no more than a few hundred inmates, Chadian Detention Center expanded into a large adjacent marshy area, which convicts drained and converted to fertile farmland while erecting high perimeter walls and the barracks inside.[90] Known both as Qinghe ["clear river"] Farm and as the Number 1 Remolding-through-Labor

---

prisoners normally arrive at their "disciplinary establishment" in handcuffs and risk being summarily shot dead if they try to leave without permission.

87. Notwithstanding the Panopticon-like external features of a tiny handful of prisons in some of China's largest cities, Frederic Wakeman Jr. finds that the approach to rehabilitating prisoners in China has tended to contrast greatly with that sketched by Foucault. See Wakeman's *Policing Shanghai, 1927–1937* (Berkeley: Univ. of California Press, 1995), p. 90.

88. Dikötter, *Crime, Punishment, and the Prison in Modern China*, p. 16.

89. Zhang Xianliang remarks that the architecture of many prison camps in northwestern China draws heavily upon the simple and ancient, pounded-earth construction techniques common in remote and impoverished villages. See *Wode Putishu* [My Bodhi Tree] (Beijing: Zuojia chubanshe, 1995), p. 267. The first half of *Wode Putishu* has been translated into English by Martha Avery as *Grass Soup* (London: Secker & Warburg, 1994). The second half of *Wode Putishu* has been translated into English by Martha Avery as *My Bodhi Tree* (London: Secker & Warburg, 1996).

90. Wu, *Laogai: The Chinese Gulag*, p. 218.

Brigade of Beijing Municipality, this unusually large camp complex has been able to provide housing and labor for over 50,000 inmates at a time, particularly after its expansion to the west in the late 1950s.[91] By the 1990s, however, Qinghe typically held about 7,000 convicts.[92] This still makes Qinghe Farm much larger than the average laogai camp, which has been estimated to contain anywhere from 1,500 to 3,000 inmates.[93] Featured prominently in autobiographical accounts by such famous ex-inmates as Harry Wu, Jean Pasqualini, and Cong Weixi, Qinghe Farm remains China's most well known prison camp.[94]

As discussed in the introduction, the PRC government formally dropped the term "laogai" from its official lexicon in December 1994, substituting the innocuously generalized "prison" [jianyu] in its place. Since that time, however, everything from popular fiction to academic writing has continued to make wide mention of the laogai, for this term has maintained both historical resonance and contemporary relevance. As a state-run law gazette noted in the wake of the 1994 terminological change, "The function, character, and role of our penal institutions remain unchanged."[95]

The Rise of PRC Camps for Reeducation through Labor

Until the mid-1950s, Chinese prisoners normally arrived at their labor camp only after having been sentenced to a certain number of years there.[96]

---

91. Ibid., p. 221. Prison camps involved in agricultural production are usually called "farms" [nongchang], though they may have sidelines in nonagricultural production.

92. Laogai Research Foundation, Laogai Handbook, 1997–1998 (Milpitas, CA: Laogai Research Foundation, 1997), p. 29.

93. Domenach, L'archipel oublié, pp. 487–488. According to Domenach, by the late 1980s there were at least 720 laogai camps, and likely a thousand or so. Incomplete and often unreliable statistics from the PRC have prevented scholars from determining exactly how many laogai camps have been in existence at any particular time—or how many prisoners theses camps have held, to the nearest thousand. For instance, Domenach points to an absurd government claim that all of Tibet contained a mere 970 prisoners in 1987 (p. 485).

94. Wu & Wakeman, Bitter Winds, pp. 99–153; Bao & Chelminski, Prisoner of Mao, pp. 176–262; Cong Weixi, Zou xiang hundun sanbuqu [The Heading into Chaos Trilogy] (Beijing: Zhongguo shehui kexue chubanshe, 1998), pp. 153–179.

95. Quoted in Margolin, "A Long March into Night," p. 541. The term "laogai" received an entry in the 2003 edition of the Oxford English Dictionary, as reported in Shijie ribao, 14 July 2003.

96. To be sure, some prisoners received a life sentence in the camps. More commonly, sentences of five, ten, or fifteen years were meted out, making the average sentence in the PRC camps considerably longer than it had been in premodern times.

Some kind of trial or tribunal was supposed to have taken place, even though the guilty verdict was a foregone conclusion. Laogai inmates were convicts and would continue to receive specific sentences from their captors for the rest of the twentieth century.

Unfortunately, PRC courts often struggled to deal with a huge backlog of criminal cases in the early 1950s, and periodic party-led campaigns of suppression against real and imagined miscreants continued to crowd detention centers during the mid- to late 1950s. CCP leaders perceived a growing need for a more streamlined approach to deal with the sort of troublemaker whom they wished to eject from his work unit and segregate from society, but whose offense was not serious enough to merit routing into the overburdened judicial system and its courts.[97] Two directives from the CCP Central Committee in 1955 and 1956 authorized the bypassing of the legal system and its procedural formalities altogether, allowing administrative units or the local police to order the removal of their less "serious" troublemakers to special prison camps for "reeducation through labor" [*laodong jiaoyang*].[98] Although these laojiao inmates were thought to deserve the punishments of forced labor and confinement, their offenses were not so serious as to put them in the same category as the laogai convicts, who were harshly defined as "enemies of the people." In order to provide a quasi-legal foundation for this existing CCP policy, the State Council promulgated a formal "decision" about reeducation through labor in 1957.[99] No limit was placed on the length of time these inmates would have to remain confined in reeducation prison camps, and prison stays of ten or even twenty years for late-1950s laojiao "initiates" were common.[100] As will be discussed in subsequent chapters, the open-ended nature of the term for *laodong jiaoyang* inmates was often so aggravating to these inmates that many of them considered commit-

97. The CCP leaders thereby resembled many of their Warsaw Pact counterparts in eastern Europe, where "administrative, non-judicial sentencing to forced labor" was quite common. See Carlton, *Forced Labor in the "People's Democracies*," p. 12.

98. Tanner, *Strike Hard!*, p. 39. For more on developments leading up to the formal establishment of reeducation through labor in 1957, see Wu, *Laogai: The Chinese Gulag*, pp. 86, 88; and Seymour & Anderson, *New Ghosts, Old Ghosts*, p. 19. Early-1950s reform schools for prostitutes provided initial models for the kind of protracted but legally informal detention that has characterized *laodong jiaoyang*. The emergence of reeducation through labor was anything but sudden; it was merely formalized by the State Council's decision of 1957.

99. Tanner, *Strike Hard!*, pp. 39–40.

100. Soon after the campaign to "let a hundred flowers bloom and a hundred schools of thought contend" in 1956 was the "anti-rightist" crackdown that swept at least several hundred thousand innocent Chinese into prison camps, many as laojiao inmates.

ting another offense that would be serious enough to merit a sentence to a laogai camp instead: at least they would have a clear idea about when their term in the laogai camp would be completed.

The indeterminate sentencing aspect of laojiao was addressed in the 1980 and 1982 restatements and amplifications of the 1957 decision: a laojiao prisoner's term would henceforth be limited to three years.[101] However, the continuing presence of a highly repressive state apparatus during the Deng-Jiang Era was manifest in the way a citizen could still be sent without a legal hearing to a labor reeducation camp for three years at the whim of the local police.

Nor was the actual treatment of the average laojiao inmate significantly less harsh than that of the laogai inmate, even though laojiao inmates were supposed to have committed less serious offenses than their laogai counterparts. The military structure of camp life was more or less the same. Both types of inmates had to "remold" themselves through hard labor and discipline, and typically lived in cramped, unsanitary, and vermin-infested barracks where they typically slept on the floor, often crowded together cheek to jowl on wooden planks. Both ordinarily subsisted on a nutritionally inadequate and often repulsive diet of coarse grain and castoff vegetables. Malnourishment, poor sanitation, and overcrowding fostered the rapid transmission of a host of serious diseases to both types of prisoners. During the unprecedented Great Leap Forward famine of 1959–62, both laogai and laojiao prisoners starved to death in huge numbers. One difference was that laojiao inmates would generally receive a fraction of their ordinary civilian pay; but they would in turn have to spend this money on some of the basic supplies and clothing that laogai convicts generally received free of charge. Prior to 1983, many camps contained both laogai and laojiao brigades, whose members would sometimes intermingle in such a way as to blur the distinction between laogai convict and laojiao inmate.[102]

101. Tanner, *Strike Hard!*, p. 41. However, it was in fact still possible to be sent back to reeducation through labor for a second offense, or to have one's existing sentence lengthened for committing an offense while in the camp.

102. Wu Hongda, *Zhongguo de Gulage,* pp. 26–27. According to Wu, even after implementation of the 1983 policy to place laojiao inmates in their own camps separate from laogai convicts, some 30% of the laojiao inmates still belonged to a brigade that shared a camp with a laogai brigade. According to Cong Weixi, the only difference he could tell between the treatment of laojiao inmates and laogai convicts was that the former did not have their heads shaved and were supposed to receive a fraction of the wages they had formerly earned from their work unit. See *Zou xiang hundun* [Heading into Chaos], vol. 1 (Beijing: Zuojia chubanshe, 1989), p. 194.

Laogai and laojiao regimens differed, yet a host of other factors had a greater impact on the conditions endured by inmates. These include the length of one's term; the amount of nutritional and moral support received from relatives and friends outside of the camp; the general political atmosphere of the times, which could range from fairly tolerant to violently repressive; national and especially local economic conditions, which could vary from relative affluence to the crisis of deadly famine; the overall management of one's own camp, which would fall somewhere on a spectrum from professional and humane to arbitrary and harsh; and the local prisoners' subculture, which could vary from peaceful and predictable to violent and treacherous.

The Rise and Steep Decline of "Forced Job Placement" for Released Inmates

Although the estimated average number of laogai and laojiao inmates nationwide during the 1990s was no more than half of what it was during the 1950s, neither of these two branches of the prison system seemed to be experiencing drastic increases or drops in its population.[103] Instead, the major decline in the size of the PRC prison system during the Deng-Jiang Era occurred within the third category of camp inmate who had completed his term but was compelled to accept "job placement in the vicinity of the camp" *[liuchang jiuye]*.[104] The PRC system of requiring many "retained ex-inmate workers" *[jiuye renyuan]* to settle down permanently in the vicinity of the prison camp to earn no more than 60 to 70% of the prevailing wages for their work was formally instituted by the State Council in 1954.[105] The *jiuye* system closely resembles its Soviet gu-

---

103. To be sure, crime and imprisonment rates were higher in urban than in rural areas, and some largely rural provinces such as Qinghai were experiencing dramatic drops in their prisoner population. On a nationwide basis, however, neither the laogai nor the laojiao camps were showing signs of having "completed their historical mission" or "withering away."

104. Harry Wu notes that retained ex-inmate workers form the third category of the camp system's "three types of personnel" *[sanlei renyuan]* in *Laogai: The Chinese Gulag*, pp. 108, 124. See also Seymour & Anderson, *New Ghosts, Old Ghosts*, p. 190. *Jiuye* is the most common version of *liuchang jiuye*, which is in turn short for *xingman shifang qiangzhixing liuchang jiuye* [mandatory job placement in the vicinity of the camp after completion of term and release]. Ex-inmates subject to *jiuye* might best be referred to as "retained ex-inmate workers."

105. The wage "discount" for retained ex-inmate workers is mentioned in Wu, *Laogai: The Chinese Gulag*, p. 114.

lag predecessor.[106] The government wanted many of its able-bodied ex-inmates to help build up the prison enterprises, to settle down permanently in the remote regions where the camps were often located, and to stay away from crowded urban areas where their counterrevolutionary thought or antisocial tendencies could be dangerously infectious.[107] According to Harry Wu, the phenomenon of the retained ex-inmate worker reflects the PRC government's tacit assumption that these ex-inmates had often not been successfully remolded into docile and obedient subjects. Perhaps many if not most of the inmates simply could not be remolded in the way Mao and his lieutenants expected them to be.[108] As Patricia Griffin notes in reference to the pre-1949 CCP prison camps, "In contrast to some Communist sources, refugee accounts reveal that conditions were intolerable enough in some camps to engender animosity rather than foster the proletarian viewpoint."[109]

The quality of life for a retained ex-inmate worker varied according to time and place, and lay somewhere on a spectrum between the poles of the laogai prisoner with no rights, on the one hand, and the free citizen with full rights and no criminal record, on the other.[110] Under the worst circumstances, which were common during the Mao Era and especially the late 1950s and late 1960s, retained ex-inmate workers were treated almost as harshly as laogai convicts, and were occasionally driven to rioting in protest.[111] During better times, a retained ex-inmate could bring in his spouse and other relatives to settle down together, travel occasionally, and enjoy at least the semblance of an ordinary life.

The death of Mao and rise to power of a more pragmatic leadership

106. Gustav Herling discusses ex-con gulag camp workers in *A World Apart*, pp. 107–108.

107. Two of the government's three major motivations are drawn from Seymour & Anderson, *New Ghosts, Old Ghosts*, p. 190. See also Wu, *Laogai: The Chinese Gulag*, pp. 109–110.

108. Wu, *Laogai: The Chinese Gulag*, p. 108.

109. See Griffin, *The Treatment of Counterrevolutionaries*, p. 125. And as Kasza might understand this situation, these released camp inmates were usually not promising recruits for their conscription society's administered mass organizations (AMOs).

110. Of course, the rights of an ordinary PRC citizen have been extremely limited by international standards, but the official denial of rights was nonetheless "socially damning and psychologically debilitating," as stressed by Seymour & Anderson, *New Ghosts, Old Ghosts*, p. 192.

111. Wu, *Laogai: The Chinese Gulag*, pp. 116–118; Seymour & Anderson, *New Ghosts, Old Ghosts*, pp. 191–193. Cong Weixi has mentioned that during harsh times in the Mao Era, retained ex-inmate workers were routinely called "second-degree laogai inmates" *[er laogai]*, as contrasted with ordinary laogai convicts or "first-degree laogai inmates" *[da laogai]*. See *Zou xiang hundun* (1989), pp. 222, 224.

in the late 1970s ushered in major positive changes for the plight of retained ex-inmate workers. In 1979, those who had not been deprived of their political rights were formally reclassified as ordinary farmers or workers.[112] In the following year, the State Council ordered that the practice of jiuye should be totally overhauled; the rules were relaxed significantly, culminating in a 1983 directive to release and send home retained ex-inmate workers whose sentences had been completed before January 1982.[113] Although the subsequent "strike-hard" crackdown on crime led to some tightening up of control over retained ex-inmate workers, this temporary backlash soon gave way to the prevailing situation, in which almost any inmate who has completed his term and wants to leave the camp and return home can do so. "By 1988," note Seymour and Anderson, "the number of people on jiuye in China was already down to under 100,000, or only about 5% of the number of actual prisoners."[114] Because the retained ex-inmate workers had sometimes amounted to at least a quarter of the total number of inmates during the Mao Era, the steep decline in the number of jiuye personnel during the Deng-Jiang Era represents the most significant nationwide downsizing of the PRC prison camp system. On the other hand, the fact that the State Council turned down a serious proposal to dismantle the jiuye system altogether in 1980 suggests that the PRC government has been determined to reserve its privilege to maintain special control over released camp inmates.

Conclusion

Prison camps under the CCP developed rapidly in the earliest guerrilla bases in Jiangxi and Yan'an to become the dominant instrument for punishing real and imagined enemies of the regime as well as ordinary criminals. Adopting a militarized structure for the prison camps and extending their productive capabilities to technologically advanced manufacturing in the Northeast during the late 1940s, the CCP drew heavily on both Soviet models and authoritarian indigenous traditions. Confronted with swelling ranks of prisoners in the wake of successive campaigns against counterrevolutionaries and other alleged miscreants, the

112. Seymour & Anderson, *New Ghosts, Old Ghosts,* p. 192.
113. Ibid., p. 193.
114. Ibid., p. 197.

CCP soon extended this laogai system to the rest of the country upon their 1949 victory in the civil war.

CCP leaders' sweeping rejection of late Qing and Republican Era legal codes and procedures during most of the 1930s and 1940s gave rise to an ad hoc, decree-based approach to adjudicating criminal cases that frustrated proponents of routinized legality throughout most of the PRC's Mao Era. Deng Era legal and penal reforms freed hundreds of thousands of prisoners who had been wrongfully incarcerated under Mao and improved overall conditions in the camps somewhat. However, the Deng-Jiang insistence upon the CCP's continued monopoly of political power prevented the emergence of an independent judiciary and the rule of law—even though a relatively routinized rule *by* law seemed to have prevailed in the PRC by the 1980s.[115] PRC prisons and labor camps continued to incarcerate many people who were innocent of any real crime, though, and conditions in many prisons remained horrendous even throughout the relatively peaceful and prosperous 1980s and 1990s. Yet in contrast with the situation in China before the 1980s, there were now plenty of ex-inmates and others to write about Chinese prisons and labor camps, often from the perspective of one-time "participant observers." Based precisely upon such writings, the next two chapters delve into the most salient aspects of life in the PRC prison camp.

115. Harold Tanner distinguishes between the rule of law and rule by law in *Strike Hard!*, p. 29. The PRC judiciary's obvious lack of independence from party control is probably the key factor in preventing the rule of law from taking root in China.

CHAPTER 3

The PRC Prison Camp (I)

From Arrest to Forced Labor

Although PRC prison camp conditions have varied along with the specific historical setting and physical location of a camp, a number of shared general patterns or phases can be discerned from memoirs, fiction, and other retrospective writings on confinement in the camps. This chapter traces these widely shared patterns of the prison camp regime from arrest through forced labor, while Chapter 4 ranges from party-state strategies of control over prisoners and struggle sessions to the final release from prison. Of course, few prisoners would have experienced all of these aspects of prison existence; the terminal phases of execution and death in confinement have affected only a minority of prisoners. Most inmates with years of prison experience would have encountered most of these conditions, however.

Arrest

PRC police organs such as the Public Security Bureau *[Gong'an ju]* and the newer People's Armed Police *[Renmin wuzhuang jingcha,* or *wujing]* have a national jurisdiction, while working in close cooperation with local security and surveillance organizations such as neighborhood committees *[jumin weiyuanhui]*. With as much as 4% of the PRC population working in some capacity for the public security authorities in 1990, the Public Security Bureau has long had the wherewithal to make quite a show of force when arresting a suspect.[1] Ex-inmates Song Shan and Wuming-

---

1. The estimate comes from an editor of the Fuzhou journal *Jingtan fengyun* [Police World]; it must include auxiliaries and support personnel, not simply uniformed police

shi, a skilled factory worker and an unemployed writer, respectively, are startled to see no fewer than eight policemen or plainclothes detectives stride into their homes for their arrest.[2] A contingent of ten policemen and plainclothes detectives arrest the GMD military intelligence officer Hong Xianheng in Wumingshi's fictional memoir *Hong sha* [Red in Tooth and Claw].[3] The contingent of policemen dispatched to arrest a suspect would seldom amount to fewer than three, the number who arrested the Shanghainese Catholic schoolgirl Wang Xiaoling in 1955.[4]

The almost inevitable handcuffing of the suspect upon arrest tends to evoke an emotional response of anxiety and shame, as it embodies the individual's loss of basic mobility and freedom to the heavy-handed machinery of the party-state dictatorship. Gao Xin, a soberly courageous leader of the June 1989 hunger strike in Tiananmen Square, contrasts the equanimity with which he faced the advancing PLA troops and tanks on June 4 with the fear he experienced when handcuffed right next to a policeman armed with an electric shock baton.[5] Wang Xiaoling recalls her parents' anguished facial expressions upon seeing the police lead her away in handcuffs, and both Gao Xin and Song Shan recall their preoccupation with sparing their relatives such a sight.[6]

Common varieties of PRC administrative detention such as "shelter and investigation" *[shourong jiancha]* do not require a formal arrest warrant, though the police may order the suspect to sign some other type of document. Even if the police officers making an arrest produce a warrant, this document would typically lack an indication of the charge. Some-

---

officers and plainclothes detectives. See Jeffrey C. Kinkley, *Chinese Justice, the Fiction: Law and Literature in Modern China* (Stanford: Stanford Univ. Press, 2000), pp. 297–298.

2. Wumingshi (pseud. of Bu Naifu, alias Bu Ning), *Hai de chengfa*, p. 9. Translated into English as *The Scourge of the Sea* (Taipei: Kuang Lu Publishing, 1985). Song Shan, *Hong qiang, hui qiang* [Red Walls, Gray Walls] (Hong Kong: Baijia chubanshe, 1986), pp. 1–2. Wumingshi was arrested in 1958, and Song Shan in 1973. Both works are presented as memoirs.

3. Wumingshi, *Hong sha*, p. 114. The condensed English version of this work is Wumingshi (pseud. of Pu Ning), *Red in Tooth and Claw: Twenty-Six Years in Communist Chinese Prisons*, trans. Tung Chung-hsuan (New York: Grove Press, 1994). *Hong sha* was written as the memoir of an ex-inmate surnamed Han whose pseudonym is Hong Xianheng. See C. T. Hsia, "Foreword," in Pu Ning, *Red in Tooth and Claw*, p. xviii.

4. Wang Xiaoling, *Many Waters: Experiences of a Chinese Woman Prisoner of Conscience* (Hong Kong: Caritas Printing, 1988), p. 42. Wumingshi reports having been rearrested in 1968 by four burly policemen at a train station; see *Zou xiang Gegeta: yijiu liuba nian shounan jishi* [Heading toward Golgotha: A True Account of My Suffering in 1968] (Taipei: Xinwen tiandi she, 1976), pp. 64–65.

5. Gao Xin, *Beiwei yu huihuang*, p. 23.

6. Wang Xiaoling, *Many Waters*, p. 43; Song Shan, *Hong qiang, hui qiang*, p. 2. Gao Xin expresses a wish to spare his fiancée the spectacle of his imminent arrest and handcuffing (*Beiwei yu huihuang*, p. 20).

times, the entire process of generating a warrant and other related paperwork has to be done at the time of release and backdated in order to accord with the procedural requirements that were overlooked at the time of arrest. This is what happened to the Tibetan intellectual and philanthropist Tashi Tsering at the hands of PRC prison authorities.[7] In response to suspects' common queries about the nature of the criminal charge and where they would be first imprisoned, the police officer would usually either say nothing or else curtly reply that the detainees would find out for themselves soon enough. For example, the police officer in charge of arresting Song Shan simply ignores her questions about the charges against her.[8] Occasionally, a police officer making the arrest would laconically volunteer the information as if reporting a finalized verdict—characterizing Wang Xiaoling as a reactionary and addressing Hong Xianheng as a spy, for example.[9] Because Hong Xianheng is on a secret mission in China for the GMD military, the PRC police officer's characterization of him as a spy in *Hong sha* is actually correct, whereas most of the other inmates featured in this chapter are innocent, at least according to internationally accepted standards of legality.

If arrested at home, the captive's removal to a detention facility would usually occur only after his dwelling had been thoroughly searched [*soucha*] and any potentially incriminating documents and other evidence had been confiscated by the police.[10] Whether or not the police bothered to reveal what the charge was, the handcuffed captive would ordinarily be whisked away by jeep or police van for an indeterminate period of incommunicado detention in a facility unknown to all but the tight-lipped police officers making the arrest.[11]

When arresting someone away from home, the PRC police have been more likely to jump the suspect and wrestle him to a waiting motor vehicle without so much as a word of explanation, even when there is no sign of physical resistance from the suspect. At times, this mode of arrest

7. See Melvyn Goldstein, William Siebenschuh, & Tashi Tsering, *The Struggle for Modern Tibet: The Autobiography of Tashi Tsering* (Armonk, NY: M. E. Sharpe, 1997), p. 139.

8. Song Shan, *Hong qiang, hui qiang*, p. 1. Similar incidents are depicted in Peng Yinhan, *Dalu jizhongying*, p. 10, and in Wumingshi, *Hai de chengfa*, p. 10.

9. Wang Xiaoling, *Many Waters*, p. 42; Wumingshi, *Hong sha*, p. 115.

10. For examples, see Peng Yinhan, *Dalu jizhongying*, pp. 7, 10; Song Shan, *Hong qiang, hui qiang*, pp. 1–2.

11. The police are less likely to jump or pin down a suspect being arrested at home than if the suspect is away from home. However, in an exception to this rule, the police who arrested Hong Xianheng in 1951 rushed forward without a word to grab him around the waist and arms as soon as he opened his front door. See Wumingshi, *Hong sha*, p. 114.

has even resembled kidnapping, such as when some plainclothes detectives from the Northeast tricked a respectable business manager and local People's Congress deputy named Zhou Jialiang into leaving his hotel in Bengbu, Anhui, and venturing onto the sidewalk outside. The detectives' ruse was to tell Zhou that one of his old business associates was waiting to speak to him in a cab outside the hotel. There he was suddenly grabbed from behind and shoved into a waiting taxicab by several burly plainclothes detectives, who tore up all the important documents in Zhou's briefcase and beat and kicked him viciously for daring to demand transfer of custody to his hometown Bengbu Public Security municipal station.[12] As a respected community leader in Bengbu, Zhou Jialiang would hardly have suffered the sort of physical abuse under the local authorities that he did at the hands of the detectives from Changchun in Jilin province (figure 1).[13]

Though the National People's Congress passed a law in 1979 forbidding the arrest of any such congress representative without prior notification of the relevant congress leadership, the plainclothes detectives from the Northeast did not implement this mandate. Zhou's sudden and unexplained disappearance caused considerable consternation among his fellow congress representatives, who were expecting to receive a significant report from him the day after he went missing.

Often, weeks or even months would pass before the new inmate's relatives or friends could find out where he or she was being imprisoned. In the case of Zhou Jialiang, the relatives' notification of arrest was simply stuffed by the taxi driver into Zhou's hotel room through a crack in the door. Back in the Mao Era, even this type of perfunctory notification of an arrested suspect's relatives was seldom bothered with.[14]

Inquiring after a new prisoner's whereabouts or raising questions about the charges at the Public Security Bureau can be hazardous, as the famous human rights activist Liu Qing discovered when making inquiries about the people arrested in November 1979 during the sale of transcripts to Wei Jingsheng's trial earlier that year.[15] After having arrested one seller

12. See Shen Jiali, "Renda daibiao Zhou Jialiang feifa jujin an zhuiji" [A Retrospective Account of the Case of People's Congress Deputy Zhou Jialiang's Illegal Detention], in Xiao Chong, ed., *Zhonggong sifa heimu,* pp. 106–108.

13. Ibid., pp. 109–110. Though innocent, Zhou had to undergo a protracted stretch of imprisonment.

14. Ibid., p. 111.

15. Liu Qing, "Sad Memories and Prospects: My Appeal to the Tribunal of the People," in *Wild Lily, Prairie Fire: China's Road to Democracy, Yan'an to Tian'anmen, 1942–1989,* ed. Gregor Benton & Alan Hunter (Princeton: Princeton Univ. Press, 1995), pp. 247–257, esp. 250.

中共公安做事永遠是偷偷摸摸，見不得光。

FIGURE I. PRC police often apply excessive force even when arresting a nonviolent suspect (from Xiao Chong, ed., *Zhonggong sifa heimu*, p. 120; courtesy of Ha Fai Yi Publishing Ltd.).

of the trial transcripts, the police went on to arrest those bystanders who dared to openly criticize this abuse of the police's authority. In a Kafka-esque move, not only did the Beijing Public Security Bureau officials insist that the transcript seller and the outspoken bystanders were legally and properly arrested, but they went on to arrest Liu Qing himself.[16] From that day forward, Liu Qing would have to endure numerous bouts of torture and four years of solitary confinement during a decade of incarceration in various prisons and labor camps.

Detention Centers and the Pressure to Confess

Occasionally, new inmates will land in a labor camp without knowing why they have been sent there; their camp cadres express boredom with the whys and wherefores, merely insisting that the inmates get right to work and follow the prison rules. The sixteen-year-old Li Yuegai thought he was being sent on a work assignment to a civilian farm in Yunnan, but it turned out to be a reeducation-through-labor camp, where he had been entered on the books as a rightist offender. After being captured during an escape attempt, he received a long sentence to the laogai.[17]

More typically, however, the public security authorities will pressure a new prisoner into making a confession at a detention center [kanshou suo, juliu suo, shourong suo] before sentencing and transporting him to a labor camp or prison for long-term incarceration.[18] The great disparity in power between the interrogator and the prisoner will usually be reinforced by having the interrogator seated on a raised platform or behind a high table, while forcing the prisoner to squat on the floor or sit on a very low stool.[19] On some occasions, the security authorities have already

16. Family of Liu Qing, "Liu Qing Is Innocent! The Public Security Bureau Is Breaking the Law!" in *Wild Lily, Prairie Fire,* pp. 244–246, esp. 244.

17. Wen Yu, *Zhongguo zuo huo* [China's Leftist Calamities] (Hong Kong: Tiandi tushu, 1994), pp. 260–261.

18. The PRC security organs' emphasis upon forcing prisoners to confess stems from similar preoccupations in the old USSR, in the early CCP guerrilla bases such as Jiangxi and Yan'an, and in premodern China. For a summary of the pressure on suspects to confess during Kang Sheng's so-called Salvation Movement [qiangjiu yundong] in early-1940s Yan'an, see Wen Yu, *Zhongguo zuo huo,* pp. 130–133.

19. A camp administrator orders the inmate protagonist Zhou Zhiming to sit on a low stool for interrogation in Lü Haiyan, *Bianyi jingcha* [The Plainclothes Detective] (Beijing: Renmin wenxue, 1985), p. 165. The same thing happened to Jean Pasqualini under interrogation; see Bao & Chelminski, *Prisoner of Mao,* p. 36. Some prison camps in Hainan that were too poor to afford chairs for interrogators would resort to seating interrogators on

decided exactly how they want the prisoner's confession to read, and merely focus on applying the types of pressure most likely to persuade the prisoner to sign their prefabricated confession. The most common approach has been the threat that an uncooperative "attitude" *[taidu]* will result in a harsh punishment, often expressed as "the road to death" *[silu yitiao]*.[20] A PRC interrogator's threats of imminent execution or of an entire life behind bars have not been at all uncommon. The former political prisoner Sidney Rittenberg is just one example of a recipient of death threats during interrogation in the PRC. The interrogator would issue one "military order" after another to Rittenberg, who "could not sit, stand, speak, move without a direct order" from that official.[21]

If such verbal threats do not achieve the intended affect, more drastic measures sometimes follow in rapid succession. For instance, some combative CCP officials and various other vigilantes in the Shanghai Maritime Academy demanded in 1969 that the demobilized PLA soldier and student Ni Yuxian sign a confession to rape, attempted murder, and arson.[22] Knowing that any one of these fabricated charges would be enough to bring him capital punishment or a long prison term if he signed the confession, Ni Yuxian managed to hold firm through vicious beatings while being suspended in mid-air by his wrists (figure 2).[23] After months of further imprisonment and mistreatment, Ni finally agreed to a compromise with his captors whereby he would be released in return for neither agreeing nor arguing with the collective decision on his case during a mass sentencing rally at the academy. To its credit, the Public Security Bureau found the evidence against Ni Yuxian too problematic to justify a conviction, and dropped its investigation of his case. However, Ni's work unit and the Shanghai Municipal Revolutionary Committee condemned Ni as a counterrevolutionary, expelled him from the Maritime Academy, and forced him to register at the local police station for the surveillance he would have to work under for the remainder of his life in the PRC.[24]

---

stools and prisoners on the ground or the floor, according to Wang Zifu, *Nü lao ziwei* [The Flavor of a Women's Prison] (Beijing: Zuojia chubanshe, 1996), p. 22.

20. Song Shan, *Hong qiang, hui qiang*, p. 3.

21. Sidney Rittenberg & Amanda Bennett, *The Man Who Stayed Behind* (New York: Simon & Schuster, 1993), pp. 403, 405.

22. Anne F. Thurston, *A Chinese Odyssey: The Life and Times of a Chinese Dissident* (New York: Scribner's, 1991), p. 238.

23. This traditional technique of suspending an "uncooperative" suspect by his bound wrists behind his back in mid-air and beating him like a punching bag is illustrated in Figure 2. See Li Baojia's (Li Boyuan, 1867–1906) late Qing novel *Huo diyu* [A Living Hell] (1906; rpt. Taipei: Guangya chuban gongsi, 1984).

24. Thurston, *A Chinese Odyssey*, pp. 245–246.

FIGURE 2. A variation of this kind of torture has been used on some PRC prisoners, such as Ni Yuxian; the captive is suspended in mid-air, hanging solely from his backward-pulled wrists (from Li Baojia, *Huo diyu*).

In the city of Wuwei in Gansu province, the Public Security Bureau was more effective in using beatings to extract a baseless murder confession in 1992 that fully met their preconceived specifications. When the framed suspect Yang Liming came up with the wrong murder weapon during his forced confession, the police resumed the beatings until Yang named the correct weapon, which happened to be scissors.[25] In his forced confession, Yang at first claimed to having stabbed the victim with

25. Yang Wei, "Gansu gong'an quda chengzhao xian qu liangming" [The Gansu Public Security Authorities Almost Took Two Lives through Forcing Prisoners to Confess], in Xiao Chong, ed., *Zhonggong sifa heimu,* pp. 170–173.

a knife rather than a pair of scissors. Though the torturing of suspects has been officially prohibited, the gap between theory and actual practice in the PRC criminal justice system has often been decidedly large.[26]

Public security authorities generally tend to be more subtle and less dependent on violence in their methods of extracting a confession. According to David Kelly, a Chinese American veteran of over two decades in the laogai camps, "The important thing was to break your spirit rather than inflict physical pain. The whole system was aimed at reducing people to ciphers, getting them to admit their errors and throw themselves on the mercy of the Communist Party."[27] In Song Shan's *Red Walls, Gray Walls,* she recounts how she refused to implicate two innocent colleagues, even after beatings by fellow prisoners and confinement in a tiny cell. Prison officials then bring in her former fiancé to attempt a softer approach.[28] When this fails, the prison cadres persuade one of Song Shan's friends to write her a letter begging her to cooperate with the government in order to bring an end to the interrogations that both of them have endured because of her noncompliance.[29] The cadres also step up their lengthy back-to-back midnight interrogations, a cumulative form of pressure that over time breaks down many prisoners' resistance to confessing and / or implicating others.[30] Finally, in the time-honored tradition of using prisoners' relatives to preach the party line, the cadres arrange for Song Shan's white-haired mother to visit the prison and try persuading her daughter to cooperate with the government's investigation, thereby securing an earlier release.[31] However, like so many other PRC prison-

26. Tanner, *Strike Hard!,* p. 194. Since the PRC authorities' use of torture includes functions other than extracting confessions, the use of torture will be further discussed in the next chapter.

27. Jay Mathews & Linda Mathews, *One Billion: A China Chronicle* (New York: Ballantine, 1983), pp. 296–297. Kelly's American missionary father died before 1949, and his Chinese mother decided to remain in China under CCP rule. After the PRC government refused Kelly's formal request to emigrate to the United States, he eventually attempted to escape by swimming to Macao, but was caught and sentenced to the laogai. Kelly was not released until 1978, at the age of thirty-seven. He had been in camps and prisons since the age of sixteen.

28. Song Shan, *Hong qiang, hui qiang,* pp. 21, 23, 38–39. Her two senior colleagues, Old Cheng and Old Lin, were party military cadres who were secretly accused by a jealous and spiteful colleague in the early 1970s of trying to organize a new "People's Party" [renmin dang].

29. Ibid., pp. 66–67.

30. Ibid., pp. 47–50.

31. Ibid., pp. 83–85. During her mother's visit, Song Shan dismisses her wounds from beatings as bruises from a fall down stairs; similarly, Harry Wu was careful to express nothing but praise for his prison administrators during a staged family visit. See Wu &

ers who have seen through the insidious lure to implicate others in the slogan "Leniency to those who confess, and severity to those who resist," Song Shan refuses to betray her innocent friends for the sake of testing the party's high-sounding promises of leniency. Needless to say, Song's refusal to participate in the framing of two of her friends resulted in being condemned to years of imprisonment and forced labor.[32]

Detention centers tend to be so crowded and uncomfortable, and the psychological pressures exerted by the cadres and activists on the prisoners so intense, that many prisoners confined there have actually looked forward to the day of being sentenced to a prison camp. After prolonged confinement in a Beijing detention center during the late 1950s, every single inmate in Jean Pasqualini's cell "was begging to be sent to the camps."[33] In 1968, An Sinan was held in a public toilet in a bus station prior to his transfer to a long-term detention center.[34]

According to a common saying among prisoners, a single month in a detention center can be the equivalent of an entire year in a labor camp.[35] Although midnight interrogation sessions are routine in detention centers and often last for hours at a stretch, these jails have almost always strictly forbidden prisoners from lying down during the daytime or even dozing off while seated. Song Shan comments at length about this strategy [zhanshu] of wearing inmates down with fatigue.[36] Reliable accounts of Shanghai's notoriously squalid Huangpu Detention Center from the early 1970s to the late 1980s indicate that unreasonably strict rules against talking or even shutting one's eyes in the daytime persisted throughout that period.[37] In the late 1950s, Jean Pasqualini was understandably glad to sign his ersatz confession and a special form indicating his willingness to join a labor camp brigade, as long as he could secure a transfer away from the grim Beijing detention center.[38] Anything seemed more bear-

Wakeman, *Bitter Winds*, p. 197. A letter from Wu's elder brother urged him to work hard on remolding himself through labor (p. 174).

32. Song Shan, *Hong qiang, hui qiang*, p. 70

33. See Bao & Chelminski, *Prisoner of Mao*, p. 47. "Activists" or "activist elements" [*jiji fenzi*] among the inmates function as eager underlings of the guards and prison administrators, disciplining and bullying the ordinary prisoners in hopes of reducing their own sentence or receiving other special favors.

34. An Sinan, *Lian yu sanbuqu*, pp. 32–33.

35. Thurston, *A Chinese Odyssey*, p. 319.

36. Song Shan, *Hong qiang, hui qiang*, pp. 47–48.

37. Thurston, *A Chinese Odyssey*, pp. 320–321; Kate Saunders, *Eighteen Layers of Hell* (London: Cassel, 1996), pp. 3–4.

38. Bao & Chelminski, *Prisoner of Mao*, p. 83.

able than more months of midnight interrogation sessions, routine struggle sessions that pitted one hapless prisoner against the harsh condemnations of the others, endless revision of his self-flagellating written confession, and a putrid, vermin-infested cell that enforced physical inactivity.

With the increasing skepticism among the younger generation in society toward the CCP and especially its moribund Leninist underpinnings, prisoners exercised growing resistance to confession during the 1990s.[39] However, the inquisitorial nature of the PRC criminal justice system combined with its dearth of effective safeguards for individual rights have forestalled the possibility that the party-state's formidable pressure on inmates to confess would "wither away" anytime soon.

Going before a Court or Tribunal

For reeducation-through-labor inmates and retained ex-inmate workers, administrative decrees rather than court judgments form the basis of the prisoner's fate, such as sentencing. During the Mao Era, this administrative sentencing would often follow closely on the heels of a public "struggle" session or denunciation rally, a relic of the old Maoist guerrilla insurgency that faded dramatically during the relatively pragmatic Deng-Jiang Era. For example, Song Shan's vivaciously maternal cell mate "Fire Wheels" (Dahuolun) feels indignant about having received a two-year sentence to reeducation through labor shortly after serving as the target of an hours-long denunciation rally.[40] In both eras, however, the administrative sentence or decision has been effectively final, as no workable mechanism for appeal exists. There was simply no avenue of appeal for a laojiao prisoner like Peng Yinhan, for example.[41]

A quietly resentful reaction was also common among those administratively sentenced to less punitive regimens than reeducation through labor. Ni Yuxian has no immediate outlet for expressing his outrage and resentment upon discovering that he has been sentenced to register as a counterrevolutionary at the local police station and do manual labor under their surveillance for the foreseeable future.[42]

Even during the Mao Era, prisoners would typically bristle inwardly

39. Seymour & Anderson, *New Ghosts, Old Ghosts,* pp. 206–207.
40. Song Shan, *Hong qiang, hui qiang,* p. 47.
41. Peng Yinhan, *Dalu jizhongying,* p. 43.
42. Thurston, *A Chinese Odyssey,* pp. 246–248.

upon receiving an administrative order for their reeducation through labor, in accord with the Chinese expression of "daring to get angry but not daring to verbalize it" *[gan nu er bu gan yan]*. Late in the Mao Era, a middle-aged female prisoner whose warden has unctuously praised the party's compassion for having given her a mere two-year sentence to reeducation through labor complains bitterly to her cell mates about this injustice just before being dragged away by guards.[43] In December 1960, Cong Weixi inwardly fumes that the "confession" already prepared for him and his wife, Zhang Hu, to sign before their sudden removal to a reeducation through labor camp is partly the result of a frame-up by an unscrupulous colleague eager to "establish merit" *[li gong]*.[44] Cong Weixi must keep his perceptions of betrayal and injustice to himself—in the presence of the entirely self-assured party leaders of his work unit and the complacent armed police officer waiting to escort the "reactionary clique" members to prison, it would be senseless and even dangerous to dispute these accusations.[45]

Laojiao inmates in Deng-Jiang Era have been emboldened enough by increasing social and economic freedoms to challenge their sentences more often than their Mao Era counterparts.[46] Unfortunately, these challenges have seldom gotten them anywhere. According to a Baimaoling (Anhui province) prisoner interviewed in a piece of literary reportage by Wang Anyi and Zong Fuxian, the Shanghai police unfairly sentenced her to a third three-year laojiao term after she admitted under oath that she had slept with her new boss at his urging.[47] She had unintentionally angered the police by originally declining to testify against her boss for womanizing, and even though she later did their bidding at the court hearing, the police would not forgive her for having been a "difficult" witness at the outset. When she protested the police's snap decision to "hit me with

43. Song Shan, *Hong qiang, hui qiang*, p. 47.

44. Cong Weixi, *Zou xiang hundun*, vol. 1 (1989), pp. 124–125. The insidious colleague at the news bureau, Luo Xinmin, had "established merit" in the eyes of the party higher-ups by implicating Cong, Zhang, and another man for supposedly having formed an anti-party "reactionary clique." By setting this trap to whisk all three of these "clique" members away to reeducation through labor, Luo gained the political merit that would help safeguard him from suffering a similar fate.

45. Ibid., p. 125.

46. Of course, Deng-Jiang Era citizens have lacked the corresponding political freedoms, as mentioned in Seymour & Anderson, *New Ghosts, Old Ghosts*, pp. 224–225.

47. Wang Anyi & Zong Fuxian, "Fengshu ling liu ri: Baimaoling nü laojiao dui caifang jishi" [Six Days on Maple Ridge: A Record of Interviews at the Baimaoling Reeducation-through-Labor Brigades for Women], in *Daqiang nei wai* [Inside and Outside the Prison Walls], no. 4 (1988): 3–9, esp. 7.

another three-year term" of laojiao, an officer merely brushed her off: "What made you give us such a hard time in the first place?"[48]

The hapless woman persuaded her well-meaning labor camp brigade leader to ask the police to reconsider the sentence, but the police declined. When asked whether she had considered appealing this latest sentence or asking for an additional investigation of her case, the inmate replied in exasperation, "In what laojiao camp has an appeal ever been of any use?"[49] As an inmate who had "entered the palace thrice" *[san jin gong]*—was on her third term in prison—she had good reason to be skeptical about the likelihood of securing justice from such appeals to the police. This twenty-seven-year-old inmate insisted that she had never committed any offense even as serious as prostitution. It seems clear that her most recent "transgression" of engaging in extramarital sex for the sake of employment security would not be considered a crime in most countries. The Shanghai police officers had originally assured her that they merely wanted her to testify against her boss, not to be considered an accomplice.

In contrast to laojiao inmates, who can be incarcerated by means of administrative decision without any due process, laogai inmates are supposed to have been convicted in court according to proper legal procedure—even though this has usually been a ceremonial affirmation of a verdict already decided behind closed doors in consultation with local party and procuratorial officials, especially during the Mao Era. Unlike a detention warrant *[juliu zheng]*, an arrest warrant *[daibu zheng]* would nearly always mean that the recipient would eventually be convicted and sentenced; the main question at that point would be the severity of one's sentence.[50]

When Song Shan was brought forward as a civilian before a military tribunal *[junshi fating]* in the early 1970s, she recognized that a guilty verdict was inevitable and requested that the tribunal make an early decision about her sentence.[51] Similarly, in the late 1950s Jean Pasqualini decided to be docile and accommodating so as to get his ceremonial trial over with quickly and start serving his foreordained laogai sentence sooner rather than later. He marveled at the naïveté of two otherwise intelligent fellow inmates who appealed their guilty verdicts; the court consequently extended

48. Ibid., p. 7.
49. Ibid.
50. An Sinan, *Lian yu sanbuqu*, p. 39.
51. Song Shan, *Hong qiang, hui qiang*, pp. 53–55. This use of a military tribunal to try civilians accused of political offenses is reminiscent of the GMD military in Taiwan prior to the ending of martial law in 1987.

their multi-year sentences to life imprisonment.[52] During the Mao Era, a prisoner who appealed a guilty verdict was allegedly betraying an opposition to remolding himself and to the government's "lenient treatment," and thus would typically have his sentence extended as punishment. Of course, this common practice was seldom made explicit, so prisoners who foolishly took written legal statutes and constitutional guarantees at face value often paid dearly for neglecting the importance of customary practices in the PRC criminal justice system. The PRC Criminal Law of 1979 drastically curtailed the CCP's customary practice of extending the sentence of a prisoner who appealed a guilty verdict. However, the highly inquisitorial nature of that regime's criminal justice system did not change.

The state-appointed criminal defense attorney has often been a pliant tool of the party-state and its procuratorate. In 1989, Gao Xin's fellow prisoners told him this joke: As a certain trial is drawing to a close and the judge is about to consider a verdict and sentence, the defense attorney stands up to make a concluding statement to the judge and his court: "I would solemnly remind Your Honor that my client has a criminal record."[53] Most defense attorneys have remained state employees who rarely challenge the procurator's case against the accused; rather, they focus on mitigating factors that might justify lenient treatment such as a shorter term of imprisonment. Private attorneys in criminal law who advocate vigorously in defense of their clients risk losing their license to practice, and may even land in jail.

In the Deng-Jiang Era, defense attorneys in the area of civil law have enjoyed more autonomy in PRC courtrooms than their counterparts in criminal law, where intrusions from the party-state are common. During Wei Jingsheng's trial in 1979, he had little choice but to take charge of his own defense in the courtroom.[54]

Even the judiciary commonly defers to intervention by party secretaries and the police. An example of the judiciary's dependent relationship with the party and the security apparatus comes from the 1992 case of Zhou Jialiang. A judge in Changchun visited Zhou in prison to offer a sort of oral plea bargain: if Zhou would plead guilty to the charge of fraud, the judge and the local Public Security Bureau would release him

52. Bao & Chelminski, *Prisoner of Mao,* pp. 80–82.
53. Gao Xin, *Beiwei yu huihuang,* p. 132.
54. Wei Jingsheng entered the courtroom with his head already shaved. Male convicts typically had shaved heads up through the early Deng Era; the fact that Wei's head was shaved before his trial date indicates that the party-state had already settled upon a guilty verdict in the time-honored PRC tradition of "verdict first, trial second" *[xian pan hou shen].*

from prison, where he was receiving beatings and other harsh treatment. Zhou refused.[55]

In the prosperous southeastern provinces far from Beijing's heavy hand, however, some Deng-Jiang Era criminal cases have been tried in ways that have limited the state's towering advantage over the individual defendant. This situation has been particularly evident in cases not perceived as threatening to state security, such as the January 1990 trial in Xiamen, Fujian, of the novelist Tang Min for libel.[56] Several provincials from outside this prominent port city had become convinced that one of Tang Min's satiric novels had slandered them, and they furiously lobbied the government to have her jailed, heavily fined, and publicly shamed in court.

Tang Min's attorney offered an effective defense that probably influenced the judges to set the monetary compensation due the plaintiffs at only 2,000 yuan, a tiny fraction of what they had expected to receive.[57] Although Tang Min was about to be sentenced to a year's imprisonment, she acted the part of a triumphant heroine both inside and outside the courtroom, flashing the "V for victory" sign and smiling for the gaggle of newspaper photographers and curious onlookers who crowded the area. Her unabashed statements inside the courtroom were defiant expressions of her innocence and the illegality of the impending libel judgment against her, and she responded to a disapproving stare from one of the judges by glaring back at him so fiercely that he soon looked the other way. The plaintiffs' hopes of publicly shaming Tang Min backfired, as the courtroom proceeding allowed her to garner publicity and achieve a moral victory over both the crestfallen plaintiffs and the startled judges. As she described her role going into the courtroom for the sentencing proceedings, "Since it's all a big act, I might as well put on a stunning performance."[58]

Transit Prisons and Transport to Camp

Great distances often separate prison camps from the population centers where prisoners have been sentenced or await relocation, and it takes time

55. Shen Jiali, "Renda daibiao Zhou Jialiang feifa jujin an zhuiji," p. 115.

56. Tang Min, *Zou xiang heping—yu zhong shouji* [Heading toward Peace—Prison Jottings] (Urumqi: Xinjiang daxue chubanshe, 1994), pp. 41–44.

57. Ibid., p. 43. Two thousand yuan would not have compensated the plaintiffs for even their legal expenses. They were obviously outraged at not having been awarded the tens of thousands of yuan that they had demanded from the defendant.

58. Ibid., p. 41.

for the bureaucracy to prepare the transfer of each prisoner's personal dossier *[dang'an]* and other necessary paperwork. A nationwide network of "detention shelters" *[shourong suo]* has served many of the same functions of the old Soviet gulag's transit prisons, though the Chinese term is more elastic. Before the PRC was established in 1949, *shourong suo* were part of the social welfare system—shelters where the poor or disadvantaged could temporarily lodge on a voluntary basis. The term still has this original meaning in most Chinese-speaking territories outside of the PRC's control, such as Taiwan.[59]

For example, the shourong suo where Peng Yinhan was confined awaiting transport to a laojiao prison camp in 1960 had been converted from a women's shelter for former prostitutes sometime after 1953, when Peng had visited it with other "returned Overseas Chinese."[60] Due to the large number of Overseas Chinese brought by PRC cadres to visit this immaculately furnished facility, which served unusually high-quality food by Shanghai standards in 1953, Peng could perceive that this facility then amounted to a Potemkin Village showcase model.[61] After its conversion to a prison, the facility lost its former sheen and took on the usual grim and crowded appearance of a detention shelter.

Like Peng Yinhan's Shanghai detention shelter, Cong Weixi's transit prison in Greater Beijing (Tucheng shourong suo) did not force prisoners to labor while they were awaiting transport to their prison camps.[62] Tucheng Detention Shelter, also known as Beiyuan Detention Center, is located in the northern suburbs of Beijing. It was built on the site of an ancient prison with rammed-earth walls, but the modern outermost wall

59. The old USSR transit-prison counterparts to the PRC's *shourong suo* are described in Aleksandr I. Solzhenitsyn, *The Gulag Archipelago, 1918–1956: An Experiment in Literary Investigation*, vol. 1, trans. Thomas P. Whitney (New York: Harper & Row, 1974), pp. 533–557.

60. Peng Yinhan, *Dalu jizhongying*, pp. 49–50. One fellow inmate believed the facility had been converted to a prison in 1958, when the anti-rightist crackdown caused a large influx of prisoners. "Overseas Chinese" [*Huaqiao*] are people of Chinese ethnicity who have a foreign passport or who reside abroad. The PRC government encourages *Huaqiao* to travel, invest, or live in China.

61. Ibid., p. 50. Peng Yinhan was originally a white-collar professional who ate above-average institutional food, and the fact that the food was so much better in this women's shelter for unskilled prostitutes suggests high government subsidies earmarked to make a good impression on visiting Overseas Chinese. The PRC government has resorted to such techniques of "impression management" to attract the capital and especially the technical expertise of many Overseas Chinese on visits there.

62. Cong Weixi, *Zou xiang hundun sanbuqu*, pp. 102, 104. In contrast to both Cong and Peng, Jean Pasqualini was forced to labor very intensively at his transit prison, Banbuqiao, in Beijing; see Bao & Chelminski, *Prisoner of Mao*, pp. 85, 89–90.

made Tucheng look very much like an ordinary state agency or office. Cong Weixi and his wife were imprisoned in this facility in 1960, about half a year later than Peng Yinhan's detention in the Shanghai transit prison. (Taipei also has a transit prison called Tucheng, but as recently as the late 1970s it was reserved for political prisoners, according to ex-inmate Chen Sanxing.[63])

In both of these urban transit prisons, ordinary criminals and vagrants greatly outnumbered political prisoners, from whom they sometimes stole food and other things, yet seldom in the brutal or menacing way that often characterized criminal zeks in the former USSR's transit prisons.[64] In general, the relations between political prisoners and ordinary offenders in PRC transit prisons seem to have been marked by less mistrust and violence than was the case in the old Soviet Union, though intellectuals in both countries have often expressed indignation at having been locked up with ordinary criminals.[65]

As in the detention centers, many prisoners in transit prisons hope for an early departure to a labor camp, where conditions tend to be less crowded and uncomfortable.[66] Cong Weixi recalls that the stench of the latrine bucket at one end of the unventilated cell was compounded by unwashed bodies, along with the placement of neighbors' stinking feet right next to one's face, for the crowding was too severe to allow prisoners to sleep with their feet facing the same direction.[67] Cong has derisively referred to the crowded transit prison tent as a "Mongolian yurt."[68]

Several writers have described how bedbugs and lice commonly bedeviled the underfed inmates in transit prisons; cadres sometimes pestered prisoners with denunciation meetings and struggle sessions as well.[69] Hunger has also been endemic among transit prison inmates—and has

---

63. Chen Sanxing, *Shaonian zhengzhi fan feichang huiyilu* [The Extraordinary Memoirs of a Youthful Political Prisoner] (Taipei: Qianwei chubanshe, 1999), p. 225.

64. Cong Weixi, *Zou xiang hundun sanbuqu*, p. 99.

65. The rapacity with which Russian criminals often treated political prisoners is described in Solzhenitsyn, *The Gulag Archipelago*, vol. 1, pp. 500–502.

66. Cong Weixi recalls a transit prisoner talking in his sleep about how he would like to be sent to any camp, even up to the border with Siberia, as long as he could leave that dreadful place. See *Zou xiang hundun*, p. 165.

67. Ibid., pp. 156–157.

68. Ibid., p. 147. Of course, Mongolian yurts would not be as crowded and uncomfortable as these prison tents.

69. Regarding vermin in the transit prisons, see Peng Yinhan, *Dalu jizhongying*, p. 55; Cong Weixi, *Zou xiang hundun*, pp. 158–159; and Wang Xiaoling, *Many Waters*, p. 45. For more on the struggle meetings there, see Cong Weixi, *Zou xiang hundun*, pp. 150–151.

been so intense that it commonly resulted in "psychological pathology," according to Cong Weixi.[70]

As in the Soviet gulag, an atmosphere of secrecy has usually pervaded the transfer of laogai convicts to a camp.[71] Inmates in a given transit prison could be sent out to a number of different prison camps, and they have often not been told of their final destination until after arriving there.[72] On more than one occasion, Cong Weixi's question about where the guards were transporting him was met with the evasive reply, "You'll find out when you get there."[73] There were good reasons for fearing dispatch to an especially distant prison camp like Xingkaihu, near the Siberian border. Living conditions there have been particularly harsh; some prisoners might be blocked from returning home after serving their term; and the likelihood of seasonal family visits is greatly diminished. Cong Weixi, for example, mentions both the hardships his elderly mother would face merely to visit him at the frigid and remote Xingkaihu Prison Camp and his anxiety about not knowing his destination.[74]

Inmates in transit prisons could sometimes make educated guesses about their final destination in the camp system, however. Shortly before GMD military officer Hong Xianheng's train trip to the camps in the early 1950s, the Shanghai transit prison cadres issued padded winter jackets and winter hats to all the laogai prisoners in his cell block. The prisoners correctly surmised that their destination must be either the Northeast or far to the west; it turned out to be the latter—the cold and arid Qinghai plateau by way of Hekou in Gansu province.[75] Several years later, in 1960, Peng Yinhan's transit prison cadres announced that the laojiao inmates would be going to camps scattered across three provinces—including Jiangxi, which turned out to be Peng's destination. This transit prison accommodated approximately 1,500 prisoners, but the population fluctu-

70. Cong Weixi, *Zou xiang hundun*, pp. 152–153.

71. The following passage comes from Varlam Shalamav, "The Lawyers' Plot," in *Kolyma Tales*, trans. John Glad (New York: Norton, 1980), pp. 151–170, esp. 160: "Where was I being taken? North or south? East or west? There was no sense asking, and besides, the guards weren't supposed to say."

72. The authorities did not give either Harry Wu or Wang Xiaoling's group of female prisoners any inkling as to their final destination, as noted in Wu & Wakeman, *Bitter Winds*, p. 99, and Wang Xiaoling, *Many Waters*, p. 96.

73. Cong Weixi, *Zou xiang hundun sanbuqu*, p. 90; for more on Cong's frustration about the cadres' senseless and unnecessary secrecy [baomi] about the prisoners' destination, see *Zou xiang hundun*, p. 169.

74. Cong Weixi, *Zou xiang hundun*, pp. 141, 167.

75. Wumingshi, *Hong sha*, p. 167. Hekou was the end of the railway line for passengers bound for Qinghai during the early 1950s, when Hong Xianheng was taken there.

ated because there were large-scale inflows and outflows on a regular basis. On the eve of Peng's departure, the cadres were unusually forthcoming; they informed the prisoners that their destination was a camp in Jiangxi province.[76]

Inmates have usually arrived at a prison camp either on foot or in the back of a truck, which has often been part of a larger convoy escorted by armed guards. The hundred women driven from a Shanghai prison to the Qingshan Knitting Factory on 4 March 1960 were all loaded into a single truck, according to Wang Xiaoling.[77] If trucks were in short supply, prisoners might occasionally be transferred from one urban prison to another on a public bus, as was experienced by Cong Weixi on 29 December 1960.[78] For camps in remote areas and especially during the major buildup of the laogai during the 1950s, rugged trails and vehicle shortages often meant that prisoners needed to march in columns for a long distance to their camp. Under more ordinary circumstances, the march from the vehicle drop-off point to the camp itself would not be inordinately long, as such treks entailed special precautions to guard against escapes.

Transport to the camps by train, nicknamed "big wheels" [dalun] in prison argot, has typically been a dirty and especially uncomfortable experience.[79] Prisoners have generally found themselves crammed like barnyard animals into windowless freight cars [tie menzi che] that have almost never been cleaned of the livestock droppings or coal dust from the previous cargo haul.[80] The only ventilation would be an envelope-sized opening or two at the top of the freight car, while some of the feces and urine from the open latrine barrel would occasionally spill out onto the floor whenever the train jolted to one side or the other. The small food rations seldom assuaged the inmates' hunger pangs, and there was so little drinking water that many prisoners felt parched and their lips cracked from dryness.[81] Relatively short freight car passages of a day or two, like Peng Yinhan's and Wang Xiaoling's, usually did not take much of a toll on the

76. Peng Yinhan, *Dalu jizhongying*, pp. 45, 51, 56.
77. Wang Xiaoling, *Many Waters*, pp. 92–93
78. Cong Weixi, *Zou xiang hundun*, pp. 142–143.
79. Ibid., pp. 168, 180.
80. Peng Yinhan, *Dalu jizhongying*, p. 58; Wumingshi, *Hong sha*, p. 167; Wang Xiaoling, *Many Waters*, p. 97. The PRC prison train transports more closely resemble the USSR gulag's "red cattle cars" than the "Stolypin cars," which were converted from passenger cars instead of ordinary freight cars. See Solzhenitsyn, *The Gulag Archipelago*, vol. 1, p. 566.
81. Wumingshi, *Hong sha*, p. 168; and Wang Xiaoling, *Many Waters*, p. 97.

prisoners, aside from the usual hunger and weariness. In contrast, Hong Xianheng's rail odyssey of over a week from Shanghai to Gansu caused a great many inmates in his freight car to fall ill.[82]

In order to prevent inmates from escaping into the crowds of a railway station, the prisoners would be loaded or unloaded either at a station platform, empty except for armed guards, or along the railway tracks several dozen meters away from the station platform. Another advantage in this kind of unloading is that the cadres would not attract unwanted attention from the general populace—a preference which also accounts for the frequency of transferring prisoners at night.[83] The way that ordinary onlookers would often whisper among themselves and stare curiously at the passing inmates under guard suggests that the comings and goings of labor camp prisoners must have been a fairly rare sight in the PRC.[84] Until the beginning of the twenty-first century, the PRC government encouraged mass rallies and public humiliation of prisoners condemned to execution, while keeping ordinary prisoners out of the public eye.

Socialization in the Prison Camp

Because the PRC prison camp is a militarily structured unit within a "conscription society" of a single-party authoritarian state, new inmates must be assigned to a particular brigade *[dui]* and group *[zu]* and accept their places within that hierarchical structure.[85] Kasza's theory of the type of authoritarian governance marked by administered mass organizations (AMOs) in the place of civil society is especially relevant to the laogai, whose inmates have often shown a lack of the submission to authority that such organizations demand.

82. Wumingshi, *Hong sha,* pp. 168–169.

83. Harry Wu describes his arrival by train in Chadian in Wu & Wakeman, *Bitter Winds,* p. 98. Concealing the loading and unloading of prisoners from the general public was also a common practice of the Soviet gulag officials, according to Solzhenitsyn, *The Gulag Archipelago,* vol. 1, p. 567.

84. Harry Wu had not seen ordinary civilians for a year when he noticed a group of them staring at him and his fellow inmates; see Wu & Wakeman, *Bitter Winds,* p. 98. Cong Weixi also notes the curious and apprehensive stares from both pedestrians and public bus riders in *Zou xiang hundun,* p. 143.

85. See Kasza's *The Conscription Society.* There is a squad chief *[banzhang]* instead of a group chief *[zuzhang]* in Cong Weixi, "Da qiang xia de hong yulan" [Reddish Magnolia Blossoms beneath the Prison Wall], in *Cong Weixi daibiaozuo* [Representative Works of Cong Weixi] (Zhengzhou: Huang He wenyi chubanshe, 1987), pp. 170–240, esp. 180.

This hierarchy has often been reinforced spatially by having an inmate sit on a very low stool or squat when called in to a cadre's office, much as a commoner had to kneel or bow before the county magistrate in a premodern *yamen*. Some relatively experienced prisoners shouted "Kneel down!" *[dunxia]* at Cong Weixi during his stage as a novice inmate, instructing him in the necessity of showing his deference in front of the prison cadre. This reminded Cong of yamen runners intimidating prisoners coming before the ancien régime's county magistrate with shouts of *tangwei* [Tremble before the power of this hall!]. Before speaking to a cadre or a guard, an inmate would usually have to preface any utterance with the military honorific, "Reporting to the squad chief" *[baogao banzhang]*, always addressing the superior by his title rather than his name in order to show respect.[86]

For the inmate to avoid conflicts and foster his integration into this mini-society, a certain amount of deference and cooperation must be shown not only to the camp cadres and guards, but also to those fellow inmates in positions of authority, particularly one's group chief *[zuzhang]*. For example, when the Delingha camp cadres decided upon a road construction project in the early 1950s, it was the group chief's responsibility to order his fellow inmates to get to work building this road between Qinghai and Tibet.[87] Indeed, the local prison subculture is something that the inmate must adapt to or at least cope with—and perhaps help shape over time, to a modest degree. Although poststructuralist "grand theorists" like Foucault have portrayed prison wardens and guards as all-powerful disciplinarians who thoroughly control their highly malleable, cipher-like prisoners, practical theorists like Norman Johnston show a more nuanced understanding of prisoners' complex and often formidable subculture. Johnston points to some of the practical limits of the power of surveillance, which Foucault sketches in mystifyingly omnipotent hues in the latter's discussion of Bentham's Panopticon: "Surveillance alone could not prevent escapes, unruly behavior, and mutual contamination . . . Distant inspection may prevent fighting, but not conniving, and from the warden's center house one can only see but not hear what is going on in the [prison] yards."[88]

Unlike the detention centers, with their emphasis on interrogating pris-

---

86. Cong Weixi, *Zou xiang hundun*, pp. 147, 194.
87. See Wumingshi, *Hong sha*, p. 172.
88. Norman Johnston, *Forms of Constraint: A History of Prison Architecture* (Urbana: Univ. of Illinois Press, 2000), pp. 2, 45.

oners and squeezing out confessions, prison camps have focused mainly on labor and production, which occupy most of the inmates' waking hours six days per week—and sometimes thirteen out of every fourteen days. In contrast with the oft-quoted slogan in camp guard manuals of "remolding first, and production second" *[gaizao diyi, shengchan di'er]*, labor would take up anywhere from eight to twelve hours of the inmates' waking hours, whereas indoctrination and study sessions would rarely exceed two hours per day. And that was during the Mao Era; by the Deng-Jiang Era, study sessions had in practice withered further as attention shifted more to the bottom line of production.[89] After all, judgments as to the effectiveness of a given prisoner's remolding were highly subjective and difficult to measure, while the camp's productive output could be quantified in yuan or some other measure that would garner wide acceptance.[90]

Therefore, a core aspect of prison camp life is the administration's setting of production targets, which each inmate group chief *[zuzhang]* implements on an individual basis among the prisoners in his specific group. The grade of an individual prisoner's food ration depends on the degree to which the production quota is fulfilled or undershot. During famine years in the Mao Era, having one's food ration cut due to missing the production quota could mean gradual starvation to death in a "goners' brigade" *[laocan dui]* like Section 585 at Qinghe Prison Camp.[91] Even during more normal times, failing to meet the production quota often results in such meager rations as to increase one's susceptibility to the many diseases that have regularly swept through the camps, including during the Deng-Jiang Era.

Some of the most important writers of the Chinese laogai have served as group chiefs or other responsible positions in the camps. Such prisoners have served in a mediating role between the camp administration and rank-and-file prisoners, thereby developing a relatively keen sense of

89. Admittedly, there were exceptions to this rule, for whenever the government launched a political movement, politics would be able to elbow economic production aside and "take command" for a spell. Yet this would eventually blow over as the imperatives of economic production again asserted themselves.

90. The difficulty of measuring or evaluating a given prisoner's progress in remolding through labor is demonstrated in Song Shan, *Hong qiang, hui qiang,* p. 233, and in Lü Haiyan, *Bianyi jingcha,* p. 325. Production, on the other hand, can simply be rendered in terms of currency (yuan) or various weights and measures, thereby garnering virtually universal acceptance.

91. For more on Section 585, see Wu & Wakeman, *Bitter Winds,* pp. 112–129. Jean Pasqualini mentions a similar goners' brigade in Bao & Chelminski, *Prisoner of Mao,* p. 207.

how the camps are run on a daily basis. Harry Wu was a group chief at both the Qinghe and Tuanhe prison camps; Cong Weixi served in this capacity at a mining camp.[92] Zhang Xianliang was the group accountant and the group chief at his prison camp in Ningxia, and also served as the occasional scribe of his camp administrators, some of whom were barely literate.[93] These writers' fictional and autobiographical accounts of their years in the camps suggest that they used their limited authority in a reasonably fair way that fostered trust and a certain amount of solidarity among the prisoners in their group. For instance, when a particularly unscrupulous prisoner who habitually informed on other inmates to the authorities went so far as to break Harry Wu's wrist in a sneak attack, the other prisoners in Wu's team later beat up this bully and threw him into a muddy ditch as a reprisal and warning.[94]

The prison subculture has also had its negative side. The government's policy to stir up mutual incrimination [jiefa] and denunciation [pipan] among the prisoners has often been so successful that it has weakened or even paralyzed inmate solidarity. Moreover, the prison administration's dependence upon inmate chiefs [laotou] to help control other prisoners has often enabled cell tyrants [yuba] to lord it over the rank-and-file like criminal kingpins. The factors that condone and even succor the intimidation tactics of cell tyrants like Tian Baoshan are discussed in the police writer Lü Haiyan's novel The Plainclothes Policeman [Bianyi jingcha]; these factors include poorly educated cadres, untrained guards, and cunning opportunism on the tyrant's part.[95]

Security is always a concern within a prison setting, requiring the prisoners' observation of the relevant disciplinary strictures. Discipline within the camps' military structure smacks of martial law, for any prisoner who attempts to scale a prison wall, slip out through a gate, or wander outside the flag-marked boundaries of a work zone may be shot dead without warning. This is exactly the scenario of the PRC's first work of the "towering wall literature" [da qiang wenxue] set amidst the imposing walls

92. Wu & Wakeman, Bitter Winds, pp. 193, 227; Cong Weixi, Zou xiang hundun, pp. 188–189..

93. Zhang Xianliang, Wode Putishu, p. 93, 152. Zhang Xianliang's alter ego first-person narrator in one novel serves as a group chief in his labor camp. See Xiguan siwang [Getting Used to Dying] (Taipei: Yuan shen chubanshe, 1989), p. 192.

94. Wu & Wakeman, Bitter Winds, pp. 226–227.

95. Lü Haiyan, Bianyi jingcha, pp. 219–221. For an informed portrayal of a cell tyrant in a women's prison camp, see Li Jian, Nüxing de xue qi [The Females' Bloody Banner], Zhuomuniao [Woodpecker], no. 4: 54–74, no. 5: 139–160, no. 6: 128–160, esp. no. 5: 142 (1989).

and guard towers of the prison camps, Cong Weixi's 1979 story "Reddish Magnolia Blossoms beneath the Prison Wall" [Da qiang xia de hong yu-lan]. This story features an old inmate who is not even trying to escape, but is shot to death without warning after climbing part way up a ladder by the prison wall—though a mediocre work, it broke a long-standing taboo on writing and publishing about the laogai in the PRC. Liu Binyan's famous 1985 work of reportage, "The Second Type of Loyalty" ["Di'er zhong zhongcheng"], opens with an eyewitness report of the 1969 execution-style murder of GMD war prisoner Li Zhirong by some Nenjiang (Heilongjiang) Prison Camp guards who deemed him insufficiently deferential when laboring close to the boundary markers.[96] Understandably, most prisoners have taken special care to avoid doing anything that might be interpreted as an escape attempt.

Prison Food and Clothing

Unlike laojiao inmates, laogai prisoners are typically issued cloth shoes and a uniform, the color and thickness of which varies according to the locale. Gray and black are the most common colors, along with dark blue.[97] Commonly etched in white on the uniform is the character for "criminal," *fan*, or sometimes the two characters for "remolding through labor," *lao* and *gai*. To make prisoners further stand out from the general populace and thus easier to nab in the aftermath of an escape, male laogai prisoners have usually had to shave their heads, unlike laojiao inmates.[98] Mao Zedong and his CCP must have inherited the old practice of shaving male convicts' heads from the Stalinist gulag and the czarist *katorga*, since in premodern China this practice was not customary.[99]

96. Liu Binyan, "Di'er zhong zhongcheng" [The Second Type of Loyalty], in *Liu Binyan zixuanji* [Liu Binyan: A Personal Selection of His Writings] (Beijing: Zhongguo wenlian chubanshe, 1988), pp. 113–156. This incident was translated by Geremie Barmé as "Murder at Nenjiang Camp," in *Seeds of Fire: Chinese Voices of Conscience,* ed. Geremie Barmé & John Minford (Hong Kong: Far Eastern Economic Review, 1986), pp. 65–67.

97. The winter clothing that the prison officials issued to Hong Xianheng and his fellow laogai inmates was all black, a common color for camp inmate garb. However, other colors such as gray and blue were also used, while laojiao inmates often wore whatever clothing they could get hold of or patch together. See Wumingshi, *Hong sha,* p. 167.

98. Duan Kewen, *"Zhanfan" zishu* [The Personal Account of a "War Criminal"] (Taipei: Shijie ribao she, 1978), p. 226; Cong Weixi, *Zou xiang hundun,* p. 194.

99. The czarist prison labor regimen concentrated in Siberia was known as *katorga,* a word deriving from the Greek term for forced labor, as of a galley slave. Stalin reintroduced this long-proscribed term in 1943. For the typical appearance of the shaved Russian convict

Underclothes, socks, hats, and jackets tend to be the responsibility of camp inmates to purchase out of the meager fraction of their ordinary wages or a small prison allowance that they may receive.[100] Because this small amount of money also has to cover necessities such as toilet paper, a toothbrush, toothpaste, soap, and a towel, PRC inmates have typically spent many of their free Sundays mending or patching their worn clothes. The late Mao Era Tibetan prisoner Tashi Tsering both patched his worn-out clothing and knitted new socks from cast-off blankets; his multi-patched prison jacket festoons the cover of his autobiography.[101] One of the most memorable exhibits at a Washington conference on the laogai in 1999 was a heavily patched jacket that had belonged to a man who had died in the camps after many years of captivity; he had bequeathed it to his son, who was fortunate enough to survive imprisonment and be released back into society.[102]

In sum, with few or no spare outfits of clothing and little water in which to wash them, laogai prisoners have spent much of their time wearing dirty and often stinking garments.[103] However, the shortage of clean and lightly worn clothing was more of a problem during the poverty-stricken Mao Era than it has been in the relatively prosperous Deng-Jiang Era.

Food is one of the aspects of prison life that most clearly distinguishes modern authoritarian conscription societies from their premodern forebears.[104] Prison wardens in imperial China and czarist Russia almost never

---

in czarist times, see Fyodor Dostoyevsky, *House of the Dead*, trans. David McDuff (1860; rpt. London: Penguin, 1985), p. 57; and in Stalinist times, see Varlam Shalamav, "The Lepers," *Graphite*, trans. John Glad (New York: Norton, 1981), pp. 181–186, esp. 184. Cong Weixi notes that laogai inmates have been traditionally forced to have their heads shaved (*Zou xiang hundun*, p. 194).

100. Song Shan received only two and a half yuan per month as a kind of allowance to cover daily necessities and clothing. See *Hong qiang, hui qiang*, p. 160.

101. Goldstein, Siebenschuh, & Tsering, *The Autobiography of Tashi Tsering*, pp. 135–136. An even more heavily patched prison outfit, that of John Liu, may be seen in the photo section after p. 112 in Saunders, *Eighteen Layers of Hell*.

102. Voices from the Laogai: Fifty Years of Surviving China's Forced Labor Camps, conference, Washington, D.C., 17–19 September 1999.

103. Zhang Xianliang, *Wode Putishu*, pp. 268–269; Wumingshi, *Hong sha*, pp. 78–79.

104. Modern conscription societies have adopted various complex food rationing schemes for the general public as well as for prisoners. In the PRC, this has greatly benefited urban residents at the expense of the majority in the countryside, who have borne the brunt of the PRC's many famines. Most of these famines stemmed from foolish policies implemented by an unaccountable single-party government, which used the rationing schemes to exert greater control over its dependent citizenry. One of the factors that made escape from the camps so untenable during the Mao Era was that an escapee would be outside of the government's rationing system and would usually be unable to afford paying high prices to buy grain on the black market. See Duan Kewen, *"Zhanfan" zishu*, pp. 226–227.

intentionally cut prisoners off from food as a method of controlling them through their shrunken and growling stomachs, as can be surmised from informed and highly critical accounts of imprisonment by Li Baojia and Fyodor Dostoyevsky.[105] Dostoyevsky criticized his nineteenth-century Siberian prison camp's vegetable soup for containing cockroaches, but he praised both the high quality and ample quantity of the camp's bread, not to mention the availability of meat—all of which stand in sharp contrast to the ordinary situation in the camps under Stalin and Mao. A prison warden would not generally prohibit relatives or friends of ordinary premodern Chinese or Russian prisoners from bringing them food on a daily basis, nor would he impose weight limitations on the food brought to inmates.

Yet in the PRC and Soviet Union, food parcels have generally been limited to one per month, and no more than 5 kilograms or so per parcel. Specific rules about the exact weight allowed for the monthly food parcel have varied from camp to camp in the PRC, but 10 catties [*jin*] (around 11 pounds, or not quite 5 kilograms) has been common. Guards or cadres would often find ways of pressuring the prisoner to share even that small amount of food with them.[106] In the PRC and the former Soviet Union, food would be stingily and bureaucratically rationed according to the political rank and productive output of a given prisoner, leaving most prisoners uncomfortably hungry much of the time—and famished almost all of the time during lean years.

The problem of hunger among laogai inmates varies greatly in intensity according to the historical period, the region, and the rationing policies of the local camp cadres. Hunger was worst during the Mao Era,

---

105. Li Baojia, *Huo diyu;* Dostoyevsky, *House of the Dead,* pp. 44–45. See also Chapter 14 of the mid-seventeenth-century novel *Xingshi yinyuan zhuan,* in which a rich gentryman bribes a jail warden to build his concubine a new jail cell, provides her with ample food, and visits her whenever he wishes. Xi Zhou Sheng (pseud.), *Xingshi yinyuan zhuan* [Marriage as Retribution, Awakening the World], 3 vols. (Shanghai: Shanghai guji chubanshe, 1981). For a study of this novel, see Yenna Wu, *Ameliorative Satire and the Seventeenth-Century Chinese Novel, Xingshi Yinyuan Zhuan—Marriage as Retribution, Awakening the World* (Lewiston, NY: Edwin Mellen Press, 1999).

106. See Wu & Wakeman, *Bitter Winds,* pp. 196–197. For more about this situation in the former USSR, see Solzhenitsyn, *The Gulag Archipelago, 1918–1956,* vol. 3, trans. Harry Willetts (New York: Harper & Row, 1976), p. 498. Even a decade after Stalin's death, food parcels for a prisoner were generally limited to one per month, of no more than 5 kilograms. In December 1963, when Solzhenitsyn asked the USSR Legislative Proposal Commission why larger and more frequent food parcels could not be allowed, the pat answer from these obviously prosperous officials was that this change would favor "rich" families and thus be unfair to "working" families.

particularly during the worst famine in world history, from 1959 to 1962, when an estimated 30 million Chinese died of starvation, nearly all in the rural areas where prison camps were usually located. Hunger has usually been worse in the inland provinces, especially those in the northwest and west, than those along the eastern seaboard. Yet the food rationing policies have applied everywhere in the PRC, and while malnutrition in the prison camps is no longer the lethal danger it was in the Mao Era, it has still remained a problem in many regions during the Deng-Jiang Era. For high-ranking political prisoners who could be of use in government propaganda or "impression management," such as the former emperor Puyi, who had been imprisoned at a special war criminals' unit at Fushun Prison in Liaoning, the daily fare was rice and sautéed vegetable and meat dishes. This would have been an almost unheard-of luxury for the ordinary rank-and-file inmate.[107]

Even during Liu Qing's imprisonment throughout the 1980s, his fellow laogai inmates could seldom eat their fill of the rancid hardtack buns *[wotou]* and half-rotten vegetable soup that was their daily fare. In the camps he was in, most of the fights that resulted in fatalities were over food. Liu notes that the ordinary prisoners' soup was typically made of partly rotten vegetables that no customers would buy at the market. It would usually lack edible oil, which is an extremely important but often missing nutritional component in the practically meatless camp diet.[108] With only two scanty meals per day being provided in many labor camps, one can understand the pervasiveness of hunger there.[109]

Even when eating the meager but less disastrous urban prison food in Beijing during 1989–90, the often famished Gao Xin once asked a veteran inmate how he could stand such prison conditions over the long term. Gao Xin would get just a taste of meat once a week, but extremely little oil, and mainly just starch and liquid.[110] Some prisons in pros-

107. See Aixin Jueluo Yutang, "Puyi yu wo shuzhi zhijian," in Aixin Jueluo Pujie et al., *Zai jizhongying de rizi: Xuantong huangdi de houbansheng* [The Days in Concentration Camps: The Latter Half of the Life of the Xuantong Emperor] (Hong Kong: Dong xi wenhua shiye chuban gongsi, n.d.), pp. 114–115.

108. Liu Qing, "The Role of Hierarchy in the Treatment of Chinese Prisoners," conference presentation, The Chinese Labor Camp: Theory, Actuality, and Fictional Representation, Univ. of California, Riverside, CA, 15 January 2000. Lai Ying also recalls that fights among her fellow female prisoners over food were very common and that prison cadres probably intercepted and consumed many inmates' food parcels during 1959–62. See *The Thirty-Sixth Way*, pp. 82–83, 89.

109. Peng Yinhan, *Dalu jizhongying*, p. 64; Song Shan, *Hong qiang, hui qiang*, p. 159; Wumingshi, *Hong sha*, pp. 173, 316.

110. Gao Xin, *Beiwei yu huihuang*, p. 50.

perous coastal regions like Xiamen were providing many of their inmates with adequate dietary oil and marginally decent institutional food by the late 1990s, but this was the exception rather than the rule for the country as a whole. Even in these relatively prosperous and well-run prisons in Fujian at the turn of the new century, grain was so overwhelmingly dominant in the prison diet that inmates frequently complained that they were unable to experience satiety from a prison meal.[111]

Zhang Xianliang's 1995 laogai memoir suggests that the state's power to withhold food from its hungry citizens can win their submission to its authority more efficiently than any ordinary form of torture.[112] Of course, much of the mass starvation that took place both in and out of the laogai camps in 1959–62 was due more to hare-brained CCP policies and actions than to conscious design. However, the hunger that has periodically pestered the vast majority of laogai prisoners since 1949 has been based on the system of stringent rationing according to the inmate's rank and labor output, along with the party-state's yearning for the dependent prisoner's total submission [juedui fucong] to its authority.[113] As a "schema of individual submission" [schéma de la soumission individuelle], to borrow Foucault's formulation, the PRC's rationing of food to laogai inmates has exerted a more thoroughgoing control over prisoners than any of the French disciplinary regimens Foucault enumerates in Discipline and

111. Tang Min provides a menu of what appears to be typical late-1990s fare at the Xiamen Detention Center in Zou xiang heping, p. 78. It should be remembered that as a literary celebrity who had no quarrel with the central government, Tang Min enjoyed unusual prosperity and received especially generous treatment in both Xiamen detention center and Fujian Women's Prison, and thus cannot be considered a typical case. As noted on pp. 207–208, many prisoners in Fujian Women's Prison continued to feel hungry much of the time, especially if their families were not wealthy enough to send them food parcels to supplement the lean prison diet.

112. Zhang Xianliang, Wode Putishu, p. 100. The CCP used hunger as a weapon at least as early as the civil war of the 1940s, according to Huang Jue, Xue xing si yi [Four Cities That Reek of Blood] (Hong Kong: Yazhou chubanshe, 1953), p. 18. CCP cadres in Guangdong would frequently recruit young beggars and street urchins [xiao gui] as utterly dependent soldiers and errand boys, and would punish them by withholding food and drink for a day if they were afraid to attack the enemy when so ordered.

113. Zhang Xianliang's old camp commissar constantly insists that "obeying the leadership" [fucong lingdao] is the prisoner's first duty, and that no knowledge can be applied without "following commands" [tinghua]. Zhang later compares the camp cadres to the harsh patriarchs of a large clan; they could behave dementedly and abnormally at times, yet their behavior had to be accepted by the entire family as an expression of their concern for the errant youths (prisoners) who have let everybody down. See Wode Putishu, pp. 20–21, 200–201. For more on food rationing as a means of control over prisoners, see Bao & Chelminski, Prisoner of Mao, p. 46.

Punish.[114] The CCP's unprecedented control over the levers of basic nour-
ishment has exacerbated and capitalized on the average Chinese personality's tendency to extend filial devotion *[xiao]* beyond the confines of the
family to a general deference before authority.[115]

If the PRC has developed a particularly advanced form of reinforcing
submission to authority through food rationing, this has simultaneously
brought about a countervailing devolution in many laogai camps toward
retrograde phenomena such as jostling over scraps and foraging for wild
foods, much as in a primitive hunting-and-gathering society. Laogai memoirs and fiction brim with casual accounts of famished Mao Era prisoners catching and devouring—raw or cooked—a wide variety of unlikely
wild animals, including field mice, crickets, locusts, toads, grapevine
worms, grasshoppers, insect larvae and eggs, and poisonous snakes.[116] The
party-state has usually prohibited and punished this sort of "foraging"
[chi qing], thereby exposing inmates to added risks as they have sought
to alleviate their hunger pangs.[117] Empty stomachs would often drive inmates to steal cucumbers, turnips, or cabbage leaves from crop fields—
and to devise ingenious stratagems to smuggle any uneaten contraband
through the inspection line back into their barracks.[118] Dimitri Panin observed a similar phenomenon during his confinement in the Soviet gulag: "The prisoners steal everything they can possibly bring back into the

114. Michel Foucault, *Surveiller et punir: naissance de la prison,* pp. 246–247. Translated
by Alan Sheridan as *Discipline and Punish: The Birth of the Prison,* 2nd ed. (New York: Vintage Books, 1995), p. 243.

115. Kuo-shu Yang, "Chinese Personality and Its Change," *The Psychology of the Chinese
People,* ed. Michael Harris Bond (Hong Kong: Oxford Univ. Press, 1986), pp. 106–170, esp.
126–127.

116. Cong Weixi himself characterizes this grim situation as "devolution" *[tuihua]* in *Zou
xiang hundun,* p. 107. See also Cong Weixi, "Yuan qu de bai fan" [White Sails Far Departed],
in *Cong Weixi daibiao zuo* [Representative Works of Cong Weixi] (Zhengzhou: Huang He
wenyi chubanshe, 1987), pp. 364–459, esp. 367, 393; Wang Ruowang, "Ji'e sanbuqu," pp. 78–
222, esp. 154–155; Song Shan, *Hong qiang, hui qiang,* p. 118; and Bao & Chelminski, *Prisoner
of Mao,* p. 242.

117. Zhang Xianliang, *Wode Putishu,* pp. 293–294.

118. During the early 1960s, two prisoners who had hidden small stolen cucumbers in
one another's rectums were caught during an inspection and punished, according to Cong
Weixi, *Zou xiang hundun,* pp. 217–218. See also Bao & Chelminski, *Prisoner of Mao,* pp. 227–
228, 253. For a comparative perspective on how Soviet gulag inmates were similarly driven
to illicit techniques to ward off starvation, see Anatoly Marchenko, *My Testimony,* trans.
Michael Scammell (New York: E. P. Dutton, 1969), pp. 236–242. Anne Thurston notes the
devastating effects that extreme hunger often has on human character, particularly an "over-
whelming selfishness" and a "callous disregard for others in one's struggle for individual
survival." See *A Chinese Odyssey,* p. 61.

camp from their places of work, or consume it on the spot."[119] Even well-educated PRC inmates would often jostle and fight with other prisoners over the little bit of gruel left at the bottom of the vat, and rummage through rubbish heaps in search of something edible.

The way laogai inmates have regularly licked their bowls clean resembles the lunch scene featuring the impoverished old illiterate farmer in the 1984 film *Yellow Earth [Huang tudi]*.[120] Eating in the camps was something that demanded one's "full concentration," and came to resemble "prayer among religious devotees," according to the narrator of Zhang Xianliang's 1985 novel *Half of Man Is Woman*. Anyone with the gall to interrupt the prisoners at this special time would encounter the same kind of furious snarls and glares that a wolf would make "if hindered from carrying off the rabbit it had caught in its jaws."[121] The competition and strife among prisoners over food has thus functioned as both a part of their punishment and a lever in the party-state's control over them by divide-and-conquer tactics.[122]

Such atavistic "remolding" in the camps functioned rather like a time machine thrown in reverse as it coarsened and dehumanized the malnourished captives at its disposal. As the painter and ex-inmate Luo Xinmin explained it, the camps were in part an expression of the CCP's long-standing "ignorant masses policy" [*yu min zhengce*, lit. "policy of deceiving the people"], whereby educated but insufficiently deferential convicts would be exiled for remolding into "the common herd of simpletons" [*tounao jiandan de qunmeng*].[123] Precisely this type of remolded simpleton appears in Zhang Xianliang's novella *Lü hua shu* [Mimosa], whose educated protagonist's intense craving for basic creature com-

119. Dimitri Panin, *The Notebooks of Sologdin*, trans. John Moore (New York: Harcourt Brace Jovanovich, 1976), p. 40.

120. Cong Weixi, *Zou xiang hundun sanbuqu*, pp. 111, 194–195, 197. *Yellow Earth* (1984) was directed by Chen Kaige. See Bonnie S. McDougall, *The Yellow Earth: A Film by Chen Kaige, with a Complete Translation* (Hong Kong: Chinese Univ. of Hong Kong Press, 1993).

121. Zhang Xianliang, *Nanren de yiban shi nüren* [Half of Man Is Woman], in *Zhang Xianliang xuanji* [An Anthology of Zhang Xianliang], vol. 3 (Tianjin: Baihua wenyi chubanshe, 1986), pp. 399–618, esp. 434. English translation by Martha Avery (New York: Norton, 1986). For another view of famished prisoners' ritualization of eating, see Cong Weixi, *Zou xiang hundun*, pp. 179–180.

122. The prison authorities' implicit strategies for control over inmates will be discussed further in Chapter 4.

123. Quoted in Cong Weixi, *Zou xiang hundun*, p. 55. Cong Weixi replies to Luo that the CCP's banishment of difficult or inconvenient citizens to the camps is entirely comparable to premodern exile [*fapei*], the only difference being that Chinese prisoners no longer had their faces tattooed.

forts has pushed aside his former interest in national affairs and world culture. "Having gone through four years of harsh collective forced labor and hunger that gave me a brush with death, various sorts of impractical ambitions . . . were all dumped into the great ocean to the east."[124] After years of semi-starvation fare in PRC prisons, the one-time ardent political idealist Sidney Rittenberg similarly came to perceive utopia as "an ideal world where I could have all the cornbread I wanted."[125] The road of ascent to a Marxian utopia where exploitation was abolished and ordinary human needs were universally met had actually metamorphosed into a twisting and plunging Hobbesian path marked by a demeaning struggle to achieve the most basic and narrow physical needs — yet couched in high-sounding, stentorian political rhetoric.

Barracks Life and Sanitation

A few top-ranking prisoners such as former CCP officials may enjoy sautéed meals in a private cell with a metal-spring bed, but the vast majority of inmates have subsisted on hardtack buns *[wotou]* and watery vegetable soup in crowded, uncomfortable, and stinking cells or barracks. Even in the model prisons to which visiting foreign dignitaries in the PRC are occasionally escorted, former hard-line Chicago Police Superintendent LeRoy Martin approvingly noted that "sanitary facilities are a bucket" and that the inmates were "locked down" most of the time they were not laboring.[126]

Though few observers would endorse Martin's favorable evaluation of ordinary PRC prison conditions, his early-1990s report on the rudimentary "sanitary facilities" and primitive conditions even within some of the model prisons is accurate and quite representative. Barracks flooring may be of cement or wood planking, but floors of bare earth or straw have also been frequently encountered, even in labor camps set up to re-

124. Zhang Xianliang, *Lü hua shu* [Mimosa], in *Zhang Xianliang xuanji*, vol. 3, pp. 161–338, esp. 220–221. English translation by Gladys Yang (Beijing: Panda Books, 1989).

125. Rittenberg & Bennett, *The Man Who Stayed Behind*, p. 400.

126. Kevin Johnson, "Get Harsh on Crime, Says Chicago's Top Cop," *USA Today,* 16 July 1991, p. 3A. Chicago's mayor disagreed with Martin's view that the PRC penal system would be an appropriate model for the United States to adopt. However, Sheriff Joe Arupaio's "tent city" for prisoners in Phoenix, Arizona, does seem to follow the PRC approach to deterring and punishing crime by making prison life quite forbidding.

ceive inmates from the largest and most prosperous cities.[127] Experienced PRC prisoners learn to move to the side of the barracks or cell that is furthest from the reeking latrine bucket, beside which the newest prisoners in the group must generally lay down their bedrolls. The two allowed daily visits to the privy are generally limited to a few minutes, even when an inmate has been left in handcuffs and/or leg irons as punishment.[128]

Instead of eating in a prison mess hall, PRC prisoners almost always take their meal while squatting in their own barracks or cell, unless their food is brought out to their work site.[129] There is enough space to eat in their cell or barracks because they typically have no furniture: nearly all PRC prisoners either sleep on the floor or on very low plank platforms, in contrast with the bunk-bed barracks arrangement in the former Soviet gulag.[130] The USSR gulag inmates in a given four-bunk unit would all have their feet facing in the same direction, but PRC laogai inmates have often been so crowded in their cell or barracks that two neighbors' unwashed feet would have to be on either side of one's head all night.[131] The standard sleeping space on the floor has often been only 30 centimeters wide, and the lack of storage space within the crowded barracks has forced most inmates to hang their simple belongings on pegs in the wall.[132] Cong Weixi was once accused of suspiciously sizing up the terrain and formally reprimanded by his transit prison group chief for having stuck his head part way out of his stuffy and stinking tent to gulp down some draughts of fresh air.[133] His revulsion for the camp's acrid odors was a common reaction of visitors and relatively new prisoners, who have often found the quarters barely fit for human habitation.[134] In contrast, veteran denizens of a camp have tended "not to notice its stench as time

127. Prisoners from Shanghai found a mud floor in their Jiangxi camp barracks; see Peng Yinhan, *Dalu jizhongying,* pp. 63–64. Inmates from Beijing found a straw-covered mud floor and tents in their transit prison in the northern suburbs of the city; see Cong Weixi, *Zou xiang hundun,* p. 149.

128. Gao Xin, *Beiwei yu huihuang,* p. 50. A handcuffed prisoner depends on the considerate assistance of a fellow inmate to help him on and off with his pants, to wipe his rear end with toilet paper, and to assist with other essential daily tasks.

129. Wumingshi, *Hai de chengfa,* p. 34.

130. Soviet gulag bunks were in units of four beds, with two spaces above and two spaces below, as illustrated in Rossi, *The Gulag Handbook,* p. 41.

131. Cong Weixi, *Zou xiang hundun,* p. 157.

132. Zhang Xianliang, *Wode Putishu,* p. 228.

133. Cong Weixi, *Zou xiang hundun,* pp. 149–150.

134. For example, Wang Xiaoling vividly recalled the stench of her cell mate and mustiness of the jail as a whole; see *Many Waters,* pp. 43–44. For a similar first impression of a reeking prison, see Peng Yinhan, *Dalu jizhongying,* pp. 63–64.

went on" *[jiu er bu wen qi chou]*, having learned to numb their olfactory sensitivities.[135]

Baths and showers for Chinese prisoners have been so rare as to hardly ever receive any mention in laogai memoirs. An exception is Zhang Xianliang's comment that he envied Soviet gulag prisoners for sometimes having had access to baths and showers, since this was totally lacking in the laogai, in his experience.[136] Most washing in the laogai has been localized to the body parts most in need of it, such as face, hands, and feet. Yet water for such purposes was often so limited as to require several prisoners to share one basin of water, which would soon turn dark gray from the accumulated filth.[137] Sanitation standards have typically been very low; even those prisoners assigned to transport and spread animal manure or human feces onto farm fields have rarely had a chance to wash their hands thoroughly with soap before eating. Moreover, inmates who have dropped food on the ground by mistake have often been expected to pick it up and eat it, in spite of the danger of ingesting roundworm eggs or disease microbes.[138] Even an inmate who faced the danger of infection from a work-related injury might have to make a very strong case to the supervisor to be allowed to take time off to see a doctor.[139]

Vermin and Disease

Blood-sucking parasites have been a widespread scourge of PRC prisoners, with bedbugs *[chouchong]* probably the most frequently encountered vermin of all.[140] Especially at night, bedbugs would commonly crawl up from cracks

135. Duan Kewen, *"Zhanfan" zishu,* p. 209.

136. Zhang Xianliang, *Wode Putishu,* p. 268.

137. Song Shan, *Hong qiang, hui qiang,* p. 13. When Song Shan was sent from her urban prison to a rural labor camp, there was somewhat more water for washing, but even so, there was only a bucketful of muddy well water in the morning and at night, since the water tap was off limits for prisoners' washing needs (pp. 129–130).

138. Duan Kewen, *"Zhanfan" zishu,* p. 208.

139. After cutting his feet on pottery shards or broken glass while toiling in the farm fields, Duan Kewen could at most hope to rinse the cut with brackish water and tie it up with a dirty cloth before hurrying back to work to prove his thorough remolding. See *"Zhanfan" zishu,* p. 200. Though Cong Weixi's finger had been cut so badly at work that the tendon was damaged, his supervisor urged him just to smear on some ointment and keep working without delay. See *Zou xiang hundun,* pp. 116–117.

140. Severe PRC prison bedbug infestations are mentioned, for example, in Cong Weixi, *Zou xiang hundun sanbuqu,* p. 321; Wang Xiaoling, *Many Waters,* p. 45; Peng Yinhan, *Dalu jizhongying,* p. 55; Wumingshi, *Hong sha,* p. 139; Wang Ruowang, *Ji'e sanbuqu,* p. 158; and An Sinan, *Lian yu sanbuqu,* p. 49. A reddish-brown parasite of the family Cimicidae, the

in the floor and floorboards or drop onto prisoners from the ceiling. Already weakened from malnourishment and hard labor, most inmates have also had their resting hours interrupted by the irritating bites of bedbugs or other blood-sucking vermin. Bedbugs swarm through some cells and barracks in teeming formations, earning the prison nickname of "tanks" *[tanke]*.[141]

Zhang Xianliang notes that lice infestations in the laogai could reach the point at which the parasites on a single inmate's underpants would be as numerous as the words on the front page of a newspaper.[142] Neither Zhang nor any laogai prisoner he knew ever received even 1 gram of insecticide to suppress these laogai lice infestations, but Zhang does recall seeing hungry inmates pick off lice and munch them down, just like the satirical figure Ah Q in Lu Xun's famous story.[143] As for fleas, they would often be so numerous as to leave red bumps all over a prisoner's body and turn his quilt purplish black with their droppings.[144]

Mosquitoes often swarmed so thickly near prisoners' irrigated fields that they formed an undulating dark gray ball.[145] Generally, camp cadres would either not notice the wildly gesticulating motions of prisoners attempting to ward off such flying parasites or look on with indifference.[146] Cadres would actually enlist the aid of mosquitoes when occasionally punishing an inmate by stripping him of clothing and leaving him tied to a tree in an infested marshy area.[147]

---

bedbug has occasionally provided some entertainment for bored prisoners, who would seek them out and smash them for sport, as Chen Sanxing often did when in a Taiwanese prison. See *Shaonian zhengzhi fan*, p. 138. Reasonable sanitation practices and an occasional fumigation with insecticides have proven effective and inexpensive methods of controlling bedbugs, but these methods have seldom been implemented in Chinese prisons. In a related incident, the commissar at Zhang Xianliang's prison camp insisted that lice were nothing to be concerned about, and that their presence was actually an auspicious indication that the infested person was in fine health; see *Wode Putishu*, p. 269.

141. An Sinan, *Lian yu sanbuqu*, p. 49.

142. Zhang Xianliang, *Wode Putishu*, p. 268.

143. Ibid., pp. 268–269. The satirical scene of Ah Q, in imitation of Whiskers Wang, picking off his lice and eating them occurs in the third section of Lu Xun's *A Q zhengzhuan* [The True Story of Ah Q] (1921–22; rpt. Hong Kong: Baili shudian, n.d.), pp. 46–48. Many literary scholars and critics have inaccurately claimed 1921 to be the year of publication of *A Q zhengzhuan*, which in reality was serialized in a Beiping (Beijing) newspaper literary supplement from 4 December 1921 through 2 February 1922. See *Lu Xun xiaoshuo ji* [A Collection of Lu Xun's Fiction], ed. Yang Ze (Taipei: Hongfan shudian youxian gongsi, 1994), p. 480.

144. Duan Kewen, *"Zhanfan" zishu*, p. 79.

145. Zhang Xianliang, *Wode Putishu*, p. 116

146. Zhang Xianliang, *Nanren de yiban shi nüren*, p. 404.

147. Zhang Xianliang, *Wode Putishu*, pp. 115–116. This form of punishment had been used since the early days of the Soviet gulag, and in China also seems to have been used by some modern warlords to punish their runaway troops.

Internal parasites such as the roundworm *[huichong]* have been a frequent hazard in prison farms where human excrement is used as fertilizer and sanitation standards for prisoners are low or nonexistent. Duan Kewen frequently saw dead roundworms when emptying the contents of privies into his fertilizer vat, and recalls having seen a live roundworm crawl out of an ailing fellow inmate's nostril.[148]

Along with poor inmate nutrition and sanitation, routine infestations of parasitic vermin and many other disease-transmitting insects such as flies and roaches have contributed to the unusually high rates of illness in PRC labor camps and prisons. Often riddled with itchy and inflamed bumps left by biting parasites, the skin of prisoners commonly becomes infected with sores, scabies, or other dermatological ailments.[149]

Especially during the Mao Era, the grossly inadequate prison diet would sometimes lead to severe ailments like beriberi, the edema *[fuzhong]* of which was marked by a heavy swelling in the legs that could spread throughout the body.[150] Scurvy from the lack of vitamins in the diet sometimes caused prisoners' teeth to fall out, and the low fiber and oil content in the food often caused severe constipation that could occasionally be fatal.[151] Severe diarrhea was even more common due to poor sanitation and the great stress on the prisoners' digestive systems—and was much more likely to be fatal.[152] Overall, digestive-tract diseases have ranked along with lung ailments (especially tuberculosis) and hepatitis as the most

148. Duan Kewen, *"Zhanfan" zishu*, p. 208.

149. George Black & Robin Munro, *Black Hands of Beijing: Lives of Defiance in China's Democracy Movement* (New York: Wiley, 1993), p. 286.

150. Cong Weixi, "Feng lei yan" [Eyes That Water from a Breeze], in *Lu hui tou* [The Deer Looks Back] (Beijing: Zhongguo qingnian chubanshe, 1988), p. 63. The second-degree swelling was so heavy in this particular case that the protagonist felt as though rocks were hanging from his legs as he walked.

151. Cong Weixi's constipation in the early 1960s once reached the point where he could not pass his hardened feces without using his finger to dig it out piece by piece from his rectum. See *Zou xiang hundun*, pp. 178–179. Jean Pasqualini had to take the same dire measures for his constipation in 1960, and he heard of relatively frail inmates who died from "trying to shit their guts out." See Bao & Chelminski, *Prisoner of Mao*, pp. 218–219. One of Harry Wu's fellow inmates, who eventually committed suicide, had been suffering from an inflamed hemorrhoid half a foot long; see Wu & Wakeman, *Bitter Winds*, p. 173. Tooth loss by prisoners such as Wei Jingsheng seems to have been due more to chronic vitamin deficiencies and a sorely inadequate diet than to poor hygiene. When imprisoned in 1712, the Qing literatus Fang Bao (1668–1749) observed that a number of prisoners fell ill and died due to the crowded and unsanitary conditions in his prison. However, Fang Bao's notes do not refer to any of the intentional nutritional deprivations or psychological pressures that PRC camp inmates have routinely experienced. See Fang's "Yu zhong zaji" [Prison Jottings], *Fang Wangxi quanji* [Collected Works of Fang Bao] (Beijing: Zhongguo shudian, 1991), pp. 352–354.

152. Zhang Xianliang, *Wode Putishu*, p. 279.

debitilitating and widespread physiological disorders in PRC labor camps and prisons.

As PRC prisoners have had to repeatedly revile one another and confess to having been less than human in their betrayal of "the people" and the infallible party, it is not surprising that mental diseases have appeared quite frequently in memoirs and fiction of the laogai. There were so many mentally ill inmates in one of the early 1960s camps that a special coeducational mental sanatorium was set up, and the violent behavior of some of the patients reflected the violently abusive political rhetoric and repression of the time.[153] The abandoned wives and other close relatives of wrongfully incarcerated prisoners were also at higher risk of developing mental disease, as suggested by a story by Liu Binyan.[154]

The prisoners whom the PRC government seems to have singled out for particularly damaging treatment health-wise have been the organizers of fledgling independent labor unions, which in official discourse are defined as insidiously illegal competitors of the party-state's mammoth in-house labor union, a classic one-size-fits-all administered mass organization. Ever since Lech Walesa's independent Solidarity Union broke the Polish Communist Party's monopoly on that nation's political power, CCP leaders have viewed all grassroots independent union organizing in the PRC as particularly dangerous subversion that must be mercilessly crushed and decapitated at once. By imprisoning and neutralizing the independent union organizers and leaders, the party-state in effect decapitates the grassroots union organization. Ironically, the party-state that has apotheosized the "workers, farmers, and soldiers" *[gong nong bing]* has suppressed the workers' right to free association far more strictly than the ancien régime did.

After the imprisoned independent union leader Han Dongfang complained in late 1989 of stomach trouble stemming from the inadequate diet, a cadre ordered an acupuncturist to treat him. This acupuncturist proceeded to stick a huge needle all the way into Han's palm from the

153. Several staff and ordinary inmates had to restrain one mentally ill inmate who was using a broom as a cudgel and as a means to smear bucketsful of human excrement from the privy all over herself, her fellow patients, and the facility. See Cong Weixi, *Zou xiang hundun,* p. 197.

154. Liu Binyan, "Diwuge chuan dayi de ren," pp. 28–35, esp. 32. In this story, the mental patient Jiang Zhenfang becomes overwrought upon seeing a photograph of her late husband Gu Tiancheng, who died in the frigid northern laogai during the famine in the wake of the Great Leap Forward. The taciturn and cautious Gu Tiancheng had been framed as an anti-party rightist by the smiling back-stabber Comrade He Qixiong, whose protégé had brought public disgrace upon Jiang with baseless boasts of having slept with her.

base of his thumb to just below his little finger, then threaded it back and forth in the wound, causing Han to gasp and "writhe in agony."[155] Early in 1990, a guard actually informed Han Dongfang that he was about to be moved where he would contract a disease, and precisely that happened: half of Han's new cell mates were racked by heavy tubercular coughing.[156] Before long, Han in fact contracted a severe case of tuberculosis, but was not hospitalized for months.[157]

A less famous independent union organizer and leader in Hunan named Li Wangyang, formerly a healthy and strong young man, was even more of a physical wreck after imprisonment than Han Dongfang. The numerous tortures and beatings Li received and the many illnesses he contracted over a decade in prison combined to shrink him from a height of 182 cm to a mere 173 cm.[158] Li's heart disease, tuberculosis, and spinal disorders of the lower back and neck were all contracted as a direct result of his mistreatment in prison. He went on a hunger strike when the government denied him medical care following his release.[159] As in the case of a prison chief's neglect of Cong Weixi's injury and illness some three decades earlier (1960), the medical care grudgingly rationed to PRC inmates has tended to be too little and too late.[160]

Sexuality

Almost by definition, prisons around the world deny the inmate access to a normal sex life.[161] As in prisons in many other countries, ordinary criminals *[xingshi fan]* who are male and relatively youthful chat yearningly about

---

155. Black & Munro, *Black Hands of Beijing*, p. 287.

156. The epidemic of tuberculosis in Han Dongfang's cell was nothing new. Jean Pasqualini estimated that almost half of the prisoners he knew in the early 1960s had tuberculosis, from which he suffered as well. See Bao & Chelminski, *Prisoner of Mao*, p. 276.

157. Black & Munro, *Black Hands of Beijing*, pp. 288, 323. Han Dongfang was eventually released from custody to receive medical treatment abroad, but the Brezhnevian condition for his release was that he would not be allowed to return to the PRC. When he later attempted to cross the border to China, Han's PRC passport was confiscated and he was forcibly sent back across the border. Han's torture at the hands of guards and even a judge will be discussed in the following chapter.

158. "Gongyun lingxiu Li Wangyang zai Hunan jueshi" [Labor Union Leader Li Wangyang Goes on a Hunger Strike in Hunan], *Shijie ribao*, 4 February 2001, p. A8.

159. Ibid.

160. Cong Weixi, *Zou xiang hundun*, pp. 115–121.

161. As with any general rule, there are some exceptions to this one, such as house arrest, brief leaves for family visits under special circumstances, and the postrelease informal

sex more than almost anything else except good food.[162] Women, intellectuals, and older male inmates in the PRC have tended to express much less longing for sex per se than to be reunited with their entire family.[163] During famines, interest in sex dwindles among all groups of prisoners, though of course there have been some individual exceptions. For example, even in 1962, when malnutrition was still widespread in the laogai and the countryside, a young male inmate in Harry Wu's group named Lu expressed strong but frustrated sexual desire, which a few years later intensified to the point of bringing on severe mental illness.[164] Zhang Xianliang has likened the rare pleasure of eating one's fill of foragings together with a cell mate during famine times to sexual gratification, and has noted a temporary revival of the dormant sexual desire at such a juncture.[165]

The problem of sexual dysfunction, particularly male impotence, has afflicted many inmates of the PRC laogai quite severely.[166] This widespread impotence seems to have stemmed from a combination of chronic undernourishment, exhaustion from long hours of daily forced labor, puritanical Maoist ideology, and the psychologically debilitating round of

---

control over jiuye personnel who may live with a spouse. A prison stay commonly leads to the extinction of whatever love relationship the prisoner may have had prior to incarceration, according to Zhu Guanghua, *Zhongxing fan: Zhongguo xibu yige daxing laogai nongchang li de mimi he gushi* [Long-Term Inmates: Secrets and Stories from a Large-Sized Labor Remolding Farm in Western China] (Chengdu: Sichuan wenyi chubanshe, 1989), p. 113.

162. As a typical straitlaced intellectual of his generation, Cong Weixi felt acutely embarrassed by the young male criminals' idle chatter about things like women's breasts and buttocks. He was even more mortified by their madcap antics such as fashioning a steamed hardtack bun in the shape of a penis and having it taken to a women prisoners' cell. See *Zou xiang hundun,* pp. 196–197.

163. Jean Pasqualini (and most of his cell mates) lost interest in sex, but he did very much appreciate a visit every year or so from his wife and son, according to Bao & Chelminski, *Prisoner of Mao,* pp. 242–243, 255–256. Song Shan cared little about her former fiancé or finding someone new; she was far more concerned about returning to her elderly mother and seeing her imprisoned brother again, according to *Hong qiang, hui qiang,* p. 85. Of course, there are exceptions; the intellectual Gao Xin is unusually candid in expressing his momentary physical attraction to a particularly shapely policewoman at the station where he was being booked, in *Beiwei yu huihuang,* p. 27. The relatively well-educated inmates in Wang Zifu's novel *Nü lao ziwei* also occasionally enjoy listening to the bawdy ditties of a prostitute upon whom they normally look down (p. 34). For the most part, however, their tepid interest in sex fits the general pattern for intellectual inmates.

164. Wu & Wakeman, *Bitter Winds,* pp. 149–150, 191–195.

165. Zhang Xianliang, *Wode Putishu,* pp. 189–190.

166. Though a less common problem in the former Soviet gulag than in China's laogai, the issue of inmate impotence does surface in some gulag memoirs. See Anatoly Marchenko, *My Testimony,* p. 171; and Jerzy Kmiecik, *A Boy in the Gulag* (London: Quartet Books, 1983), p. 151.

mutual vilification and self-denunciation.[167] Jean Pasqualini reckons that impotence had struck most of the laogai prisoners whom he knew well enough to judge, himself included. He adds that sexuality was even more "ideologically incorrect" in the camps than in the society on the outside.[168] Zhang Xianliang's controversial 1985 novel *Half of Man Is Woman* brought wide attention to the lingering problem of inmate impotence, which appears to have resulted in part from having to delay his own first sexual experience to the age of thirty-nine.[169] Cong Weixi suffered from impotence for almost two decades, well after his exoneration in the late 1970s.[170] The immediate catalyst was the traumatic experience of his wife's second attempted suicide and his own handcuffing and confinement in a tiny punishment cell in 1970, though the general contributing factors mentioned above had set the stage for his protracted sexual dysfunction. Cong Weixi did not finally recover from impotence until the early 1990s, when he was close to sixty years of age.[171]

Retained ex-inmate workers *[jiuye renyuan]* have often been able to settle down with a spouse in the vicinity of a prison camp, though at times even these couples have been forced to sleep apart in separate men's and women's dormitories. After Harry Wu married Shen Jiarui as fellow jiuye inmates, a clampdown in the government policy at their labor camp led to the requirement that all married couples sleep in separate rooms in the men's and women's dormitories. Before that, such couples had been able to live together under the same roof, and there was eventually a return to a less strict policy.[172]

In some of the remote far western campside regions where men greatly outnumbered women, practically the only way some retained ex-inmate workers could obtain a wife was to purchase one from a black-market trafficker in women.[173] This bride price would vary anywhere from a few

167. Zhang Xianliang emphasizes the factor of a poor diet in causing impotence; see *Wode Putishu*, p. 189. He adds that inmates from all different backgrounds seemed to view the rare opportunity for a good meal together, such as in celebration of the Lunar New Year, as a compensation for their sexual dysfunction.

168. Bao & Chelminski, *Prisoner of Mao*, p. 243. The unbridled licentiousness of Mao Zedong's private life rivaled that of the former emperors who had inhabited his Zhongnanhai imperial palace, but his preaching to the masses was unctuously puritanical.

169. An entire volume of critical articles about *Half of Man Is Woman* came out in the wake of the national controversy this novel stirred up. Chen Zhuoru, ed., *Ping "Nanren de yiban shi nüren"* [Critiques of *Half of Man Is Woman*] (Yinchuan: Ningxia renmin chubanshe, 1987).

170. Cong Weixi, *Zou xiang hundun sanbuqu*, pp. 357–360.

171. Ibid., p. 406.

172. Wu & Wakeman, *Bitter Winds*, pp. 238–241.

173. Wumingshi, *Hong sha*, pp. 362–363.

hundred yuan in the 1950s to a four-figure sum or even more during the Deng-Jiang Era, and the trafficked women would typically hail from relatively impoverished rural areas.

Aside from jiuye workers and a smattering of high-ranking prisoners who have received special visiting privileges, opportunities for heterosexual relations among prisoners have been extremely rare, especially in the puritanical atmosphere of the Mao Era. For instance, Cong Weixi and his wife, Zhang Hu, were finally allowed to stay together alone at night for the first time in nine years in 1969—though on the straw-lined mud floor of a stinking pigsty, this was not exactly a passionate reunion.[174]

The rare heterosexual activity that has occurred has usually been between a camp cadre or guard and a female prisoner, such as that between a visiting female inmate actress and a local cadre in Zhang Xianliang's camp.[175] Prisoners could use their knowledge of such illicit affairs as a handle over the cadre for obtaining special privileges; thus the risks involved in such trysts were greater in the outwardly puritanical Mao Era Chinese laogai than in the old Soviet gulag.[176] Lai Ying was similarly able to use the implicit threat of publicly exposing a Guangdong camp cadre's unwanted fondling of her as a means of forcing him to back off and leave her alone henceforth.[177] In spite of the even greater risks involved, on very rare occasions a special duty prisoner would manage to have an illicit tryst with a female dependent of the camp administration.[178]

Among ordinary prisoners still awaiting their release in the PRC, homosexuality has been far more common than heterosexuality, whether among men or women. Violently puritanical reactions to homosexuality were not uncommon in the Mao Era.[179] In 1960 at Qinghe Camp, Jean Pasqualini was nauseated when he witnessed the sudden and close-

174. Cong Weixi, *Zou xiang hundun sanbuqu*, pp. 332–334.

175. Zhang Xianliang, *Wode Putishu*, p. 59.

176. Ibid., pp. 59–60. Camp officials who sexually exploited female prisoners in the old Soviet gulag were more likely to get in trouble for offenses other than lasciviousness, according to Solzhenitsyn, *The Gulag Archipelago, 1918–1956*, vol. 2, pp. 545–546.

177. Lai Ying, *The Thirty-Sixth Way*, pp. 34–35, 39, 52, 109. Lai Ying's description suggests that fondling and other forms of harassment directed at female prisoners by male guards and cadres were quite common in some Guangdong prisons and camps in the 1950s and 1960s. The use of mostly female guards and prison cadres in women's camps such as Baimaoling in Anhui has discouraged such types of sexual harassment.

178. Liu Zongren recounts the assignation he witnessed between a special duty prisoner and the wife of a guard in *Hard Time: Thirty Months in a Chinese Labor Camp* (San Francisco: China Books, 1995), pp. 207–208.

179. Homosexuality is at the top of the list of Sun Xiaoli's five "minor cultural phenomena among criminals"; the list also includes malingering, self-mutilation, suicide, and tattooing. See *Zhongguo laodong gaizao zhidu de lilun yu shijian*, pp. 256–260.

up execution of an inmate barber for having had sex with a nineteen-year-old boy.[180] However, other camp cadres during that period seem to have been more apt to condone inmate homosexuality, especially when it fit smoothly into the hierarchical pattern of a cell tyrant taking his pleasure with younger or more submissive prisoners, often in return for gifts of food.[181] In the more prosperous Deng-Jiang Era, numerous cell tyrants have continued to indulge in a disproportionate amount of homosexual behavior, partly because they can provide submissive inmates with a variety of favors, including protection from rival prison bullies or gangs.[182]

Though not approving of all this, contemporary PRC theorists and writers tend to take a less intolerant approach, relative to the Mao Era, acknowledging that a certain amount of homosexuality is a "natural phenomenon" in a prison environment.[183] However, some Deng-Jiang Era prison administrators have not protected minors from becoming the unwilling sex objects of cell tyrants. Gao Xin notes with horror a case around 1990 in which a twelve-year-old boy was placed together in a cell with some adult hooligans and was repeatedly raped by them.[184]

Forced Labor

The academic "grand theory" of disciplining prisoners by means of a "uniform" regimen of forced labor generally treats these "disciplinary objects" as a sort of undifferentiated mass or "mass phenomenon," as Fou-

180. Bao & Chelminski, *Prisoner of Mao,* pp. 189–190. The cadre's major motive in executing the barber with a bullet through the head for such a trivial offense (if even an offense) was almost certainly "killing a chicken to scare the monkeys" *[sha ji jing hou],* a traditional method of securing submission to authority. The execution also fits into the pattern of draconian punishments aimed chiefly at working people during the Mao Era as outlined by Frank Dikötter, "Crime and Punishment in Post-Liberation China," pp. 147–159.

181. Wumingshi, *Hong sha,* pp. 360–361. One bout of anal homosexual intercourse *[ji-jian]* would cost about ten hardtack buns or a pound of wheat in the 1950s in Qinghai.

182. Fan Shidong, "The Sex Life of Prisoners in Prisons and Labor Camps," conference presentation, The Chinese Labor Camp: Theory, Actuality, and Fictional Representation, Univ. of California, Riverside, CA, 15 January 2000.

183. Sun Xiaoli, *Zhongguo laodong gaizao zhidu de lilun yu shijian,* p. 256. Popular writers on the laogai have often treated homosexuality mostly as a substitute for an unavailable heterosexuality; see Zhu Guanghua, *Zhongxing fan,* pp. 105–108. This is not to say that homosexuality was being condoned by the 1990s. Tang Min's prison wardens warned the female inmates against "making friends" *[jiao pengyou],* a euphemism for relations that might develop into homosexuality. See Tang Min, *Zou xiang heping,* pp. 156–158.

184. Gao Xin, *Beiwei yu huihuang,* pp. 114–115.

cault put it.[185] As a major forerunner of the latter-day grand theorists, Karl Marx also treated criminals in an abstract manner, as a largely undifferentiated mass whose "sole means of betterment" was "productive labor" of a forced and generalized character.[186]

While there is a slight connection between this shopworn abstract theory and actual practice, serious contemporary research has tended to focus instead on the significantly differentiated workforce of convicts that prison authorities typically manage in a multi-tiered fashion.[187] Any PRC prison camp cadre depends heavily on inmate group chiefs [zuzhang] to manage production at the level of individual and small-team work assignments, allowing them relatively more access to him and other special privileges, while also expecting more from them in the way of responsibility and self-discipline. The cadres' graded treatment of inmates also depends on such factors as activist feats [jiji xingdong] in the interest of the prison authorities, how a work assignment or quota is fulfilled, adherence to prison rules, general obedience, proper ideological conformity, backstage support and other networking resources [guanxi], fame, and personal wealth.[188] Although a major policy shift or change at the top of the pyramidal power structure can have a fairly uniform and broad impact on the "mass" of inmates, everyday practices are based on a more differentiated disciplinary approach. For instance, a given cadre wields disciplinary techniques that are differentiated according to a prisoner's rank, state of health, special talents, particular shortcomings, and other factors. Also, the menu of disciplinary techniques and the favored selections from that menu often differ from one region and historical period to another.

In the summer of 1960, Zhang Xianliang's brigade leader in his Ningxia labor camp shows him special favor by including him within the small elite of prisoners whose job is to pick through piles of edible weeds for the common soup pot.[189] The cadre threatens that anyone who does

185. Foucault, *Discipline and Punish*, pp. 116, 219.

186. Robert C. Tucker, ed., *The Marx-Engels Reader*, 2nd ed. (New York: Norton, 1978), p. 541.

187. Dirk Van Zyl Smit & Frieder Dünkel, "Conclusion: Prison Labour—Salvation or Slavery?" in *Prison Labour: Salvation or Slavery?* pp. 335–347, esp. 345.

188. Personal and family wealth could be a liability during the Mao Era, but ever since then it has increasingly become the means for buying favored treatment both from fellow inmates and prison authorities.

189. Until the Deng Era, when CCP statements occasionally admitted that government actions and policies were almost entirely responsible for the 1959–62 famine, the official government line was that bad weather was the chief culprit of what was termed the "natural

not meet the quota of 25 catties for a day's work will receive no dinner, but there is no prohibition against uprooting the entire plant and counting the soil clinging to its roots as part of the overall weight.[190] The cadre does not expect those inmates who are seriously ill from malnutrition to meet the quota, but he does not need to mention this aspect of differentiated treatment in so many words. The distinction between the sick inmates *[bing hao]* and the favored ones *[shou zhaogu de]* in better health is clear to everyone.[191] Above average in height yet so emaciated as to weigh under 100 pounds, Zhang is considered healthy enough to have to meet the quota.[192] Zhang is relatively satisfied with his labor assignment. After all, picking through weeds is far better than toiling all day in the camp's rice paddies, where inmates have to wade around knee-deep in alkali-rich water that causes painful skin inflammations—or hauling his weight in dirt over long distances, a particularly grueling task.[193]

In many other camps, not filling one's work quota would result in confinement within a tiny punishment cell.[194] Another possible consequence of missing the production target was to have one's daily food ration cut by 10 or 20%; at the very least, one would receive a stern warning to shape up fast or face a reduction in food rations. To his chagrin, Jean Pasqualini learned that he would have to work at a feverish pace in order to avoid a punitive reduction in his food ration at Beijing's Banbuqiao Detention and Transit Center. In Qinghe Camp, a prison cadre threatened one of Pasqualini's fellow inmates with having his ration lowered to only 18 catties of grain per month.[195]

---

disaster" *[ziran zaihai]*. Zhang Xianliang wryly comments that he cannot figure out why the weather in his region was especially fine precisely at the time that the rest of the country was suffering from the terrible weather that was responsible for the famine. Perhaps Mother Nature was especially fond of him and his fellow starving inmates. See *Wode Putishu*, p. 32.

190. Ibid., pp. 32–33.

191. Ibid., p. 32.

192. Ibid., p. 9. At that time, Zhang Xianliang weighed only 44 kilograms, which for a twenty-three-year-old man meant that he was the very picture of a pitifully emaciated concentration camp inmate.

193. Ibid.

194. Sun Ping, Li Honglin, & Hui Xiping, *Zhongguo jianyu ren* [Chinese Prisoners] (Xi'an: Shaanxi renmin chubanshe, 1989), p. 163.

195. See Bao & Chelminski, *Prisoner of Mao*, pp. 87–88, 194. One catty is slightly more than a pound, and approximately half a kilogram. Of course, a major political change like the advent of the Cultural Revolution would sometimes cause all of the inmates' food rations to decline indiscriminately, as mentioned by a former Xinjiang camp inmate in Sun Ping, Li Honglin, & Hui Xiping, *Zhongguo jianyu ren*, p. 162.

On the other hand, overfulfilling your work quota in a sustained way might lead to an increase in the quality or the amount of one's food allotment, or perhaps promotion to group chief or some other responsible post.[196] Taking the Stakhanovite road to overfulfilling work quotas could be a dangerous choice during serious food shortages, though: the extra calories burned up at the work site might exceed the enhanced caloric intake from an increased ration.

Becoming a group chief or attaining some other special position has often given the fortunate inmate a chance to slack off and delegate his burden to the rank-and-file prisoners. Wumingshi mentions some of the occupations in which skilled inmates often received special privileges that indirectly shortchanged the rank-and-file, such as accountant, doctor, carpenter, cook, and blacksmith.[197] Inmate doctors who treat cadres can sometimes enjoy such perquisites as sleeping in a private room and eating the same large food portions as a cadre.[198] Occasionally, some inmate group chiefs have taken the responsibilities of their position very seriously, and may work as hard or even harder than most of their fellow inmates.[199] One cadre who appointed Cong Weixi group chief had to caution him against overexerting himself and thereby increasing the risk of suffering an injury.[200]

In some countries, a major justification of prison labor is its connection with job training. Theoretically, at least, the prisoner could transfer the skills learned in prison to a job in society after release. However, this function of prison labor has rarely been emphasized in the PRC, though at least some discussion of job training in prison has emerged since the end of the Mao Era. Inmates who happen to be doctors or bricklayers might well be put to work plying their old trade after landing in the camps, but there would be precious little training in new job skills unless that training fit the prison enterprise's needs. Individual-centered job training to improve the prisoner's employment prospects after release has seldom entered the picture, though of course many ex-inmate workers have

196. About 30 of the 285 prisoners in Pasqualini's Qinghe brigade were rewarded for exceeding production quotas with the receipt of a special "health preservation diet" that contained some precious horsemeat and edible oil—and none of the useless fillers like ground corn cobs that most inmates were fed. See Bao & Chelminski, *Prisoner of Mao,* pp. 217–218.

197. Wumingshi, *Hong sha,* pp. 360–361.

198. Cong Weixi, *Zouxiang hundun sanbuqu,* p. 164.

199. For instance, there is no evidence in the writings of either Zhang Xianliang or Harry Wu that either man used his position as group chief to slack off at the expense of his fellow inmates. The same, of course, appears to be true of Cong Weixi.

200. Cong Weixi, *Zou xiang hundun sanbuqu,* p. 220.

been retained in jiuye status, especially during the Mao Era. This is one of the reasons why most of the newly released camp inmates who have successfully found employment during the Deng-Jiang Era have become individual proprietors [getihu]. Forced labor in prison camps would not prepare them for a particular line of work, nor would their original work unit want them back, so they would usually wind up working at something almost totally unrelated to their job tasks in the laogai. In this sense, Deng-Jiang Era ordinary criminals who are released from the camps have resembled their intellectual confreres, who certainly have not continued digging ditches or spreading manure on farm fields following their release.

The following chapter completes this study's examination of life in the PRC prison camp, leading up to the inmate's final release from imprisonment and return to society.

CHAPTER 4

The PRC Prison Camp (II)

From Struggle Sessions to Release or Death

The Party-State's Implicit Strategies for Control over Prisoners

Routine actions of the laogai authorities have often served to erode the inmate's sense of identity, especially the capacity for independent moral judgment. By replacing an inmate's name with a three- or four-digit number, prison authorities have diminished their captives from decision-making subjects to the objects of the authorities' commands and punishment. When ordered to pin a paper strip with his number, 273, to his chest, Cong Weixi feels as though he were "a death-row inmate awaiting the executioner's bullet, and had already bid mankind a final farewell. The only difference is that the condemned inmates on their way to the execution ground have their name placards tied onto their backs."[1] As a camp inmate, Cong Weixi feels that he has "devolved" *[tuihua]* to the status of a barnyard animal, and even envies a local workhorse for its ample food and freedom from denunciation and other human woes.[2] Taking the dehumanizing barnyard metaphor further, the way that a camp cadre pries open inmates' mouths to check for evidence of unauthorized foraging reminds Zhang Xianliang of how a breeder would personally inspect the inside of a horse's mouth before purchasing it.[3]

The inmate Zhang Yonglin of *Mimosa* has noticed a similar shrinkage

---

1. Cong Weixi, *Zou xiang hundun,* p. 161.
2. Ibid., p. 107.
3. Zhang Xianliang, *Wode Putishu,* p. 17.

of self, along with an increasing dependence upon and identification with the prison wardens. Zhang has become so habituated to following the cadres' orders in his prison camp that he is subconsciously "unaccustomed to the lack of control and berating" by camp cadres following his release: "I felt that I still needed to follow someone who controlled and led me."[4] When Zhang Xianliang's brigade leader makes him bow low and pulls him around in circles with a rope, his former identity as a self-respecting intellectual has vanished. "I could no longer use my brain to think rationally, but was completely under the control of habitual servitude. Neither ashamed nor indignant, I obediently circled around behind the brigade leader, as if I truly were a dog or a donkey."[5]

In retrospect, Zhang Xianliang views the crumbling of his defense mechanisms during the remolding process as the precursor to the shattering of the prisoner's personality, here compared to the breaking of an egg: "When a person identifies with the authority figure who oppresses and tortures him, obediently allowing that authority figure to order him about, the defense mechanisms in his psychology and personality will completely collapse. This system of defense mechanisms is extremely fragile, just like an eggshell. When an eggshell shatters from an impact, the liquid essence spills away and dries out."[6] Numerous writers of the laogai have summarized the PRC prison system's basic if implicit credo for its prisoners with the classical phrase, "meekly submitting to adversity [wrought by the higher-ups]" *[ni lai shun shou]*.[7]

Prison authorities have often utilized the modern-day educated Chinese person's tendency toward what Geremie Barmé has called "self-loathing" to manipulate a prisoner into confessing his own "crimes" and implicating others, even to the point of gross fabrication.[8] Wang Meng satirizes this variety of manipulation by having his partially sinicized Uighur protagonist respond enthusiastically to his Han Chinese interrogator's demands for an ever-more self-abasing confession in "Maimaiti Chuzhang yishi" [The Anecdotes of Section Chief Maimaiti]: "It was I who started both the First and Second World Wars. What's more, I'm

4. Zhang Xianliang, *Lü hua shu,* in *Zhang Xianliang xuanji,* vol. 3, p. 174.

5. Zhang Xianliang, *Wode Putishu,* p. 52.

6. Ibid., p. 238.

7. Cong Weixi, *Zou xiang hundun,* p. 163; Zhang Xianliang, *Wode Putishu,* p. 180.

8. Geremie Barmé, *In the Red: On Contemporary Chinese Culture* (New York: Columbia Univ. Press, 1999), pp. 265–272. Barmé traces the origins of this tendency to the late Ming period (late sixteenth and early seventeenth centuries), specifying important modern authors who embody this mode of thought, in particular Lu Xun and Bo Yang.

now preparing to start World War Three."[9] In a more serious vein, Zhang Yonglin of *Mimosa* often curses himself at night for having followed his instinct for self-preservation and behaved in a cunning and deceitful manner during the day. This inmate believes that he is doomed to suffer on account of having inherited his cunning and deceit from his ideologically reprehensible "bourgeois" ancestors.[10] The numbing grind of unproductive manual labor has also contributed to feelings of inferiority and worthlessness among inmates, especially intellectuals, who find their powers of concentration and analysis to have withered under the dulling effects of physical fatigue and hunger.[11]

Unsanitary prison conditions have typically had a dehumanizing effect on educated prisoners. The mud floor and lack of wooden planks in Wumingshi's prison in the fairly prosperous region of Hangzhou Bay left him no alternative but to lie down on the floor "like a dog"; he found his cell inferior to even the pig pens he had seen.[12] Funding constraints have been partly to blame for the remarkable filth, overcrowding, and discomfort of most PRC prisoners. However, metropolitan prison administrators' common failure to supply prisoners with such basics of hygiene as a wash basin and soap fits into a long-standing pattern of malign neglect directed at the less-than-human "elements" under their custody. For example, even in the wealthy city of Beijing during the relatively prosperous 1990s, prison officials summarily rejected Wang Juntao's requests for such simple amenities as a change of clothing, a washbasin, and soap.[13]

Keeping prisoners in a state of perpetual deprivation in terms of their basic living conditions not only serves as a daily reminder of the inmates' marginally human status, but saves government funds and intensifies many prisoners' desire to receive somewhat better treatment through servile behavior. The deferential "bowing and bending over" before authority that the ex-convict narrator of *Half of Man Is Woman* deems fundamental to the remolding he underwent has been complemented by the

9. Wang Meng, "The Anecdotes of Section Chief Maimaiti," 1–30, esp. 20. Original version in *Wang Meng xiaoshuo baogao wenxue xuan* [An Anthology of Wang Meng's Fiction and Reportage] (Beijing: Beijing chubanshe, 1981), pp. 177–191.

10. Zhang Xianliang, *Lü hua shu*, pp. 187, 212–215.

11. Zhang Xianliang, *Wode Putishu*, pp. 256–268; Wumingshi, *Hai de chengfa*, pp. 48–50; Wumingshi, *Hong sha*, pp. 311–312.

12. Wumingshi, *Hai de chengfa*, pp. 21, 25.

13. Though Wang was suffering from hepatitis at that time, the authorities at Beijing Prison Number Two dismissed his requests for medical treatment with the retort that his prison file contained no record of sickness. See Black & Munro, *Black Hands of Beijing*, pp. 324–325.

heavy-handed self-criticism and mutual denunciation among prisoners that the authorities have typically demanded.[14] According to Liu Binyan's experience of mandatory mutual denunciation among political prisoners, such divide-and-conquer tactics of the party-state "have made the ranks of their political enemies split apart and crumble."[15] The camp authorities' repeated exhortations to "atone for your crime by establishing merit" [ligong shuzui] has often created a vicious cycle of mutual accusation and secret denunciation that has enabled a handful of cadres to exert especially tight control over a crowd of inmates.[16]

"Study" and Struggle Sessions

Just as the forced labor performed by PRC convicts is typically organized around small groups [xiao zu] of ten to fifteen prisoners each, so obligatory sessions of party-line indoctrination or "study" [xuexi] have usually focused on the small group.[17] "Indoctrination" would probably be a more accurate rendition of xuexi than the literal meaning of "study," especially within the coercive context of a PRC prison, since the party line from the authorities or their selected reading materials is by definition absolutely correct. As one former inmate has put it, "The reasoning goes like this: competent authorities have thought out and elaborated their mingling [command], the official line of action, according to scientific criteria— you are intelligent, devoted to the welfare of the masses, and diligent about your xuexi; therefore, it follows that you simply must agree with the evidence of government syllogisms."[18] "Study" is a broad enough term to include efforts to improve prison inmates' technical skills and literacy, but these have almost always paled in importance beside political and moral indoctrination, both in theory and in practice.[19]

---

14. Zhang Xianliang, *Nanren de yiban shi nüren*, in *Zhang Xianliang xuanji*, vol. 3, p. 611.

15. Liu Binyan, *Liu Binyan zizhuan* [The Autobiography of Liu Binyan] (Taipei: Shibao wenhua chuban, 1989), p. 124.

16. Zhang Xianliang, *Wode Putishu*, pp. 78–79, 298. Because well-educated prisoners have often played a leading role in the mutual denunciation sessions, a prison cadre was more likely to appoint these prisoners to be small-group chiefs [xiao zuzhang].

17. Martin K. Whyte analyzes the small group as a vehicle for sociopolitical control in *Small Groups and Political Rituals in China* (Berkeley: Univ. of California Press, 1974).

18. See Eleutherius Winance, *The Communist Persuasion: A Personal Experience of Brainwashing*, trans. Emeric A. Laurence (New York: P. J. Kennedy & Sons, 1959), pp. 27–28.

19. The primacy of politics in xuexi under Mao's rule was also apparent in urban areas outside of prison walls, though to a less intense degree. See Chad Hansen, "Punishment

Mao Era totalitarianism marked the apogee of what Robert Jay Lifton has called PRC cadres' "all-or-nothing . . . psychology of totalism" in orchestrating an agitated atmosphere "saturated with individual confessions" and mutual denunciations within a given small group of prisoners.[20] The colloquialism "brainwashing" *[xi nao]* in Lifton's title was coined in China around the time of the PRC's founding in 1949, according to Edward Hunter.[21] The typical Kafkaesque Mao Era situation "was like that of a man taken suddenly from his ordinary routine and placed in a hospital for the criminally insane, where he is accused of a horrendous but vague crime which he is expected to recognize and confess; where his assertion of innocence is viewed as a symptom of his disease, as a paranoid delusion; and where every other inmate-patient is wholly dedicated to the task of pressuring him into a confession and a 'cure.'"[22] Even with the major downplaying of Maoist attempts at attitudinal remolding of the citizenry during the relatively pragmatic Deng-Jiang Era, manuals and regulations for laogai cadres and guards *[laogai gan jing]* have invariably placed politics at the head of the list of subjects for prisoners to "study."[23] Whenever the regime feels threatened enough to launch a campaign of political indoctrination, as it did in the wake of the 1989 nationwide antidictatorship protests, "study" sessions have been temporarily revived or stepped up to intimidate and ferret out the party-state's real and imagined challengers.[24]

As for the many prison camps in the Deng-Jiang Era that have dropped

and Dignity in China," *Individualism and Holism: Studies in Confucian and Taoist Values,* ed. Donald J. Munro (Ann Arbor: Center for Chinese Studies, Univ. of Michigan, 1985), pp. 359–383, esp. 375. For a novel that incisively probes Beijing intellectuals' encounters with political *xuexi* in the 1950s, see Yang Jiang, *Xi zao* [Taking a Bath] (Hong Kong: Sanlian shudian, 1988).

20. Robert Jay Lifton, *Thought Reform and the Psychology of Totalism: A Study of "Brainwashing" in China* (New York: Norton, 1963), pp. 129, 262. Lifton defines "totalism" as "a tendency toward all-or-nothing emotional alignments" (129).

21. Edward Hunter, *Brainwashing: The Calculated Destruction of Men's Minds* (New York: Vanguard Press, 1953), p. 4.

22. Lifton, *Thought Reform and the Psychology of Totalism,* p. 70.

23. *Laogai gongzuo,* pp. 61–62. Politics also heads the list of subjects for inmate "study" in the November 1990 "Regulations Concerning the Behavior of Criminals Undergoing Remolding"; see Seymour & Anderson, *New Ghosts, Old Ghosts,* pp. 241–247, esp. 245.

24. There was a revival of the obligatory "study session" in Gansu in 1989–90, according to Seymour & Anderson, *New Ghosts, Old Ghosts,* pp. 41–42. Tang Min has little to report about political study sessions in her late 1990s prison stay in Fujian, but notes that the limited after-hours literacy education available to her fellow female prisoners did not seem to ameliorate the chronic state of petty conflict and vindictiveness among them. See *Zou xiang heping,* p. 161.

political indoctrination in practice (if not in theory), they have seldom substituted or promoted another subject of study, but instead focused mostly on economic production along with maintaining order and stability in the prison.[25] In spite of some official PRC rhetoric to the contrary, education and job training for prisoners have been extremely low priorities at both the national and local level in the northwestern provinces that Seymour and Anderson researched.

According to a 1994 international survey cited by Henriksson and Krech, the official PRC respondent claimed that *all* of that country's prisoners "receive education in prison" and *all* were given "opportunities for skills and trade training." Significantly, however, the PRC respondent left blank the following question about how many trade instructors were employed per hundred prisoners, since it would have been stretching the truth too far to come up with an ersatz figure for something that hardly exists.[26] Similarly, the obligatory after-dinner meetings in Tang Min's late-1990s Fujian prison focused on discussions of how production had gone that day, with occasional exhortations to "struggle" *[douzheng]* against inmates who had indulged in thievery or some other mundane crime.[27]

With this contemporary trend of downplaying political indoctrination, the PRC laogai has become more similar to the prison systems in other countries, including the former Soviet gulag. One of the few positive features of the Soviet gulag was that it nearly always left prisoners' minds alone in spite of forcing their bodies to labor.[28] Russia's gulag almost never compelled its inmates to preach, listen to propaganda, or write self-criticisms and confessions, as Solzhenitsyn recalls with rare fondness.[29] Gus-

---

25. Seymour & Anderson, *New Ghosts, Old Ghosts,* pp. 92, 168.

26. Helena Henriksson & Ralph Krech, "International Perspectives," *Prison Labour: Salvation or Slavery?,* ed. Dirk van Zyl Smit & Frieder Dünkel, Oñati International Series in Law and Society (Aldershot, U.K.: Ashgate, 1999), pp. 297–312, esp. 301–302.

27. Tang Min, *Zou xiang heping,* p. 146. The "struggle" *[douzheng]* leveled against the woman inmate accused of thievery seems much less intense than a Mao Era "struggle session" *[pidou hui],* apparently consisting only of pressure to write an admission of wrongdoing.

28. To be sure, open slander of the USSR authorities could land a prisoner in deep trouble if overheard by a stool pigeon (*ermu* in Chinese). Solzhenitsyn had to avoid moving his lips when memorizing poetry during the day to avoid being reported to the authorities by a prison stool pigeon; see *The Gulag Archipelago,* vol. 3, p. 100.

29. Solzhenitsyn was especially pleased to discover that inmates were not obliged to attend political meetings, as ordinary citizens in Soviet society were. See *The Gulag Archipelago,* vol. 2, p. 607. Cong Weixi, who dismisses Solzhenitsyn as being too full of "hatred" to acknowledge the more humane aspects of prison camp life, must have read *The Gulag Archipelago* superficially and selectively. See *Zou xiang hundun,* p. 188.

tav Herling agrees that most Russian gulag prisoners at least enjoyed the freedom of silence, but he recalls being forced to watch Soviet propaganda movies that nauseatingly extolled the glories of manual labor.[30]

Back in Mao Era China, however, indoctrination sessions were usually taken extremely seriously, especially in prisons and labor camps. For Jean Pasqualini, the thought-remolding regimen anchored by "never-ending" indoctrination and struggle sessions amounted to the "main distinction between [PRC] prison camps and those built by the Soviets."[31]

The indigenous origins of the Maoist indoctrination sessions may be traced all the way back to the Song dynasty's development of the *xiangyue* lecture system, in which government appointees throughout the Celestial Empire would exhort the local people to conform with Confucian moral precepts in their daily life.[32] Another factor may be the common traditional Chinese view of human nature as being "very malleable and influenced by the larger society."[33] Moreover, twentieth-century technological advances in communication and transportation set the stage for the PRC government and its ideology to successfully penetrate well below the county level in a sustained manner for the first time.[34] Most importantly, Mao's overweening ambition led him to press harder than his Soviet predecessors toward the implementation of the utopian Marxist-Leninist idea that the human being is a wholly malleable creature, the mere embodiment of historical and materialist forces. In implementing indoctrination sessions throughout China's cities and towns, Mao was acting on his baseless utopian assumption that the Chinese people amounted to "a blank sheet of paper" on which the party-state could write "the most beautiful words."[35]

Whether termed a "study session" *[xuexi ban]* or a "meeting to admit errors in daily life" *[shenghuo jiantao hui],* an indoctrination session in

30. Gustav Herling, *A World Apart,* 2nd ed., trans. Andrzej Ciozkosz (New York: Arbor House, 1986), p. 157.

31. Bao & Chelminski, *Prisoner of Mao,* p. 232.

32. Whyte, *Small Groups and Political Rituals in China,* p. 20. The lectures throughout the empire on the Kangxi emperor's Sacred Edict served a similar function of moralistic exhortation in the mid- to late Qing period.

33. Paul S. Ropp, "The Distinctive Art of Chinese Fiction," in *Heritage of China: Contemporary Perspectives on Chinese Civilization,* ed. Paul S. Ropp (Berkeley: Univ. of California Press, 1990), pp. 309–334, esp. 314.

34. Jonathan D. Spence, *Chinese Roundabout: Essays in History and Culture* (New York: Norton, 1992), p. 225.

35. Perhaps the best expression of Mao's patronizing view of the Chinese people as malleable clay and in need of remolding was his characterization of them as "both poor and blank" *[yi qiong er bai].*

prison typically demands universal participation. Often held after dinner so as not to interfere with productive labor and work quotas, these
meetings could be called at the whim of a prison cadre. The leader of the
meeting, either a cadre or a high-ranking fellow inmate, would intro-
duce the topic for discussion or else summarize a party newspaper article or an excerpt from Mao Zedong's writings. The leader would next
ask everyone to present their views *[biaotai,* short for *biaoshi taidu,* literally "express one's attitude"] and admit how they or their fellow inmates have failed to act in accordance with this or that Maoist principle
in their daily life.

As Zhang Xianliang's memoir illustrates, inmates are not free to remain silent, since that would usually lead to activist prisoners' *[jiji fenzi]*
heated accusations that the recalcitrant participant dares not reveal his politically sinister thoughts.[36] One of the scheming activists at Zhang's meeting attempts to "gain merit" *[li gong]* in the eyes of his superiors by taking the usual denunciatory line in confronting a silent participant: "The
more somebody won't talk, the more he brims with hatred for the party
and socialism."[37] When it is Zhang's turn to express his opinion, he takes
a moderate approach of pointing to a fairly insignificant flaw, fastening
upon his fellow inmate's very minor shortcoming of dawdling during
meals.[38] Such a mild comment makes Zhang look like an observant and
responsible member of his group, but will not significantly worsen the
current struggle target's predicament or likely punishment.[39] As the
scribe *[jilu]* of the group, Zhang eventually hands in his written summary
of the meeting to the brigade leader or some other cadre.[40] A written summary of a study session was not always required, for some prison officials
preferred an oral summary or simply left the matter in the hands of the
group chief. In other cases, individual members of a group might be singled out to write an "admission of personal wrongdoing" *[jiantao],* as re-

36. Instead of remaining silent during a confessional *[jiaoxin]* study session in the late
1950s, Duan Kewen denies that he has committed any crime. Another war prisoner does
the same, but most of the others try to take the middle path of admitting to very minor
oversights. See *"Zhanfan" zishu,* pp. 273–276.

37. Zhang Xianliang, *Wode Putishu,* p. 82. This denunciation echoes Comrade He Qixiong's vilification of the cautiously silent "rightist" intellectual Gu Tiancheng in Liu Binyan's
story "The Fifth Man in the Overcoat," in *People or Monsters?,* pp. 79–97.

38. Zhang Xianliang, *Wode Putishu,* p. 83.

39. Zhang prefers to remain as silent as possible during such meetings, and usually comes
forth with just enough mild criticism of himself and others to keep from becoming the main
target of severe criticism.

40. Zhang Xianliang, *Wode Putishu,* p. 84.

counted in the memoir of the Catholic ex-inmate Peter Bangjiu Zhou. Along with writing admissions of personal wrongdoing, prisoners often "were obliged to denounce, accuse, and criticize their fellow prisoners" in these study sessions.[41]

As soon as all of the negative attention in a "study session" becomes focused on a single culprit or two in a sustained manner, as is the case in the episode described above, it may sometimes evolve quickly into a full-blown struggle session [pidou hui], in which heated denunciations are sometimes compounded by threats or acts of physical violence. Alternatively, a prison cadre may call a small or large struggle session without such a prelude of "study," or there may be an interval in between stages of "study" and struggle. For example, Cong Weixi's prison camp memoirs indicate that there was no prelude to a certain struggle session called against a thief.[42] Nor is there any "study" prelude to a struggle session called against the political prisoner protagonist blamed for painting an overly scrawny pig in Cong's novel The Deer Looks Back.[43]

During a "study" session, the person receiving criticism usually makes a substantial verbal response of some sort.[44] In contrast, objects of a struggle session are typically expected to bow their heads contritely, bend forward at the waist, and succinctly confess their guilt [ren zui].[45] The required parts of the struggle session ritual include the stage or platform where the bowed objects of the struggle stand contritely next to gesticulating and slogan-shouting cadres or other leaders, along with the audience seated nearby, who parrot the slogans in a shouted refrain. For example, Song Shan remarks that all seventy-six times she was subjected to a struggle session in front of thousands of people, the format of the event was exactly the same.[46] The protagonist in Cong Weixi's Lu hui tou also remarks on the dull sameness of the struggle sessions. Neither of these individuals seems to be the least bit ashamed of such denunciation, for it seems to be little more than a bizarre public performance. Wumingshi's prison memoir compares the struggle sessions he witnessed and endured

41. Peter Bangjiu Zhou, Dawn Breaks in the East: A Benedictine Monk's Thirty-Three Year Ordeal in the Prisons of Communist China in Defense of His Faith (Upland, CA: Serenity, 1992), p. 83.

42. Cong Weixi, Zou xiang hundun, pp. 180–181.

43. Cong Weixi, Lu hui tou, pp. 144–146.

44. Duan Kewen responds verbally in "Zhanfan"zishu, pp. 174, 182. Some of Song Shan's fellow inmates also defend themselves verbally from the accusations that activist stool pigeons have made to a prison cadre. See Hong qiang, hui qiang, pp. 163–164.

45. Cong Weixi, Lu hui tou, p. 145.

46. See Song Shan, Hong qiang, hui qiang, pp. 124–125.

to on-stage performances, and wonders how the Maoists could have invented such a strange social practice.[47]

There are numerous optional components of the struggle session. The cadres often cut the food ration of their objects of struggle, who may feel faint from hunger. Restraining devices such as shackles, handcuffs, and a tight rope around the neck may add to the prisoners' discomfort and underline their identity as political outcasts.[48] Heavy objects may be hung with wire or rope around the prisoners' necks to make them stoop even lower, thereby intensifying their shame.[49] The cadre masters of ceremony may intone a litany of the prisoners' supposed crimes from a prepared text or shout rhetorical questions of an accusatory nature at the prisoners.[50] Finally, the cadres or activist elements in struggle sessions may sometimes physically abuse the prisoners, such as pricking them in the scalp with a tack, yanking an ear, or delivering punches and kicks.[51]

This physical abuse in Mao Era struggle sessions could easily escalate to the level of a prisoner sustaining a bone fracture or even life-threatening injuries. In one particularly violent struggle session, an activist prisoner broke Harry Wu's left arm with a sudden blow from a spade handle. Though there was an unwritten prohibition against using tools as cudgels in a struggle session, none of the cadres punished the activist prisoner for having broken the rule. Before having his arm broken, Wu had been beaten, kicked, and subjected to the very common "jet plane" [zuo penqi shi] torture, in which the prisoner is ordered to hold the painful posture of bending deeply at the waist with both hands raised high behind the back.[52] During a cold winter in Qinghai in the 1950s, an unrepentant object of struggle was reportedly stripped of his clothing and forced to keep standing until he collapsed and eventually froze to death on the snow-covered ground.[53]

It is tempting to consign all of the ritualistic violence and cruelty that often accompanied Mao Era struggle sessions to the past, especially the

47. Wumingshi, *Hai de chengfa*, p. 63.

48. Song Shan, *Hong qiang, hui qiang*, pp. 122–124.

49. Cong Weixi, *Lu hui tou*, pp. 145–146.

50. Song Shan, *Hong qiang, hui qiang*, pp. 124–125; Wumingshi, *Hai de chengfa*, pp. 61–63.

51. The pricking in the head with tacks during a struggle session is portrayed in Zhang Xianliang's novella *Tu lao qinghua*, pp. 3–89, esp. 76. The other listed varieties of physical abuse appear in Wumingshi's memoir *Hai de chengfa*, pp. 64–67.

52. Wu & Wakeman, *Bitter Winds*, pp. 225–226. This type of torture has also been described by Wang Yitao, *Wushige wenyijia zhi si* [The Death of Fifty Writers and Artists] (Hong Kong: Ming bao chubanshe, 1989), pp. 14–15.

53. Wumingshi, *Hong sha*, pp. 63–64.

early 1950s—what Jean-Luc Domenach aptly terms the Founding Terror of the PRC.[54] Official PRC histories routinely portray the period from 1949 to 1956 as a golden age in PRC cultural history, as if the lives of at least a million landlords and "rich" farmers who were struggled to death do not count.[55] The notion of the early 1950s as a golden age in the PRC has been restated or implied quite frequently, and has even been applied to that country's prison system.[56] The idea of the golden 1950s has been enshrined formally in such documents as the CCP's 1981 "Resolution on Certain Questions" about Mao Zedong's career, in which Mao's "incorrect" actions are said to have occurred almost entirely after 1956.[57] This golden-age myth has often appeared in the writing of establishment intellectuals such as Cong Weixi, who nostalgically notes his idolization of Mao and ignorance of the formative Yan'an period's political repression.[58] In 1998, Cong Weixi continued to express his gratitude for the party's having cast him down to "the lowest depths of society for twenty years," suggesting that the CCP has nothing to apologize for or to regret in its past conduct.[59] These statements embody a number of questionable assumptions, including the idea that problems involving rural landholding patterns and intellectual dissent somehow had to be solved in a significantly more violent and ruthless way in the PRC than they were handled in most other countries around the world, including many other countries and territories in and around the Western Pacific Rim.

The PRC government has not yet paid any heed to calls from respected intellectuals for the establishment of a museum commemorating the victims of the Cultural Revolution, when the struggle session was commonly utilized.[60] Perhaps the twenty-first-century CCP desire to sweep

54. Janusz Bugajski also notes the CCP's "mass terror" in the early years of the PRC, criticizing Chinese and foreign apologists for the heavy-handed methods of Maoist rural collectivization, as these apologists resemble those who have brushed off Stalin's liquidation of the Russian kulaks. "They share the assumption that there was no alternative to the forced development model," Bugajski writes. See *Fourth World Conflicts: Communism and Rural Society* (Boulder, CO: Westview Press, 1991), p. 52.

55. Rummel estimates that approximately 4.5 million landlords and rich peasants were killed during the CCP Land Reform; see *China's Bloody Century*, pp. 222–223.

56. See, for example, Sun Ping et al., *Zhongguo jianyu ren*, p. 163.

57. See Richard Baum, *Burying Mao: Chinese Politics in the Age of Deng Xiaoping* (Princeton: Princeton Univ. Press, 1994), p. 135.

58. Cong Weixi, *Zou xiang hundun*, pp. 10–11.

59. Cong Weixi, *Zou xiang hundun sanbuqu*, p. 481.

60. The famous veteran writers Xiao Qian and Ba Jin began making public requests for such a museum in the mid-1980s. See Philip F. Williams, "Chinese Cannibalism's Literary Portrayal: From Cultural Myth to Investigative Reportage," *Tamkang Review: A Quarterly*

the withered but once flourishing institution of the struggle session under the rug of history is not unrelated to the callousness toward human suffering still manifested in the endless round of record-breaking executions from the "strike-hard" crackdowns.[61]

Prison Argot

The laogai has brought a variety of curious coinages into the Chinese language with its prison argot. It is true, as Whyte notes, that the CCP prison authorities have gone considerably further than their Soviet gulag counterparts in inhibiting the growth of an inmate subculture, but the long-term presence of prison argot must qualify Whyte's almost Foucauldian claim of PRC prisoners' total dominance by the official prison culture.[62] Unfortunately, no Chinese dictionary equivalent to Jacques Rossi's *Gulag Handbook* has yet appeared. This section provides an introduction to such terms, focusing on coinages that have been mentioned only briefly or in passing elsewhere.[63]

PRC prisoners are routinely assigned a three- or four-digit identification number *[daihao],* and often treated less as a full-fledged person than as a number or an "untrustworthy element" *[bu ke xinren fenzi].*[64] "Number" *[hao]* became virtually synonymous with "prisoner," but as a bound morpheme in its grammatical usage, *hao* must be attached to another syllable in order to make sense in ordinary conversation.[65] Therefore, inmates speak of a "male prisoner" *[nanhao]* versus a "female pris-

of Comparative Studies of Chinese and Foreign Literatures 27.4 (1997): 421–442, esp. 423, 435–436.

61. Amnesty International reported in July 2001 in the wake of numerous executions during the latest strike-hard campaign that the PRC executed "more people in the past three months than the rest of the world over the past three years." See Marianne Bray, "China Out-Kills the World, Says Amnesty," *CNN.com* 6 July 2001, www.cnn.com/2001/WORLD/asiapcf/east/07/06/china.executions/index/html.

62. Martin King Whyte, "Corrective Labor Camps in China, *Asian Survey* 13.3 (1973): 253–269, esp. 269.

63. The Chinese character glossary may be of help in reading this section.

64. Cong Weixi had to call out his daihao of 273 after lining up for roll call; see *Zou xiang hundun,* p. 194. When ordering Song Shan out of her prison cell for interrogation, the guard would refer to her by her daihao of 638; see *Hong qiang, hui qiang,* p. 2. The PRC government has considered it entirely proper for all "untrustworthy elements" to be assigned "forced labor" *[qiangzhi laodong];* see Cong Weixi, *Zou xiang hundun sanbuqu,* pp. 312, 314.

65. For a more detailed explanation of bound morphemes and some examples of them, see Yuen Ren Chao, *A Grammar of Spoken Chinese* (Berkeley: Univ. of California Press, 1968), pp. 168–169.

oner" *[nühao]*, and a "new prisoner" *[xinhao]* versus an "old-timer" (behind bars) *[laohao]*.[66] Similarly, there are "sick prisoners" *[binghao]*, "fellow prisoners" *[tonghao]*, "study-leading prisoners" *[xuexihao]*, and "escaped prisoners" who have slipped away *[liuhao]* or run away *[taohao]*.[67]

The other common use of the bound morpheme *hao* is for prison cells and barracks. Prison argot often refers to prisoners' "barracks" *[laofang]* as a *haozi*.[68] A tiny isolation cell *[jinbishi]* is variously termed a "punishment cell" *[yanguanhao]*, a "small cell" *[xiaohao]*, or a "critical self-examination cell" *[fanxinghao]*.[69] Aside from referring to male or female prisoners, *nanhao* can mean a cell or barracks for male prisoners, while *nühao* can refer to a cell or barracks for female inmates.[70]

A number of other terms refer to prisoners, sometimes in a humorous manner. The honorific bound morpheme *ye*, meaning "grandfather," or "master," is often used in prison argot for a "thief" *[foye]* and a "hooligan" *[mangye]*.[71] Intellectuals *[zhishi fenzi]* may also be jokingly labeled "shit-eaters" *[chi shi fenzi]*.[72] Prison manuals refer to "recidivists" as *leifan* or *guanfan*, but prisoners use the ironic slang phrases "twice entered the palace" *[er jin gong]* and "thrice entered the palace" *[san jin gong]*.[73] An elderly male prisoner may be referred to as an "old hat" *[lao mao]*, which is also a slang term for an old man's genitalia.[74] Laogai inmates still serving their sentences are known as "primary labor remoldees" *[da laogai]*, while retained ex-inmate workers are dubbed "secondary labor remoldees" *[er laogai]*.[75] When a husband-and-wife team of "secondary labor

66. Cong Weixi, *Zou xiang hundun*, pp. 150–152, 157.

67. Ibid., pp. 141, 143, 181; Cong Weixi, *Zou xiang hundun sanbuqu*, p. 312; Cong Weixi, *Lu hui tou*, pp. 47, 152, 168, 190; Gao Xin, *Beiwei yu huihuang*, p. 79. The prison administration forced many inmates to refer to their cell mates as "classmate" *[tongxue]*, especially in the Mao Era. See Wumingshi, *Hai de chengfa*, p. 60.

68. Zhang Xianliang, *Nanren de yiban shi nüren*, p. 405.

69. Cong Weixi, "Diqige shi yaba" [The Seventh One Is a Mute], in *Cong Weixi daibiaozuo* [Representative Works of Cong Weixi] (Zhengzhou: Huang He wenyi chubanshe, 1987), pp. 80–100, esp. 86, 88; Cong Weixi, *Zou xiang hundun sanbuqu*, pp. 299, 360, 364, 388; Cong Weixi, *Lu hui tou*, pp. 115, 146, 148.

70. Cong Weixi, *Zou xiang hundun*, p. 144.

71. Ibid., pp. 167, 181, 184.

72. Ibid., pp. 136, 184; Cong Weixi, "Diqige shi yaba," pp. 89, 92.

73. Cong Weixi, *Zou xiang hundan*, pp. 166–168. *San jin gong* refers to anyone who has been sentenced to prison three or more times. In practice, this term and *er jin gong* are used much more commonly for ordinary criminals than for political prisoners.

74. Cong Weixi, "Da qiang xia de hong yulan," pp. 170–240, esp. 181; Cong Weixi, "Yuan qu de baifan," pp. 364–459, esp. 373.

75. Cong Weixi, *Duan qiao* [The Collapsed Bridge] (Beijing: Zuojia chubanshe, 1986), pp. 85, 205; Cong Weixi, *Zou xiang hundun*, pp. 222, 224. Less commonly, *da laogai* refers to high-ranking prisoners with special privileges, such as former cadres; see Wumingshi,

remoldees" are permitted to live together under the same roof outside the proverbial "big wall" *[da qiang]* encircling the prison camp, they are called "a labor-remolding couple" *[shuang laogai].*[76]

Because Chinese laogai prisoners have generally had to bow more deeply to authority than their counterparts in the Soviet gulag, Chinese prison argot generally lacks the gulag subculture's rich body of invective and slang aimed at prison administrators and guards. However, for decades prison guards have often been nicknamed "thunder guys" *[leizi].*[77] On-duty guards and prison cadres usually carry a pair or two of handcuffs, which are nicknamed "iron bracelets" *[tie zhuo]* or "bracelets" *[zhuozi].*[78] Prison slang is also used for high-ranking inmates such as cell or barracks "chiefs" *[tou ren]* who have power over other inmates, yet are still at the beck and call of prison cadres and guards.[79] Prisoners whose individual status is ambivalent or ill-defined, such as cell chiefs whose interests coincide with the cadres instead of their fellow inmates, have often been nicknamed "hermaphrodites" *[yinyang ren].*[80] Like cell chiefs, "uncapped rightists" *[zhai mao youpai]* enjoyed a higher status than ordinary rightists during the Mao Era, but they were still under suspicion and not necessarily on the path to early release or exoneration. The removal of the official label of "rightist" from the "uncapped rightists" did not free them from the stigma of their former classification, nor of the imperative to serve out their term.

However, laogai prisoners would vent some of their resentment for the government's treatment of them as human "rubbish" *[feiliao]* by describing their prison camp as a "garbage bin" *[laji xiang].*[81] Underfed and overworked inmates would sometimes refuse to get up from their sleeping space to go to work or "pretend to be a dead dog" *[shua si gou].*[82]

Hong sha, p. 344. During the 1960s and 1970s, many of the *er laogai* political prisoners were "uncapped rightists" *[zhai mao youpai].* These in-between types were no longer in as low and vulnerable position as ordinary rightists, but the label of political deviant still followed behind them everywhere like a tail *[weiba].*

76. Cong Weixi, *Zou xiang hundun sanbuqu,* pp. 332, 386, 409; Cong Weixi, *Lu hui tou,* pp. 12, 158, 163. As a metonym, the "big wall" *[da qiang]* may also refer to a prison camp in its entirety.

77. Cong Weixi, *Lu hui tou,* p. 160; Gao Xin, *Beiwei yu huihuang,* p. 138. By 1990, the term "thunder guys" was increasingly being used for plainclothes guards and detectives.

78. Cong Weixi, *Zou xiang hundun sanbuqu,* p. 154.

79. Cong Weixi, *Zou xiang hundun,* pp. 76–79, 83, 98–101, 115–118, 120–121.

80. Ibid., p. 106. Tang Min notes that a late-1990s female inmate with an angular figure and hair cut short like a male was admiringly referred to as a "hermaphrodite" *[yinyang ren];* see *Zou xiang heping,* p. 156.

81. Cong Weixi, "Yuan qu de baifan," pp. 401, 413, 438.

82. Zhang Xianliang, *Wode Putishu,* pp. 23, 47, 234, 246.

When inmates are foraging for wild foods to supplement the meager camp diet, they "eat green" *[chi qing]*, an expression that refers to the color of chewed weeds inside the prisoners' mouths.[83] Poking fun at their unending toil, prisoners have often sardonically likened their "forced labor" *[qiang lao]* to "repairing Planet Earth"*[xiu Diqiu* or *xiuli Diqiu];* and they refer to themselves as "Planet Earth repairmen" *[Diqiu xiuli gong].*[84] If a male prisoner looks too despondent about his fate, an ordinary criminal inmate may try to cheer him up by saying, "Don't go hanging down your head to settle accounts with your cock" *[bie dalazhe naodai he Lao Er suan zhang].*[85]

When all the prisoners in a given camp are moved together to a different camp, this is sometimes known as "carrying the whole nest away" *[lian wo duan].*[86] If transport of prisoners requires train travel, they usually refer to the train *[huoche]* as "big wheels" *[da lun].*[87] The somewhat similar round shape of laogai convicts' shaved heads comes vividly across in the expression "bald gourds" *[tu piao].*[88]

If the destination is the execution ground instead of a camp, the hapless inmate receives a bullet in the back of the head—in prison argot, "eats a black date" *[chi hei zao].*[89] Northern Chinese prisoners often refer to this kind of execution as "spilling out" *[mao'er],* for the bullet's force typically blows off part of the top of the skull, out of which the dead convict's brains spill to the ground.[90] A less drastic punishment that is akin to a struggle session is euphemistically termed a "help meeting" *[bangzhu hui],* in which the "help" can range from shouted demands for confession to physical abuse.[91] The most virulent among the various types of struggle sessions directed against prisoners have included the "beat-the-demons meeting" *[da gui hui]* and the "beat-the-tigers meeting" *[da hu hui].*[92]

---

83. Ibid., pp. 16–17.

84. Wumingshi, *Hai de chengfa,* p. 50; Cong Weixi, *Lu hui tou,* p. 163; Cong Weixi, *Zou xiang hundun,* pp. 55, 70; Cong Weixi, *Zou xiang hundun sanbuqu,* p. 314. *Qiang lao* is the abbreviated form of *qiangzhi laodong* [forced labor].

85. Cong Weixi, *Zou xiang hundun,* pp. 162, 243. *Lao Er* [Old Number Two] is prison slang for the male genitals.

86. Cong Weixi, *Lu hui tou,* p. 74.

87. Cong Weixi, *Zou xiang hundun,* pp. 168, 180.

88. Gao Xin, *Beiwei yu huihuang,* p. 79. The entire expression could be rendered as "shearing the head to look like a bald gourd" *[tui tu piao].*

89. Cong Weixi, *Zou xiang hundun,* p. 168; Cong Weixi, *Duan qiao,* p. 253.

90. Gao Xin, *Beiwei yu huihuang,* p. 30.

91. Cong Weixi, *Lu hui tou,* p. 190.

92. Cong Weixi, *Zou xiang hundun sanbuqu,* pp. 255, 293; Wumingshi, *Hai de chengfa,* pp. 60–62.

One of the most common types of punishment for the objects of such struggle meetings has been the modern-day equivalent of "being exposed in public with a cangue around your neck" *[daijia shizhong]*, namely "posing for a photograph" *[zhaoxiang]* in an uncomfortable and demeaning posture. With memories of such mistreatment and encounters with malnutrition and other hardships, it is little wonder that many released inmates continue to suffer from the psychological imbalance known as the "post-laogai syndrome" *[laogai houyizheng]*.[93] Like Post Traumatic Stress Disorder, this syndrome is often marked by a pervading sense of anxiety and suspicion, along with recurring memories of painful or frightening experiences. In this syndrome, sudden and often uncontrollable recollections of dreadful imprisonment are often combined with symptoms such as insomnia and impotence. Confused, even paranoid thoughts are also fairly common, especially during the early stages of the post-laogai syndrome.[94]

The Isolation Cell

Though less terrifying than a prison beating and not as mind-numbing as a marathon interrogation session, solitary confinement in a tiny *jinbi shi* or *xiao hao* [isolation cell] could often cause more damage to the inmate's physical and mental health over the long term.[95] Often nicknamed "the cooler" in Soviet Russian accounts due to its greater exposure to the elements, this "jail within a jail" would confine the inmate with his or her thoughts and little else in round-the-clock claustrophobic discomfort.[96] Prison authorities have enjoyed broad discretion in resorting to this form of punishment, often using it when they were dissatisfied with the prisoner's response to their insistent demands for a sufficiently abject and detailed confession.[97] However, a prisoner's confinement in an isolation cell

93. Cong Weixi, *Duan qiao*, pp. 253.

94. Lifton, *Thought Reform and the Psychology of Totalism*, pp. 32–36.

95. Ai Bei uses the less common variant of *xiao haozi* for "isolation cell" in her novella *Nü lao* [A Women's Prison] (Taipei: Yuan shen chubanshe, 1990), pp. 108, 166. Translated into English as *Red Ivy* by Howard Goldblatt in *Red Ivy, Green Earth Mother* (Salt Lake City: Peregrine Smith Books, 1990), pp. 61–145.

96. Solzhenitsyn, *The Gulag Archipelago*, vol. 1, pp. 113–114. Russian prisoners in isolation or punishment cells received no food, either, until their third day of confinement, though they were usually released by the fifth day—two days earlier than the Chinese norm.

97. This was the case for well-known political prisoners such as Wang Juntao, Chen Ziming, and Harry Wu, as well as for less famous inmates such as the writer Song Shan. See her *Hong qiang, hui qiang*, p. 20.

would occasionally be wholly due to external circumstances. The dissident poet Huang Xiang landed in a *xiao hao* in June 1989 simply because his Wangwu prison camp wardens in Guizhou were tightening security across the board in the wake of nationwide antigovernment protests that spring.[98]

While PRC guidelines state that no prisoner should be held in an isolation cell for more than seven days at a stretch, in practice such confinement has been routinely extended to several months for such elite 1990s political prisoners as the entrepreneurial activists Chen Ziming and Wang Juntao.[99] One GMD military intelligence officer spent two of his twenty-six-years in the laogai at the bottom of a dry and totally dark well.[100] Four of the ten years that the noted political dissident Liu Qing spent in prison during the 1980s were in a particularly mind-numbing variety of solitary confinement.[101] During one stretch in the 1970s, Song Shan was locked in a punishment cell for forty days, during which time she was taken out eleven times for bruising struggle sessions.[102] Duan Kewen was forced to rewrite his confession yet another time during his sixteen-day confinement in an isolation cell that was so secret that the cadre ordered him not to tell any of his fellow inmates about where he had been.[103]

Wu Hongda's September 1965 confinement in a Tuanhe laogai isolation cell lasted a seemingly modest eleven days, but was so arduous that Wu decided that death was a better option. He refused all food after the seventh day; and the only way the guards could keep him alive in that tiny cell was by force-feeding him through a tube stuck down his throat

98. Huang Xiang, "Huang Xiang," in *Voices from the Laogai: Fifty Years of Surviving China's Forced Labor Camps* (Washington, D.C.: Laogai Research Foundation, 2000), pp. 42–43.

99. Black & Munro, *Black Hands of Beijing*, p. 324. Sun Xiaoli pegs the maximum detention in an isolation cell at fifteen days, though he admits that this limit has often been exceeded and mentions a case where such detention lasted 317 days. See *Zhongguo laodong gaizao zhidu de lilun yu shijian*, pp. 168–169.

100. Hong Xianheng is the pseudonym of the GMD military officer whose twenty-six-year ordeal is portrayed in a semibiographical novel. For more about his solitary confinement in a dry well, see Wumingshi, *Hong sha*, pp. 22–44.

101. Robert Bernstein, Introductory Comments, *Voices from the Laogai*, pp. 17–19.

102. Song Shan, *Hong qiang, hui qiang*, p. 135.

103. Duan Kewen, *"Zhanfan" zishu*, pp. 186–188. In fact, Duan did not mention his stay in an isolation cell, nor did any of his fellow inmates ask about why he had disappeared for over two weeks. Secretiveness had become a habit among prisoners who had witnessed harsh punishments being administered for minor transgressions or nothing at all under Maoist rule.

by way of one nostril. Wu's isolation cell was basically an empty cage that was exposed to the elements, measuring a meter in width and height and two meters in length. The floor was part concrete and part dirt, with no bedding or blankets at all to ward off the frigid cold at night. There was no bucket to urinate or defecate in, and no food or water until his third day of confinement. On the seventh day, the warden kicked Wu for not having implicated his cell mates in his abject confession of guilt for having written letters to Mao Zedong.[104]

Isolation cells are designed for discomfort. Often little more than a coffin-sized cage, such a cell forces the inmate to crawl for locomotion — when he is not sprawled out "like a dog" on the cement or dirt floor.[105] Some punishment cells are so cramped and cage-like that prisoners cannot even stretch out their legs, but must crouch or curl up when locked inside.[106] Even in Beijing's Qincheng Prison, the PRC's elite jail for top-level political prisoners, the 1990s isolation cells stank from the open sewer running through them, were crawling with lice and other blood-sucking parasites, and afforded no protection from either winter cold or summer heat.[107] Refused a change of clothing or even a wash basin and soap in these unsanitary conditions, Chen Ziming soon developed seborrheic dermatitis, Wang Juntao contracted hepatitis B, and labor leader Han Dongfang languished with untreated tuberculosis.[108]

For the prisoner who had long been confined in a particularly crowded, stinking, and noisy barracks, the isolation cell could occasionally seem almost like a quiet refuge. That was the rather unusual reaction of the 1970s political prisoner Song Shan as she lay in such a cell recovering from bloody wounds she had just sustained from two beatings and a horse-whipping at the hands of "activist" prisoners doing the bidding of cadres.[109] And though the GMD military officer who spent two years at the bottom of a dry well encountered such problems as temporary blindness, he experienced his confinement as a respite from the interrogation and torture he had regularly suffered beforehand.[110] On the whole, how-

104. Wu & Wakeman, *Bitter Winds*, pp. 182–184.

105. Ibid., p. 181.

106. Cong Weixi, *Duan qiao*, p. 191.

107. Black & Munro, *Black Hands of Beijing*, p. 324.

108. Ibid., pp. 323–325, 328.

109. Song Shan, *Hong qiang, hui qiang*, pp. 18–19. The prison authorities had ordered some ordinary criminal inmates of the "activist" type to *bangzhu* [help] Song Shan — a euphemism for vigorously beating up a supposedly recalcitrant prisoner.

110. Wumingshi, *Hong sha*, p. 26.

ever, the acute privations of confinement in an isolation cell have led most Chinese prisoners to view it as a particularly debilitating and dreadful type of punishment.[111]

Bruising "Help" from Activist Prisoners

Prison camp manuals and propagandistic tracts regularly claim that the PRC correctional system's guiding principle of *shehuizhuyi rendaozhuyi* [socialist humanitarianism] prevents the physical mistreatment of inmates.[112] Prior to the Deng-Jiang Era, the typical self-congratulatory term for a policy of forced prison labor was *geming rendaozhuyi* [revolutionary humanitarianism], as cited in an anonymously authored "internally circulated" *[neibu]* manual for camp cadres and guards.[113] The idea that remolding through labor was the utmost in "humanitarian" correctional policy was also fulsomely advocated by the gentlemanly Zhou Enlai.[114] However, overseas reporting and even PRC state-controlled media reports of widespread inmate beatings helped lead to the passage of the PRC's 1994 Prison Law, in which Article 14 specifically forbids the beating of prisoners.[115] The frequency of inmate beatings seems to have decreased markedly in the wake of that law.[116] Yet such a routine prison practice over decades of PRC rule is not likely to dwindle into insignificance anytime soon, as demonstrated by the repeated

111. Even retained ex-inmate workers *[er laogai]* fear being locked in a punishment cell for violating regulations, according to the narrator of Cong Weixi's novel *Duan qiao*, pp. 213–214. In the middle of the night, the head of a local farmers' production brigade has just stolen some of the labor camp's harvested rice, over which the narrator was standing guard. After the narrator tries to stop the theft, he gets beaten up and horsewhipped by the brigade head and his underlings, and the brigade head threatens to murder the narrator if he dares to report the theft to his prison camp brigade leader. However, the narrator is tempted to ring the emergency bell due to the severe penalty for failing to report such a theft—being labeled a "destructive element" *[pohuai fenzi]*.

112. See, for example, Shao Mingzheng et al., *Zuifan lun* [On Criminality] (Huairou: Zhongguo Zhengfa Daxue chubanshe, 1989), pp. 466, 468. The prohibition against the mistreatment of prisoners had already been stated in "Zhonghua renmin gongheguo laodong gaizao tiaoli" (1954), item 5, as cited in Wu Hongda, *Zhongguo de Gulage*, p. 88.

113. *Laogai gongzuo*, p. 21.

114. Sun Xiaoli, *Zhongguo laodong gaizao zhidu de lilun yu shijian*, pp. 36–37, 39–40.

115. Seymour & Anderson, *New Ghosts, Old Ghosts*, p. 253.

116. According to anonymous Xinjiang prison camp inmates' letters that were smuggled out of China, wardens and cell bosses chastened by the 1994 Prison Law had mostly stopped beating prisoners there by 1996. See Seymour & Anderson, *New Ghosts, Old Ghosts*, p. 180.

beatings of imprisoned nonviolent Falun Gong practitioners since July 1999.[117]

Wardens and guards have been especially prone to resort to inmate beatings and other heavy-handed measures during periods of party-state clampdowns on real or perceived threats to the social or political order, such as during the ongoing cycle of "strike hard" *[yan da]* campaigns and crackdowns on unauthorized organizations.[118] Prison cadres and guards have frequently made use of high-ranking activist prisoners or trusties to handle the dirty work of administering a beating to a prisoner they find difficult, often by instructing them to "help" *[bangzhu]* the recalcitrant inmate.[119] In the former Soviet gulag, camp authorities' calls for "help" from activist inmates often served the same function of tacitly ordering them to physically abuse a targeted prisoner.[120] Such collaboration with prison authorities increases the likelihood of winning a reduction in sentence *[jianxing]* by "leaning close to the government" *[kaolong zhengfu]*; activists also have a chance to vent their own frustrations on the prisoner to whom a guard or cadre has decided to teach "a lesson" *[jiaoxun]*.[121] PRC political prisoners have often been singled out for such physical abuse at the hands of ordinary criminal inmates.[122] Regardless of the prohibitions that appear in camp cadre manuals and legal handbooks, orchestrated inmate violence has all too often been considered an acceptable and even lauded form of discipline.[123] Activist

117. David Ljunggren, "Canadian Falun Gong Follower Says Tortured in China," *Reuters World News*, 22 January 2001, dailynews.yahoo.com/h/nm/20010118/wl/canada_china_dc_1.html. Sixty-year-old sculpture professor Zhang Kunlun served less than two months of a three-year sentence for Falun Gong activities at a Shandong prison camp, but the beatings and mistreatment from guards were so bad that his battered left leg did not heal for three months.

118. Harold M. Tanner refers to the "extra-legal pressure . . . brought to bear in order to force the inmate to confess and to express contrition," in *Strike Hard!*, p. 149. Tanner also refers to "the frequent resort to torture" in order to squeeze out confessions from PRC prisoners during the 1980s (p. 186).

119. See Wumingshi, *Hai de chengfa*, p. 67; Song Shan, *Hong qiang, hui qiang*, p. 11; and Cong Weixi, *Lu hui tou*, p. 190. Of course, camp cadres may also speak of "help" in its ordinary, non-coercive sense, as in Peng Yinhan, *Dalu jizhongying*, p. 135. And among a small number of high-ranking convicts, especially the foreigners and top GMD military officers and officials who were given especially light treatment, cadres' calls for "help" typically led to denunciations, not beatings, as revealed in Duan Kewen, *"Zhanfan" zishu*, p. 207.

120. Andrei Sinyavsky, *A Voice from the Chorus*, trans. Kyril Kitzlyon & Max Hayward (New York: Farrar, Straus & Giroux, 1976), p. 103.

121. Song Shan, *Hong qiang, hui qiang*, p. 129.

122. James V. Feinerman, "Deteriorating Human Rights in China," *Current History* 89.548 (1990): 265–269, 279–280.

123. Song Shan, *Hong qiang, hui qiang*, p. 129.

苦毆打犯人索規例

FIGURE 3. Veteran prisoners may sometimes beat
new inmates without the authorities showing any
concern (from Li Baojia, *Huo diyu*).

prisoners' beating of another inmate at the behest of a cadre has often
been taken as an expression of their "good attitude" and "positive acceptance of remolding."

The cadre or guard who orchestrates a beating can tighten discipline
while absolving himself of responsibility in the event that serious injuries
to the inmate result—in which case a prisoner activist or two may be
blamed. For example, after Harry Wu's arm was broken by activist Fan
Guang, the cadre who had instigated the beating did not seem to suffer
any negative consequences. However, Wu's friends from his group later
cornered Fan and gave him a thrashing for having injured Wu so badly.
The cycle of retaliation was kept among the prisoners so that it would
not embroil the cadres and guards in a controversy with a united group

of prisoners—a divide-and-conquer strategy.[124] A premodern version of this practice—where prison authorities are indifferent to the beating going on within the prison walls—is portrayed in Figure 3.

The activists whom the cadres incite to beat Song Shan and some of her fellow female inmates all appear to be "hooligans" *[liumang]*, or ordinary criminals.[125] Yet fairly well educated prisoners have also often turned in their fellow inmates for alleged misdeeds *[jiefa]* and sometimes actively "helped" cadres beat other prisoners. From Zhang Xianliang's perspective, intellectual prisoners were more likely than ordinary criminals to attack other prisoners' ideology or report others' misdeeds to the cadres.[126] A certain well-educated activist prisoner in Wumingshi's camp named Li had beaten several prisoners at the cadres' behest before Wumingshi found an opportunity to make Li the object of struggle for the first time.[127] "Having tasted the flavor of being struggled" instead of merely attacking others at the behest of cadres, Li retreated from his zealous activism and came to be accepted into the group of ordinary non-activist prisoners over time.[128] This rapprochement marked the triumph of a modest degree of "unity" *[tuanjie]* over the self-defeating cycle of seeking revenge *[baochou]* among these camp inmates.[129] The declining influence of Mao Zedong's combative ideology in the decades since his death has resulted in more instances of such unity among prisoners.

Torture at the Hands of Prison Guards and Officials

Though technically illegal, the torture of prisoners by PRC prison guards and cadres has been widely practiced during the Deng-Jiang Era, even in "advanced" and prosperous cities such as Beijing and Shenzhen.[130] Judge Zhang Xin has estimated that 90% of the early-1990s inmates in the Shenzhen Detention Center were tortured during their interrogations in

124. Wu & Wakeman, *Bitter Winds,* pp. 226–227.

125. Song Shan, *Hong qiang, hui qiang,* pp. 11, 129, 134–135.

126. See Zhang Xianliang, *Wode Putishu,* pp. 45–47, 116.

127. Wumingshi, *Hai de chengfa,* pp. 85–89. Wumingshi did not get involved in the physical violence, according to his account, but simply put Li on the defensive with clever argumentation. Another prisoner whom Li had previously beaten returned the favor now that Li was the latest target of struggle.

128. Ibid., p. 90.

129. Ibid., p. 91.

130. See William F. Schulz, "Cruel and Unusual Punishment," *New York Review of Books,* 24 April 1997, pp. 51–54.

order to squeeze a confession out of them.[131] Aside from forcing prisoners to confess to offenses they may not necessarily have committed, torture has been commonly used to punish prisoners for either breaking prison rules or simply not having measured up to a correctional officer's expectations. As punishment for the Shenzhen laojiao camp having failed a health inspection in the early 1990s, many prisoners were lined up and beaten ten strokes each on the buttocks by a guard wielding a "redemption bastinado" *[ganhua gun]*. They would receive twice this number of blows if they made mistakes in their work.[132]

Many of these types of torture in PRC prisons differ little from traditional methods described in historical treatises and Qing dynasty novels such as Li Baojia's *A Living Hell,* and have sometimes been derided by prisoners as "old-fashioned torture" *[tu xing].*[133] One of the most common traditional instruments of torture has been the bamboo or wooden bastinado *[gunzi],* though it has lost much ground to the high-tech electric shock baton or taser *[diangun,* short for *dianji jinggun]* since the 1970s. Prison guards and cadres used the old-fashioned bastinado for beatings more frequently in the 1950s and 1960s than during the Deng-Jiang Era.[134]

131. For example, the judge Zhang Xin and the university professor Gao Xin both witnessed and experienced torture in prisons in Shenzhen and Beijing in the 1990s. See Zhang Xin, "Yige beipo wangming tianya de Zhonggong faguan de xuelei kongsu" [The Moving Account of a CCP Official in the Judiciary Who Was Forced to Flee for His Life], in *Zhonggong sifa heimu,* pp. 318–319; and Gao Xin, *Beiwei yu huihuang,* pp. 51, 55, 66, 107, 125–126. The Canadian professor Zhang Kunlun was tortured with electric shocks at an eastern Shandong laogai camp in 2000 as part of the crackdown on the Falun Gong. See Ljunggren, "Canadian Falun Gong Follower Says Tortured in China." See also Figure 4.

132. Zhang Xin, "Yige beipo wangming tianya de Zhonggong faguan de xuelei kongsu," pp. 315–325, esp. 318.

133. The heroine of a novel set partly in the Xinjiang desert laogai receives a bout of what she calls "old-fashioned torture" after going on a hunger strike *[jueshi];* see Fu Xuwen, *Yige nüqiu de zibai* [The Vindication of a Woman Prisoner] (Beijing: Zhongguo qingnian chubanshe, 1989), p. 126. The author, who had been a correspondent attached to the Public Security Bureau for several years, was aware of the particular frequency of torture in much of the Xinjiang laogai—which resulted in a particularly egregious murder in May 1991 and ignited a lethal prison camp riot in February 1989. See Fan Shidong, "Dui Xinjiang laogaidui caojian renming de jianjuxin" [A Letter Implicating the Xinjiang Laogai Brigades for Treating Human Life as Cheap], in *Zhonggong sifa heimu,* pp. 375–379; Li Xianguo, "Zhenjing quanguo zhengfa xitong de Xinjiang dabaoyu" [The Large Prison Uprising That Shocked the Entire Nation's Political and Legal Authorities], in *Zhonggong sifa heimu,* pp. 407–413.

134. See, for example, Wumingshi, *Hong sha,* p. 64. A PRC policeman wants to strike a recaptured Russian prisoner with the bastinado, but is beaten to the punch by a mob of angry civilian onlookers in Ha Jin, "The Russian Prisoner," *Ocean of Words* (New York: Vintage, 1996), pp. 134–164, esp. 162–163. For an example of a Deng-Jiang Era beating with a bastinado by a camp cadre in 1982, see Qian Guoyao et al., *Tamen fanle shenme zui? Xingshi*

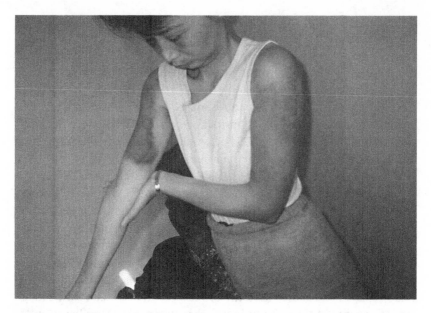

FIGURE 4. This nonviolent Falun Gong practitioner was beaten at the behest of authorities in a laojiao camp (courtesy of Falun Dafa Information Center).

Bastinados have also been used quite often to mete out "rebel justice," such as when Rae Yang and her fellow Red Guards beat a rape suspect to death in Guangzhou in 1966.[135] One modern variation of striking an inmate with a bastinado has been to beat a prisoner with a rifle stock, as a guard did to the political prisoner Li Jiulian around 1970.[136]

Another traditional technique used in some PRC prisons has been to lash a prisoner with a horsewhip. In 1969, a political prisoner named Chen Ye, who handed a bowl of water to a thirsty fellow inmate confined in a punishment cell, was horsewhipped by a guard more than forty times, leaving bloody welts all over his upper body.[137] The relative frequency of horsewhipping vis-à-vis the bastinado may derive partly from the fact that

anli fenxi [What Crime Did They Commit? Analysis of Exemplary Criminal Cases] (Shanghai: Zhishi chubanshe, 1984), p. 220.

135. Rae Yang, *Spider Eaters* (Berkeley: Univ. of California Press, 1997), p. 138.

136. Hu Ping (b. 1948), *Zhongguo de mouzi*, p. 52.

137. Cong Weixi, *Zou xiang hundun sanbuqu*, pp. 279–280. Song Shan was horsewhipped during her second bout of torture, as noted in *Hong qiang, hui qiang*, p. 18. Another female prisoner is depicted as receiving a horsewhipping in Fu Xuwen, *Yige nüqiu de zibai*, p. 128.

these two traditional varieties of corporal punishment had become almost interchangeable by the time of the Qing dynasty.[138]

The contemporary punitive use of heavy manacles around the ankles also has an ancient lineage, though the sharp edges of the manacles and their tendency to cut painfully into the skin seems to be an intentional modern design. Gao Xin notes that the skin around his ankles was often bloody and painful due to the sharp-edged manacles he had to wear as punishment for having joined the 1989 protest at Tian'anmen Square. He found it especially cruel that another prisoner had to wear 40-pound shackles even while he was outdoors performing forced labor.[139] The fact that PRC prisoners' accounts contain so many more complaints about sharp-edged manacles and handcuffs than do premodern or Republican Era prisoners' accounts suggests that the sharp-edged instruments are a relatively recent addition to the Chinese jailer's tool kit.

Some traditional varieties of torture in the PRC require the use of rope—a commonly used instrument of restraint and torture, especially when handcuffs have not been readily available.[140] In "hanging a chicken by its feet" [diao ji zhua], the prisoner's wrists would be tied behind his back, and a rope would be fastened between his wrists and the rafters of a building or a high tree limb (figure 5). Finally, he would suddenly be hung up with all his body weight supported by his wrists.[141] The pain from this torture is so excruciating that the prisoner often screams just before losing consciousness. If he remains hanging long enough, his arms will start pulling out of their shoulder sockets. Ni Yuxian underwent an even worse variety of this torture than what Cong Weixi witnessed, for Ni, as noted in Chapter 3, was repeatedly kicked and beaten while hanging from his wrists.[142]

Alternatively, nothing but rope is needed to truss the prisoner up so tightly along the torso so as to injure or even dislocate his shoulders and cause him to black out from pain.[143] Rope was also required to tie the prisoner to a "tiger bench" [laohu deng], a rack-like device for stretching leg

138. Bodde & Morris, Law in Imperial China, p. 97.

139. Gao Xin, Beiwei yu huihuang, pp. 55, 107.

140. Wu Hongda, Zhongguo de Gulage, p. 89.

141. Cong Weixi, Zou xiang hundun sanbuqu, p. 432.

142. Thurston, A Chinese Odyssey, pp. 239–240.

143. An example of being suspended from the wrists is in Wumingshi, Hong sha, p. 117. For more about the second type of rope torture, performed in a Shaanxi prison camp, see Wu & Wakeman, Bitter Winds, pp. 231–232. The victim of this particular kind of torture would usually faint and collapse to the ground within a minute after the rope trussing him up was pulled taut.

FIGURE 5. "Hanging a chicken by its feet" [*diao ji zhua*] is often followed by a beating (from Li Baojia, *Huo diyu*).

tendons to the breaking point that was sometimes known as a "tendon-pulling bed" [*ba jin chuang*] in premodern times (figure 6).[144]

Another type of torture practiced in some PRC camps and prisons is functionally equivalent to its premodern predecessor, but its specific forms and terminology have changed over time. This type of punishment was designed both to punish the offender and to deter the local populace by placing the culprit on "shameful public display" [*shi zhong*] in some kind of uncomfortable posture or restraining device. The devices ranged from

144. Wumingshi, *Hong sha,* p. 131. The tiger bench somewhat resembles the European rack, which was especially dreaded during the Inquisition.

FIGURE 6. A "tiger bench" [*laohu deng*], or "tendon-pulling bed" [*ba jin chuang*] (from Li Baojia, *Huo diyu*).

the yoke-like cangue around the neck to the dreaded "stand-up cage" [*zhan long*]; a decapitated prisoner might even have his severed head displayed atop a pole in the local marketplace.[145] The modern-day equivalent in the laogai was to make the prisoner "pose for a photo" [*zhaoxiang*] by being kept tied to a post or a tree in a public space where he would be exposed to the elements and have no food or water for a long duration.[146] The

145. A 1934 story by Wu Zuxiang refers to the slow strangulation of a convict within a "stand-up cage." See Philip F. Williams, *Village Echoes: The Fiction of Wu Zuxiang* (Boulder: Westview Press, 1993), p. 88.

146. Zhang Xianliang witnessed this form of torture in his prison camp various times in 1958; see *Wode Putishu*, p. 115. The inmate protagonist of Cong Weixi's novel *Lu hui tou* also suffers this torture; he is tied up naked to a post under the blistering summer sun and is defenseless against swarms of mosquitoes (pp. 143–153).

derisive comments from passersby would be particularly hard to bear if the prisoner had been stripped partially or totally naked, which has sometimes been done for the purpose of exposing practically all of his skin to swarming mosquitoes.[147] Another common variation, termed "controlling the blood" *[kong xue]*, was to tie the prisoner to a long and sturdy carrying pole, and then to turn him nearly upside down at around a 75-degree angle.[148] In a Deng-Jiang Era holdover from the Cultural Revolution, some prisoners have been punished by having to hold themselves for an extensive time in the uncomfortable "jet plane posture" *[zuo feiji* or *penqi shi]*, as described in the section on struggle sessions.[149]

The other type of physical torture in some PRC prisons and labor camps employs fairly high-tech devices of recent vintage. Probably the most intimidating is the taser, or electric shock baton *[diangun]*, which allows a guard or cadre to knock a prisoner to the ground or inflict intense pain with very little effort.[150] Wu Hongda notes that camp cadres and guards would often use electric shock batons to torture "opponents of remolding," and would apply shocks to prisoners' mouths and genitalia for a particularly intimidating effect.[151] Aside from its agonizing effects on the prisoner's nervous system, an electric shock baton sometimes has a powerful enough charge to cause burns on the skin or even cardiac arrest.[152]

Another intimidating tool of the trade is the modern set of self-tightening and sharp-edged handcuffs, which cut more and more deeply into the prisoner's skin and flesh around his wrists if he accidentally or intentionally puts pressure on the chain connecting the two cuffs.[153] An even worse danger with these handcuffs is having the circulation in a hand or arm overly constricted; this has led to permanent disability and disfigurement in some prisoners, such as Peter Bangjiu Zhou. As a punishment

---

147. Cong Weixi, *Lu hui tou*, p. 150; Zhang Xianliang, *Wode Putishu*, pp. 115–116. The GMD sometimes punished desertion by tying up a naked or practically naked prisoner in an area infested with mosquitoes.

148. Zhang Xianliang, *Wode Putishu*, p. 115.

149. Gao Xin, *Beiwei yu huihuang*, p. 51.

150. Li Xianguo, "Zhenjing quanguo zhengfa xitong de Xinjiang dabaoyu," p. 407.

151. Wu Hongda, *Zhongguo de Gulage*, p. 89.

152. Ljunggren, "Canadian Falun Gong Follower Says Tortured in China."

153. Cong Weixi's wrists were bleeding quite severely due to wearing such sharp handcuffs in an isolation cell, as recounted in *Zou xiang hundun sanbuqu*, p. 360. Prison cadre manuals typically forbid handcuffing behind the back or handcuffing as punishment for anything except egregious violations of prison rules, but a huge gap yawns between ideals and practices in this area. See *Laogai gongzuo*, p. 57.

for not confessing his thought crimes, Zhou's captors handcuffed his hands behind his back for twenty-nine days straight. The wounds on his wrists festered and attracted maggots, and eventually the loss of circulation caused by the self-tightening handcuffs disfigured and crippled him permanently.[154] Finally, some PRC prison guards use modern plastic-coated chains to beat difficult prisoners, which enables them to inflict painful internal injuries without leaving any tell-tale marks on the prisoner's body.[155]

In some ways, the threat of torture that hangs over both political prisoners and ordinary criminals in the contemporary PRC is reminiscent of the way some political prisoners were treated during the worst days of martial law under the GMD in Taiwan.[156] The political prisoner Bo Yang's GMD military interrogators told him that he could be beaten to death at any time the authorities desired, and this would simply be reported as a suicide. The Canadian professor and Falun Gong practitioner Zhang Kunlun was told almost exactly the same thing by his Shandong laogai interrogator in 2000: "If you were beaten to death, we could simply bury you and tell the outside world you had committed suicide."[157]

Resistance

In light of the severe measures often taken against prisoners who resist the orders of prison cadres and guards, most resistance has been of a passive or indirect nature. It has been far less dangerous to loaf on the job [dai gong] than to complain openly about being treated like a draught animal that has no control over where it lives and works.[158] Camp inmates have sometimes complained bitterly among themselves that the prison cadres "kill people with a wooden knife" [yong mu daozi sha ren] by presiding over

154. Zhou, *Dawn Breaks in the East*, pp. 56–58. Gao Xin did not suffer such extreme mistreatment, but was punished by having to wear a pair of special rigid handcuffs [si chuai] that are usually reserved for death row inmates. See *Beiwei yu huihuang*, pp. 29–30.

155. An Sinan, *Lian yu sanbuqu*, p. 44.

156. The beating and torture of some political prisoners under GMD martial law in Taiwan is described in Bo Yang & Zhou Bise, *Bo Yang huiyilu* [The Memoirs of Bo Yang] (Taipei: Yuanliu, 1996), pp. 275–276.

157. Ljunggren, "Canadian Falun Gong Follower Says Tortured in China."

158. An unusual labor camp inmate who frankly told a camp cadre that he did not care to go on being a draught animal and did not support the party or the government had his sentence increased [jia xing] to death, and was executed a few months later. See Wumingshi, *Hong sha*, pp. 380–382.

the prolonged and sometimes fatal wasting away of prisoners' bodies under the unrelenting stress of a woefully inadequate diet and hard forced
labor.[159] Opportunistic work slowdowns thus have been about the most
common type of passive resistance, as cadres and guards can hardly supervise the entire work site all of the time, and malnourished prisoners have
little or no personal stake in the camp's profitability. Camp cadres have typically been aware of this, as can be seen by one warden's list of ten common ways inmates avoid hard work.[160] Even activist inmates tend not to
report fellow inmates to the warden for slacking off, since they too must
conserve the limited amount of energy they have derived from the poor
food, and they too are doing unremunerated labor. Labor in hilly terrain
or among buildings and other objects that obscure the cadres' line of sight
makes this type of tactical self-preservation [zi jiu] more possible for the
prisoners, who have often needed to conserve precious calories.[161] These
prisoners would often speed up or slow down their work pace in direct
relation to the camp cadre's distance from them, and would extend their
time away from work with unhurried trips to the latrine or tool shed.[162]

Production quotas tied to food rations and various prison privileges have
typically functioned as a powerful work incentive. Yet there have often been
tricky ways for inmates to get around them and beat the system in a manner reminiscent of Soviet Russian *tufta*.[163] If the quota for agricultural materials is determined by weight, for example, inmates could pull plants up
by the roots and count the soil clinging to the roots as part of the total
weight harvested.[164] If a pile of collected dirt or plant material were to have
its volume determined by a measuring stick, a prisoner assigned the task
of accounting, such as Zhang Xianliang, could make a shorter but otherwise identical copy of the measuring stick to be used in lieu of the original one. The cadre who was Zhang's brigade leader was too dimwitted to
see through his trick, unlike his group chief, who as a fellow inmate decided to let it pass, even sharing a secret chuckle with Zhang about this

159. Zhang Xianliang, *Wode Putishu*, p. 70.

160. Bao & Chelminski, *Prisoner of Mao*, pp. 253–254.

161. Wumingshi, *Hong sha*, p. 98. Seymour & Anderson note that veteran laogai prisoners have usually "spent years figuring out ways to slacken off without notice." See *New
Ghosts, Old Ghosts*, p. 198.

162. Bao & Chelminski, *Prisoner of Mao*, pp. 253–254; Wumingshi, *Hong sha*, p. 98.

163. *Tufta* refers to trickery that makes the results of work appear better than they actually are. For instance, a worthless brush pile could be topped by a layer of good logs, and
the whole pile could be counted as logs. See Robert Conquest, *Kolyma: The Arctic Death
Camps* (Oxford: Oxford Univ. Press, 1979), pp. 166–167.

164. Zhang Xianliang, *Wode Putishu*, p. 32.

clever ruse. Zhang's shortened measuring stick made it seem as though his group had accomplished much more than they actually had.[165]

In another tactic, a production quota could be met without using some or all of the provided materials, which could be quietly stashed somewhere for the prisoner's personal use. Some ground barnyard millet *[baizi]* used as construction paste was carried off in this way by a crafty camp inmate who later made it into coarse griddle cakes to help stave off his hunger pangs.[166]

Some types of counterproductive or destructive inmate behavior do not bring the inmates any rest time or material benefit. However, occasional acts of casual vandalism may relieve inmates' emotional frustration and need not negatively impact the fulfillment of the brigade's production quotas. In *Half of Man Is Woman,* for example, unknown inmates from another brigade vandalize some of the irrigation channels and crop field embankments that the protagonist's group has painstakingly constructed. These other inmates appear to see no harm in ruining something that inmates from another brigade will need to fix later on. They lack the material incentives to preserve agricultural infrastructure that a family farmer in a market economy would have.[167]

In order to be relieved temporarily from the drudgery of unremunerated toil, laogai prisoners have come up with numerous schemes to feign an illness. When prisoners felt less hungry from lying down all day and eating half rations than they would from working all day with full rations, as many as one in ten would feign sickness *[zhuang bing]*.[168] A fever in excess of 38°C (100.4°F) has generally been deemed sufficiently serious to warrant at least one day off from work in the camp infirmary.[169] To increase the reading on the thermometer just before having their temperature taken, some prisoners would exercise vigorously, guzzle a lot of hot water, or rub the thermometer briskly on a warm surface, to name but a few typical stratagems.[170] Many prisoners who want even more time off

165. Ibid., pp. 187–188.

166. Zhang Xianliang's semi-autobiographical narrator Zhang Yonglin does this in *Lü hua shu,* pp. 191, 243.

167. Zhang Xianliang, *Nanren de yiban shi nüren,* pp. 434–435.

168. This was the case in Peng Yinhan's *laojiao* camp in the early 1960s, according to *Dalu jizhongying,* p. 151. Wumingshi's methods of feigning sickness in a labor camp are outlined in *Hai de chengfa,* pp. 83–84.

169. An Sinan, *Lian yu sanbuqu,* p. 71.

170. Ibid., p. 71. There are jokes about the thermometer being dipped in hot water just before its placement in the prisoner's mouth, resulting in absurd temperature readings of 42°C (107.6°F).

work have gone so far as to injure or mutilate themselves *[zi shang zi can]*, often swallowing some kind of hard or noxious object that makes them unfit for labor and necessitates prompt medical attention.[171] One laogai hospital had over 130 such cases during a four-year span in the 1980s, and there were even more self-mutilation cases over the same period that were handled by the local camp infirmaries. Apparently, most of these 130 cases required surgery. An inmate at the Pailou laogai camp in Xinjiang had developed a kind of injection that would cause symptoms similar to hepatitis if injected near the liver. He injected himself and fifteen other inmates—most were indeed hospitalized, but soon required treatment for serious complications that they had not originally anticipated.[172]

A more direct but extremely dangerous kind of resistance has been to refrain from throwing oneself on the mercy of the party, refusing to confess to an offense that either had not been committed or else would not be considered a crime by international standards.[173] Prison cadres often label this kind of difficult inmate an "ace opponent of remolding" *[fan gaizao jianzi]*.[174] For example, Wei Jingsheng spent the better part of two decades in prison partly because he refused to back away from expressing his political values or confess to a set of crimes that he had not actually committed.[175] Hunger strikes have sometimes been an effective way of showing the authorities how resistant a prisoner can be to demands for confession or to intolerable living conditions, but such strikes typically elicit a response of painful force-feeding, often through a tube forced down the prisoner's throat.[176] Some nonviolent political prisoners have paid the ultimate price

171. Sun Xiaoli, *Zhongguo laodong gaizao zhidu de lilun yu shijian*, pp. 258–259.

172. Zhu Guanghua, *Zhongxing fan*, pp. 10–14.

173. Because of the heavy-handed measures often used in the PRC criminal justice system to pressure prisoners to confess, one cannot fault those who do submit to such pressure and confess to an offense they did not commit. It is more difficult to sympathize with those who give into pressure to implicate people who are innocent, but torture and other forms of duress make this kind of behavior understandable, if not laudable.

174. Qiu Zhu, "Shengming de 'leiqu'—yuzhong jishi zhi san" [The "Mined Zone" of Life—Three Prison Accounts], *Da qiang nei wai*, no. 2 (1989): 10–15, esp. 10.

175. See, for example, Wei Jingsheng's March 1984 appeal of his verdict in his book *Wei Jingsheng yuzhong shuxin ji* [A Collection of Wei Jingsheng's Letters from Prison] (Taipei: Shibao wenhua, 1997), pp. 152–154. For the English translation, see Wei Jingsheng, *The Courage to Stand Alone: Letters from Prison and Other Writings,* trans. Kristina M. Torgeson (New York: Viking Penguin, 1997), pp. 84–85. Earlier in the 1970s, Song Shan was sentenced to eighteen years for refusing to confess to charges of counterrevolution; see *Hong qiang, hui qiang*, p. 127.

176. One of the longest hunger strikes was that by the Jiangxi dissident Li Jiulian in 1975, for a total of seventy-three days. See Hu Ping, *Zhongguo de mouzi*, p. 126. See also Liu Qing's personal experience of a prison force-feeding in Liu Qing, "Qianyan" [Preface], in Wei Jingsheng, *Wei Jingsheng yuzhong shuxin ji*, p. 57.

for refusing to confess, as with the two Jiangxi women dissidents Li Jiu-lian and Zhong Haiyuan, who were executed in the late 1970s.[177]

As a form of resistance, escape has typically been an unlikely option. All of the usual physical features of a prison camp militate against it—high boundary walls, barbed wire, observation towers, heavy gates, armed guards, and police dogs.[178] Except for an outright assault on a cadre or guard, an escape attempt is typically considered the most serious violation a prisoner can commit.[179] Escapees may be legally shot dead in the act, and if captured alive are typically punished severely upon recapture by cadres and guards, who fear escape-related demerits on performance evaluations from their superiors.[180] Yet inmates are generally allowed to move about within a work site and walk back and forth to the barracks, which provides an occasional opportunity to flee.[181] Rarely, a prisoner like the Xinjiang camp inmate Li Zhiying becomes something of an "escape specialist" *[taopao zhuanjia];* he broke out more than half a dozen times, earning extensions of his sentence and other punishments along the way.[182]

Lai Ying is one of the few ex-inmate writers who made a successful and permanent escape from the laogai; she swam along the coast to Macao after a lengthy period of traveling and lying low in Guangdong.[183] The

177. Hu Ping, *Zhongguo de mouzi,* pp. 156, 174.

178. A fairly small number of prison camps in remote areas did not have either high walls or barbed wire and were not very carefully guarded. See Zhang Xianliang, *Wode Putishu,* pp. 266–268.

179. Zhang Xinxin & Sang Ye, "Zai tong yidu gao qiang houmian" [Behind the Same Prison Walls], in *Beijing ren: Yibaige putong ren de zishu* [Beijingese: Personal Accounts of a Hundred Ordinary Persons] (Shanghai: Shanghai wenyi chubanshe, 1986), pp. 363–376, esp. 364.

180. In the Deng-Jiang Era, the leadership's stress on reducing prison escapes to the lowest possible number has meant that more than two escapes per year from a given laogai camp can have serious negative consequences for its cadres and guards, particularly if the escapee has not been caught within twenty-four hours. The camp cadres and guards thus go all out to recapture the escaped convict, as is portrayed in Qiu Feng, "Zhuibu zhi ye" [Night of the Pursuit], *Dianshi, Dianying, Wenxue,* no. 5 (1990): 61–72, esp. 69. An example of a camp escapee who was tortured after his capture is Chen Ye, a former colleague of Cong Weixi's at the *Zhongguo qingnian bao;* see *Zou xiang hundun sanbuqu,* pp. 279–281.

181. Nonetheless, popular PRC magazines designed for inmates and security personnel to read such as *Da qiang nei wai* typically emphasize the futility of escape and the ruthlessness of some escapees. The escaped inmates in the following work of reportage are either captured and executed or else cornered and driven to suicide: Qiu Zhu, "Shengming de 'leiqu,'" pp. 10–15, esp. 12, 14–15.

182. Zhu Guanghua, *Zhongxing fan,* pp. 85–87.

183. Lai Ying, *The Thirty-Sixth Way.* Lai Ying thereupon settled down in Hong Kong, where she had family and friends. David Kelly attempted to swim to Macao, but was caught and thrown into the laogai for over two decades, as related in Mathews & Mathews, *One Billion,* pp. 296–297.

inmate protagonists in Cong Weixi's novels sometimes daringly escape from the camps, in contrast to his own personal experience as a quite cautious "model" *[mofan]* prisoner.[184] However, Cong does write admiringly about the unusual experiences of his friend and fellow "rightist" inmate Zhang Zhihua, who escaped and supported himself for quite some time before being arrested for selling ration coupons on the black market; subsequently, he was thrown back into the camps.[185] In contrast, Zhang Xianliang's fictional characters seldom even think of escaping from prison, but the author himself managed to slip away from his rather poorly guarded Ningxia camp for several hours one morning after he found himself unexpectedly alone and unsupervised in his barracks; during his temporary reprieve, he gorged himself on watermelon.[186] Because Zhang Xianliang returned to camp that day before he was counted missing and wrote an effective "admission of wrongdoing" *[jiantao]* to his lax and rather affable brigade leader, his half-day joyride outside the perimeter of the camp was not counted as a bona fide escape.[187] Another prison writer offers an almost total inversion of Zhang Xianliang's experience, portraying alarmed cadres and guards engaging in a frantic search outside the camp walls for a prisoner whom they assume has escaped, but who has actually returned early from the work site to the camp infirmary on account of intestinal pain.[188]

Probably the least common type of inmate resistance consists of physical attacks on laogai cadres or guards, either individually or as a group in a prison riot. Such physical attacks on laogai *ganjing* are very rare; also, ex-inmate novelists and memoir writers are mostly intellectuals who take

184. For instance, the protagonist Suo Hongyi escapes from the camp where he has been held as a retained ex-inmate worker in Cong Weixi's novel *Lu hui tou,* pp. 170–171; his exit is described as simply having "left the camp" *[li chang]* rather than improperly "escaping" *[taopao].* However, this escapee has obviously left no forwarding address with the camp authorities. Cong Weixi's memoirs of camp life, *Zou xiang hundun sanbuqu,* suggest that he went much further in "staying close to the government" *[kaolong zhengfu]* than someone like Zhang Xianliang, who admits having tried and sometimes succeeded in beating the system that was keeping him malnourished and locked away from society for no good reason.

185. Cong Weixi, *Zou xiang hundun sanbuqu,* pp. 204–209. Another fellow inmate who escaped from a laogai camp, Jiang Baochen, made it all the way to Yunnan and had almost crossed the border out of China when he was caught and thrown back in the camp. See *Zou xiang hundun sanbuqu,* pp. 424–430.

186. Zhang Xianliang, *Wode Putishu,* pp. 123–124.

187. Ibid., pp. 126–127. Zhang Xianliang intentionally bypassed his relatively strict group chief and passed his admission of wrongdoing directly to the lax brigade leader, with whom he was on fairly good terms.

188. Qiu Feng, "Zhuibu zhi ye."

a dim view of violence in general.[189] The punishment for such an act has often been execution, especially if a cadre or guard has been killed. This happened when a 1950s camp cadre in Qinghai who was overseeing a mountain road construction project was killed by an inmate for having so disregarded inmate safety that many prisoners had suffered broken bones or death from falls.[190] The large-scale prison camp riots of more recent vintage generally stem from similar pent-up inmate frustrations over unreasonably heavy-handed treatment by various cadres and guards at a particular camp. A prison camp riot on 8 February 1989 in the southeastern Taklamakan Desert in Xinjiang was ignited by the cadres' increased beatings of prisoners right around the lunar calendar New Year's holiday. A group of more than eighty prisoners took over the prison camp for eighteen hours, killing some camp employees and activist prisoners before the riot was suppressed with outside reinforcements.[191] Perhaps the largest PRC prison riot to date took place on 3 July 1997 at the Ya'an camp complex, Sichuan's second largest.[192] An intensified pattern of corruption and physical abuse by the prison administration triggered a massive riot that allowed over two hundred inmates to escape and left nearly five hundred people dead, including seventeen armed police and security personnel.[193]

Inmate Death and Its Aftermath

The PRC laogai system has not experienced a death rate as high as that of Stalin's gulag, with the possible exception of the terrible nationwide famine years of 1959–62. Nor has any single PRC labor camp achieved the notoriety of Stalin's most deadly prisons, such as Kolyma and

189. Gao Xin does occasionally "attack with words," however, as in a denunciatory poem about an abusive guard that he scratches on his cell wall; see *Beiwei yu huihuang,* pp. 221–222. Laogai *ganjing* are camp cadres and guards.

190. Wumingshi, *Hong sha,* pp. 88–90. The inmate who killed the cadre was beaten to death.

191. Li Xianguo, "Zhenjing quanguo zhengfa xitong de Xinjiang dabaoyu," pp. 406–413.

192. The information about the Ya'an prison riot is based on a panel discussion at the Annual Meeting of the Association for Asian Studies, Washington, D.C., 27 March 1998.

193. Early in the prison riot, inmates torched the electricity generation plant, thereby leaving a huge area within the camp complex in total darkness. Troops were called in from major cities such as Chengdu, and helicopters and armored personnel carriers were brought in. In addition to the deaths mentioned above, nearly two hundred security personnel were injured before the riot could be put down about a day and a half after it had begun.

Vorkuta. Yet memoirs and fiction by former camp inmates tend to include a variety of brushes with death, witnessing of death, and fears of never emerging from prison alive.[194] Although the PRC camps were far more potentially lethal during the Mao Era, they have remained dangerous places during the Deng-Jiang Era—prisoners such as Gao Xin have worried about the possibility of execution, while others who entered prison in good health soon developed serious or even life-threatening medical conditions.[195]

In the memoir *My Bodhi Tree,* Zhang Xianliang makes an ironic aside to the reader on the precariousness of life in the camps; he had awakened one morning in 1960 to discover that one of his fellow malnourished inmates had died in his sleep in the barracks: "It was precisely as the Great Leader had said: 'Human death is a common occurrence.'" Unlike his matter-of-fact group chief, Zhang was initially shocked to discover that one of his fellow inmates had just died. However, he soon grew so accustomed to death in the camps that he even marked this development with the title of his 1989 novel *Xiguan siwang* [Getting Used to Dying].[196] A former inmate in a Qinghai laogai camp in the 1950s notes that the deaths from hunger, cold, and sickness seemed as numerous as fallen blossoms at the end of spring.[197] Inmates who starved to death or died of illnesses in their weakened state during the early 1960s would frequently be carried away and piled onto carts and deposited in sheds to await group burial, usually in mass graves.[198] A former inmate in a Gansu camp recalls the large number of prisoners who died from hunger there, along with those who were too weak to help the cadres dispose of the corpses. "At first, it was the prisoners who carried their fellow inmates' corpses out of the barracks; later, the cadres had to do all the carrying."[199]

Zhang Xianliang, too, at first helped carry inmate corpses out for burial in his Ningxia camp during the famine, but early one morning, having slipped into a comatose state due to the starvation diet, he was mistaken for a corpse as he lay immobile and silent in his barracks.[200] Zhang

194. For example, Jean Pasqualini often feared he would never get out of prison alive; see Bao & Chelminski, *Prisoner of Mao,* p. 98.

195. Gao Xin, *Beiwei yu huihuang,* p. 24.

196. Zhang Xianliang, *Wode Putishu,* p. 85. Hitler enjoyed being referred to as "The Leader"; Mao Zedong preferred the title "Great Leader" *[weida de lingxiu].*

197. Wumingshi, *Hong sha,* p. 93.

198. Cong Weixi, *Zou xiang hundun,* pp. 233–234; Bao & Chelminski, *Prisoner of Mao,* pp. 192–195; Wu & Wakeman, *Bitter Winds,* pp. 102–107, 127–129.

199. Sun Ping et al., *Zhongguo jianyu ren,* p. 162.

200. C. T. Hsia, "Chang Hsien-liang [Zhang Xianliang] as Author and Hero: A Study of His *Record of My Emotional Life,*" p. 7, verified this incident at his presentation to the

was carried outdoors and loaded onto a donkey cart piled high with inmate corpses; he was then taken to a storage shed, where he was lugged onto a large pile of corpses awaiting burial. Gradually, he regained consciousness, and somehow managed to muster enough strength to crawl out from the pile of corpses and lie at rest near the door of the shed. When the burial detail returned to load up the corpses for burial, they noticed Zhang's odd position near the door and discovered that he was still breathing, if faintly. They reported their discovery to the camp doctor—a fellow inmate himself, as is typical—who had them bring Zhang to the infirmary for a successful treatment with restorative nutriments.

Many laogai inmates have the physical endurance to withstand difficult conditions in the laogai, but they lose the psychological will to go on living through such hardship, and commit suicide. Though more frequent in the Mao Era than the Deng-Jiang Era, suicide was the cause of death in thirty-five cases of inmate mortality at one camp in Anhui between 1986 and 1989.[201] The immediate causes of suicide have varied a great deal. Rope torture and repeated struggle sessions catalyzed one suicide in Qinghai, while prolonged semi-starvation and the fear of dying a "hungry ghost" led a prisoner in Ningxia to take his own life.[202] Some retained ex-inmate workers have used their suicides as a gesture of protest against the government by committing the act in a symbolic place like the nation's capital, much like a wronged Chinese daughter-in-law making the ultimate parting gesture of defiance toward her abusive mother-in-law.[203] Seeing nothing but endless frustrations and disappointments awaiting them in their future, other inmates have instead taken their own lives in an unobtrusive way.[204]

According to a laogai manual for cadres and guards, a dead prisoner's

International Conference on Literature, Politics and Society in Mainland China, Taipei, Taiwan, May 1989. The incident was also included in two of Zhang Xianliang's novels. A labor camp cook confirms with the protagonist Zhang Yonglin that he is indeed the one who "crawled out from within a pile of corpses" in *Lü hua shu*, p. 169. The incident is treated in much more detail, though interspersed with other incidents and reflections, in *Xiguan siwang*, pp. 184–185.

201. Sun Xiaoli, *Zhongguo laodong gaizao zhidu de lilun yu shijian*, p. 259.

202. Wumingshi, *Hong sha*, pp. 378–379; Zhang Xianliang, *Wode Putishu*, pp. 138–140. According to Buddhist teachings, the sufferings of "hungry ghosts" *[egui]* who had starved to death are worse than other types of hellish existence in the hereafter.

203. The comparison with a wronged daughter-in-law's suicide is the authors', while Cong Weixi emphasizes the element of protest in the chemist Zheng Guangdi's suicide in *Zou xiang hundun sanbuqu*, p. 256.

204. This is how Harry Wu's friend and fellow Tuanhe inmate Ao Naisong committed suicide. See Wu & Wakeman, *Bitter Winds*, pp. 188–189, 268.

ash urn or corpse is supposed to be held for the deceased's relatives to pick up within a prescribed period of time. If nobody comes to pick up the inmate's remains within that time, then they are supposed to be buried in a marked grave.[205] In actual practice, however, countless deceased inmates have been buried in unmarked graves, and sometimes have been simply abandoned where they died.[206] For example, the corpse of the Jiangxi dissident Li Jiulian was left to lie where she collapsed after being executed in 1977. Her family members were too apathetic to go pick up Li's corpse, the government did not bother with it, and a local sexual deviant brutally mutilated it with a knife where it lay unattended that night. This desecration of the corpse caused outrage among people who knew how courageous and principled Li Jiulian had been.[207]

Cong Weixi once discovered that the deceased inmates' names on the grave markers in his Hebei camp had been rendered illegible due to weathering—they had simply been scrawled on bricks in the first place.[208] Some of the relatives of inmates who had died in the camp had complained to Cong about not being able to find their loved ones' remains.

In the wake of the massive death toll as a result of the PRC's misguided Great Leap and rural commune policies, growing outrage and unrest within society prompted the government investigating teams to look into the elevated death rate at the camps. Zhang Xianliang's Ningxia camp commissar cleverly saved himself and his local colleagues from any blame: just before an investigating team arrived at the Ningxia prison camp to look into the causes for the spike in inmate deaths from starvation and related disorders, the commissar locked a group of inmate doctors and nurses overnight in a room full of deceased inmates' medical records. The commissar told them to change the cause of death on the medical records (usually intestinal ailments) to sicknesses affecting organs unrelated to the digestive system.[209] At the same time, the commissar had to deal with another death-related problem. The cadres had been simply dumping the bodies of dead inmates into unmarked collective graves, but the relatives of the deceased were coming to the camp in search of their loved ones' remains. These relatives began filing formal complaints that they could not find these remains. Zhang and some

205. *Laogai gongzuo*, pp. 44–45.

206. The rocky terrain and bitter cold in Qinghai meant that many of the inmate corpses could not be buried; see Wumingshi, *Hong sha*, p. 93.

207. Hu Ping, *Zhongguo de mouzi*, 157–159.

208. Cong Weixi, *Zou xiang hundun*, pp. 233–234.

209. Zhang Xianliang, *Wode Putishu*, pp. 289–290.

other inmates were put to work digging up skeletons for the relatives to pick up. The camp cadres did not know the identity of any of the skeletons, of course, and decided to tell the visiting relative—most often a wife—that whichever skeleton she picked out from those on display in the storage shed was indeed the remains of her dead husband.[210]

These clever solutions to problems related to high death rates in the camps spur Zhang to add some ironic comments. The fact that none of the prisoners had bothered the cadres about how the issue of their remains should be disposed of proves that these prisoners had been properly remolded. On the other hand, the fact that the dead inmates' relatives complained about not having been allowed to pick up these remains shows that these citizens outside of the camp had not been properly remolded.

Recent advances in medical technology have contributed to the rise of a new controversy over the disposition of the remains of PRC prisoners who died under state custody. Since the 1970s, the typically nonconsensual removal of organs such as kidneys and corneas from executed PRC prisoners for purposes of medical transplantation has become increasingly widespread.[211] The policy on harvesting prisoners' organs was formalized by the Supreme People's Court and various other governmental bodies in a written regulation dated 9 October 1984.[212] Human Rights Watch/ Asia has estimated that from 2,000 to 3,000 such organ extractions from executed convicts have taken place annually, making such prisoners the chief source of organ transplantation in the PRC.[213]

Fiction and literary reportage from the 1980s played a significant role in bringing the problem of organ harvesting to a broad readership. Cao Guanlong's story "Three Professors" *[San'ge jiaoshou]* portrays an amoral and ambitious professor of ophthalmology in Shanghai who masterminds a cornea transplant in order to curry favor with a half-blind public secu-

210. Zhang Xianliang, *Xiguan siwang,* pp. 255–256.

211. For more on the issue of consent in the harvesting of executed prisoners' organs, see the Laogai Research Foundation, *Communist Charity: A Comprehensive Report on the Harvesting of Organs from the Executed Prisoners of the People's Republic of China* (Washington, D.C.: Laogai Research Foundation, 2001), pp. 30–33.

212. Zuigao renmin fayuan et al., "Guanyu liyong sixing zuifan shiti huo shiti qiguan de zhanxing guiding" [Provisional Regulations Regarding the Use of Executed Criminals' Corpses or Organs within the Corpses], 9 October 1984. The government agencies responsible for these regulations include the Supreme People's Court, the Supreme People's Procuratorate, the Ministry of Public Security, the Ministry of Justice, and the Ministry of Public Health.

213. "Crime and Vivisection: A New Human-Rights Report Claims That Convicts Are Used as Organ Donors," *Time,* 5 September 1994.

rity chief.[214] This professor appears to show personal concern for a young male prisoner nicknamed "Glass," but all the modest improvements to Glass's inadequate prison diet are merely for the sake of maintaining the health of Glass's eyes up to his time of execution. In accord with common practice in the PRC, the authorities in this story hardly feel a need to receive the death row prisoner's voluntary written consent before harvesting organs from his body. Glass is trussed up, executed, and his corneas are deftly removed by the professor, who later performs a picture-perfect cornea transplant for the ailing public security chief.[215] Although this story concludes with a fanciful "karmic-whiplash" twist, its basic scenario was plausible enough to provoke a few letters of protest from Shanghai surgeons.[216] These doctors insisted that they had never willingly participated in such a cruel and deceitful practice as that described in the story—thereby implying that they had performed such organ transplants only on orders from the higher-ups.[217] Mark Baber, an ex-inmate of Shanghai Number One municipal prison during the early 1990s, noted signs of systematic organ harvesting: death row inmates were given a specially enhanced diet and regular medical attention that ordinary prisoners did not receive.[218]

The process of performing an organ extraction from a death row convict unfolds with the kind of detail and precision that only an eyewitness account can provide in Hu Ping's book-length literary reportage *Zhongguo de mouzi* [China's Eyes Unpeeled].[219] The author bases his account on his in-depth interview of a guard who accompanied the Jiangxi schoolteacher and prisoner of conscience Zhong Haiyuan to the execution ground in 1978.[220] While riding there in the police van, the guard

214. Cao Guanlong, "San'ge jiaoshou" [Three Professors], *Anhui wenxue*, no. 1 (1980): 17–31. For English version see Cao Guanlong, "Three Professors," trans. John Berninghausen, in *Roses and Thorns: The Second Blooming of the Hundred Flowers in Chinese Fiction, 1979–80,* ed. Perry Link (Berkeley: Univ. of California Press, 1984), pp. 111–145, esp. 130–145.

215. Glass's execution is modeled on that of a historical figure who was killed during the Cultural Revolution for having made minor but "counterrevolutionary" changes to a model revolutionary opera.

216. At the end of the story, the public security chief drowns himself to escape from the "fire" in his new corneas, which comes from Glass's eleventh-hour outrage over the ambitious ophthalmologist's ruse.

217. Perry Link, introduction to the English translation of "Three Professors," *Roses and Thorns,* pp. 111–112.

218. Saunders, *Eighteen Layers of Hell,* pp. 50–51.

219. Hu Ping's *Zhongguo de mouzi* first appeared in the PRC literary journal *Dangdai* [Contemporary Age], no. 3 (1989): 7–72. All citations are from the reprinted 1990 edition published by Tiandi tushu in Hong Kong.

220. Ibid., pp. 160–182.

felt Zhong's body tremble with pain as a medic wielding a large metal veterinarian's syringe administered three shots in her buttocks of what must have been a kidney-preserving chemical. All this occurred without any explanation to Zhong Haiyuan herself, who had no idea that she was about to have her kidneys cut out and transplanted into the body of a high-ranking military officer's ailing son. After the public security authorities shot Zhong point-blank in the right side of her back and rushed her to the waiting ambulance's operating table, her heart kept beating until most of the kidney extraction process had been concluded.[221] The young male kidney recipient did not survive even a year after his transplant operation.

Zhong Haiyuan was posthumously "exonerated" *[pingfan]* of her supposed ideological crimes. As Zhang Zanning of the Jiangxi Province School of Social Medicine argues, Zhong's harsh fate remains a "painful memory" of the problems involved with obtaining organs from executed convicts.[222]

However, the combination of PRC citizens' increasing prosperity, party-state connivance in organ harvesting, technical advances in transplant procedures, and longer survivability among recipients since the late 1970s have significantly increased the demand for executed prisoners' kidneys. A PRC doctor's 1993 firsthand account of harvesting organs and numerous body parts from an executed prisoner indicates that nothing more than a wobbly lump of the dead prisoner's midriff section was left to cremate after all the "useful" parts had been removed and placed in various bags and containers.[223]

Prisoners' corpses have also been disposed of in other unseemly ways. During the Great Leap famine years, Hong Xianheng knew of cases in which chunks of inmates' corpses were either knowingly cannibalized or else sold under the guise of camel flesh or horse meat to unsuspecting customers.[224]

The treatment of executed prisoners like Zhong Haiyuan as little more than state property to be disposed of expediently derives in part from the party-state's extremely instrumentalist view of the laogai prisoner as

---

221. Removal of the organs for transplant prior to the death of the donor improves the prospects for a successful transplant, but obviously amounts to a severe violation of medical ethics and legal norms.

222. Laogai Research Foundation, *Communist Charity*, p. 115.

223. Zhang Zhu, "Shiwan huoji—xingchang ge shen!" [Most Urgent! Cutting Out Kidneys at the Execution Grounds], *Zhonggong sifa heimu*, pp. 121–128, esp. 124–126.

224. Wumingshi, *Hong sha*, pp. 346–348.

"useful material" *[youyong zhi cai]*.[225] Some prison cadres' avowed determination to "make full use of the things at your disposal" *[wu jin qi yong]*, a phrase often directed at inmates, appears to be the animating spirit at this juncture.[226] The Deng-Jiang Era emphasis on placing top priority on economic production and downplaying remolding may have exacerbated the tendency to take a remarkably mercenary view of the prisoner's worth even after his or her death.[227]

Release Back into Society

Prior to the vast downsizing of the jiuye system of forcibly retaining ex-inmates in the vicinity of prison camps as heavily supervised workers during the late 1970s and especially the 1980s, most PRC labor camp prisoners could not return to society as free citizens with full political rights. These retained ex-inmate workers tended to work and live under so many restrictions and fears of periodic political clampdowns that people in general referred to their condition as "secondary laogai" *[er laogai]*.[228] If given a choice, most released PRC prisoners have preferred ending or bypassing jiuye status and leaving the camps behind for good, so this laudable downsizing of the jiuye system has greatly expanded the possibilities for ex-inmates to reintegrate into society.[229] The post-Mao government's formal decriminalization of the private economic sector has meant that released prisoners in search of a job are no longer limited to a choice between acceptance by a state-controlled work unit—the default being their old prison enterprise, where they would become retained ex-inmate workers—versus risky trading on the black market.[230] In the Deng-Jiang

225. Prisoners are characterized as "useful material" for socialist construction in *Laogai gongzuo*, p. 4.

226. Cong Weixi, *Zou xiang hundun*, p. 118.

227. Qiu Feng suggests that many Deng-Jiang Era camp cadres are so busy with "utilizing prisoners for production" to pay for prison maintenance and administrators' salaries that they neglect most other functions of the prison. See "Zhuibu zhi ye," p. 68.

228. Shao Mingzheng, ed., *Laogai faxue gailun* [An Outline of Labor Remolding Law] (Beijing: Zhongguo Zhengfa daxue chubanshe, 1990), p. 264. Some former urban inmates such as Song Shan argue that there was very little difference between ordinary inmates and released ex-inmate workers; see *Hong qiang, hui qiang*, p. 188. Yet in relatively rural prison camps such as those where Cong Weixi, Zhang Xianliang, and Harry Wu served as jiuye personnel, there was quite a bit more socializing and freedom of movement than what ordinary inmates experienced.

229. Song Shan, *Hong qiang, hui qiang*, p. 187; An Sinan, *Lian yu sanbuqu*, p. 214.

230. Dealing in grain coupons on the black market led to the escaped inmate Zhang Zhihua's rearrest and further imprisonment in the 1960s, according to Cong Weixi, *Zou xiang*

Era, released prisoners have been free to find employment in the PRC's growing private sector, quite often as small individual proprietors *[getihu]* engaged in peddling or small-scale production.[231] Most of the women prisoners in one late-1980s novel discuss how they plan to support themselves after release by becoming individual proprietors, chiefly in the garment industry; this seems like "almost the only way out" *[chulu]* of their predicament.[232]

However, as in the United States, the "ex-con" label has long been a burden to many released prisoners. Chinese society has generally taken a dim view of these ex-inmates, who are disparagingly labeled as "criminals who have completed their term" *[xing man fanren]* or "released laogai criminals" *[laogai shifang fan]*.[233] More neutral-sounding official terms for released convicts in the Deng-Jiang Era, such as "personnel who have completed their sentences" *[xing man shifang renyuan]*, have seldom achieved the common currency of the more colloquial expressions, which end with "criminal" *[fanren or zuifan]*.[234] Some commentators have suggested replacing the various pejorative terms for "criminal" with *jianyu ren*, the neutral neologism for "prisoner," as a way of reducing societal prejudice against these inmates, but it remains to be seen whether popular discourse would truly embrace this new coinage.[235] Moreover, a mere change in terminology would not necessarily alter common images of present and past inmates as "the dregs of society" *[shehui zhazi]* who are somehow less than human due to their alleged lack of ordinary "human feelings" *[ganqing]*.[236] Incendiary governmental rhetoric and stepped-up arrests during the seemingly interminable "strike-hard" campaigns against crime have not helped PRC citizens become more charitable toward former prisoners. The Deng-Jiang Era Public Security Bureau's internal classification of released laogai and laojiao inmates as a core *zhongdian*

hundun sanbuqu, p. 208. If Zhang had left prison twenty or more years later instead, he would have likely steered clear of the black market and supported himself by some kind of legal business activity such as peddling or trading.

231. See, for example, Thomas Gold, "Urban Private Business and China's Reforms," *Reform and Reaction in Post-Mao China: The Road to Tiananmen*, ed. Richard Baum (New York: Routledge, 1991), pp. 84–103.

232. Li Jian, *Nüxing de xue qi*, p. 150.

233. See, for example, An Sinan, *Lian yu sanbuqu*, pp. 214–215. An abbreviated but less common variant of *laogai shifang fan* is *lao shi fan*.

234. Shao Mingzheng, ed., *Laogai faxue gailun*, p. 266.

235. Sun Ping et al., *Zhongguo jianyuren*, pp. 171–172.

236. Ibid., p. 1. These negative stereotypes do not extend to the families and friends of former prisoners. Particularly in the Deng-Jiang Era, the relatives and friends of prisoners can sometimes be quite supportive of them, as evidenced in Tang Min, *Zou xiang heping*, pp. 288, 290.

renkou [special population] subject to unusually intense police surveillance and control has become an open secret in PRC society.[237] As a result, released inmates have often reported intense frustration over their treatment as *erdeng gongmin* [second-class citizens] by both the police and society in general.[238]

As recently as the late 1990s in a relatively prosperous urban locale within Fujian province, the husband of the imprisoned and recently released writer Tang Min warned her that she probably had no future in her own country. Some other relatives and friends went further, urging Tang to go abroad and settle down there at the earliest opportunity.[239] If Tang had done so, she would have risked being blacklisted and prevented from returning to the PRC as long as that nation's authorities suspected her of involvement in "antigovernment activities" overseas.[240] Even released prisoners who have been formally exonerated of their alleged crimes have seldom felt free of their dangerously checkered past or "tail" *[weiba],* which seems to follow them wherever they go within their country.[241]

At the individual level, many released inmates drag behind them another tail—post-traumatic stress disorder (PTSD), key symptoms of which include "behavioral reenactments" of past responses to a traumatic situation and "the reappearance of traumatic memories in the forms of flashbacks."[242] In Bei Dao's story "The Homecoming Stranger," the traumatized released inmate continues to suffer the terror of looming punishment from the authorities at his old laogai camp, in spite of assurances from his family that he is now safe in his old home after a two-decade or-

237. Michael R. Dutton, *Streetlife China* (Cambridge: Cambridge Univ. Press, 1998), p. 69.

238. Ge Fei, *Erdeng gongmin: ji Gongheguo diyici yanda* [Second-Class Citizens: A Record of the (PRC) Republic's First Strike-Hard Campaign] (Chengdu: Chengdu chubanshe, 1992).

239. Tang Min, *Zou xiang heping,* pp. 289–290. Tang Min rejected the advice to leave the PRC upon her release from prison; for her reasoning, see pp. 290–291.

240. The PRC State Council reportedly issued a secret decree in October 1993 outlawing the return of politically active PRC citizens in eight categories who were residing overseas. For details, see John F. Copper & Ta-ling Lee, *Coping with a Bad Global Image: Human Rights in the People's Republic of China, 1993–1994* (Lanham, MD: University Press of America, 1997), p. 60.

241. One of Harry Wu's college students warned him to remain mindful of his "tail" in 1979, according to Wu & Wakeman, *Bitter Winds,* p. 263.

242. Bessel A. Van der Kolk & Onno Van der Hart, "The Intrusive Past: The Flexibility of Memory and the Engraving of Trauma," *Trauma: Explorations in Memory,* ed. Cathy Caruth (Baltimore: Johns Hopkins Univ. Press, 1995), pp. 158–182, esp. 176.

deal in the laogai. The old released inmate keeps his fears at bay by means of behavioral enactments of past self-protective behavior. Because his children can hardly understand what he has been through in the camps, they react with amazement and exasperation at the way their old father compulsively burns what he mistakenly imagines to be self-incriminating jottings on cigarette packs.[243]

Other laogai narratives express ex-inmate writers' PTSD by means of flashbacks or recurrent images from traumatic memory that keep coming back to haunt them. Unlike ordinary memories, which become vague or generalized over time, memories of traumatic situations tend to change very little, largely because the person troubled by these memories cannot readily assimilate them into the normal patterns of his understanding. In Zhang Xianliang's fiction, images of gun barrels and the terror of being shot to death recur frequently enough to merit their classification as traumatic images. The gun barrel is always aimed in the direction of his protagonist, and often glows with a sinister dark blue glint.[244]

The treatment that former inmates receive after their release sometimes looms large in their decisions about such pressing matters as whether to leave the PRC or write about their experiences in prisons and labor camps. After her release from a Jiangxi prison camp in the mid-1970s, the dissident Li Jiulian seemed ready and willing to try to "live like everyone else,"[245] but her political "tail" prevented her from resuming a normal social life, getting married, or receiving a well-deserved job transfer.[246] She then continued speaking out about local political injustices stemming from the Cultural Revolution, and before long was rearrested and thrown back into the camps, from where she never returned.

Gao Xin's prison cadres accurately warned him just before his release in 1990 that his case had not been concluded and that he would henceforth

243. Bei Dao (pseud. of Zhao Zhenkai), "Guilai de moshengren," in *Bodong* (Hong Kong: Zhongwen daxue chubanshe, 1985), pp. 149–166, esp. 155–157. Translated into English by Bonnie S. McDougall & Susan Ternent Cooke as "The Homecoming Stranger" in *Waves: Stories by Bei Dao,* ed. Bonnie S. McDougall (New York: New Directions, 1990), pp. 9–26, esp. 15–17.

244. Zhang Xianliang, *Tu lao qinghua,* p. 21; *Nanren de yiban shi nüren,* pp. 445, 598, 599; *Xiguan siwang,* pp. 15, 131, 233, 310.

245. The former Soviet working-class dissident Anatoly Marchenko was often urged by relatives and hometown friends to play it safe and "live like everyone else" after his release from the gulag. Yet he insisted on writing about his experiences and maintaining his contacts with intellectuals and other dissidents. This resulted in Marchenko's rearrest and eventual death in captivity. See *To Live like Everyone,* trans. Paul Goldberg (New York: Holt, 1989).

246. Hu Ping, *Zhongguo de mouzi,* pp. 54–60.

bear the "tail" of residential surveillance.[247] Gao's interrogator brusquely admonished him to "talk less" [shao shuohua] following his release, lest they should meet again back in prison.[248] No longer welcome at his state job in the university, Gao Xin indeed temporarily spoke less. Yet he wrote more: his book about his prison experiences and decision to go abroad were direct responses to government pressure. A somewhat similar situation occurred in Peng Yinhan's case nearly three decades earlier, for his old work unit in Shanghai refused to assign him a job following his release from reeducation through labor.[249]

Zhang Xianliang had no work unit to which he might return after release from the camps in the late 1970s, so he busied himself with attempting to find a unit that would accept him.[250] After many difficulties, he finally found a cadre who took him into his work unit and assigned him a teaching job. Yet after only a month, the cadre ordered Zhang back to his original labor camp unit due to concerns about his inability to receive a formal exoneration from the authorities. Though Zhang was assigned to a teaching job there, he would have remained little more than a retained ex-inmate worker unless he were to find a way to persuade the provincial party leadership in Ningxia to grant him an exoneration. He finally caught the provincial leadership's eye in 1979 by writing a series of short stories that were published by the leading local literary journal, Shuofang, and received the cherished exoneration in recognition of his talent. Zhang's emergence on the literary scene was highly fortuitous, but his fiction's common motifs of Mao Era political suppression and the lot of prison camp inmates could have been predicted, as these were tied up with his motivations for writing in the first place.

Released laogai prisoners on the verge of leaving the PRC for Hong Kong, Taiwan, or some other overseas destination where they had some kind of connection were often treated to a few fine meals or even some sightseeing. From time to time, these released convicts would be plied with smiling exhortations to maintain a "united front" [tongyi zhanxian] in support of the PRC government.[251] At other times, the PRC author-

247. Gao Xin, Beiwei yu huihuang, p. 241. In addition to placing Gao Xin under surveillance, the public security authorities placed a sign that read "no admission for foreign visitors" [waibin zhibu] in front of Gao's residence.

248. Gao Xin, Beiwei yu huihuang, pp. 241–242.

249. Peng Yinhan, Dalu de jizhongying, pp. 216–217.

250. Zhang Xianliang, "Man zhi huangtang yan" [Pages Full of Preposterous Words], Zhang Xianliang xuanji, vol. 1 (Tianjin: Baihua wenyi chubanshe, 1985), pp. 187–194, esp. 191.

251. Wumingshi, Hong sha, pp. 400–402. Usually referred to as tongzhan, united-front work is designed to help complete the unification of China across the Taiwan Strait on

ities have determined that an overseas-bound released laogai camp inmate would be an unworthy object of such a charm offensive, and instead sternly warned the individual not to divulge "secrets" or "talk irresponsibly" about their prison experiences after relocating abroad.[252]

Whether writers of the Chinese laogai have remained in the PRC or emigrated, they have had a number of motivations for revisiting their memories of imprisonment instead of cultivating a safe amnesia, as the authorities would have generally preferred. The next chapter explores the motivations behind this body of writing and other aspects of literary dynamics.

Beijing's terms, and is the relatively diplomatic counterpart of the PRC's long-standing threat to attack Taiwan militarily if it were to formally declare its independence from the PRC.

252. Zhou, *Dawn Breaks in the East,* p. 120.

CHAPTER 5

Prison Writings

From Taboo-Enforced Silence to Active Development

During the Mao Era, prison writings set in the contemporary PRC amounted to a kind of "forbidden zone" *[jinqu]* that local authors gave a wide berth. Even foreigners who dared flout this unwritten rule were likely to encounter retaliation in their dealings with the highly image-conscious party-state.[1] Merely for having written a book review of Jean Pasqualini's laogai memoir *Prisoner of Mao* in 1973, Harvard historian John Fairbank was denied a visa for a long-awaited trip to the PRC. Fairbank was disappointed but appropriately unapologetic, and a decade and a half later wrote a book review of Zhang Xianliang's prison camp novel *Half of Man Is Woman.*[2]

For an actual PRC prisoner to send out critical writings about a contemporary labor camp for publication abroad, even during the relatively "open" *[kaifang]* post–Mao Era, is extremely risky, both for the writer and for anyone who helps him. Liu Qing, who by the 1990s had emigrated to New York to engage in human rights advocacy, received four years in solitary confinement and other forms of harsh treatment in his labor camp as punishment for having smuggled out such a text in 1981.[3]

1. The informal taboo against portraying the PRC prison in that country's literature and art was finally shattered in 1979 by Cong Weixi's "Da qiang xia de hong yulan," a hackneyed story that nonetheless broke the ice for more memorable efforts to follow.

2. John Fairbank, "Roots of Revolution," *New York Review of Books,* 10 November 1988, pp. 31–33, esp. 32–33. Fairbank's applications for a PRC visa in subsequent years were routinely approved.

3. Liu Qing, "Prison Memoirs" [Yuzhong shouji], ed. Stanley Rosen & James Seymour, *Chinese Sociology and Anthropology* 15.1–2 (1982–83): 3–181, esp. 13–173.

Curiosity had long been building up both at home and abroad about a far-flung prison system based on forced labor that had incarcerated untold millions since 1949 — everyone from disgraced high cadres and intellectuals to the lowest strata of petty thieves and hoodlums. Among its other achievements, the vigorous post-Mao cultural thaw of the late 1970s and early 1980s gave rise to the first PRC fiction and reportage about Mao Era prison camps by writers such as Cong Weixi, Zhang Xianliang, and Liu Binyan. By the mid-1980s, a significant enough body of work had emerged to receive the subgenre classification of "prison wall literature" *[da qiang wenxue]*, with an entire volume of critical essays written about a single controversial novel in this subgenre.[4] From the late 1980s on, a rich memoir literature unfolded, written in part by the prison wall novelists themselves. Moreover, an increasing number of memoirs and popular novels about contemporary Deng-Jiang Era prisons appeared in the late 1980s and 1990s to complement the retrospective Mao Era focus of the early prison wall novelists.

Four Categories of Prison Writings

The prison writings analyzed in this interdisciplinary study fall into four major categories, the first pair of which is nonfictional, while the third and fourth are fictional.[5] Each will be introduced below, with discussion of the varying types of motivation at work behind these writings.

The first category consists of memoirs, diaries, collections of letters, autobiographies, and testimonials written by former PRC prison inmates. A significant amount of this nonfictional material has a contemporary Deng-Jiang Era focus, such as Wei Jingsheng's collected prison letters, Liu Qing's account of his arrest and his reflections on prison camp life, Gao Xin's memoirs of his arrest and several months' incarceration as a political prisoner, and Tang Min's recollections of her trial and imprisonment for libel. However, because intellectuals were far more likely to land in prison under the dictatorship of the Mao Era than under Deng and his successors, writings in this category about Mao Era imprisonment

4. See Li Qian, *Teding shiqi de da qiang wenxue* [Prison Wall Literature of a Certain Period] (Shenyang: Liaoning daxue chubanshe, 1988). The 1985 novel that attracted so much attention was Zhang Xianliang's *Nanren de yiban shi nüren*, in *Zhang Xianliang xuanji*, vol 3.

5. There is also some PRC poetry that deals with prison settings, such as that by Wuming-shi and Huang Xiang, but it is outside the scope of this study, which focuses on prose writings.

have been even more prominent. Among the most significant are those by Lai Ying (1969), Jean Pasqualini (1973), Duan Kewen (1978), Peng Yinhan (1984), Wumingshi (1985), Song Shan (1986), Cong Weixi (1989/1998), Harry Wu (1994), and Zhang Xianliang (1995).[6]

The second type of prison writing, also nonfictional, includes reportage, journalistic writings, and interviews penned by authors who either have never been imprisoned in the laogai or else focus almost exclusively on recounting the cases of prisoners other than themselves. Writings of this type sometimes come from the hand of serious novelists like Wumingshi and Wang Anyi or accomplished reportage writers like Hu Ping.[7] More often, though, they aim at a popular readership and are penned by lesser-known writers and journalists such as Sun Ping and Zhu Guanghua, both of whom have interviewed a number of laogai inmates.

The third type of prison writing is fiction by former prison inmates. While necessarily imaginative in nature, it is often semi-autobiographical or semibiographical in nature, depending on whether the author draws more on personal experience or the recounted recollections of fellow inmates in creating a given literary narrative. The major writers in this category are Zhang Xianliang and Cong Weixi, though Liu Binyan and some others have written an occasional prison wall piece. Because of Zhang's and Cong's frequent use of prison camp settings, the novelist Wang Meng has somewhat facetiously labeled Cong Weixi "the father of [PRC] prison camp literature" *[da qiang wenxue zhi fu]* and anointed Zhang Xianliang "the younger uncle of prison camp literature" *[da qiang wenxue zhi shu]*. *Da qiang wenxue*, also known as "towering wall literature," a term referring to PRC literature set amidst the high walls of prison camps, grew fastest during the 1980s.[8] The contemporary critic Li Qian compares prison camp literature with "wound literature" *[shanghen wenxue]*, and

6. Some commentators have claimed that Jean Pasqualini's was the first laogai prison memoir (see Bao & Chelminski, *Prisoner of Mao*), and the only work comparable to Liu Qing's *Prison Memoirs* as of 1982. See Rosen & Seymour's introduction to Liu Qing's *Prison Memoirs*, pp. 3–9, esp. 8. In fact, Lai Ying's *The Thirty-Sixth Way* (1969) is comparable to Liu Qing's memoirs and predates *Prisoner of Mao* by four years.

7. Hu Ping's *Zhongguo de mouzi* focuses on reconstructing and analyzing the cases of the imprisoned and executed political activists Li Jiulian and Zhong Haiyuan. However, Hu also recounts how he himself was wrongly imprisoned and physically abused (pp. 201–202) and how his father and sister were implicated as a result (pp. 203–204).

8. Zhang Xianliang, "Guanyu shidai yu wenxue de sikao—zhi Cong Weixi" [Thoughts about Literature and Its Epoch—A Letter to Cong Weixi], in *Zhang Xianliang xuanji*, vol. 3, pp. 689–695, esp. 689. See Kyna Rubin, Introduction to Wang Ruowang, *Hunger Trilogy*, pp. xiii–xiv, xxxiv–xxxv; and Philip F. Williams, "'Remolding' and the Labor-Camp Novel," *Asia Major* 4.2 (1991): 133–149, esp. 146.

finds prison wall literature by the likes of Zhang Xianliang and Cong Weixi has much more focus and a deeper sense of history, since it usually stresses reflective thought [fansi].[9]

The fourth type of prison writing consists of fiction or drama that is set in prison camps, but has been penned by writers who appear not to have experienced imprisonment in the laogai. It includes fairly serious works, such as a major novel by Lü Haiyan, along with more popular works by authors like Ai Bei, Fu Xuwen, and Wang Zifu.

Although all four types of prison writings figure in this book's analysis of the PRC prison camp, special emphasis has been placed on writings by former prisoners (the first and third types), some of whom spent as long as two decades in the camps. While exceptions exist, the first type, nonfiction, is perhaps the most authentic and authoritative in its firsthand description of prison camp regimens and subcultures.[10] Fiction by former prisoners presents a simulation of prison camp life that encourages readers to imagine how they themselves might react to the quandaries the various protagonists face. Though based to some extent on the authors' personal experiences and other related events in prison camps, their shaping of the subject matter to fit literary conventions and achieve literary effects can dilute the testimonial or historical value of the work. These authors' personal experiences include careful social observation of the camp milieu and conversations with both inmates and camp administrators, not to mention the reading of other literature pertaining to prison camps since their release.

Interviews with camp inmates and other writings in the second category (reportage by writers who have not been inmates) can provide valuable firsthand accounts of prison life. Reportage can also offer factual background material on various prisons and their inmates, along with statistics provided by camp cadres and other government functionaries. Yet on the whole, this kind of material does not offer an in-depth or sustained account of prison life from the inmate's perspective. The journalist authors often write on the basis of observations obtained from a brief visit that is controlled by camp cadres to emphasize the positive aspects and downplay the negative features of the camp. Furthermore, depending on the

9. Li Qian, *Teding shiqi de da qiang wenxue*, p. 19. "Wound literature" refers to a type of PRC writing from the early post-Mao years that focuses upon suffering caused by the violence and chaos of the Cultural Revolution (1966–76).

10. Any memoir or autobiography contains a certain amount of subjective bias, but this problem can be mitigated by such scholarly practices as checking against alternative sources.

political affiliation and motives of the journalists, reportage can vary a great deal in terms of candor and depth of observation. Some reportage appears to be written to satisfy superficial aspects of the popular readership's curiosity about prison and prisoners, while at the same time reiterating the official party line that the government and its cadres are effectively remolding prisoners and reducing recidivism.[11] Understandably, this type of reportage typically condemns prisoners' passive and active resistance to their forced labor regimen, for its sympathies often reside more with prison cadres and guards than with inmates. Yet such reportage can be informative and even entertaining in relating how particular prisoners engaged in criminal activity, received punishment after their arrest, and succeeded or failed at attempts to adjust themselves to the camp regimen.[12] This reportage can also be "pedagogical," or cautionary, in the sense that it warns readers against the temptations of criminal activity and reassures them of the government's effectiveness in combating crime.

The fourth type of prison writings, fiction by non-inmates, can also be somewhat informative and pedagogical, but in comparison with the third type, it tends to be more entertaining than serious in purpose. These non-inmate writers often want to broaden their portrayals of society to include prison environments, and may be interested in a kind of layman's sociological exploration of prison culture, as is the case with Wang Zifu and Ai Bei. Ai Bei has also chosen to write about female prisoners because of her interest in the status and literary representation of women. She uses the female penitentiary as a symbol of how Chinese women still seem to be "imprisoned" in their society's traditionalistic structuring of gender relationships.[13] Finally, while a desire for public recognition or at least commercial success exists to some extent within all four types of prison writing, commercial leanings tend to be relatively stronger in the fourth type.[14]

Ex-inmates' Motivations for Writing

A complex web of motives has impelled ex-inmates to write about their labor camp experiences in the first and third categories of prison writing

---

11. For example, Gu Xiaoyan, *Zhongguo de jianyu* (Shenyang: Jilin renmin chubanshe, 1988); Sun Ping et al., *Zhongguo jianyu ren;* and Zhu Guanghua, *Zhongxing fan.*

12. See, for example, Gu Xiaoyan, *Zhongguo de jianyu.*

13. See, for example, the discussion in Ai Bei, *Nü lao,* pp. 117–119.

14. In her preface, Ai Bei makes a point of thanking all the people who have purchased her book, no matter what their motives may have been. Ai Bei, "Zixu," in *Nü lao,* p. 3.

(nonfiction and fiction by ex-inmates). Camp inmates who survived especially harsh periods such as the great famine of 1959–62 have sometimes felt duty-bound to preserve the memory and succor the relatives of those wronged inmates who died or otherwise disappeared in the camps. For instance, this seems to be the driving motivation of the ex-inmate protagonist of Liu Binyan's story "Diwuge chuan dayi de ren"—a feature that Liu Binyan has often embraced in his career as a journalist and writer.

Numerous former inmates have wanted to use their writings to shed light on the shadowy laogai system, most aspects of which have been shrouded in secrecy from ordinary PRC citizens and foreigners alike, making it considerably more poorly understood internationally than either the former Soviet gulag or Hitler's concentration camps. Both Cong Weixi's *Zou xiang hundun sanbuqu* and Zhang Xianliang's *Wode Putishu* provide a combination of narrative and commentary on life in the camps that is mildly reminiscent of Solzhenitsyn's *Gulag Archipelago,* to which they directly allude from time to time, with Zhang generally making the more perceptive cross-cultural comparisons. Along somewhat similar lines, Harry Wu recalls that the disappointing paucity of books and studies of the PRC prison system that he encountered in mid-1980s U.S. university libraries was a spur for him to write about the laogai.

Most ex-inmate writers have wanted to illustrate how educated and law-abiding citizens could easily become snagged and engulfed in the PRC regime's prison machinery, with all the sufferings and uncertain outcomes that this has normally entailed.[15] Those who were incarcerated in labor camps during the Mao Era have also wished to reveal their understanding of what lay below the idealistic veneer of platitudes about remolding and "study" sessions—especially the arbitrariness, callousness, and deception that were built into the camp system.[16] Serious reforms were needed of a system in which the occasional kindness of certain cadres and fellow inmates paled beside the general round of treatment that has encouraged mutual suspicion and hostility, incubated material deprivation and disease, and treated the individual inmate like an interchangeable cog in a machine.[17] Some inmates have been compelled to insist that instead of being "remolded" into a higher state of being, the camps have

15. An Sinan, "Houji" [Epilogue], in *Lian yu sanbuqu,* p. 217.

16. See, for example, Wumingshi, *Hai de chengfa,* pp. 32, 54–58; Yang Jiang, *Ganxiao liuji* [Six Chapters from a Cadre School] (Hong Kong: Guangjiaojing chubanshe, 1981), p. 67; and Cong Weixi, *Zou xiang hundun,* pp. 55, 59–60.

17. See Cong Weixi, *Zou xiang hundun,* pp. 76–81, and Zhang Xianliang, *Wode Putishu,* pp. 45–46, 82.

mostly pressured them to "devolve" to a more primitive modus vivendi marked by outer subservience, inner ruthlessness, and calculating self-absorption.[18]

On the other hand, a select group of highly privileged inmate writers have expressed mostly praise for the prison system and its functionaries. It should be noted that the Fushun Prison cadres and guards in charge of high-ranking prisoners of war such as the last Manchu emperor were considerably more educated and better trained than the norm. The autobiography of the last Manchu emperor, Aixin Jueluo Puyi (Aisin Gioro Puyi), describes in detail how he was treated very kindly by the patient CCP laogai cadres, along with the process of being "remolded" into a "new man" who repented his crimes of collaboration with the Japanese military conquerors.[19] Puyi also notes how the prison cadres helped him change from a conceited and good-for-nothing figurehead of an emperor into a useful citizen with a "correct" political ideology.[20] In a similar way, the former high-ranking GMD military officer Shen Zui rewarded his captors for their decidedly lenient treatment of him with a wholehearted transfer of his loyalty to the PRC, where he was content to settle down in comfortable retirement following his release. Shen attributes the CCP's success in remolding a select group of former GMD officers to its provision of excellent living arrangements for them, along with its scheduling of frequent field trips for them to witness the industrial and agricultural achievements under the CCP.[21]

However, both Aixin Juelo Puyi and Shen Zui are quite exceptional cases that cannot form the basis of general statements about conditions in the camps. They were prisoners of war who had expected to receive severe and mostly justifiable punishment for collaborating with enemy invaders or leading armies into battle against the Chinese Communists during the civil war. Instead, they were given preferential treatment in prison and a special amnesty after being confined for only a decade or so. Their

18. See Zhang Xianliang, *Wode Putishu,* pp. 26, 31, 166–167, 297–298; and Cong Weixi, *Zou xiang hundun,* pp. 86–87.

19. Aixin Jueluo Puyi is also known as Aisin Gioro Puyi. He was the Japanese militarists' puppet ruler of Manchukuo during the 1930s and the first half of the 1940s, and his collaboration was second in seriousness only to that of Wang Jingwei, who was the puppet leader of the bulk of China under Japanese military occupation during the Second World War.

20. Aixin Jueluo Puyi, *Wode qianbansheng* [The Former Half of My Life] (1964; rpt. Beijing: Qunzhong chubanshe, 1983), pp. 417–556.

21. Shen Zui, *Zhanfan gaizao suo jianwen,* vol. 2, p. 3.

gratitude thus led to their willing self-transformation into properly deferential followers of the CCP.[22] In addition to serving as living examples in the CCP's showcase of "remolded model prisoners," they wrote about their successful stories of remolding, thereby serving as useful instruments of the CCP's "United Front" *[tongzhan]* strategy to co-opt the people of Taiwan and win international approval for the CCP's self-styled humanitarianism. Of course, Puyi's and Shen Zui's memoirs have some historical value; Shen Zui has assembled a number of vivid and occasionally humorous vignettes of his fellow inmates, also prominent former GMD military officers.[23] However, since the memoirs of Puyi and Shen Zui have served primarily as CCP propaganda for the laogai's self-proclaimed success in remolding prisoners, these two memoirs present very little that can be used in the overall evaluation of Mao Era prison camps.

In contrast with Puyi and Shen Zui, who were on the losing side of deadly political and military struggles, the majority of the laogai ex-inmate authors committed no internationally recognized offense, and should not have been detained or imprisoned in the first place. Furthermore, their experiences in the Mao Era forced labor camp were usually so harsh as to result in wariness and concealed resentment of the party-state's iron hand, not the "remolding" into "new socialist men" that has been so often advertised. Reading these ex-inmate writings side by side with the sanitized prison manuals for cadres and guards and their idealized vision of a forced labor prison, one realizes how great the disparity between theory and practice can be. The lofty "socialist humanitarianism" touted in camp cadre manuals does not often trickle down to the ground on which the actual prisoners in the ex-inmates' accounts are standing.

In his study of life in the Nazi death camps, Terrence Des Pres groups Holocaust memoirs together with other memoirs of extreme autocratic

22. Hu Juren suspects that Mao Zedong was employing the strategy of psychological manipulation in his especially mild treatment of these high-ranking prisoners of war. See Hu Juren, "Ba" [Epilogue], in Shen Zui, *Zhanfan gaizao suo jianwen*, pp. 334–335.

23. On one occasion, the prison cadre who was giving Shen Zui and his colleagues political instruction intoned a crude Maoist slogan these prisoners had never heard before: "Take off your pants and cut off your tail" *[tuo kuzi ge weiba]*. "Tail" is a metaphor for the bad ideology of the precommunist society that people are supposedly dragging along with them. However, when unsuccessfully trying to use a Beijing pronunciation variant for "tail" *[yiba]*, the cadre mispronounced it as "cock" *[jiba]*, making the sentence come out as "Take off your pants and cut off your cock" *[tuo kuzi ge jiba]*. Until this was finally explained to the anxious prisoners several days later, they thought the cadre was serious about this threat and began to assume that the ultimate punishment for their "war crimes" was going to be castration *[gongxing]*. See Shen Zui, *Zhanfan gaizao suo jianwen*, vol. 1, pp. 57–58.

suppression, such as those of Soviet gulag survivors.[24] Yet David Patterson argues for a fundamental distinction between the two types of memoirs, according to whether the suppression was based on political or ontological factors. In other words, Patterson claims that gulag prisoners tended to be punished on account of what they had allegedly done, while Holocaust prisoners were deemed guilty simply because of who they were in the Nazi scheme of group identity.[25] Of course, this distinction should not be overplayed; Stalin often imprisoned or exiled potential enemies en masse on the basis of mere group affiliation, such as Poles, Balts, Chechens, Cossacks, kulak farmers (similar to Mao's "rich farmers"), and repatriated prisoners of war. Similarly, Hitler imprisoned or executed many so-called "Aryans" who opposed him politically, not simply members of ethnic or religious groups that he had marked out for destruction, such as Jews and gypsies.

The PRC laogai prisoners' situation under the Mao dictatorship bore a closer resemblance to that of their Soviet counterparts than to the Jewish prisoners of the Nazi concentration camps. Admittedly, some Chinese groups such as male rural landlords were indeed singled out by Mao Zedong for virtual annihilation, much like the kulaks under Stalin and the gypsies under Hitler.[26] However, most PRC prisoners have been punished on the basis of actions they allegedly performed rather than as a consequence of their group affiliation.[27] Political factors have loomed large

24. Terrence Des Pres, *The Survivor: An Anatomy of Life in the Death Camp* (New York: Oxford Univ. Press, 1976).

25. David Patterson, *Sun Turned to Darkness: Memory and Recovery in the Holocaust Memoir* (Syracuse, NY: Syracuse Univ. Press, 1998), p. 4. In regard to the Holocaust as an ontological category, Patterson draws on Piotr Rawicz and Emil L. Fackenheim.

26. One major difference between the Hitlerian and Maoist approaches to liquidating enemy groups is that Hitler aimed for a total liquidation, including the elderly and even children in his genocidal executions. Mao instead aimed to decapitate an enemy group such as rural landlords by stirring up nationwide vigilante executions of adults, mostly males, while leaving most of the women and children alive to eke out their lives in a state of impoverishment and sociopolitical disgrace.

27. Yet because of the CCP belief in the absurd "Blood-Line Theory" *[xuetong lun]* or "Theory of Class Pedigree" *[chushen lun]*, some people were executed not for what they did but for what they were—because they belonged to the bourgeois class, they were intellectuals, or their parents belonged to the landlord class or some other vilified group. In this sense, the Chinese case parallels the Holocaust: Jewish death camp inmates were exterminated on the basis of what they were instead of what they did. In 1966, a young student named Yu Luoke had the courage to write an essay entitled "Chushen lun" [The Theory of Class Pedigree] to oppose such a dangerous and simple-minded schema for the political pigeonholing of citizens. As a result, he was imprisoned and executed in 1970. See Wen Yu, *Zhongguo zuo huo,* pp. 558–563.

in the motivation for ordering arrests under both Stalin and Mao, and neither leader executed as large a percentage of the prison camp population as did Hitler. Nevertheless, while Mao's laogai was considerably less deadly than Stalin's gulag, the PRC camp system saw a significant number of prisoners slowly exterminated while in confinement through such means as starvation, illness, overwork, exposure, and torture.

Unlike many Holocaust memoirs and some gulag testimonials, laogai memoirs rarely mention God or express yearnings for God or other deities.[28] Instead of wrestling with the possible religious significance of their suffering, laogai writers tend to focus on the sociopolitical and ethical aspects of confinement. This tendency resonates with the largely secular foundations of law and ethics in Chinese culture that were discussed in Chapter 1.

Still, similarities can be discerned in these different types of prison memoirs. Like Holocaust and gulag memoirs, Chinese laogai memoirs exhibit a strong interest in moral issues. An important motivation for the Chinese ex-inmates to write about their experience has been a sense of moral duty. Aware of how the CCP has attempted to conceal its errors and has urged its citizenry to forget about the recurring suppression of basic civil rights in the PRC's history, the survivor-authors feel the need to publicize the truth and preserve those memories. In their memoirs, they bear witness to [jianzheng] the injustice that has befallen themselves, their families, and various other inmates.[29] Some memoir writers recount how some of the most famous intellectuals of their day were deprived of dignity and died wretchedly in prison.[30] Others reveal how they were subjected to inhumane treatment for long periods of time—deprived not only of freedom but also the fulfillment of basic human needs—as they un-

28. An exception to the general rule of little interest in religion among the Chinese laogai writers and most other inmates has been the many Catholics thrown into the laogai, especially during the 1950s. Protestants and Muslims have also been incarcerated, the latter being relatively common in China's western provinces, where Zhang Xianliang's labor camps were situated. Prisoners with a strong religious faith seem to have handled the inevitable hardships of camp life with more calm and courage than the norm. Cong Weixi expresses his admiration for the courage and selflessness of Ying Mulan, a female inmate doctor and a devout Catholic, in *Zou xiang hundun sanbuqu*, pp. 413–421.

29. See, for example, Wumingshi, "Yige dalu qiutu de yishiliu—*Hai de chengfa* xupian, Xiashaxiang jizhongying xinling jingyan" [The Stream of Consciousness of a Mainland Prisoner—A Supplement to *Punishment of the Sea*, the Mental Experience of Xiashaxiang Concentration Camp], in *Hai de chengfa*, pp. 114–115.

30. For example, Cong Weixi records his grief during a deathbed encounter with Lü Ying, a well-respected writer who died in prison when he was just fifty-five years old. *Zou xiang hundun sanbuqu*, pp. 312–316, esp. 315–316.

derwent forced labor in conditions that wore down both the body and the mind.[31]

A typical memoir of the Mao Era prison camps often functions as testimony or exposé. It bears witness to the chaos and confusion experienced by prisoners and their families during those years that were peppered with harsh political campaigns. The change from a relatively orderly existence to a suddenly chaotic state was both drastic and traumatic: innocent, even patriotic people were condemned as rightists, worthy intellectuals were imprisoned for having dutifully responded to Mao's call to make minor criticisms of the party, and decent values were trampled.[32] For Cong Weixi, who appropriately titled his memoir *Zou xiang hundun* [Heading into Chaos], the world had indeed turned upside down when he and his wife, both patriots who had been loyal to the party, were thrown into prison camps. The calamity fractured a previously harmonious family—he was separated from his wife, son, and widowed mother, and thereby utterly unable to perform his roles as husband, father, and son. Cong Weixi often records his incessant worries about his family, particularly the devastating imprisonment of his wife, who repeatedly attempted suicide. In splitting numerous families apart on the flimsiest of pretexts, the CCP indeed "struck hard" at basic family values long considered to be of central importance in Chinese civilization. Laogai memoir writers have almost invariably noted their anguish over this coercive separation from close relatives.[33]

Extending this concern for ruptured families from themselves to others, these writers also record the traumatic separation between some of their fellow inmates and their families. Cong Weixi relates in touching detail the deep bond between his fellow inmate Han Dajun and Han's old mother, and how they both suffered when Han was imprisoned. At one juncture, Han Dajun suddenly received a transfer to a faraway camp. When his mother heard the news, she boarded a bus in order to visit him

31. For instance, see An Sinan, *Lian yu sanbuqu*, pp. 46–50; and Cong Weixi, *Zou xiang hundun*, pp. 115–120. Though not his own memoir, Wumingshi's *Hong sha* is also a good example. See Yenna Wu, "Expressing the 'Inexpressible': Pain and Suffering in Wumingshi's *Red Sharks (Hong sha)*," conference presentation, The Chinese Labor Camp: Theory, Actuality, and Fictional Representation, University of California, Riverside, CA, 15 January 2000.

32. Cong Weixi, *Zou xiang hundun*, pp. 12–19.

33. For example, Yang Jiang reports sorely missing her daughter and husband in her *Ganxiao liuji*; Song Shan and Zhang Xianliang express how they longed to see their mothers again in *Hong qiang, hui qiang* and *Wode Putishu*, respectively. Gao Xin expresses his anguish at being separated from his fiancée in *Beiwei yu huihuang*.

a last time at his old labor camp prior to this move to a distant region. Han Dajun was already on a truck departing from his old camp when he spotted his mother in a bus traveling in the opposite direction. Han impulsively jumped out of the truck to chase after his mother's bus, in complete disregard of the risk he was taking. Unfortunately for them both, Han was soon arrested and handcuffed by some guards.[34]

Even in the Deng-Jiang Era, an especially pronounced separation of prisoners from their family members remains to some extent. Gao Xin finds it extremely inhumane that even in the "Reform Era," a prisoner sentenced to death is not usually allowed to bid farewell to his family before his execution. Gao cites a case related to him by a fellow inmate who witnessed a scene of a death row inmate's final encounter with his family. This particular young man, who had recently gotten married, had been condemned to death. His wife briefly glimpsed him through a window of the prison van in which he was being taken to that Beijing prison's notorious K-Building, yet the couple had no chance to bid each other a final farewell or clasp one another's hands one last time. Although both husband and wife were weeping, the guards had no sympathy for them. The wife and her two brothers then mounted bikes and pedaled quickly behind the lumbering prison van, calling for the husband to look back for a last glimpse. Although the prisoner was strictly forbidden from gazing out of the barred van window, he insisted on looking back at his wife, even though a guard kept striking him in the face until blood from cuts on his face dripped down to mix with his tears.[35]

Ex-inmate writers often relate the adverse changes wrought on their bodies and emotional lives. Zhang Xianliang repeatedly mentions his pathetically emaciated body and his constant hunger. Zhang describes himself as so hungry and scrawny that he weighed a mere 44 kilograms in 1960. Similarly, at the beginning of *Lü hua shu,* the starved protagonist Zhang Yonglin—the narrative persona of author Zhang Xianliang—is 178 centimeters tall, but weighs only 44 kilograms.[36]

Remarking upon the physical toll taken by the camps, Cong Weixi discusses how carrying heavy loads on a pole in the laogai left scars and permanent lumps on his shoulders and neck. Cong goes on to describe his permanently deformed finger due to an injury in his labor camp.[37]

34. Cong Weixi, *Zou xiang hundun sanbuqu,* pp. 286–290, esp. 288–289.

35. Gao Xin, *Beiwei yu huihuang,* pp. 47–49.

36. Zhang Xianliang, *Wode Putishu,* pp. 3, 9, 123, 246; *Lü hua shu,* p. 163.

37. Cong Weixi, *Zou xiang hundun,* pp. 58, 120. See also Peng Yinhan's description of adverse changes in prisoners' bodies in *Dalu jizhongying,* p. 81.

Many of the memoirs and fictional works feature groups of hungry, emaciated, and filthy prisoners who are dressed in shabby and patched clothes as they fall in and out of line for roll call and toil at heavy labor for long hours.[38] Writing in a vein that David Wang has called "grotesque realism," the authors sketch many disturbing portraits of inmates at various stages of illness and starvation, as well as the corpses of prisoners who could not withstand the rigors of the camp regimen.[39] At times, a prisoner's appearance would deteriorate so much in the camps that relatives and friends could barely recognize him, and an occasional glance at a mirror would leave him mortified and despondent.[40]

Cong Weixi recalls that he was ordinarily calm to the point of numbness in the face of deaths among his fellow inmates. Yet for the first time he felt dumbstruck and was moved to silent tears at the deathbed of the emaciated literary scholar Lü Ying: "Formerly of larger physique than the norm, Lü Ying had shrunk to the size of a dwarf. To put it even more accurately, he had become a mummy incapable of any movement other than shallow breathing . . . In front of this barely living corpse of a Lü Ying, I lost the composure that unforgiving Life had given me."[41]

Such unforgiving conditions gave rise to Cong Weixi's decades-long bout with impotence. Zhang Xianliang similarly dramatizes the conscious sexual repression *[bie]* and subsequent impotence *[yangwei]* of a male inmate in his *Half of Man Is Woman*. These inmates' problems stem from tangible traumatic or extreme situations encountered in adulthood, not some sort of conjectural Freudian "unconscious repression" that inevitably dates back to the inmates' childhood. Even some scholars within the psychoanalytic tradition have recognized that Freudian dogma about the centrality of the patient's childhood experiences and notions about a hypothetical "unconscious repression" do not tally with either advances in the brain and behavioral sciences or the problems affecting their patients with post-traumatic stress disorder (PTSD). Van der Kolk and Van der Hart point to the more cogent hypothesis by the eminent psychia-

38. For example, Wumingshi, *Hai de chengfa*, pp. 52–53; Cong Weixi, *Zou xiang hundun*, pp. 178–180; and Wumingshi, *Hong sha*, pp. 57–62, 78–82, 319–322.

39. Wang, *Fin-de-Siècle Splendor*, p. 251; Zhang Xianliang, *Wode Putishu*, pp. 85, 154–155, 218–220, 251–252, 279, 296. See also Peng Yinhan, *Dalu jizhongying*, p. 82; An Sinan, *Lian yu sanbuqu*, pp. 60–61; and Wumingshi, *Hong sha*, pp. 97–99, 106, 310–312, 336–343, 346–348.

40. See Wumingshi, *Hai de chengfa*, pp. 106–107; Peng Yinhan, *Dalu jizhongying*, p. 212; and Yang Jiang, *Ganxiao liuji*, pp. 12–13.

41. Cong Weixi, *Zou xiang hundun sanbuqu*, p. 315.

trist Pierre Janet that psychopathology sometimes develops from painful, recurring memories of an extreme situation.[42]

According to these memoirs and novels, the psychological toll of prolonged confinement in the camps could be even more onerous than the physical deterioration that inmates endured. Even highly esteemed professionals and intellectuals would often see little alternative but to compromise their dignity in order to survive.[43] For the sake of self-preservation under the thumb of the camp's inadequate food quotas, they often resorted to stealing and fighting over food, foraging for wild plants and animals, and scavenging for moldy scraps in garbage heaps.[44] Some laogai writers claim that many psychological problems of prisoners have arisen because their most basic needs went unfulfilled for years on end.[45] Cong Weixi sadly observes that many intellectuals exhibited what he termed "the post-famishment syndrome" *[ji'e houyizheng]:* after having suffered extreme hunger, they always felt famished and wanted to eat anything, including foul scavenged things they would have never even looked at twice under normal conditions.[46]

Under the harsh famine conditions of many Mao Era camps, Zhang Xianliang and Cong Weixi often witnessed death at close proximity.[47] Their memoirs and fiction seem partly an attempt to exorcise or at least ameliorate the emotional damage from these disturbing memories. Zhang Xianliang relates how it took a long time for him to grow accustomed to seeing corpses in the barracks or elsewhere in the camp.[48] One day, in an attempt to pilfer food from a parked truck, Zhang reached up to grab what he thought would be a daikon radish or an edible cabbage root. What he had actually grabbed was a dead man's frozen arm; only then did Zhang realize that the truck had been loaded with stiff naked corpses. This encounter with death was so disturbing that after he was released, he would often grow nauseated at the mere sight

42. See Van der Kolk & Van der Hart, "The Intrusive Past," p. 158.

43. See, for example, Wumingshi, *Hai de chengfa,* pp. 92–93; Cong Weixi, *Zou xiang hundun,* pp. 59, 104–112; and his *Zou xiang hundun sanbuqu,* pp. 197–201.

44. Cong Weixi, *Zou xiang hundun sanbuqu,* pp. 193–198. Zhang Xianliang, *Wode Putishu,* pp. 278–279.

45. See, for example, Wumingshi, *Hong sha,* pp. 336, 343, 360, 363; Zhang Xianliang, *Wode Putishu,* pp. 129–130, 151–152, 135–136; and Cong Weixi, *Zou xiang hundun sanbuqu,* pp. 130, 320.

46. Cong Weixi, *Zou xiang hundun sanbuqu,* pp. 194, 197.

47. See Zhang Xianliang, *Wode Putishu,* pp. 85–86; and Cong Weixi, *Zou xiang hundun sanbuqu,* pp. 158–160, 316–321, 395.

48. Zhang Xianliang, *Wode Putishu,* pp. 85–86.

of butchered chicken or ducks, and thus eventually became a near-vegetarian.[49]

Some memoir writers recall a nagging fear of losing their identity, of general regression and devolution, and of becoming less than human, or even no longer human.[50] They would sometimes realize that they were losing the virtue and decency so crucial to their former sense of identity within society. Zhang Xianliang admits having sometimes resorted to scheming and deception in order to obtain a bit more food; he was aware of his degenerating and decaying sense of self, yet could not do anything about it.[51] Cong Weixi laments, "After entering the labor camp brigade, I have been whittled by the carving knife of this life into my non-self *[fei wo]*."[52]

While feeling helpless about having lost his former identity, Cong also notes that this reaction was widespread among professionals and intellectuals in the camps at that time. Since intellectual achievement was very much tied up with such a person's individual identity, many professionals were psychologically at sea in the prison camp.[53] Indeed, the laogai was wasting their educational training and most productive years with manual chores that any able-bodied illiterate could do as well or better than they.[54]

Life in the labor camps often revealed character flaws in the laogai writers' own peers amongst the imprisoned professionals and intellectuals. Both Cong Weixi and Zhang Xianliang repeatedly observe how the ordinarily muted unscrupulousness and lack of mutual respect among many intellectuals often came bubbling to the surface in prison camps. In order to strive for a higher position in the camp's hierarchy of prisoners or to accumulate merit for a possible reduction in their sentences, educated inmates often utilized their intellects to inform on others as the cadres' stool pigeons, or cruelly attacked the target of a struggle session.[55] Well-educated prisoners often behaved more unscrupulously than ordinary criminal inmates in this regard, according to both Cong and Zhang.

49. Ibid., pp. 154–156.

50. See Wumingshi, *Hai de chengfa,* p. 27; Zhang Xianliang, *Wode Putishu,* pp. 129–130, 173–174; and Cong Weixi, *Zou xiang hundun,* pp. 18, 107.

51. Zhang Xianliang, *Wode Putishu,* pp. 248–249.

52. Cong Weixi, *Zou xiang hundun sanbuqu,* p. 299.

53. Zhang Xianliang, *Wode Putishu,* pp. 236–238.

54. See, for example, Wumingshi, *Hai de chengfa,* p. 48; and Zhang Xianliang, *Wode Putishu,* pp. 256–257.

55. See Zhang Xianliang, *Wode Putishu,* pp. 297–298; and Cong Weixi, *Zou xiang hundun,* pp. 76–81, 98–100.

In a similar vein, the urban-based prison writers' forced mingling with ordinary working-class inmates in the camps sometimes opened their eyes to problems in the society and the government that they had not previously perceived.[56] On the face of it, this development might seem to accord with Mao Zedong's oft-repeated imperative that urban intellectuals "learn from workers, farmers, and soldiers" *[xiang gongnongbing xuexi]*. Yet the lessons that the inmate writers learned from their prison sojourns at the lower depths of society often differed dramatically from what Mao would have hoped, for the poverty, hunger, and repression so widespread in the countryside seemed largely the result of Mao's failed rural policies.[57] An Sinan went so far as to claim that he was "remolded" by his prison camp experiences at society's lower depths from a naïve follower of the CCP into a hardened ex-inmate who had broken totally with the CCP in favor of values based on respect for the individual citizen.[58]

Of course, laogai memoir writers and novelists who agree that they learned much of value and novelty during the hardships of incarceration have not been inclined to recommend imprisonment for their readers' edification. Friends of both Zhang Xianliang and Cong Weixi have told them that their years of suffering in prison camps provided them with a huge amount of writing material. Cong Weixi has tended to agree with such sentiments, particularly during the ebullient finale *[guangming de weiba]* of his laogai memoirs, though the somber and aggrieved tone in which he earlier recounts the incident of being handcuffed in a punishment cell forms quite a contrast.[59] Zhang Xianliang insists that if he were to compare the few literary fruits resulting from his laogai experiences with the long period of his arduous incarceration, "the loss far outweighs the gain."[60]

Some of the laogai writers have been spurred to record what they

56. Zhang Xianliang, *Wode Putishu,* pp. 46–47.

57. Cong Weixi relates how some peasant women were stealing peaches from the orchards tended by prisoners. Three of the women played a shameless trick on him when he caught them in the act. Cong also describes in detail a proletarian nicknamed "Loosehand He" [He Dana], who was a callous and deceitful habitual thief. See Cong's *Zou xiang hundun sanbuqu,* pp. 242–243 and 301–307, respectively. See also Yang Jiang, *Ganxiao liuji,* pp. 21, 24–25.

58. An Sinan, *Lian yu sanbuqu,* pp. 96–97.

59. Cong Weixi, *Zou xiang hundun sanbuqu,* pp. 509–510. The veteran writer Sun Li told Cong Weixi that his personal misfortune in the camps was a boon to his literary career, a sentiment that Cong's literary peer and close friend Liu Shaotang has also expressed.

60. Zhang Xianliang, "Man zhi huangtang yan," in *Zhang Xianliang,* vol. 1, pp. 187–194, esp. 187.

heard and saw by the specific requests of fellow inmates to pen an accurate account of prison camp life. An old inmate named Pei Lianzhen once told Cong Weixi the following: "You used to be a journalist and writer. You must conscientiously commit this span of history to memory. If someday you're able to write again, you must put all this down on paper without mixing in any falsehood. Doing so won't be muckraking, but rather an action on behalf of China's future."[61] Cong Weixi himself has written that by "reflecting" *[fansi]* at length on modern Chinese cultural history and offering personal judgments of it in his writings, he can help prevent the "historical tragedy that is already past" from ever recurring in China.[62] From a less sanguine perspective on how far the PRC criminal justice system advanced during the Deng Era, Wumingshi (Bu Naifu) expresses the hope that his readers in Taiwan and abroad will have no illusions about how the laogai helped the CCP consolidate its power—and how the camps remain a formidable tool of intimidation and repression in the PRC.[63]

A sense of moral duty also impelled Hu Ping to write *Zhongguo de mouzi*, a work of reportage about the ill-fated dissidents Li Jiulian and Zhong Haiyuan, who were executed in the late 1970s and exonerated posthumously. Hu Ping had previously garbled some of the information in one of the two cases, and desired to set the record straight. More important, however, was his desire that these nonviolent dissidents' legitimate political endeavors and the government's harsh suppression of them be more widely known. One editor frankly informed Hu Ping that while the topic was important and well researched, he lacked the courage to risk angering the party authorities by publishing it.[64] Hu Ping did eventually find a PRC journal editor who would publish this work, the writing of which also served a cathartic function. Prior to Hu Ping's completion of the first draft of his full-length reportage on the 1970s Jiangxi

61. Cong Weixi, *Zou xiang hundun sanbuqu*, p. 293.

62. Cong Weixi, "Wenxue de meng—da Yanhuo" [My Dream of Literature—A Reply to Yanhuo], in *Cong Weixi yanjiu zhuanji* [A Specialized Collection of Research on Cong Weixi's Writings], ed. Liu Jinyong & Fang Fuxian (Chongqing: Chongqing chubanshe, 1985), pp. 67–81, esp. 77. Of course, many historians and criminal justice scholars would disagree with Cong Weixi that the "historical tragedy" of the laogai was simply over and done with after Deng Xiaoping's rise to power.

63. Wumingshi, "Zixu (1)" [Preface (1)] and "Zixu (2)" [Preface (2)], in *Hong sha*, pp. 1–12 and 13–20, respectively. See also his "Prologue: The Secret of the Cave," in Pu Ning, *Red in Tooth and Claw*, pp. xxv–xxvii; and Jonathan D. Spence, "In China's Gulag," *New York Review of Books* 42.13 (10 August 1995): 15–18.

64. Hu Ping, *Zhongguo de mouzi*, pp. 6–7.

dissidents, he would grow somewhat agitated each time he recalled the rank injustice meted out to Li Jiulian and Zhong Haiyuan.[65]

On rare occasions, laogai writers have managed to keep a diary or a personal journal, even though almost any writings and books have been subject to confiscation in the camps. It required considerable courage for a laogai inmate to write; Liu Qing suffered years of solitary confinement and other types of punishment and torture in retaliation for having smuggled out an account of his arrest and confinement in the early 1980s. Zhang Xianliang was also well aware of the strict censorship in his camp and the danger he was courting by keeping a diary from 11 July to 20 December 1960. He took care in writing mostly about mundane activities that were unlikely to arouse suspicion, and placed special emphasis on paraphrasing the announcements of camp cadres. Zhang's diary avoided any mention of controversial subjects such as escape attempts, ideologically incorrect remarks, theft, and malingering.[66] For Zhang Xianliang, one of the driving forces in keeping a diary was the desire to keep some kind of record of how his young adulthood was passing him by. The laconic expressions in his diary serve as condensed seeds of thought that would later trigger his recollection of numerous other related events of that period. The act of keeping a diary was partly an attempt to preserve his identity as an intellectual. It was also cathartic—in his diary he could express some of his emotions, including the venting of mild anger and frustration—albeit in a cautious and restrained manner.

The Prison Camp Stay as a Transitional Device

The prison camp occasionally surfaces as a secondary motif in literary works outside of the four categories discussed above. In many works of contemporary Chinese fiction, the labor camp serves as little more than a device that advances the plot, often by signifying a protagonist's transition from one mode of existence to another. Under these circumstances, little or nothing in the way of a coherent prison camp setting emerges. For example, in Li Bihua's 1989 novel *Bawang bie ji* [Farewell, My Concubine], a prison camp in Fujian province serves merely as the transition point between the opera actor Duan Xiaolou's wretched life in the PRC as a "manufactured deviant" and his relatively carefree existence afterward

65. Ibid., p. 6.
66. Zhang Xianliang, *Wode Putishu*, p. 130.

in Hong Kong.[67] Unlike Xiang Yu, the tragic and ultimately suicidal ancient military hero whom Xiaolou had often played onstage, Xiaolou was
more than willing to escape across the waters to a safe haven (Hong Kong)
on the other side, and did not care to die for a country (PRC) that had
rejected him.[68] Appearing as little more than a site that provides inadequate food and demands hard and thankless labor in return, Xiaolou's
prison camp has no other function than to symbolize how Mao Era China
has rejected him.[69]

Some major protagonists of Gu Hua's novels, such as Qin Shutian and
Tian Faqing, also suffer terms in prison camps, but again no coherent
prison setting emerges.[70] Novels such as *Furong zhen* [Hibiscus Town]
and *Fanpanzhe* [The Rebel] instead focus on what happens before and
after the protagonist's term in a labor camp. The prison term functions
as a key reversal in the plot from which the protagonist rebounds to vindi-
cate himself as having been a worthy member of his community all along.
There is much moral irony along the way, since Qin Shutian and Tian
Faqing are both thrown into the camps for having performed virtuous
acts that only seemed punishable through the warped lens of Maoist in-
tolerance for artistic refinement and legal business practices.

The "rightist" intellectual Qin Shutian's so-called crime during the
Cultural Revolution is to have married Hu Yuyin, an upstanding, widowed tofu seller who was in political disgrace due to Maoist suppression of private commerce, even at the most basic level of a single-family
shop in a small town or village. The farm production brigade leader Tian

67. Li Bihua (Lillian Li), *Bawang bie ji* [Farewell, My Concubine] (Taipei: Huang guan
chubanshe, 1989), pp. 121–123. A more precise translation of this novel, the plot of which
differs in striking ways from the filmscript of Chen Kaige's 1993 award-winning film of the
same title, would be "The Hegemon Bids His Mistress Adieu." Sidney Greenblatt describes
much of the ferreting out of targets for criticism and denunciation during Maoist rectification campaigns as the "manufacture" and "recruitment" of deviance in "The Manufacture
of Deviance," *Deviance and Control in Chinese Society*, ed. Amy Wilson, Sidney Greenblatt,
and Richard Wilson (New York: Praeger, 1972), pp. 82–120. According to international
norms of criminality, most of these targets of rectification would be considered innocent.

68. Li Bihua, *Bawang bie ji*, p. 124.

69. Xiaolou's perception that his country had unfairly rejected him as a thought criminal resonates with the most controversial scene in Bai Hua's 1979 filmscript *Kulian* [Unre-
quited Love]. For more discussion of the 1981 political campaign against Bai Hua and his
filmscript, see Perry Link, *The Uses of Literature*, pp. 28–29; and Chapter 5 of Michael S. Duke,
Blooming and Contending: Chinese Literature in the Post-Mao Era (Bloomington: Indiana
Univ. Press, 1985).

70. Qin Shutian and his wife, Hu Yuyin, are the two major protagonists of Gu Hua's
Furong zhen [Hibiscus Town] (Beijing: Renmin wenxue chubanshe, 1981). Tian Faqing is
the protagonist of Gu Hua's *Fanpanzhe* [The Rebel] (Taipei: Yuanliu chuban shiye, 1989).

Faqing's supposed transgression in agricultural economics during the mid-1970s was to implement the production responsibility system *[bao chan dao hu]*, which became an official PRC policy in 1978–80 but was still considered an illegal and evil capitalistic practice under Mao Zedong and Hua Guofeng.[71] Neither protagonist is grateful to the authorities for having given them an early release, for they naturally resent having been wrongfully incarcerated and unfairly stuck with the label or "tail" of a "released labor-remolding criminal" *[laogai shifang fan]*.[72] Tian Faqing even asks the laogai cadre who has brought him the good news of a reduction of sentence and early release whether or not this amounts to an exoneration. The stolid farmer lets his displeasure show when the cadre laughs in his face and condescendingly replies that the exoneration policy was not designed for farmers in remote rural areas.[73] After Tian Faqing returns on foot to his village from the camp, he secretly vows that he will punch out any local man who dares use his criminal record as a handle over him—even if it means a second term in the camps.[74]

In sum, the term in a labor camp is something that Gu Hua portrays only in occasional snippets of the protagonist's memories as a spur to the search for vindication and a restoration of the ordinary social position and normal family life that the protagonist deserves. As is the case with Li Bihua, Gu Hua's novel draws upon the laogai camp as a kind of harsh reversal in the protagonist's fortunes that helps explain his motivations and actions after returning to ordinary society—but that need not be fleshed out as a setting in its own right.

Structural Features of Prison Wall Fiction

The interweaving of the narrative present with the past has emerged as a dominant structural characteristic of prison wall fiction by both Cong Weixi and Zhang Xianliang. Cong Weixi tends to begin a story with an event from the narrative present—by which time the narrator or protag-

71. See David Zweig, *Freeing China's Farmers,* pp. 12–16; and Richard Baum, *Burying Mao,* pp. 68–69. The decollectivization of PRC agriculture began in the late 1970s as a grass-roots movement that was protected by the top provincial leaders in Anhui and Sichuan, and that was finally institutionalized on a national level in the 1980s.

72. Gu Hua, *Fanpanzhe,* p. 11.

73. Ibid., p. 10.

74. Ibid., p. 64.

onist has already been released from his prison camp.[75] As the story continues, somebody or something in the narrative present serves as a trigger of memories that lead to a flashback of the past, with its grimly fas-
cinating setting of the prison camp. The trigger of past memories could
be an encounter with one of the narrator's old friends or fellow ex-
inmates; it could also arrive in the form of a question, an object such as
a letter, an image, or a landscape. For example, in Cong Weixi's 1988 novel
The Deer Looks Back [Lu hui tou], the soldier who escorts the prisoner Suo
Hongyi asks Suo about his eye, which is watering from a breeze, and
this question reminds Suo of the famine year in 1960 when his left eye
was injured.[76] It is often through the consciousness and the emotional
response of a character or narrator that the "somebody" or "something"
becomes a trigger.[77]

The story finally concludes with a return to narrative present, which
may have its own separate plot line and usually contains something in the
way of commentary or summary. This structure resembles the *"recherche"*
of a younger self and the "prose reminiscences" that Lu Xun often utilized in his May Fourth fiction during the early 1920s.[78]

Interweaving has been an important device in traditional Chinese
fictional aesthetics. A number of late imperial novelists paid much attention to achieving narrative coherence through the techniques of fore-
shadowing and echoing.[79] Occasionally, a late imperial novelist may employ flashbacks—a character's memory of a past event, for example—in
order to provide more information or a different perspective, or else to
compare or contrast the fictional present with the past.[80] Yet nowhere in

75. The "narrative present" does not literally mean the very moment the narrator is telling
the tale or writing the story, but is very close in time to when the narrative is being recounted.

76. Cong Weixi, *Lu hui tou,* p. 14. Suo Hongyi's eye injury causes his left eye to water
whenever encountering a breeze.

77. For example, the protagonist Suo Hongyi in Cong Weixi's novel *The Deer Looks Back*
and the narrator Ye Tao in Cong's novellas "White Sails Far Departed" ["Yuan qu de bai
fan"] and "Snow Falls Silently on the Yellow River" ["Xue luo Huang He jing wusheng"].
See "Yuan qu de bai fan," pp. 364–459; and "Xue luo Huang He jing wusheng," in *Xue luo
Huang He jing wusheng* (Beijing: Zhongguo wenlian chuban gongsi, 1984), pp. 1–93.

78. Leo Ou-fan Lee, *Voices from the Iron House: A Study of Lu Xun* (Bloomington: Indiana Univ. Press, 1987), pp. 64–65; and Marston Anderson, "The Morality of Form: Lu Xun
and the Modern Chinese Short Story," in *Lu Xun and His Legacy,* ed. Leo Ou-fan Lee (Berkeley: Univ. of California Press, 1985), pp. 32–53, esp. 32.

79. Yenna Wu, "Repetition in *Xingshi yinyuan zhuan," Harvard Journal of Asiatic Studies*
51.1 (June 1991): 58–59.

80. For a discussion of echoes and flashbacks in the seventeenth-century novel *Xingshi
yinyuan zhuan,* see ibid., pp. 74–76.

late imperial fiction can we find such frequent and intricate interlinking of past and present, and such long, extended flashbacks as those that pepper Cong Weixi's works. Cong Weixi has apparently learned some of these techniques from reading Euro-American and twentieth-century Chinese fiction.[81]

Short stories by Cong Weixi have generally exhibited the rather straightforward structural pattern of $present_1$-past-$present_2$. "The Seventh One Is a Mute" [Diqige shi yaba] (1980) begins with Zhang Longxi, the commissar of a laogai farm, feeling anxious and dispirited because he is aware that times have changed from the familiar old days under Mao.[82] Zhang Longxi fears that the camp inmates who are about to be exonerated might expose his misdeeds after they are released and return to society.

An old woman cadre from Beijing thereupon arrives to escort a newly exonerated "rightist" professor named Yang Ya—a pun on *yang ya*, "pretend to be mute"—back to his old university to resume his academic career. Realizing that Yang knows of Zhang's past misconduct and might report him to the authorities, Zhang Longxi grows alarmed and suffers from insomnia that night.[83] Having aroused the reader's curiosity about Zhang's insomnia, Cong Weixi then moves back eight years, to 1970, when Yang Ya entered Zhang Longxi's camp as a new prisoner.[84] Cong gives an extended chronological narrative of how Yang Ya defiantly expresses his innocence by refusing to speak for several years, during which time the avaricious Zhang mistreats this apparent mute in various ways.[85]

After informing the reader of the reason for Zhang's sleeplessness, Cong Weixi brings the story back to the fictional present: Zhang Longxi has prepared a going-away feast for Yang Ya and the woman cadre in a fake and ostentatious display of goodwill. Zhang learns from the cadre that Yang was actually just pretending to be mute all those years in the camp in order to express his "utmost contempt" for those who had wrong-

---

81. Cong Weixi mentions some of the Euro-American literary works that influenced his fiction in "Xiaoshuo shi xingxiang siwei de yishu" [Fiction Is the Art of Imagery and Thought], *Beijing wenxue* 11 (1983): 52–53.

82. See Cong Weixi, "Diqige shi yaba," pp. 80–100.

83. Ibid., pp. 80–83.

84. Cong Weixi may have gotten his chronology somewhat mixed up in this story. Cong mentions that Yang Ya entered the camp in 1970 (p. 84) and behaved like a mute for six years (p. 100). Yet later on p. 100, Cong also mentions the return of the previous commissar due to the decision made at The Third Plenum of the Eleventh Central Committee [Sanzhong quanhui], which took place in December 1978.

85. Cong Weixi, "Diqige shi yaba," pp. 84–96.

fully imprisoned him. Yang subsequently arrives at the banquet wearing his prison uniform, which is soiled with human excrement from the camp privies that Zhang has regularly made him empty for fertilizer. The dwarfish Zhang Longxi hurries to extend his hand in an attempt to shake hands with Yang Ya in a hypocritical show of friendliness. Instead of extending his hand, the tall inmate professor raises his mud-smeared right foot to the same height as Zhang's extended right hand. Zhang is speechless and does not know how to respond to this public humiliation. Yang Ya uncorks his long-suppressed fury with some stentorian farewell comments: "Do you feel that this foot is an insult to you?! It may be smeared with mud, but it is cleaner than every single part of your soul! Do you understand, Commissar Zhang?!"[86] In addition to Yang's venting of anger and disgust, Cong Weixi concludes the story with Zhang Longxi's ouster from the laogai camp administration and his replacement by a far more trustworthy commissar who had been wrongly dismissed during the Cultural Revolution. The temporal interweaving of present$_1$-past-present$_2$ also provides a pattern of result$_1$-cause-result$_2$. The past is not simply in a static juxtaposition with the present, but serves dynamically as an explanation of result$_1$ and a catalyst for result$_2$. This tightly structured story thus achieves poetic justice and effectively creates a dramatic climax.

In a novella or novel, Cong Weixi often performs several shifts between narrative present and past before concluding the work in the narrative present. A sort of prelude that is set in the narrative present establishes the tone at the beginning of the novel, while a finale in the narrative present provides a reasonable resolution or otherwise satisfies the reader's curiosity. This structure could be schematized in the following way: prelude-present$_1$-past$_1$-present$_2$-past$_2$-present$_3$-past$_3$-present$_4$-past$_4$-present$_5$-ending. Cong Weixi either numbers each block of present-past narratives or provides a section heading for each one.[87] One critic has characterized the typical structure of Cong Weixi's fictional narrative as a "fishing-net structure" [tuowang shi jiegou]. According to this model, the narration of the present events is the head rope of the fishing net, and the memory of the past forms the net's meshes; the author cuts up the past in temporal order and hangs up each piece on the separate links to the present.[88] Were

86. Ibid., pp. 97–100, esp. 100.

87. For example, Cong Weixi uses numbers to section off the different blocks of narratives in his novella "Footprints Left on the Seashore" [Yiluo zai haitan de jiaoyin] (1980) and his novel Lu hui tou. See "Yiluo zai haitan de jiaoyin," in Cong Weixi daibiaozuo, pp. 241–363.

88. Zhang Zaixuan, "Tiaochu laotao, keyi qiuxin," cited in Li Qian, Teding shiqi de da qiang wenxue, p. 183.

the reader to extract all the short pieces of the narrative present, she would find that they progress slowly in time to form a relatively short but complete episode. The episodes of the narrative past may also be extracted to form a fairly chronological and almost unified story.[89] In general, the episodes of the "past" are much longer than the pieces of the "present," and constitute the bulk of the overall story.

Cong's novella "Snow Falls Silently on the Yellow River" [Xue luo Huang He jing wusheng] (1983) begins with a letter written to the participant-narrator Ye Tao by his ex-inmate friend Fan Hanru. The letter prompts Ye Tao to embark on a westward train to visit Fan at a small town near the Yellow River. While en route in the train, Ye gazes intently at the chicken feather that Fan had enclosed in the envelope. The feather triggers Ye's distant memory of the time when he first made Fan's acquaintance, on a train that was conveying both of the "rightists" to a prison camp for reeducation through labor.[90] The stubbornly patriotic and upright Fan has been working as his labor camp's sole chicken farmer, and one night is rewarded for his hard work with the bonanza of fourteen eggs. He wakes Ye up at midnight to share a feast of boiled eggs with him, and urges Ye to remember their meal together.[91] Recalling this part of the past, Ye now understands why Fan has enclosed the feather in his letter.

In the second segment of the "present," the landscape outside the train window serves as the trigger to another episode from the past. Ye Tao sees that the smoke from his train seems to be embracing the clouds, and reflects on the way similar objects in nature tend to commingle. Then he wonders why Fan Hanru and his longtime girlfriend Tao Yingying have not yet gotten married, considering all the hardships they have weathered together.[92] Through the narrator's sight of an image in nature, his reflection on it, and the memory evoked by it, Cong Weixi takes his reader back to the story of how Fan initially became acquainted with and interested in Tao.[93]

Cong Weixi's emphasis shifts from visual to aural stimuli in the third stage of the "present." Late at night, the narrator is kept awake by other passengers' loud snoring. Yet he insists that the primary reason he cannot sleep is his preoccupation with Tao Yingying, who has made a very

89. See also the discussion in Li Qian, *Teding shiqi de da qiang wenxue*, p. 184.
90. Cong Weixi, "Xue luo Huang He jing wusheng," pp. 1–3.
91. Ibid., pp. 4–11.
92. Ibid., p. 12.
93. Ibid., pp. 12–25.

deep impression upon him. He then continues to remember how Fan and Tao fell in love with each other.[94] The narrator subsequently relates the various tribulations suffered by Fan and Tao, as well as the final release of Ye and Fan from the prison camp, by repeating several more times the pattern of a present sight or sound reminding him of related past events.

In the last part of the novella, as the narrator's train (in the narrative present) approaches the town, he remembers leaving the small town three years ago.[95] Ye Tao recalls how Fan had told him about the end of his love affair: Tao Yingying finally confessed to Fan why the government had imprisoned her—she had supposedly betrayed China when attempting to flee by swimming across a river at the PRC's border with another country. Because she knew how solemnly patriotic Fan was, she felt so ashamed about her past that she would not dare marry him—even though she was now a retained ex-inmate medical worker at the camp, and thus free to marry.[96] In the end, Ye finds Tao's farewell letter in Fan's dormitory room—Tao has requested a transfer and is preparing to move to another camp.

It may seem that Cong Weixi appears to simply mix and match various truncated episodes in the narrative present with those of the narrative past, but the structure of his fiction is far from merely mechanical. He takes pains in varying the circumstances surrounding the main character's retrieval of memories so as to arrange contrasting points of departure. Cong Weixi is also very careful in handling the focal level of his fiction.[97] He either has a relatively omniscient narrator narrating consistently through a protagonist's focus, or he uses a first-person participant-narrator as the major focalizer.[98] His frequent use of a first-person participant-narrator is especially effective in leading the narrative to unfold and cohere organically. By having his participant-narrator access memories by reflecting on something he sees or hears, Cong makes smooth transitions to his narration of episodes in the past.

94. Ibid., pp. 25–40.

95. Ibid., p. 84.

96. Ibid., pp. 84–90.

97. See Gérard Genette, *Figures III* (Paris: Éditions du Seuil, 1972), pp. 203–211; and Hanan, *The Chinese Vernacular Story*, p. 17.

98. The term "focalizer" refers to the character who sees and reflects on what he sees. For example, the narrator in Cong Weixi's 1980 novella "Footprints Left on the Seashore" narrates primarily through the observations of the protagonist Lu Buqing. By contrast, Cong's novella "Baiyun piaoluo tianmu" (1983) uses a first-person participant-narrator. See "Yiluo zai haitan de jiaoyin" and "Baiyun piaoluo tianmu" [White Clouds Descending from Heaven], in *Cong Weixi daibiaozuo*, pp. 241–363 and 460–546, respectively.

The structure of two interwoven narrative lines proves advantageous vis-à-vis linear chronological narration, particularly in a story in which memories of long-past events loom so large in importance. Instead of telling a story about the prison camp in a dry, straightforward manner, this structure allows the author to complicate the plot, along with making the story more suspenseful and intriguing. It is perhaps natural for Cong Weixi to have chosen this kind of structure, since he has written virtually all of his laogai-based fiction only *after* his release and exoneration—and thus in retrospect. Cong Weixi also mentions that he adopted first-person narration for his novella "White Sails Far Departed" not because he "deliberately chose a certain technique," but "entirely because of the natural revelation of his true feelings." Once he started writing the novella, he could not stop, because "he was too familiar with these characters he was describing."[99] Because of the combined use of retrospection and first-person participant-narration, his fiction reads a bit like autobiography, and the narrator seems to be closely identified with the author at times. Indeed, even Cong Weixi concurs that "White Sails Far Departed" has the flavor of an "autobiographical novel."[100]

Of course, the author is not likely to have experienced everything described in the story, and probably has simply drawn inspiration from the people and events he observed or heard about during his imprisonment. He has certainly altered some of the phenomena that he actually witnessed or heard of during his imprisonment in order to design fictional incidents that fit the plot in accord with his artistic purposes and tenor of thought.[101] Yet the use of a first-person participant-narrator—especially a narrator who seems so familiar with the other characters—contributes to the sense of authenticity in the story, making the work seem rooted in firsthand observation and personal experience. The fact that Cong Weixi gives the first-person participant-narrator in many works the same name, Ye Tao, further underscores the apparent authenticity of the story and the resemblance between the author and his narrative persona.[102]

99. Cong Weixi, "Guanyu 'Yuanqu de baifan'" [About "White Sails Far Departed"], in *Cong Weixi yanjiu zhuanji*, p. 65.

100. Cong Weixi, "Wenxue de meng—da Yanhuo," p. 76.

101. See, for example, Cong Weixi's admission about his alteration of events in "Guanyu 'Yuanqu de baifan,'" pp. 65–66.

102. See Cong's "Yuan qu de bai fan" (written in 1975, published in 1983), "Xian gei yisheng de meiguihua" [Roses in Dedication to a Doctor] (1979), "Yiluo zai haitan de jiaoyin" (1980), "Ranshao de jiyi" [Blazing Memories] (1981), "Meiyou jia'niang de hunli" [A Wedding without the Bride] (1981), "Xue luo Huang He jing wusheng" (1983), "Baiyun piaoluo tianmu" (1983), and *Duan qiao* (1984).

Zhang Xianliang adopts a similar structural approach in certain prison camp novels such as *Tu lao qinghua* [Passionate Words from a Village Prison] (1980), where a sudden and unexpected reencounter with a former female prison guard in a railway station triggers the participant-narrator's memories of events in his prison camp from more than a decade earlier. These troubled memories of the past form the bulk of the novel, while the return to the narrative present occurs only in the dénouement, located in the novel's final few pages.[103] In somewhat later works of prison wall fiction such as *Lühuashu* [Mimosa] and *Nanren de yiban shi nüren* [Half of Man Is Woman],[104] Zhang Xianliang begins with a preface in the narrative present and then shifts abruptly to the past, using a relatively naïve narrative perspective of a young prison camp inmate.[105] Each novel concludes with a return to the narrative present and the perspective of a more adequate and mature narrator.[106]

In writing his 1980 story "Body and Soul" [Ling yu rou],[107] Zhang Xianliang avoided an overly straightforward mode of narration, which would have seemed "dull, flat, and monotonous," yet he hesitated in adopting Western-style stream of consciousness—which was "not yet suited to the majority of our [Chinese] readers." He finally decided to try out a fresh narrative technique: "Chinese-style stream of consciousness combined with Chinese-style collage or patchwork illustration *[pintie hua]*. That is to say, the flowing stream of consciousness would have to take the form of narrative incidents, and there would have to be threads of plot stretching across the interstices between the various patches of the patchwork illustration."[108]

"Body and Soul" begins in the fictional present. As the protagonist Xu Lingjun proceeds to go out with his wealthy father and the old man's secretary to a nightclub, words and images of the present time remind Xu

103. Zhang Xianliang, *Tu lao qinghua*, pp. 3–89, esp. 4–8, 85–89.

104. Zhang Xianliang, *Nanren de yiban shi nüren*, pp. 400–402, 618.

105. See Yenna Wu, "The Interweaving of Sex and Politics in Zhang Xianliang's *Half of Man Is Woman*," *Journal of the Chinese Language Teachers Association* 27:1/2 (1992): 1–27, esp. 7–9.

106. Zhang Xianliang, *Lü hua shu* and *Nanren de yiban shi nüren*, in *Zhang Xianliang xuanji*, vol. 3, pp. 161–338, 399–618, esp. 162, 334–338, 400–401, 618.

107. Zhang Xianliang, "Ling yu rou," in *Zhang Xianliang xuanji*, vol. 1, pp. 138–165. Translated by Philip F. C. Williams as "Body and Soul," in *Prize-Winning Stories from China, 1980–1981*, ed. W. C. Chau (Beijing: Foreign Languages Press, 1985), pp. 58–92.

108. Zhang Xianliang, "Xinling he routi de bianhua" [The Transformation of Mind and Body], in *Zhang Xianliang xuanji*, vol. 1, p. 200. On p. 196, Zhang mentions that in his youth he was very much influenced by Euro-American literature.

of his past, especially his life with his wife and daughter. The line of the past is woven into the line of the present until near the end of the story, when Xu decides not to go abroad to help run his father's lucrative business, instead returning to his familiar home in a small village.

Zhang Xianliang's *Half of Man Is Woman* employs stream of consciousness and nonchalant fantasy in the scene where the protagonist, Zhang Yonglin, discusses politics with the horse he is tending, as well as in the various lengthy conversations Zhang has with such historical figures as Song Jiang, Zhuang Zi, and Karl Marx.[109] Yet it is in *Getting Used to Dying* where Zhang Xianliang plunges most fully into fragmented stream-of-consciousness narration, as well as making a more daring experiment with a narrative based on "patchwork illustration." As previously demonstrated, Cong Weixi carefully splices together snippets of episodes in such a way that the ordinary reader can easily follow the two interwoven lines of the present and the past. In contrast, Zhang Xianliang appears to have ventured beyond his early determination to cater to the tastes of the majority of Chinese readers when writing *Getting Used to Dying*. The work still consists of interwoven strands of the present and the past, but the snippets of the present and the past are patched together much more arbitrarily. Moreover, the later novel's points of transition between present and past are considerably more abrupt than what one finds in Cong Weixi's works or any of Zhang Xianliang's previous works. Readers may not always be able to splice the plot strands back together with ease, though they may be able to understand and respond to individual episodes.[110]

Zhang Xianliang's depiction of the first-person participant-narrator's "post-laogai syndrome" *[laogai houyi zheng]* is especially compelling.[111] For instance, he cannot readily readjust to the outside society, which has changed so much during the two decades of his imprisonment. Moreover, in line with the classic symptoms of post-traumatic stress disorder (PTSD), fearful memories of witnessing death in the camps frequently accost him unexpectedly, and he gropes unsuccessfully to communicate his feelings about the past to those who have never endured the laogai.

---

109. See Zhang Xianliang, *Nanren de yiban shi nüren*, pp. 510–516, 529–537.

110. The translator of this novel has changed the numbering of the chapters and added a title to each chapter in order to provide guidance to the reader. See Zhang Xianliang, *Getting Used to Dying*, trans. Martha Avery (New York: Harper Collins, 1991).

111. For a fine portrayal of an ex-inmate who suffers from post-laogai syndrome, see also Cong Weixi, "Linjie de chuang" [The Window Facing the Street], in *Cong Weixi daibiaozuo*, pp. 144–169.

Cathy Caruth discusses the "literality" and recurring nature of traumatic memories (such as Zhang's), and recognizes their resistance to interpretation by old Freudian theories of "unconscious repression." As one of the unfalsifiable hypotheses that are legion in Freudianism, the notion of "unconscious repression" is at odds with everything that experimental psychologists know about traumatic memories and PTSD. Harold Bloom rightly approaches Freud as a "mythologist," for "speculation, rather than theory, is Freud's mode."[112]

Zhang Xianliang's late-1990s story "Unable to Awaken" [Wufa suxing] continues to address memories of death in the camps and the ex-inmate's post-laogai syndrome, as in Getting Used to Dying, again employing the technique of stream of consciousness and juxtaposing present and past events.[113] Though similarly challenging, this story presents the reader with fewer puzzling conundrums than Getting Used to Dying, since the targets of its satire are quite clear-cut.

The Romantic Laogai Camp

Among novels and stories with a prominent prison camp setting, some take considerable poetic license in the introduction of a love interest. Given that many retained ex-inmate workers have in fact married or had extramarital sexual relations on the outskirts of the camp where they have been formerly imprisoned, this is not an altogether implausible scenario. However, when prison camp novelists arrange for an inmate protagonist to win the amorous attentions of an endearing woman connected with the prison administration, they have embraced the literary convention of "the romantic prison"[114] and turned aside from the ordinary labor camp routines highlighted in Solzhenitsyn's masterpiece One Day in the Life of Ivan

112. See Caruth's introduction to Trauma: Explorations in Memory, pp. 4–6; and Harold Bloom, "Freud: Frontier Concepts, Jewishness, and Interpretation," in Trauma: Explorations in Memory, pp. 113–127, esp. 113.

113. Zhang Xianliang, "Wufa suxing" [Unable to Awaken], in Xinhua wenzhai, no. 1 (1996): 75–86.

114. See Victor Brombert, The Romantic Prison: The French Tradition (Princeton: Princeton Univ. Press, 1978); Tomas Venclova, "Prison as a Communicative Phenomenon: The Literature of Gulag," Comparative Civilizations Review 2 (1979): 65–73; Hugh McClean, "Walls and Wire: Some Notes on the Prison Theme in Russian Literature," International Journal of Slavic Linguistics and Poetics 25–26 (1982): 253–265; Kinkley, "A Bettelheimian Interpretation," 83–113, esp. 106; and Yenna Wu, "Women as Sources of Redemption in Chang Hsien-liang's Camp Fiction," Asia Major 4.2 (1991): 115–131.

Denisovich.[115] What Victor Brombert and some other scholars of Western literature call "the romantic prison" is a literary, nonhistorical scenario representing the triumph of the unfairly ostracized protagonist over the sociopolitical forces that have consigned him to the lowest depths of society among common criminals.[116]

In order to overcome the natural apathy and disdain of the object of his love—the woman at the opposite end of the prison hierarchy—the inmate protagonist must prove his basic decency and desirability through tangible means. This sort of protagonist within "the romantic prison" has established his personal worth under much more trying circumstances than the societal norm and thus tends to garner the reader's sympathy and even admiration. Such an inmate hero usually refrains from taking advantage of his erotic opportunities, but the mere fact of his access to a willing sexual partner from the elite represents a victory over the prison regimen, with its rule of celibacy and its generally dehumanizing treatment of inmates.[117]

Laogai fiction of the post–Mao Era has made up for the premodern Chinese novel's lack of male inmate characters who invert the prison hierarchy in this way.[118] PRC writers who have utilized the romantic prison

115. Cong Weixi has dismissed Solzhenitsyn for his supposedly unrestrained ire and negativity in *The Gulag Archipelago* and *Cancer Ward*, but obviously would not be able to make the same claim about *One Day in the Life of Ivan Denisovich*. To our knowledge, neither Cong Weixi nor Zhang Xianliang has mentioned the latter novel.

116. In *The Romantic Prison,* Brombert specifically mentions the common motif of "love at a distance (often for the jailer's daughter)," pp. 9, 76–77. The political dissidents and former prison camp inmates Wang Xizhe (PRC) and Doan Viet Hoat (Vietnam) have maintained that one of the most demeaning aspects of prison life for intellectuals is being confined with poorly educated common criminals. See Wang Xizhe, "Wang Xizhe," and Doan Viet Hoat, "Political Prisoners in Vietnam," in *Voices from the Laogai,* pp. 72–74, esp. 73, and 140–142, esp. 140.

117. As Hugh McClean points out, the topos of "the male prisoner being succored by an attractive female from the imprisoning camp" surfaced repeatedly not only in major written works such as Pushkin's *The Prisoner of the Caucasus,* but also in oral accounts such as Prince Vladimir of Kiev's imprisoning of the noble hero Il'ja Muromec. Muromec enjoyed visits and gifts of food from none other than the prince's own daughter. See "Walls and Wire," pp. 256–257. This literary motif might not seem related to the grim reality of imprisonment, but one fairly reliable eyewitness account reports a mid-1970s sexual tryst between a special duty prisoner and a prison guard's wife in the giant prison camp complex of Chadian (Qinghe) in Hebei province. See Liu Zongren, *Hard Time,* pp. 207–208.

118. We have not come across any examples of love spanning the prison hierarchy in a "romantic prison" in premodern Chinese fiction. Nor have we seen any such examples in prominent fictional works from the Republican Era, though it is likely, in view of the strong foreign influence at that time, that some lesser-known works from that period broach this theme.

topos include both middlebrow writers and serious novelists. The most prolific of these writers of the romantic prison is Cong Weixi. In *The Deer Looks Back*, Cong Weixi creates a love interest between the veteran "rightist" prisoner Suo Hongyi and an attractive but impoverished *mangliu* [migrant rover] woman named Li Cuicui.[119] They meet when he is working at a lime kiln, presumably outside the camp's walls. As they become closer friends, Cuicui goes so far as to offer him sex, but he demurs out of a desire to keep their relationship platonic and due to his fear of entangling her in his political troubles.

Their close friendship continues, nevertheless, even after Cuicui manages to receive a marriage proposal from Hongyi's prison camp warden, Section Chief Zheng Kunshan. After her marriage to Zheng, Cuicui continues to make secret visits to the lime kiln to slip Hongyi food to supplement his meager rations.[120] Cuicui also assures Hongyi that if Zheng Kunshan keeps on "remolding" the prisoners so heavy-handedly, she will use her position as wife to "remold" Zheng in turn.[121] Under his wife's influence, Zheng indeed lightens his regimen of discipline over the prisoners.

With Zheng's approval, Hongyi's supposed crime is watered down to the point at which he can change his status from prisoner to retained ex-inmate worker and live on the outskirts of the prison camp. He has long disagreed with Cuicui's advice to escape from the prison camp, but when the outbreak of the Cultural Revolution in 1966 threatens to reverse Hongyi's improved status as a jiuye worker, he finally accepts her counsel and flees from the camp. Even though the couple never physically consummate their love, Li Cuicui and Suo Hongyi have inverted the process of remolding, for this warden's wife has reserved most of her emotional attachment *[ganqing]* for a mere inmate, thus confounding the hierarchical norms of their prison society.

If the warden's wife does not offer her affections to the male inmate protagonist in this kind of romantic prison novel, then the next most likely candidate is the warden's daughter. This is the scenario of the 1988 story "Xue ji" [Blood Sacrifice], by the middlebrow crime writer Liang Peimin.[122] A handsome, youthful, and unmarried mining engineer named

119. Cong Weixi, *Lu hui tou.*

120. Cuicui's visits to Hongyi must remain clandestine, for when Zheng Kunshan was first married to her, he would sometimes compare counterrevolutionaries in the labor camp to snakes and criticize them for being untrustworthy. His outlook only gradually becomes more moderate. See, for example, *Lu hui tou,* pp. 48–49.

121. Ibid., p. 49.

122. Liang Peimin, "Xue ji" [Blood Sacrifice], *Zhongguo fazhi wenxue* [Chinese Rule-of-Law Literature] 6 (1988): 85–93.

Heihu is sentenced to the laogai for five years for having punched a corrupt cadre who had hurled obscenities at him. Because of often skimpy state subsidies during the Deng-Jiang Era, laogai wardens have needed to make their camp enterprise operations as cost-effective as possible. The warden in charge of Heihu's camp mine, Liu Feng, is thus happy to be presented with a talented young specialist in engineering. As might have been hoped, Heihu's advanced training and youthful vigor enable him to discover many new mineral veins in the mine. Warden Liu Feng thus wins recognition and praise from his superiors for his prison enterprise's considerable growth in production.

Unfortunately, the warden cannot find anyone among the nonconvict mine workers who is both willing and able to serve as Heihu's apprentice. Liu Feng thus faces the likely prospect of production declining once Heihu's five-year term has been completed. In desperation, the warden tells his own twenty-year-old daughter, Liu Lu, to serve as Heihu's apprentice for the sake of learning some of the young engineer's prospecting skills. Liu Lu at first objects to the idea of working alongside a mere prisoner, but her father manages to gain her acquiescence by stressing that even hardened criminals can be remolded into solid citizens through the hard work and considerate guidance that he has provided to them in the camp.

Though Heihu attempts to maintain a businesslike decorum in his work alongside Liu Lu, over time a friendship with overtones of intimacy begins to develop between them, especially after Heihu risks his life to grapple with a would-be rapist who assaults Liu Lu inside the mine. After she discovers that Heihu's crime amounted to no more than losing his temper on one occasion with an abusive and corrupt local cadre, her feelings of attraction to the young engineer grow stronger.

Liu Lu secretly decides to marry Heihu after his release from the mining labor camp, and continually asks her father whether or not it is the CCP's policy to reduce the sentences of prisoners like Heihu who have outstanding achievements on the production front. Liu Feng agrees with his daughter and processes all the sentence-reduction paperwork. Yet on the very day that Liu Feng receives the higher-ups' approval of Heihu's one-year sentence reduction, the older man overhears a private conversation between the two young people in which his daughter broaches the possibility of marrying Heihu after his release from prison. The warden furiously orders his daughter to accompany him out of the mine, and proceeds to tear up Heihu's one-year reprieve notification letter in front of her eyes. When Liu Lu throws the original arguments he had made to her about the dignity of remolded prisoners back in her father's face, the old warden merely reiterates his pronouncement that no daughter of his is going to marry a lousy ex-convict.

"Blood Sacrifice" ends on a melodramatic note, with Heihu sacrificing his own life to save Liu Lu during a subsequent cave-in in the mine shaft. The prison authorities then falsely report that Heihu died as he was attempting to rape Liu Lu, who was still recovering from exposure and dehydration in the local hospital. Yet just as Heihu's corpse is being perfunctorily lowered into an unmarked grave, Liu Lu appears on the scene to restore Heihu's good name by informing the bystanders of the genuine facts about his self-sacrifice.

In this story, the emotional attachment of the warden's female relative for the inmate protagonist fails to influence, much less transform, the warden, in contrast with the case in Cong Weixi's *The Deer Looks Back*. The very thought of having an ex-inmate as a son-in-law is enough to goad Warden Liu Feng into "flying into a rage based on feelings of shame" *[xiu er cheng nu]*. His position as a patriarch *[jiazhang]* with almost unlimited authority allows him to dispense with the bureaucratic routinization that emphasizes playing by the codified rules, especially when he impulsively rips to shreds the document approving Heihu's early release. The broad discretion enjoyed by laogai cadres in lengthening or shortening prison terms finds dramatic expression here—and in this particular aspect of the story's scenario, the portrayal is not hyperbolic or far-fetched.

A more complicated unfolding of the romantic prison motif occurs in Zhang Xianliang's 1980 novel *Passionate Words from a Village Prison*.[123] The plot features an unlikely but dramatic triangular relationship between a male prisoner, a female guard, and the camp authorities, as represented by both the male warden and a male guard. To be sure, female PRC prison guards are normally used only to supervise women inmates, though Zhang Xianliang recalls having encountered one gun-toting female guard during the Cultural Revolution.[124] In the backwoods prison camp depicted in this novel, the camp authorities bend the rules in order to employ one

123. Zhang Xianliang, *Tu lao qinghua*, pp. 3–89. Although no English translation has yet appeared, there is a translation into Japanese under the same title by Ôsato Hiroaki (Tokyo: Nihon Ajia Bungaku Kyôkai, 1993), pp. 109–270.

124. Zhang Xianliang, *Xie xiaoshuo de bianzhengfa* [The Dialectics of Writing Fiction] (Shanghai: Shanghai wenyi chubanshe, 1987), p. 74. The female guard in Zhang's male brigade was in the military, which during the late 1960s and early 1970s had taken over various governmental functions from the partially decimated bureaucracy. Zhang indicates that a Soviet Russian movie entitled *The Forty-First* contains a plot similar to that of *Tu lao qinghua*, though he had not seen that movie before writing this novel.

of the unmarried young female relatives of an associate of the warden, Liu Jun.[125] The attractive peasant guard Qiao Anping is assigned to supervise the protagonist and other male prisoners, as there are no women inmates in the camp.

The educated and handsome young inmate protagonist Shi Zai and his cell mates fear that Warden Liu Jun will continue to torture fellow inmates to death, as he has just murdered an imprisoned official under torture, reporting appendicitis as the cause of death. Shi Zai decides to join his fellow inmate Old Qin's scheme to send a letter exposing the truth to the murdered official's widow, Wang Yufang, in the hope that she will press the case with higher officials and get the entire barracks of inmates transferred to a different camp. The problem is how to send out such a dangerous letter, since all mail is opened and read carefully by the camp administration before being delivered. At Old Qin's behest, Shi Zai uses Qiao Anping's attraction to him as a way to persuade her to smuggle the letter out, falsely claiming that the widow Wang Yufang is his aunt. Qiao Anping also plans to steal the male guard Wang Fuhai's keys in order to let Shi Zai escape from prison, so he can elope with her. Yet before either the prison transfer or the planned escape can take place, a routine interrogation of Shi Zai by Warden Liu Jun and a visiting official plunges Shi Zai into a state of panic.

Instead of bearing up under interrogation, the easily intimidated Shi Zai cravenly gives in almost at once and confesses even before a hand is laid upon him. What is worse, he implicates Qiao Anping as the conduit for the letter he smuggled out. More seriously, Shi Zai reveals the scheme involving Qiao Anping's planned theft of Wang Fuhai's keys and her scheme to help him escape. The ruthless warden angrily punishes Qiao Anping by raping her after he catches her in the act of stealing the keys, and later on forces Qiao into a very unhappy marriage with the uncouth drunk of a guard Wang Fuhai. Some weeks later, Qiao Anping sends a letter to Shi Zai indicating that she does not believe the rumors that he was the one who implicated her. Yet Shi Zai does not have the integrity to apologize to her or even to admit that he in fact implicated her.

In an unusual departure from this literary mode's standard portrayal of the inmate protagonist as a sympathetic figure, Zhang Xianliang creates a pathetic anti-hero in Shi Zai, whose unprincipled use of Qiao Anping as a tool for political intrigue mirrors the CCP cadres' use of Shi Zai as a convenient object of class struggle. Unlike Suo Hongyi and Heihu,

125. Zhang Xianliang, *Tu lao qinghua,* p. 34.

in *The Deer Looks Back* and "Blood Sacrifice," respectively, Shi Zai seems to have lowered his ethical standards to the level of the worst camp cadres in his midst—an understandable if regrettable turn of affairs, considering the wretched conditions of his imprisonment. Because he is a philosophical materialist, there is no god or goddess from whom Shi Zai can beg forgiveness at the conclusion of the novel. Yet when he substitutes the term "people" *[renmin]* for the term "God" *[Shangdi]* in the standard phrase, "God help me" ("People help me"), one senses that his remorse is shallow and insincere.[126]

Zhang Xianliang has thus transformed a romantic topos of regeneration and renewal into an anti-romantic theme of moral degradation and self-deceiving illusions, thereby undercutting the supposed moral superiority of the wrongfully incarcerated protagonist. The incarcerated victim can all too easily strike a bargain with the prison chief—in this case, at the expense of a guileless and vulnerable woman connected with the camp administration. A hardened or "remolded" prisoner like Shi Zai finds it easier to betray this woman's confidence than to face even the possibility of suffering a beating or some other torture. Unlike the romantic heroism that many of Cong Weixi's inmate protagonists exude, Zhang Xianliang's inmate anti-heroes such as Shi Zai often manifest the sort of craven shiftiness and irresponsibility that is a common result of long-term abuse in the worst labor camps.

However, laogai fiction writers typically offer a less grim variation of the romantic prison motif. The warden's daughter in "Blood Sacrifice" actually practices the ideals that her father had merely preached about maintaining respect for camp inmates as fellow human beings capable of virtuous conduct. Cong Weixi's *The Deer Looks Back* also presents the scenario of a female relative of a prison warden risking her reputation and social status out of love for a decent male inmate. Although Li Cuicui is far more successful than Liu Lu in her intervention on behalf of her favored prisoner, both works' evocation of the romantic prison reveal that by the last decades of the twentieth century, this European motif had been integrated into Chinese literature. Ironically, the walled-off world of China's labor camps—which by the twenty-first century seems such an anomaly in an age of instantaneous worldwide communication and a global network of market-based mixed economies—has provided the setting for fiction that has reduced the distance between Chinese and Western literary traditions.

126. Ibid., p. 89.

Conclusion

Since the early 1990s, many Chinese ultra-nationalists, both inside and outside the PRC government, have developed an increasingly heated and one-sided discourse of Chinese victimization at the hands of various foreign powers, who in the state-controlled press become easy scapegoats for predominantly internal Chinese problems. To be sure, there is an inglorious history of Western and Japanese imperialist acts in China that span from the 1830s to the 1940s. Still, to react to international criticism of China's human rights record by focusing almost exclusively on the negative aspects of foreign powers' interactions with China since the 1830s may betray an unbalanced and somewhat chauvinistic approach to cross-cultural relations.

Although China suffered a high death toll from its various border wars since 1949 and especially the Japanese military invasion of 1937–45, even these figures are dwarfed by the number of Chinese people who have died as a direct result of internal governmental policies and actions. Jean-Louis Margolin has provided a moderate estimate of the number of PRC deaths directly resulting from PRC governmental actions: 6 to 10 million.[1] Margolin's figure includes hundreds of thousands of Tibetan deaths, but excludes the late-1940s civil war, the multitudes who died in prisons and labor camps, and the approximately 30 million deaths from the Great Leap Forward famine. Margolin's figures resonate with those of R. J. Rummel, a demographer who has ranked the regimes of both Mao

1. Margolin, "China: A Long Journey into Night," p. 463.

Zedong and Chiang Kai-shek among the world's four most lethal in the twentieth century.[2]

Yet in order to gloss over the severely tarnished history of over a half century of CCP rule, since the early 1990s the PRC's state-controlled press has been required to maintain an embarrassed silence during the anniversaries of internal CCP-driven disasters such as the Cultural Revolution and the Great Leap Forward famine. Instead, the government has resoundingly commemorated the anniversaries of earlier instances of foreign invasion—especially that of the early Showa Era Japanese military.[3]

Tensions between China and its neighbors have naturally heightened in the wake of such developments as the increasingly outspoken PRC depiction of China as an eternally innocent and aggrieved victim on the one hand, and its anachronistic caricature of the contemporary Japanese as early Showa Era militarists, on the other.[4] This pattern of rhetorical xenophobia has combined with a more aggressive military stance vis-à-vis China's neighbors to create a higher level of anxiety about security in the Western Pacific region than was generally the case during the Deng Era.[5] An examination of the PRC's prison camp system serves as a telling reminder that a significant number of China's worst scourges over the past century were largely self-inflicted ones—as has been the case with most of the world's nations, including the other major powers.[6]

2. Rummel, *Death by Government,* p. 105. Though Rummel's figure of 15 million deaths in CCP-run labor camps appears to be too high, it amounts to less than half of the likely death toll of the Soviet gulag. Even if Rummel's figures were significantly reduced, they would still amount to more than the number of Chinese deaths from the Japanese military's invasion of China during the 1930s and 1940s. Shalom's estimates are considerably lower in *Deaths in China Due to Communism: Propaganda versus Reality.* Shalom's work can be considered more objective than his chief object of criticism, Richard L. Walker, *The Human Cost of Communism in China* (Senate Committee on the Judiciary, Internal Security Committee, See 92nd Congress, 1st session, 1971). However, some of Shalom's estimates have proven to be far too low, such as his estimate of 5.5 million deaths in the Great Leap Forward famine (pp. 57, 61)—this undershoots the actual death toll by a factor of five or six. Moreover, Shalom's categorical denial of common criminals' brutalizing of political prisoners in the Chinese laogai is demonstrably false (p. 104). One source for Shalom's categorical judgments about the relations between ordinary criminal inmates and political prisoners is Whyte, "Corrective Labor Camps in China," 253–269, esp. 261–262.

3. Edward Friedman, "Preventing War between China and Japan," *What if China Doesn't Democratize? Implications for War and Peace,* ed. Edward Friedman & Barrett L. McCormick (Armonk, NY: M. E. Sharpe, 2000), pp. 114–115; Williams, "Chinese Cannibalism's Literary Portrayal," p. 423.

4. Friedman, "Preventing War between China and Japan," pp. 104, 125 n.21.

5. See also Geremie Barmé, *In the Red,* pp. 255–280.

6. Poland and Tibet are obvious exceptions, but this observation would apply to major powers such as the United States, Russia, Japan, and Britain.

In light of the impressive expansion of the Chinese people's social and economic freedoms since the death of Mao Zedong, it might seem that the PRC criminal justice and prison systems are bound to move much closer to international norms as well. Such a view could be reinforced by the impressive rollback of the jiuye job placement system since 1980, along with some provincial leaders' downsizing of their laogai systems, as in Qinghai province. By 1994, the PRC government had enacted tougher laws against the beating and torture of prison inmates, and even formally discarded the term "laogai" in favor of *jianyu* [prison]. Before long, many of the most famous and determined political dissidents such as Wei Jing-sheng were at last released from prison and allowed to make a one-way "trip abroad for medical treatment" *[baowai jiuyi]*. Finally, the vast majority of laogai prisoners can be classified as ordinary criminal convicts rather than political prisoners, causing the Deng-Jiang Era's prisons and labor camps to look more "normal" by international standards than their Mao Era counterparts.[7]

Yet there are a number of reasons for skepticism about such a sanguine assessment. While Taiwan's impressive advances in democracy have proven that the strongly authoritarian aspects within China's cultural inheritance can be overcome, the CCP shows no signs of moderating its insistence on retaining an absolute monopoly on political power. Traditional Chinese political culture's lack of the concept of a loyal opposition party or grouping has played a significant role in the preference for a single-party dictatorship under both Chiang Kai-shek's GMD and Mao Zedong's CCP. A key point of difference is that Chiang Kai-shek's less hidebound GMD successors in Taiwan eventually lifted the ban on opposition parties and accepted the voting public's decision to turn them out of the top executive offices in 2000. In contrast, Mao Zedong's CCP successors still impose long prison terms and harsh treatment on anyone who dares organize an opposition party, even when such a party is explicitly peaceful and nonviolent in its program or charter. One of the PRC's sacrosanct "four upholds" *[sige jianchi]* in the Deng-Jiang Era has been that the Chinese political system must remain under the "leadership of the Chinese Communist Party," which in practice means under the thorough control of the CCP.

7. Amnesty International estimates that as of summer 2001, there were at least 6,000 political prisoners in the PRC, and probably many more. We speak of "ordinary criminal convicts" because of the nature of the charges leveled against them, not because we assume that a large majority of these people are actually guilty of a serious offense.

The Leninist-Stalinist ideology of vertically structured one-party dictatorship has taken firm root in the soil of the authoritarian Chinese political tradition, while mostly eradicating the moderating vestiges of this tradition such as the remonstrating official and his horizontal networks of support. Compared to their ancestors in premodern China, "intellectuals in the PRC have been a social stratum or group with few established horizontal connections," argues Timothy Cheek, for the party-state has typically "prohibited individual or interest group politics."[8]

With the PRC judiciary being as utterly dependent upon CCP officials as practically any other branch of the PRC government, PRC criminal trials have remained mostly scripted theater in which the verdict has already been decided in advance. The minimal legal procedures of even such mockeries of justice as Wei Jingsheng's two criminal trials can be dispensed with through the continuing administrative sanction of laojiao. Laojiao incarceration stripped Mao Era prisoners like Cong Weixi and Harry Wu of two decades of their freedom, and locked up the Deng Era dissident Liu Qing for a decade.[9]

The PRC government's incendiary anti-foreign rhetoric and absolutist approach to the question of national sovereignty can easily dismiss as "gross interference in China's internal affairs" United Nations High Commissioner for Human Rights Mary Robinson's modest request to dismantle and eventually abolish China's practice of reeducation through labor.[10] It was no accident that the PRC government's 1957 "decision" to implement reeducation was merely restated in the Deng Era and has remained in force under Jiang Zemin and Hu Jintao as well. Though no longer a totalitarian state since the end of the Mao Era, the PRC remains a police state that extends extraordinary discretionary powers of warrant-free detention and informal sentencing to the Public Security Bureau and certain other security organs. While a fair number of police officers and laogai guards and cadres have been prosecuted under the 1993 prohibition against beating and torturing prisoners, this practice still continues unpunished in many places, and is facilitated by high-tech devices such as electric shock batons.

8. Timothy Cheek, "Habits of the Heart: Intellectual Assumptions Reflected by Chinese Reformers from Deng Tuo to Fang Lizhi," *Changes in China: Party, State, and Society,* ed. Shao-chuan Leng (Lanham, MD: University Press of America, 1989), pp. 117–143, esp. 124.

9. Wei, Cong, Wu, and Liu would disagree with one another on many issues, but they share the experience of wrongful incarceration and an abiding concern about China's future.

10. Christopher Bodeen, "China Urged to End Labor Camps," *Associated Press,* 27 February 2001, sg.news.yahoo.com/010226/igay/html.

Large-scale exonerations of PRC political prisoners remain almost entirely limited to inmates who were framed during the Mao Era. Deng-Jiang Era political prisoners who have received a reduction in sentence on condition that they go abroad for medical treatment risk immediate arrest or deportation if they dare return to PRC. This situation greatly resembles the Brezhnev leadership's handling of many Soviet dissidents in the 1970s, and illustrates how the PRC's development in matters of criminal justice and tolerance of dissent lag decades behind that of many of its neighbors in Asia, including countries with a similarly authoritarian cultural heritage.

In light of these severe shortcomings of the PRC criminal justice system, the yawning gap between the high-sounding theory of labor camp manuals for cadres and the actual treatment of PRC prisoners in specific camps and prisons deserves close attention.[11] This book's critical use of prison memoirs and fiction set in labor camps brings a human face back into discussions that have sometimes gotten bogged down in dry statistics and uncritically received bureaucratic formulations. After sampling the memoirs of Song Shan and Liu Qing or the major laogai novels by the likes of Lü Haiyan, the reader knows better than to accept the received academic wisdom that PRC prisons do not allow ordinary criminal cell tyrants to lord it over political prisoners.[12] The colorful PRC prison argot that can be culled from the memoirs of such inmates as Gao Xin, Zhang Xianliang, and Cong Weixi reveals that a PRC prison subculture exists, however much the PRC government and some Western scholars might wish to deny it. Though some Western scholars join the PRC government in suggesting that the Deng-Jiang Era laogai is vastly different from its Mao Era predecessor, prison memoirs and fiction suggest some

---

11. As Seymour & Anderson note, PRC prison conditions vary so much across place and time that "any general claim regarding how good or bad prison conditions are . . . must be limited to actual cases . . ." See *New Ghosts, Old Ghosts,* p. 220. Despite this variability, prisons share a strong dependence on the party-state that the PRC government has cultivated in the general citizenry, and especially among prisoners under its direct control. Moreover, scholars in the social sciences such as Seymour have made some use of prisoners' letters, but seem to have made little attempt to test their hypotheses with prison writings such as memoirs and fiction. Such materials should be considered an important part of this documentation of prison conditions, particularly in light of stringent restrictions on scholars' access to such prisons.

12. Martin King Whyte came to such a problematic conclusion on the basis of what seems to have been an excessively narrow sample of Hong Kong refugee interviewees in 1970. See "Corrective Labor Camps in China," pp. 253–269. Ten years after Whyte's article was published, it was still being taken as authoritative. See Rosen & Seymour's notes to the translation of Liu Qing, *Prison Memoirs,* p. 180 n. 22.

striking continuities.[13] These continuities exist at the national level, where the Deng-Jiang leaders have passed up opportunities to (1) replace the Maoist notion of "remolding prisoners" with something more practical and unambiguous, and less militarized in its structure and approach; (2) abolish the jiuye system of retaining ex-inmate workers in the camp's vicinity, instead of merely downsizing it; (3) discontinue laojiao administrative detention, instead of simply limiting it to repeatable terms of three years; and (4) make prison labor more relevant to the skills prisoners could use after release, instead of assigning them whatever manual labor is expedient or profitable, as in the Mao Era.[14] At the local level, the continuities between the Mao Era and the Deng-Jiang Era include most of the aspects of prison life surveyed in Chapters 3 and 4, with the most notable exception being the Deng-Jiang Era's downplaying of Maoist ideological remolding in favor of bottom-line economic results. For instance, much continuity exists in terms of inmate hierarchy, at the top of which is the cell tyrant, as well as in terms of a great deal of the prison argot. To be sure, Deng-Jiang Era prisoners have rarely starved to death, as they did in droves during the 1959–62 famine, but the problems of physical abuse, inadequate nutrition, and especially disease in Deng-Jiang Era prisons have remained quite serious in numerous locales, including some in urban areas.

Cultural insularity can sometimes be harmless, such as when the PRC government announced in 1997 that Deng Xiaoping's state funeral would be off limits to foreigners, including ambassadors and visiting heads of state.[15] Yet this government's common tactic of inveighing against international criticism of its still largely Maoist criminal justice and prison systems as imperialist meddling or an "anti-China" conspiracy is far from innocent. A stubborn refusal to overhaul an outmoded criminal justice system that has generated the massive amount of needless suffering so

13. Seymour & Anderson generally stress the differences between the Mao Era and Deng-Jiang Era prisons while tending to overlook or downplay the many continuities.

14. After all, early in the Deng Era, the PRC government formally discarded the "official formulation" [tifa] of "remolding" [gaizao] in connection with ordinary PRC intellectuals within society, realizing that the concept had done more harm than good in nation building when leveled at ordinary intellectuals during the Mao Era. What exactly makes "remolding" so much more effective when leveled at prisoners in camps rather than ordinary intellectuals in society has not been adequately explained. It would seem that as a top-down process, remolding is used by the powerful against the lowly and the relatively weak. In the Deng-Jiang Era, prisoners necessarily remained weak and subject to constant manipulation, while intellectuals saw their social position rise considerably over what it had been under Mao.

15. Moreover, it was at least possible for the uninvited foreign dignitaries to watch Jiang Zemin's eulogy of Deng Xiaoping on television.

evident from laogai memoirs and fiction is tantamount to proclaiming that similar injustices should continue to occur in China over the foreseeable future. Alternatively, a PRC government sincerely bent upon reducing future miscarriages of justice would discard the obscurantist myth of "Asian values" and incorporate a great many of the procedural safeguards and principles of judicial independence that already exist in neighboring powers ranging from New Delhi to Tokyo.[16] There is little doubt as to which of these two courses of action most of the laogai novel and memoir writers would prefer to see.

16. Immanuel C. Y. Hsu criticizes the mythical notion of uniquely "Asian values" in *The Rise of Modern China,* 6th ed. (New York: Oxford Univ. Press, 2000), pp. 1001–1003.

Bibliography

Western-Language Nonfiction

Adler, Jacob. *The Urgings of Conscience: A Theory of Punishment*. Philadelphia: Temple Univ. Press, 1991.

Anderson, Marston. *The Limits of Realism: Chinese Fiction in the Revolutionary Period*. Berkeley: Univ. of California Press, 1990.

———. "The Morality of Form: Lu Xun and the Modern Chinese Short Story." In *Lu Xun and His Legacy*, ed. Leo Ou-fan Lee, pp. 32–53. Berkeley: Univ. of California Press, 1985.

Andreski, Stanislav. *Military Organization and Society*. Berkeley: Univ. of California Press, 1971.

Armstrong, Nancy, and Leonard Tennenhouse, eds. *The Violence of Representation: Literature and the History of Violence*. London: Routledge, 1989.

Bakken, Borge. *The Exemplary Society: Human Improvement, Social Control, and the Dangers of Modernity in China*. Oxford: Oxford Univ. Press, 2000.

Bao Ruo-wang, and Rudolph Chelminski. *Prisoner of Mao*. 1973; rpt. Harmondsworth: Penguin, 1976.

Barmé, Geremie. *In the Red: On Contemporary Chinese Culture*. New York: Columbia Univ. Press, 1999.

———, and John Minford, eds. *Seeds of Fire: Chinese Voices of Conscience*. Hong Kong: Far Eastern Economic Review, 1986.

Barnett, A. Doak. *Communist China: The Early Years, 1949–55*. New York: Praeger, 1964.

Baum, Richard. *Burying Mao: Chinese Politics in the Age of Deng Xiaoping*. Princeton: Princeton Univ. Press, 1994.

———, ed. *Reform and Reaction in Post-Mao China: The Road to Tiananmen*. New York: Routledge, 1991.

Becker, Jasper. *The Chinese: An Insider's Look at the Issues Which Affect and Shape China Today*. New York: Oxford Univ. Press, 2002.

Bentham, Jeremy. *The Panopticon Writings.* Ed. Miran Bozovic. London: Verso, 1995.

Benton, Gregor. *Mountain Fires: The Red Army's Three-Year War in South China, 1934–1938.* Berkeley: Univ. of California Press, 1992.

———, and Alan Hunter, eds. *Wild Lily, Prairie Fire: China's Road to Democracy, 1942–1949.* Princeton: Princeton Univ. Press, 1995.

Bernstein, Robert. "Introductory Comments." In *Voices from the Laogai: Fifty Years of Surviving China's Forced Labor Camps,* pp. 17–19. Washington, D.C.: Laogai Research Foundation, 2000.

Besançon, Alain. "Why Is the Twentieth Century the Century of Concentration Camps?" International Conference on Human Rights in North Korea. Seoul, Korea, 1–3 December 1999.

Black, George, and Robin Munro. *Black Hands of Beijing: Lives of Defiance in China's Democracy Movement.* New York: Wiley, 1993.

Bloom, Harold. "Freud: Frontier Concepts, Jewishness, and Interpretation." In *Trauma: Explorations in Memory,* ed. Cathy Caruth, pp. 113–127. Baltimore: Johns Hopkins Univ. Press, 1995.

Bo Yang (pseud. of Guo Yidong). "The Wonderful Chinaman." In *The Ugly Chinaman and the Crisis of Chinese Culture,* trans. and ed. Don J. Cohn and Jing Qing. St. Leonards, Australia: Allen and Unwin, 1992.

Bodde, Derk, and Clarence Morris. *Law in Imperial China Exemplified by 190 Ch'ing Dynasty Cases.* Cambridge: Harvard Univ. Press, 1967.

Bodeen, Christopher. "China Urged to End Labor Camps." Associated Press, 27 February 2001. sg.news.yahoo.com/010226/igay/html.

Bond, Michael Harris, ed. *The Psychology of the Chinese People.* Oxford: Oxford Univ. Press, 1986.

Brandt, Conrad, Benjamin Schwartz, and John K. Fairbank. *A Documentary History of Chinese Communism.* Cambridge: Harvard Univ. Press, 1952.

Bray, Marianne. "China Out-Kills the World, Says Amnesty." CNN.com 6 July 2001. www.cnn.com/2001/WORLD/asiapcf/east/07/06/china.executions/index/html.

Briggs, John, Christopher Harris, Angus McInnes, and David Vincent. *Crime and Punishment in England: An Introductory History.* New York: St. Martin's Press, 1996.

Brombert, Victor. *The Romantic Prison: The French Tradition.* Princeton: Princeton Univ. Press, 1978.

Brooks, E. Bruce, and A. Taeko Brooks. *The Original Analects: Sayings of Confucius and His Successors.* New York: Columbia Univ. Press, 1998.

Brzezinski, Zbigniew. *The Grand Failure: The Birth and Death of Communism in the Twentieth Century.* New York: Scribner's, 1989.

Buchanan, Allen E. *Marx and Justice: The Radical Critique of Liberalism.* Totowa, NJ: Rowman and Allanheld, 1982.

Bugajski, Janusz. *Fourth World Conflicts: Communism and Rural Society.* Boulder, CO: Westview Press, 1991.

Bunyan, James. *The Origins of Forced Labor in the Soviet State, 1917–1921: Documents and Materials.* Baltimore: Johns Hopkins Univ. Press, 1967.

Butterfield, Fox. *Alive in the Bitter Sea.* New York: Times Books, 1982.

Carlton, Richard K., ed. *Forced Labor in the "People's Democracies."* New York: Mid-European Studies Center, 1955.

Caruth, Cathy. Introduction. In *Trauma: Explorations in Memory,* ed. Cathy Caruth, pp. 3–12. Baltimore: Johns Hopkins Univ. Press, 1995.

———, ed. *Trauma: Explorations in Memory.* Baltimore: Johns Hopkins Univ. Press, 1995.

Chao, Yuen Ren. *A Grammar of Spoken Chinese.* Berkeley: Univ. of California Press, 1968.

Cheek, Timothy. "Habits of the Heart: Intellectual Assumptions Reflected by Chinese Reformers from Deng Tuo to Fang Lizhi." In *Changes in China: Party, State, and Society,* ed. Shao-chuan Leng, pp. 117–143. Lanham, MD: University Press of America, 1989.

Chow Ching-wen. *Ten Years of Storm: The True Story of the Communist Regime in China.* New York: Holt, Rinehart and Winston, 1960.

Coetzee, J. M. "Idleness in South Africa." In *The Violence of Representation: Literature and the History of Violence,* ed. Nancy Armstrong and Leonard Tennenhouse, pp. 119–139. London: Routledge, 1989.

Cohen, Jerome Alan, ed. *Contemporary Chinese Law: Research Problems and Perspectives.* Cambridge: Harvard Univ. Press, 1970.

———. *The Criminal Process in the People's Republic of China, 1949–1963: An Introduction.* Cambridge: Harvard Univ. Press, 1968.

Cohn, Dorrit. "Optics and Power in the Novel." *New Literary History* 26.1 (1995): 3–20.

Conquest, Robert. *Kolyma: The Arctic Death Camps.* Oxford: Oxford Univ. Press, 1979.

Copper, John F., and Ta-ling Lee. *Coping with a Bad Global Image: Human Rights in the People's Republic of China, 1993–1994.* Lanham, MD: University Press of America, 1997.

Courtois, Stéphane, et al., eds. *The Black Book of Communism: Crimes, Terror, Repression.* Trans. Jonathan Murphy and Mark Kramer. Cambridge: Harvard Univ. Press, 1999.

Courtois, Stéphane, and Jean-Louis Panné. "The Comintern in Action." In *The Black Book of Communism: Crimes, Terror, Repression,* ed. Stéphane Courtois et al., trans. Jonathan Murphy and Mark Kramer, pp. 271–332. Cambridge: Harvard Univ. Press, 1999.

"Crime and Vivisection: A New Human-Rights Report Claims That Convicts Are Used as Organ Donors." *Time,* 5 September 1994.

Deacon, Richard [Donald McCormick]. *A History of the Chinese Secret Service.* London: Frederick Muller, Ltd., 1974.

Deng Xiaoping. *Report on the Rectification Campaign.* Beijing: Foreign Languages Press, 1957.

Des Pres, Terrence. *The Survivor: An Anatomy of Life in the Death Camp.* New York: Oxford Univ. Press, 1976.

Dikötter, Frank. "Crime and Punishment in Post-Liberation China: The Prisoners of a Beijing Gaol in the 1950s." *China Quarterly* 149 (1997): 147–159.

———. *Crime, Punishment, and the Prison in Modern China*. New York: Columbia Univ. Press, 2002.

Doan Viet Hoat. "Political Prisoners in Vietnam." In *Voices from the Laogai: Fifty Years of Surviving China's Forced Labor Camps*, pp. 140–142. Washington, D.C.: Laogai Research Foundation, 2000.

Domenach, Jean-Luc. *Chine: l'archipel oublié* [China: The Forgotten Archipelago]. Paris: Librairie Arthème Fayard, 1992.

Duke, Michael S. *Blooming and Contending: Chinese Literature in the Post-Mao Era*. Bloomington: Indiana Univ. Press, 1985.

Dutton, Michael R. *Policing and Punishment in China: From Patriarchy to "the People."* Cambridge: Cambridge Univ. Press, 1992.

———. *Streetlife China*. Cambridge: Cambridge Univ. Press, 1998.

———, trans. "The Basic Character of Crime in Contemporary China." *China Quarterly* 149 (1997): 160–177.

Eastman, Lloyd E. *The Abortive Revolution: China under Nationalist Rule, 1927–1937*. Cambridge: Harvard Univ. Press, 1974.

———. *Seeds of Destruction: Nationalist China in War and Revolution, 1937–1949*. Stanford: Stanford Univ. Press, 1984.

Ekirch, A. Roger. "Great Britain's Secret Convict Trade to America, 1783–1784." *The American Historical Review* 89.5 (1984): 1285–1291.

Fairbank, John. "Roots of Revolution." *New York Review of Books* 10 November 1988, 31–33.

Faligot, Roger, and Rémi Kauffer. *The Chinese Secret Service*. Trans. Christine Donougher. London: Headline Books, 1989.

Family of Liu Qing. "Liu Qing Is Innocent! The Public Security Bureau Is Breaking the Law!" In *Wild Lily, Prairie Fire: China's Road to Democracy, Yan'an to Tian'anmen, 1942–1989*, ed. Gregor Benton and Alan Hunter, pp. 244–246. Princeton: Princeton Univ. Press, 1995.

Fan Shidong. "The Sex Life of Prisoners in Prisons and Labor Camps." Trans. Yenna Wu. Conference presentation. The Chinese Labor Camp: Theory, Actuality, and Fictional Representation. Univ. of California, Riverside, 15 January 2000.

Farías, Victor. *Heidegger and Nazism*. Ed. Joseph Margolis and Tom Rockmore. Philadelphia: Temple Univ. Press, 1989.

Feinerman, James V. "Deteriorating Human Rights in China." *Current History* 89.548 (September 1990): 265–269, 279–280.

Felman, Shoshana, and Dori Laub. *Testimony: Crises of Witnessing in Literature, Psychoanalysis, and History*. New York: Routledge, 1992.

Finkelstein, David. "The Language of Communist China's Criminal Law." In *Contemporary Chinese Law: Research Problems and Perspectives*, ed. Jerome Alan Cohen. Cambridge: Harvard Univ. Press, 1970.

Foucault, Michel. *Discipline and Punish: The Birth of the Prison*. Trans. Alan Sheridan. 2nd ed. New York: Vintage Books, 1995.

———. *Surveiller et punir: naissance de la prison*. Paris: Éditions Gallimard, 1975.

Friedman, Edward. "Preventing War between China and Japan." In *What if China*

Doesn't Democratize? Implications for War and Peace, ed. Edward Friedman and Barrett L. McCormick, pp. 99–128. Armonk, NY: M. E. Sharpe, 2000.

Friedman, Edward, Paul G. Pickowicz, and Mark Selden. *Chinese Village, Socialist State.* New Haven: Yale Univ. Press, 1991.

Fyfield, J. A. *Re-educating Chinese Anti-Communists.* New York: St. Martin's Press, 1982.

Garland, David. *Punishment and Welfare: A History of Penal Strategies.* Aldershot, U.K.: Gower, 1985.

Genette, Gérard. *Figures III.* Paris: Éditions du Seuil, 1972.

Gold, Thomas. "Urban Private Business and China's Reforms." In *Reform and Reaction in Post-Mao China: The Road to Tiananmen,* ed. Richard Baum. New York: Routledge, 1991.

Goldman, Merle. "Confucian Influence on Intellectuals in the People's Republic of China." In *Confucianism and Human Rights,* ed. Wm. Theodore de Bary and Tu Weiming, pp. 261–269. New York: Columbia Univ. Press, 1997.

Goldstein, Melvyn, William Siebenschuh, and Tashi Tsering. *The Struggle for Modern Tibet: The Autobiography of Tashi Tsering.* Armonk, NY: M. E. Sharpe, 1997.

Greenblatt, Sidney. "The Manufacture of Deviance." In *Deviance and Control in Chinese Society,* ed. Amy Wilson, Sidney Greenblatt, and Richard Wilson, pp. 82–120. New York: Praeger, 1972.

Griffin, Patricia E. *The Chinese Communist Treatment of Counterrevolutionaries: 1924–1949.* Princeton: Princeton Univ. Press, 1976.

Hanan, Patrick. *The Chinese Vernacular Story.* Cambridge: Harvard Univ. Press, 1981.

Hansen, Chad. "Punishment and Dignity in China." In *Individualism and Holism: Studies in Confucian and Taoist Values,* ed. Donald J. Munro, pp. 359–383. Ann Arbor: Center for Chinese Studies, Univ. of Michigan, 1985.

Hayford, Charles W. *To the People: James Yen and Village China.* New York: Columbia Univ. Press, 1990.

Hazard, John. *Communists and Their Law.* Chicago: Univ. of Chicago Press, 1969.

Henriksson, Helena, and Ralph Krech. "International Perspectives." In *Prison Labour: Salvation or Slavery?* ed. Dirk van Zyl Smit and Frieder Dünkel, pp. 297–312. Oñati International Series in Law and Society. Aldershot, U.K.: Ashgate, 1999.

Herling, Gustav. *A World Apart.* 2nd ed. Trans. Andrzej Ciozkosz. New York: Arbor House, 1986.

Ho Ping-ti. *Studies on the Population of China, 1368–1953.* Cambridge: Harvard Univ. Press, 1957.

Holm, David. *Art and Ideology in Revolutionary China.* Oxford: Clarendon Press, 1991.

Hsia, C. T. "Chang Hsien-liang [Zhang Xianliang] as Author and Hero: A Study of His *Record of My Emotional Life.*" Conference presentation. International Conference on Literature, Politics and Society in Mainland China. Taipei, Taiwan, May 1989.

———. "Foreword." In Pu Ning (pseud. Wumingshi), *Red in Tooth and Claw:*

Twenty-Six Years in Communist Chinese Prisons, trans. Tung Chung-hsuan, pp. xi–xxiii. New York: Grove Press, 1994.

Hsiao, Kung-chuan. *Rural China: Imperial Control in the Nineteenth Century.* Seattle: Univ. of Washington Press, 1967.

Hsu, Cho-yun. "The Spring and Autumn Period." In *The Cambridge History of Ancient China: From the Origins of Civilization to 221 B.C.,* ed. Michael Loewe and Edward L. Shaughnessy. Cambridge: Cambridge Univ. Press, 1999.

Hsu, Immanuel C. Y. *The Rise of Modern China.* 6th ed. New York: Oxford Univ. Press, 2000.

Huang, Philip C. C. *Code, Custom, and Legal Practice in China: The Qing and the Republic Compared.* Stanford: Stanford Univ. Press, 2001.

Huang, Ray. *China, a Macro History: Turn of the Century Edition.* Armonk, NY: M. E. Sharpe, 1997.

Huang Xiang. "Huang Xiang." In *Voices from the Laogai: Fifty Years of Surviving China's Forced Labor Camps,* pp. 38–43. Washington, D.C.: Laogai Research Foundation, 2000.

Hucker, Charles O. *China's Imperial Past.* Stanford: Stanford Univ. Press, 1975.

Hunter, Edward. *Brainwashing: The Calculated Destruction of Men's Minds.* New York: Vanguard Press, 1953.

Jacobs, James B. "United States of America: Prison Labour, a Tale of Two Penologies." In *Prison Labour: Salvation or Slavery?* Ed. Dirk van Zyl Smit and Frieder Dünkel, pp. 269–280. Oñati International Series in Law and Society. Aldershot, U.K.: Ashgate, 1999.

Jenner, W. J. F. *The Tyranny of History: The Roots of China's Crisis.* London: Penguin, 1992.

Johnson, Kevin. "Get Harsh on Crime, Says Chicago's Top Cop." *USA Today,* 16 July 1991.

Johnston, Norman. *Forms of Constraint: A History of Prison Architecture.* Urbana: Univ. of Illinois Press, 2000.

———. *The Human Cage: A Brief History of Prison Architecture.* New York: Walker and Co., 1973.

Kasza, Gregory J. *The Conscription Society: Administered Mass Organizations.* New Haven: Yale Univ. Press, 1995.

Keightley, David N. "Public Works in Ancient China: A Study of Forced Labor in the Shang and Western Chou." Ph.D. dissertation, Columbia Univ., 1972.

———. "The Shang: China's First Historical Dynasty." In *The Cambridge History of Ancient China: From the Origins of Civilization to 221 B.C.,* ed. Michael Loewe and Edward L. Shaughnessy. Cambridge: Cambridge Univ. Press, 1999.

Kinkley, Jeffrey C. "A Bettelheimian Interpretation of Chang Hsien-liang's [Zhang Xianliang] Concentration Camp Novels." *Asia Major* 4.2 (1991): 83–113.

———. *Chinese Justice, the Fiction: Law and Literature in Modern China.* Stanford: Stanford Univ. Press, 2000.

Kirby, William C. "The Internationalization of China: Foreign Relations at Home and Abroad in the Republican Era." In *Reappraising Republican China,* ed. Frederic Wakeman Jr. and Richard Louis Edmonds, pp. 179–204. Oxford: Oxford Univ. Press, 2000.

Kmiecik, Jerzy. *A Boy in the Gulag.* London: Quartet Books, 1983.

Ladany, Laszlo. *The Communist Party of China and Marxism, 1921–1985: A Self-Portrait.* Stanford: Hoover Institution Press, 1988.

———. *Law and Legality in China: The Testament of a China-Watcher.* Ed. Marie-Luise Näth. Honolulu: Univ. of Hawaii Press, 1992.

Lai Ying. *The Thirty-Sixth Way.* Trans. Edward Behr and Sidney Liu. Garden City, NY: Doubleday, 1969.

Laogai Research Foundation. *Communist Charity: A Comprehensive Report on the Harvesting of Organs from the Executed Prisoners of the People's Republic of China.* Washington, D.C.: Laogai Research Foundation, 2001.

———. *Laogai Handbook, 1997–1998.* Milpitas, CA: Laogai Research Foundation, 1997.

Lee, Leo Ou-fan. *Voices from the Iron House: A Study of Lu Xun.* Bloomington: Indiana Univ. Press, 1987.

———, ed. *Lu Xun and His Legacy.* Berkeley: Univ. of California Press, 1985.

Leng, Shao-chuan. *Justice in Communist China: A Survey of the Judicial System of the Chinese People's Republic.* Dobbs Ferry, NY: Oceana Publications, 1967.

Levi, Primo. *The Drowned and the Saved,* trans. Raymond Rosenthal. New York: Simon and Schuster, 1988.

Lifton, Robert Jay. *Thought Reform and the Psychology of Totalism: A Study of "Brain-washing" in China.* New York: Norton, 1963.

Link, Perry. "Introduction." In *Roses and Thorns: The Second Blooming of the Hundred Flowers in Chinese Fiction, 1979–80,* ed. Perry Link. Berkeley: Univ. of California Press, 1984.

———. Introduction to "Three Professors." In *Roses and Thorns: The Second Blooming of the Hundred Flowers in Chinese Fiction, 1979–80,* ed. Perry Link, pp. 111–112. Berkeley: Univ. of California Press, 1984.

———. *The Uses of Literature: Life in the Socialist Chinese Literary System.* Princeton: Princeton Univ. Press, 2000.

Liu Binyan. *A Higher Kind of Loyalty.* Trans. Zhu Hong. New York: Random House, 1990.

Liu Qing. "Prison Memoirs" [Yuzhong shouji]. Ed. Stanley Rosen and James Seymour. *Chinese Sociology and Anthropology* 15.1–2 (1982–1983): 3–181.

———. "The Role of Hierarchy in the Treatment of Chinese Prisoners." Trans. Philip F. Williams. Conference presentation. The Chinese Labor Camp: Theory, Actuality, and Fictional Representation. Univ. of California, Riverside, 15 January 2000.

———. "Sad Memories and Prospects: My Appeal to the Tribunal of the People." In *Wild Lily, Prairie Fire: China's Road to Democracy, Yan'an to Tian'anmen, 1942–1989,* ed. Gregor Benton and Alan Hunter, pp. 247–257. Princeton: Princeton Univ. Press, 1995.

Liu Zongren. *Hard Time: Thirty Months in a Chinese Labor Camp.* San Francisco: China Books, 1995.

Ljunggren, David. "Canadian Falun Gong Follower Says Tortured in China." Reuters World News, 22 January 2001. dailynews.yahoo.com/h/nm/20010118/wl/canada_china_dc_1.html.

Loewe, Michael. "The Heritage Left to the Empires." In *The Cambridge History of Ancient China: From the Origins of Civilization to 221 B.C.,* ed. Michael Loewe and Edward L. Shaughnessy. Cambridge: Cambridge Univ. Press, 1999.

Lötveit, Trygve. *Chinese Communism, 1931–1934: Experience in Civil Government.* 2nd ed. London: Curzon Press, 1979.

Lubman, Stanley B. *Bird in a Cage: Legal Reform in China after Mao.* Stanford: Stanford Univ. Press, 1999.

MacCormack, Geoffrey. *The Spirit of Traditional Chinese Law.* Athens: Univ. of Georgia Press, 1996.

Mao Tse-tung. "On the People's Democratic Dictatorship." *Selected Works of Mao Tse-tung.* Vol. 4. Beijing: Foreign Languages Press, 1961.

Mao Zedong. "Report on an Investigation of the Peasant Movement in Hunan, March 1927." *Selected Works of Mao Zedong.* Vol. 1. Beijing: Foreign Languages Press, 1965.

Marchenko, Anatoly. *My Testimony.* Trans. Michael Scammell. New York: E. P. Dutton, 1969.

———. *To Live like Everyone.* Trans. Paul Goldberg. New York: Holt, 1989.

Margolin, Jean-Louis. "China: A Long Journey into Night." In *The Black Book of Communism: Crimes, Terror, Repression,* ed. Stéphane Courtois et al., trans. Jonathan Murphy and Mark Kramer, pp. 463–546. Cambridge: Harvard Univ. Press, 1999.

Marr, David G., ed. *Reflections from Captivity: Phan Boi Chau's "Prison Notes" and Ho Chi-minh's "Prison Diary."* Trans. Christopher Jenkins, Tran Khanh Tuyet, and Huynh Sanh Thong. Athens: Ohio Univ. Press, 1978.

Marx, Karl, and Friedrich Engels. "Critique of the Gotha Program." In *Basic Writings on Politics and Philosophy,* ed. Lewis S. Feuer, pp. 112–132. Garden City, NY: Anchor Books, 1959.

Mathews, Jay, and Linda Mathews. *One Billion: A China Chronicle.* New York: Ballantine, 1983.

McClean, Hugh. "Walls and Wire: Some Notes on the Prison Theme in Russian Literature." *International Journal of Slavic Linguistics and Poetics* 25–26 (1982): 253–265.

McGowen, Randall. "Punishing Violence, Sentencing Crime." In *The Violence of Representation: Literature and the History of Violence,* ed. Nancy Armstrong and Leonard Tennenhouse, pp. 140–156. London: Routledge, 1989.

McKnight, Brian E. *Law and Order in Sung China.* Cambridge: Cambridge Univ. Press, 1992.

———, and James T. C. Liu, trans. *The Enlightened Judgments, Ch'ing-ming Chi: The Sung Dynasty Collection.* Albany: State Univ. of New York Press, 1999.

McMullen, David L. "The Real Judge Dee." Lecture. Harvard Univ., Cambridge, 11 March 1991.

Megill, Allan. *Prophets of Extremity: Nietzsche, Heidegger, Foucault, Derrida.* Berkeley: Univ. of California Press, 1985.

Meijer, Marinus Johan. "Abuse of Power and Coercion." In *State and Law in East Asia: Festschrift Karl Brüger,* ed. Dieter Eikemeier and Herbert Franke. Wiesbaden: Otto Harrassowitz, 1981.

Merquior, J. G. *Foucault.* London: Fontana Press/Collins, 1985.

Nathan, Andrew J. *Chinese Democracy.* Berkeley: Univ. of California Press, 1985.

O'Brien, Patricia. *The Promise of Punishment: Prisons in Nineteenth-Century France.* Princeton: Princeton Univ. Press, 1982.

Panin, Dimitri. *The Notebooks of Sologdin.* Trans. John Moore. New York: Harcourt Brace Jovanovich, 1976.

Patterson, David. *Along the Edge of Annihilation: The Collapse and Recovery of Life in the Holocaust Diary.* Seattle: Univ. of Washington Press, 1999.

———. *Sun Turned to Darkness: Memory and Recovery in the Holocaust Memoir.* Syracuse, NY: Syracuse Univ. Press, 1998.

Peerenboom, R. P. *Law and Morality in Ancient China: The Silk Manuscripts of Huang-Lao.* Albany: State Univ. of New York Press, 1993.

Pusey, James. *China and Charles Darwin.* Cambridge: Harvard Univ. Press, 1983.

Reynolds, Douglas R. *China, 1898–1912: The Xinzheng Revolution and Japan.* Cambridge: Harvard Univ. Press, 1993.

Rhoads, Edward J. M. *Manchus and Han: Ethnic Relations and Political Power in Late Qing and Early Republican China, 1861–1928.* Seattle: Univ. of Washington Press, 2000.

Rittenberg, Sidney, and Amanda Bennett. *The Man Who Stayed Behind.* New York: Simon and Schuster, 1993.

Rocca, Jean-Louis. *L'empire et son milieu: la criminalité en Chine populaire* [The Empire and Its Milieu: Criminality in China]. Paris: Plon, 1991.

Ropp, Paul S. "The Distinctive Art of Chinese Fiction." In *Heritage of China: Contemporary Perspectives on Chinese Civilization,* ed. Paul S. Ropp, pp. 309–334. Berkeley: Univ. of California Press, 1990.

Rossi, Jacques. *The Gulag Handbook: An Encyclopedia Dictionary of Soviet Penitentiary Institutions and Terms Related to the Forced Labor Camps.* Trans. William A. Burhans. New York: Paragon House, 1989.

Rubin, Kyna. Introduction to Wang Ruowang, *Hunger Trilogy,* pp. xi–xxxvii. Armonk, NY: M. E. Sharpe, 1991.

Rummel, R. J. *China's Bloody Century: Genocide and Mass Murder since 1900.* New Brunswick, NJ: Transaction, 1991.

———. *Death by Government.* New Brunswick, NJ: Transaction, 1994.

Saunders, Kate, ed. *Eighteen Layers of Hell.* London: Cassel, 1996.

Schoenhals, Michael. *Doing Things with Words in Chinese Politics: Five Studies.* Berkeley: Institute of East Asian Studies, Univ. of California, 1992.

Schoppa, R. Keith. *Blood Road: The Mystery of Shen Dingyi in Revolutionary China.* Berkeley: Univ. of California Press, 1995.

Schulz, William F. "Cruel and Unusual Punishment." *New York Review of Books,* 24 April 1997, 51–54.

Scott, James C. *Weapons of the Weak: Everyday Forms of Peasant Resistance.* New Haven: Yale Univ. Press, 1985.

Seybolt, Peter J. "Terror and Conformity: Counterespionage Campaigns, Rectification, and Mass Movements of 1942–43." *Modern China* 12.1 (1986): 39–73.

Seymour, James D., and Richard Anderson. *New Ghosts, Old Ghosts: Prisons and Labor Reform Camps in China*. Armonk, NY: M. E. Sharpe, 1998.

Shalom, Steven Rosskam. *Deaths in China due to Communism: Propaganda versus Reality*. Tempe: Arizona State Univ. Center for Asian Studies Monograph Series, 1984.

Sinyavsky, Andrei. *A Voice from the Chorus*. Trans. Kyril Kitzlyon and Max Hayward. New York: Farrar, Straus and Giroux, 1976.

Sofsky, Wolfgang. *The Order of Terror: The Concentration Camp*. Trans. William Templer. Princeton: Princeton Univ. Press, 1997.

Solzhenitsyn, Aleksandr I. *The Gulag Archipelago, 1918–1956: An Experiment in Literary Investigation*. Vol. 1. Trans. Thomas P. Whitney. New York: Harper and Row, 1974.

———. *The Gulag Archipelago, 1918–1956: An Experiment in Literary Investigation*. Vol. 2. Trans. Thomas P. Whitney. New York: Harper and Row, 1975.

———. *The Gulag Archipelago, 1918–1956: An Experiment in Literary Investigation*. Vol. 3. Trans. Harry Willetts. New York: Harper and Row, 1976.

Spence, Jonathan D. *Chinese Roundabout: Essays in History and Culture*. New York: Norton, 1992.

———. *God's Chinese Son: The Taiping Heavenly Kingdom of Hong Xiuquan*. New York: Norton, 1996.

———. "In China's Gulag." *New York Review of Books*, 10 August 1995, 15–18.

Storey, Robert. *Mimesis and the Human Animal: On the Biogenetic Foundations of Literary Representation*. Evanston, IL: Northwestern Univ. Press, 1996.

Tanner, Harold M. "China's 'Gulag' Reconsidered: Labor Reform in the 1980s and 1990s." *China Information: A Quarterly on Contemporary Chinese Studies* 9.2–3 (1994–1995): 40–71.

———. "Policing, Punishment, and the Individual: Criminal Justice in China." *Law and Social Inquiry: Journal of the American Bar Foundation* 20.1 (1995): 277–303.

———. *Strike Hard! Anti-crime Campaigns and Chinese Criminal Justice, 1979–1985*. Ithaca: Cornell Univ. East Asian Series, 1999.

Thurston, Anne F. *A Chinese Odyssey: The Life and Times of a Chinese Dissident*. New York: Scribner's, 1991.

———. *Enemies of the People: The Ordeal of the Intellectuals in China's Great Cultural Revolution*. Cambridge: Harvard Univ. Press, 1988.

Toynbee, Arnold J. *Armenian Atrocities: The Murder of a Nation*. London: Hodder and Stoughton, 1915.

Tucker, Robert C., ed. *The Marx-Engels Reader*. 2nd ed. New York: Norton, 1978.

Van der Kolk, Bessel A., and Onno Van der Hart. "The Intrusive Past: The Flexibility of Memory and the Engraving of Trauma." In *Trauma: Explorations in Memory*, ed. Cathy Caruth, pp. 158–182. Baltimore: Johns Hopkins Univ. Press, 1995.

Van der Sprenkel, Sybille. *Legal Institutions in Manchu China: A Sociological Analysis*. London: Athlone Press, 1962.

Van Zyl Smit, Dirk, and Frieder Dünkel. "Conclusion: Prison Labour—Salvation or Slavery?" In *Prison Labour: Salvation or Slavery?* ed. Dirk van Zyl Smit and Frieder Dünkel, pp. 335–347. Oñati International Series in Law and Society. Aldershot, U.K.: Ashgate, 1999.

Venclova, Tomas. "Prison as a Communicative Phenomenon: The Literature of Gulag." *Comparative Civilizations Review* 2 (1979): 65–73.

Voices from the Laogai: Fifty Years of Surviving China's Forced Labor Camps. Washington, D.C.: Laogai Research Foundation, 2000.

Wakeman, Frederic Jr. *Policing Shanghai, 1927–1937.* Berkeley: Univ. of California Press, 1995.

———. "A Revisionist View of the Nanjing Decade: Confucian Fascism." In *Reappraising Republican China,* ed. Frederic Wakeman Jr. and Richard Louis Edmonds, pp. 141–178. Oxford: Oxford Univ. Press, 2000.

———, and Richard Louis Edmonds, eds. *Reappraising Republican China.* Oxford: Oxford Univ. Press, 2000.

Waldron, Arthur. *The Great Wall of China: From History to Myth.* Cambridge: Cambridge Univ. Press, 1990.

Waley-Cohen, Joanna. *Exile in Mid-Qing China: Banishment to Xinjiang, 1758–1820.* New Haven: Yale Univ. Press, 1991.

Walker, Richard L. *The Human Cost of Communism in China.* Senate Committee on the Judiciary, Internal Security Committee, 92nd Congress, 1st session, 1971.

Wang, David Der-wei. *Fin-de-Siècle Splendor: Repressed Modernities of Late Qing Fiction, 1849–1911.* Stanford: Stanford Univ. Press, 1997.

Wang Ruowang. *Hunger Trilogy.* Trans. Kyna Rubin with Ira Kasoff. Armonk, NY: M. E. Sharpe, 1991.

Wang Xiaoling. *Many Waters: Experiences of a Chinese Woman Prisoner of Conscience.* Hong Kong: Caritas Printing, 1988.

Wang Xizhe. "Wang Xizhe." In *Voices from the Laogai: Fifty Years of Surviving China's Forced Labor Camps,* pp. 72–74. Washington, D.C.: Laogai Research Foundation, 2000.

Weber, Max. *The Protestant Ethic and the Spirit of Capitalism.* Trans. Talcott Parsons. London: Allen and Unwin, 1976.

Wei Jingsheng. *The Courage to Stand Alone: Letters from Prison and Other Writings.* Trans. Kristina M. Torgeson. New York: Viking Penguin, 1997.

Wei, William. *Counterrevolution in China: The Nationalists in Jiangxi during the Soviet Period.* Ann Arbor: Univ. of Michigan Press, 1985.

White, Lynn T., III. *Policies of Chaos: The Organizational Causes of Violence in China's Cultural Revolution.* Princeton: Princeton Univ. Press, 1989.

Whyte, Martin K. "Corrective Labor Camps in China." *Asian Survey* 13.3 (1973): 253–269.

———. *Small Groups and Political Rituals in China.* Berkeley: Univ. of California Press, 1974.

Wilbur, C. Martin. *Slavery in the Former Han Dynasty, 206 B.C.–25 A.D.* Chicago: Field Museum of Natural History Anthropological Series no. 34, 1943.

Williams, Philip F. "Can We Paradigm? The Mimetic Heresy and Some Other

Imbroglios in Recent Western-Language Academic Studies of Modern Chinese Literature." *Tamkang Review: A Quarterly of Comparative Studies of Chinese and Foreign Literatures* 30.3 (2000): 111–148.

———. "Chinese Cannibalism's Literary Portrayal: From Cultural Myth to Investigative Reportage." *Tamkang Review: A Quarterly of Comparative Studies of Chinese and Foreign Literatures* 27.4 (1997): 421–442.

———. "Ingraining Self-Censorship and Other Functions of the Laogai, as Revealed in Chinese Fiction and Reportage." In *Voices from the Laogai: Fifty Years of Surviving China's Forced Labor Camps,* pp. 97–104. Washington, D.C.: Laogai Research Foundation, 2000.

———. "'Remolding' and the Labor-Camp Novel." *Asia Major* 4.2 (1991): 133–149.

———. "Some Provincial Precursors of Popular Dissent Movements in Beijing." *China Information: A Quarterly on Contemporary Chinese Studies* 6.1 (1991): 1–9.

———. *Village Echoes: The Fiction of Wu Zuxiang.* Boulder, CO: Westview Press, 1993.

Winance, Eleutherius. *The Communist Persuasion: A Personal Experience of Brainwashing.* Trans. Emeric A. Laurence. New York: P. J. Kennedy and Sons, 1959.

Windschuttle, Keith. *The Killing of History.* New York: Free Press, 1996.

Wittfogel, Karl A. *Oriental Despotism: A Comparative Study of Total Power.* New Haven: Yale Univ. Press, 1957.

Womack, Brantly. "Media and the Chinese Public: A Survey of the Beijing Media Audience." *Chinese Sociology and Anthropology* 18.3–4 (1986).

Wright, Arthur F. *The Sui Dynasty.* New York: Knopf, 1978.

Wu, Hongda Harry. *Laogai: The Chinese Gulag.* Boulder, CO: Westview Press, 1992.

Wu, Harry, and Carolyn Wakeman. *Bitter Winds: A Memoir of My Years in China's Gulag.* New York: Wiley, 1994.

Wu, Yenna. *Ameliorative Satire and the Seventeenth-Century Chinese Novel, Xingshi Yinyuan Zhuan—Marriage as Retribution, Awakening the World.* Lewiston, NY: Edwin Mellen Press, 1999.

———. "Expressing the 'Inexpressible': Pain and Suffering in Wumingshi's *Red Sharks* (Hongsha)." Conference presentation. The Chinese Labor Camp: Theory, Actuality, and Fictional Representation. University of California, Riverside, 15 January 2000.

———. "The Interweaving of Sex and Politics in Zhang Xianliang's *Half of Man Is Woman.*" *Journal of the Chinese Language Teachers Association* 27.1/2 (1992): 1–27.

———. "Ironic Intertextuality in *Six Chapters from a Floating Life* and *Six Chapters from Life at a Cadre School.*" *Journal of the Chinese Language Teachers Association* 26.2 (1991): 51–80.

———. "Repetition in *Xingshi yinyuan zhuan.*" *Harvard Journal of Asiatic Studies* 51.1 (1991): 55–87.

———. "Women as Sources of Redemption in Chang Hsien-liang's Camp Fiction." *Asia Major* 4.2 (1991): 115–131.

Wumingshi (pseud. of Bu Naifu, alias Bu Ning /Pu Ning). "Prologue: The Secret of the Cave." In Pu Ning, *Red in Tooth and Claw: Twenty-Six Years in Commu-*

nist Chinese Prisons, trans. Tung Chung-hsuan, pp. xxv–xxvii. New York: Grove Press, 1994.

———. *Red in Tooth and Claw: Twenty-Six Years in Communist Chinese Prisons.* Trans. Tung Chung-hsuan. New York: Grove Press, 1994.

———. *The Scourge of the Sea.* Taipei: Kuang Lu Publishing, 1985.

Xu Xiaoqun. "The Fate of Judicial Independence in Republican China, 1912–37." *China Quarterly* 149 (1997): 1–28.

Yang Jiang. *Six Chapters from My Life "Downunder."* Trans. Howard Goldblatt. Seattle: University of Washington Press, 1984.

Yang, Kuo-shu. "Chinese Personality and Its Change." In *The Psychology of the Chinese People,* ed. Michael Harris Bond, pp. 106–170. Hong Kong: Oxford Univ. Press, 1986.

Yang, Rae. *Spider Eaters.* Berkeley: Univ. of California Press, 1997.

Zhang Xianliang. *Grass Soup.* Trans. Martha Avery. London: Secker and Warburg, 1994.

———. *My Bodhi Tree.* Trans. Martha Avery. London: Secker and Warburg, 1996.

Zhou, Peter Bangjiu. *Dawn Breaks in the East: A Benedictine Monk's Thirty-Three Year Ordeal in the Prisons of Communist China in Defense of His Faith.* Upland, CA: Serenity, 1992.

Zweig, David. *Freeing China's Farmers: Rural Restructuring in the Reform Era.* Armonk, NY: M. E. Sharpe, 1997.

Western-Language Fiction

Ai Bei. *Red Ivy, Green Earth Mother.* Trans. Howard Goldblatt. Salt Lake City: Peregrine Smith Books, 1990.

Bei Dao (pseud. of Zhao Zhenkai). *Waves: Stories.* Trans. Bonnie S. McDougall and Susette Ternent Cooke. New York: New Directions, 1990.

Cao Guanlong. "Three Professors." Trans. John Berninghausen. In *Roses and Thorns: The Second Blooming of the Hundred Flowers in Chinese Fiction, 1979–80,* ed. Perry Link, pp. 111–145. Berkeley: Univ. of California Press, 1984.

Chen Yingzhen. "Mountain Path." Trans. Nicholas Koss. In *"Death in a Cornfield" and Other Stories from Contemporary Taiwan,* ed. Ching-Hsi Perng and Chiu-kuei Wang. Hong Kong: Oxford Univ. Press, 1994.

Ching-Hsi Perng, and Chiu-kuei Wang, eds. *"Death in a Cornfield" and Other Stories from Contemporary Taiwan.* Hong Kong: Oxford Univ. Press, 1994.

Dostoyevsky, Fyodor. *House of the Dead.* Trans. David McDuff. 1860; rpt. London: Penguin, 1985.

"Eternal Prisoner under the Thunder Peak Pagoda." Trans. Diana Yu. In *Traditional Chinese Stories: Themes and Variations,* ed. Y. W. Ma and Joseph S. M. Lau, pp. 355–378. 1986; rpt. Boston: Cheng and Tsui, 1996.

Gao Xiaosheng. "Li Shunda Builds a House." Trans. Ellen Klempner. In *The New Realism: Writings from China after the Cultural Revolution,* ed. Lee Yee, pp. 31–55. New York: Hippocrene Books, 1983.

Ha Jin. "The Russian Prisoner." In *Ocean of Words.* New York: Vintage, 1996.

Lee, Lillian (Li Pik-wah/Li Bihua). *Farewell to My Concubine* [Bawang bie ji]. Trans. Andrea Lingenfelter. New York: William Morrow, 1993.

Lee Yee, ed. *The New Realism: Writings from China after the Cultural Revolution.* New York: Hippocrene Books, 1983.

Li Yu. *Silent Operas.* Trans. Patrick Hanan. Hong Kong: Chinese Univ. of Hong Kong Press, 1990.

Link, Perry, ed. *Roses and Thorns: The Second Blooming of the Hundred Flowers in Chinese Fiction, 1979–80.* Berkeley: Univ. of California Press, 1984.

Liu Binyan. "The Fifth Man in the Overcoat." Trans. John S. Rohsenow with Perry Link. In Liu Binyan, *"People or Monsters?" and Other Stories and Reportage from China after Mao,* ed. Perry Link, pp. 79–97. Bloomington: Indiana Univ. Press, 1983.

———. "Murder at Nenjiang Camp." Trans. Geremie Barmé. In *Seeds of Fire: Chinese Voices of Conscience,* ed. Geremie Barmé and John Minford. Hong Kong: Far Eastern Economic Review, 1986.

———. *"People or Monsters?" and Other Stories and Reportage from China after Mao.* Ed. Perry Link. Bloomington: Indiana Univ. Press, 1983.

Liu E. *The Travels of Lao Ts'an.* Trans. Harold Shadick. Ithaca: Cornell Univ. Press, 1952.

Ma, Y. W., and Joseph S. M. Lau, eds. *Traditional Chinese Stories: Themes and Variations.* 1986; rpt. Boston: Cheng and Tsui, 1996.

McDougall, Bonnie S. *The Yellow Earth: A Film by Chen Kaige, with a Complete Translation.* Hong Kong: Chinese Univ. of Hong Kong Press, 1993.

Shalamav, Varlam. "The Lawyers' Plot." In *Kolyma Tales,* trans. John Glad, pp. 151–170. New York: Norton, 1980.

———. "The Lepers." In *Graphite.* Trans. John Glad. New York: Norton, 1981.

Shi Nai'an, and Luo Guanzhong (attrib.). *Outlaws of the Marsh.* Trans. Sidney Shapiro. Bloomington: Indiana Univ. Press, 1981.

Wang Meng. "The Anecdotes of Section Chief Maimaiti: 'Black Humor' of the Uighurs." Trans. Philip F. Williams. *Journal of Asian Culture* 8 (1984): 1–30.

Zhang Xianliang. "Body and Soul." Trans. Philip F. C. Williams. In *Prize-Winning Stories from China, 1980–1981,* ed. W. C. Chau, pp. 58–92. Beijing: Foreign Languages Press, 1985.

———. *Getting Used to Dying.* Trans. Martha Avery. New York: HarperCollins, 1991.

———. *Half of Man Is Woman.* Trans. Martha Avery. New York: Norton, 1986.

———. *Mimosa.* Trans. Gladys Yang. Beijing: Panda Books, 1987.

Nonfiction in East Asian Languages

Aixin Jueluo Puyi 愛新覺羅 · 溥儀. *Wode qianbansheng* 我的前半生 [The Former Half of My Life]. 1964; rpt. Beijing: Qunzhong chubanshe, 1983.

Aixin Jueluo Yutang 愛新覺羅 · 毓嶂. "Puyi yu wo shuzhi zhijian" 溥儀與我叔侄之間. In Aixin Jueluo Pujie 愛新覺羅 · 溥傑 et al., *Zai jizhongying de rizi:*

Xuantong huangdi de houbansheng 在集中營的日子：宣統皇帝的後半生 [The Days in Concentration Camps: The Latter Half of the Life of the Xuantong Emperor]. Hong Kong: Dong xi wenhua shiye chuban gongsi, n.d.

An Sinan 安思南. *Lian yu sanbuqu* 煉獄三部曲 [The Purgatory Trilogy]. Taipei: Zhongguo dalu zazhishe, 1985.

Bao Jialin 鮑家麟 (Chia-lin Pao Tao). "Ming mo Qing chu de Suzhou cainü Xu Can" 明末清初的蘇州才女徐燦 [The Late-Ming to Early-Qing Talented Suzhou Woman Xu Can]. In Wang Chengmian 王成勉, ed., *Ming-Qing wenhua xinlun* 明清文化新論 [New Theories of Ming-Qing Culture], pp. 455–475. Taipei: Wenjin chubanshe, 2000.

Bao Ziyan 包子衍 and Yuan Shaofa 袁紹發, eds., *Huiyi Xuefeng* 回憶雪峰 [Remembering Feng Xuefeng]. Beijing: Zhongguo wenshi chubanshe, 1986.

Bo Yang 柏楊 (pseud. of Guo Yidong 郭衣洞). *"Choulou de Zhongguoren" fengbo* 《醜陋的中國人》風波 [The "Ugly Chinaman" Controversy]. Beijing: Zhongguo Huaqiao chuban gongsi, 1989.

Bo Yang 柏楊 and Zhou Bise 周碧瑟. *Bo Yang huiyilu* 柏楊回憶錄 [The Memoirs of Bo Yang]. Taipei: Yuanliu, 1996.

Cai Shuheng 蔡樞衡. *Zhongguo xingfa shi* 中國刑法史 [A History of Chinese Punishment]. Nanning: Guangxi renmin chubanshe, 1983.

Chen Duxiu 陳獨秀. "Tongxin" 通信 [Editorial Correspondence]. *Xin qingnian* 新青年 [La Jeunesse] 1.1 (September 1915): 1–2.

Chen Sanxing 陳三興. *Shaonian zhengzhi fan feichang huiyilu* 少年政治犯非常回憶錄 [The Extraordinary Memoirs of a Youthful Political Prisoner]. Taipei: Qianwei chubanshe, 1999.

Chen Zhuoru 陳琢如, ed. *Ping "Nanren de yiban shi nüren"* 評《男人的一半是女人》 [Critiques of *Half of Man Is Woman*]. Yinchuan: Ningxia renmin chubanshe, 1987.

Cong Weixi 從維熙. "Guanyu 'Yuanqu de baifan'" 關於遠去的白帆 [About "White Sails Far Departed"]. In Liu Jinyong 劉金鏞 and Fang Fuxian 房福賢, eds., *Cong Weixi yanjiu zhuanji* 從維熙研究專集 [A Specialized Collection of Research on Cong Weixi's Writings]. Chongqing: Chongqing chubanshe, 1985.

———. "Wenxue de meng—da Yanhuo" 文學的夢—答彥火 [My Dream of Literature—A Reply to Yanhuo]. In Liu Jinyong and Fang Fuxian, eds., *Cong Weixi yanjiu zhuanji* [A Specialized Collection of Research on Cong Weixi's Writings], pp. 67–81. Chongqing: Chongqing chubanshe, 1985.

———. "Xiaoshuo shi xingxiang siwei de yishu" 小說是形象思維的藝術 [Fiction Is the Art of Imagery and Thought]. *Beijing wenxue* 北京文學 11 (November 1983): 52–56.

———. *Zou xiang hundun* 走向混沌 [Heading into Chaos]. Vol. 1. Beijing: Zuojia chubanshe, 1989.

———. *Zou xiang hundun sanbuqu* 走向混沌三部曲 [The Heading into Chaos Trilogy]. Beijing: Zhongguo shehui kexue chubanshe, 1998.

"Di ji" 帝紀 [Imperial chronicles]. In *Sui shu* 隋書 [Official History of the Sui Dynasty]. *Ershiwu shi* 二十五史 [The Twenty-Five Histories]. 2nd ed. Taipei: Kaiming shudian, 1965.

Duan Kewen 段克文. *"Zhanfan" zishu* 戰犯自述 [The Personal Account of a "War Criminal"]. Taipei: Shijie ribao she, 1978.

Ershiwu shi 二十五史 [The Twenty-Five Histories]. 2nd ed. Taipei: Kaiming shudian, 1965.

Fan Shidong 范似棟. "Dui Xinjiang laogaidui caojian renming de jianjuxin" 對新疆勞改隊草菅人命的檢舉信 [A Letter Implicating the Xinjiang Laogai Brigades for Treating Human Life as Cheap]. In Xiao Chong, ed., *Zhonggong sifa heimu* [The Dark Side of the Chinese Communist Legal System], pp. 375–379. Hong Kong: Xiafei'er guoji chuban gongsi, 1998.

Fang Bao 方包. "Yu zhong zaji" 獄中雜記 [Prison Jottings]. In *Fang Wangxi quanji* 方望溪全集 [Collected Works of Fang Bao], pp. 352–354. Beijing: Zhongguo Shudian, 1991.

Gao Xin 高新. *Beiwei yu huihuang: yige "Liu si" shounanzhe de yu zhong zhaji* 卑微與輝煌：一個六四受難者的獄中札記 [Disgrace and Glory: Prison Jottings of a Victim of "June Fourth"]. Taipei: Lianjing, 1991.

Ge Fei 革非. *Erdeng gongmin: ji Gongheguo diyici yanda* 二等公民：記共和國第一次嚴打 [Second-Class Citizens: A Record of the (PRC) Republic's First Strike-Hard Campaign]. Chengdu: Chengdu chubanshe, 1992.

"Gongyun lingxiu Li Wangyang zai Hunan jueshi" 工運領袖李旺陽在湖南絕食 [Labor Union Leader Li Wangyang Goes on a Hunger Strike in Hunan]. *Shijie ribao* 世界日報, 4 February 2001, A8.

Gu Xiaoyan 顧笑言. *Zhongguo de jianyu* 中國的監獄 [China's Prisons]. Shenyang: Jilin renmin chubanshe, 1988.

Guo Moruo 郭沫若. *Nuli zhi shidai* 奴隸之時代 [The Era of the Slave System]. Beijing: Renmin chubanshe, 1974.

Hu Juren 胡菊人. "Ba" 跋 [Epilogue]. In Shen Zui, *Zhanfan gaizaosuo jianwen*, vol. 2, 332–337. Hong Kong: Baixing wenhua shiye youxian gongsi, 1987.

Hu Ping 胡平 (b. 1947). *Ren de xunhua, duobi, yu fanpan* 人的馴化、躲避與反叛 [Taming of the Human, and the Responses of Evasion and Rebellion]. Hong Kong: Yazhou kexue chubanshe, 1999.

Hu Ping 胡平 (b. 1948). *Zhongguo de mouzi* 中國的眸子 [China's Eyes Unpeeled]. Hong Kong: Tiandi tushu, 1990.

Huang Jinlin 黃金麟. *Lishi, shenti, guojia: jindai Zhongguo de shenti xingcheng (1895–1937)* 歷史，身體，國家：近代中國的身體形成(1895–1937) [History, Body, and Nation: The Formation of the Modern Chinese Body (1895–1937)]. Taipei: Lianjing chuban shiye gongsi, 2000.

Huang Jue 黃覺. *Xue xing si yi* 血腥四邑 [Four Cities that Reek of Blood]. Hong Kong: Yazhou chubanshe, 1953.

Jia Zhifang 賈植芳. *Yu li yu wai* 獄裡獄外 [In and out of the Prisons]. Shanghai: Shanghai yuandong chubanshe, 1995.

Laogai gongzuo 勞改工作 [The Work of Remolding through Labor]. Beijing: Qunzhong chubanshe, 1983.

Li Ao 李敖. "Jianyu xue Tucheng" 監獄學土城 [Learning from the Tucheng Prison]. In Liu Qing 劉青 et al., eds., *Dalu Taiwan zuo lao ji* 大陸臺灣坐牢記

[Accounts of Imprisonment in the Mainland and Taiwan], pp. 95–158. Hong Kong: Baixing banyuekan, 1983.

Li Jiafu 李甲孚. *Zhongguo fazhi shi* 中國法制史 [A History of China's Legal System]. Taipei: Lianjing chuban shiye gongsi, 1988.

Li Qian 李倩. *Teding shiqi de da qiang wenxue* 特定時期的大牆文學 [Prison Wall Literature of a Certain Period]. Shenyang: Liaoning daxue chubanshe, 1988.

Li Xianguo 李現國. "Zhenjing quanguo zhengfa xitong de Xinjiang dabaoyu" 震驚全國政法系統的新疆大暴獄 [The Large Prison Uprising in Xinjiang That Shocked the Entire Nation's Political and Legal Authorities]. In *Zhonggong sifa heimu,* ed. Xiao Chong, pp. 406–413. Hong Kong: Xiafei'er guoji chuban gongsi, 1998.

Liang Qichao 梁啓超. *Xin min lun* 新民論 [On Renovating the People]. Taipei: Zhonghua shuju, 1978.

Liu Binyan 劉賓雁. "Di'er zhong zhongcheng" 第二種忠誠 [The Second Type of Loyalty]. In Liu Binyan, *Liu Binyan zixuanji* 劉賓雁自選集 [Liu Binyan: A Personal Selection of His Writings], pp. 113–156. Beijing: Zhongguo wenlian chubanshe, 1988.

———. *Liu Binyan zizhuan* 劉賓雁自傳 [The Autobiography of Liu Binyan]. Taipei: Shibao wenhua chuban, 1989.

Liu Qingbo 劉清波. *Zhonggong laodong gaizao de pipan* 中共勞動改造的批判 [A Critique of the Chinese Communists' Remolding through Labor]. Taipei: Zhengzhong shuju, 1975.

Lü Simian 呂思勉. *Zhongguo tong shi* 中國通史 [A General History of China]. Shanghai: Kaiming shudian, n.d.

Mao Zedong 毛澤東. "Lun renmin minzhu zhuanzheng: jinian Zhongguo gongchandang ershiba zhounian" 論人民民主專政：紀念中國共產黨二十八週年 [On the People's Democratic Dictatorship: In Commemoration of the Twenty-Eighth Anniversary of the Founding of the Chinese Communist Party]. In *Mao Zedong xuanji* 毛澤東選集 [Selected Works of Mao Zedong], vol. 4, pp. 1468–1482. Beijing: Renmin chubanshe, 1991.

———. "Shijian lun" 實踐論 [On Practice]. In *Mao Zedong xuanji,* vol. 1, pp. 282–298. Beijing: Renmin chubanshe, 1991.

Peng Yinhan 彭銀漢. *Dalu jizhongying* 大陸集中營 [The Mainland Concentration Camp]. Taipei: Shibao wenhua chuban, 1984.

Qi Li 齊禮, ed. *Shan-Gan-Ning bianqu shilu* 陝甘寧邊區實錄 [True Accounts from the Shaanxi-Gansu-Ningxia Border Region]. Yan'an?: Jiefang she, 1939.

Qian Guoyao 錢國耀 et al. *Tamen fanle shenme zui? Xingshi anli fenxi* 他們犯了什麼罪?－刑事案例分析 [What Crimes Did They Commit? Analysis of Exemplary Criminal Cases]. Shanghai: Zhishi chubanshe, 1984.

Qiu Zhu 秋竹. "Shengming de 'leiqu'—yuzhong jishi zhi san" 生命的雷區－獄中紀實之三 [The "Mined Zone" of Life—Three Prison Accounts]. *Da qiang nei wai* 大牆內外 [Inside and Outside the Prison Walls], no. 2 (1989): 10–15.

Shangrao jizhongying 上饒集中營 [Shangrao Concentration Camp]. Shanghai: Shanghai renmin chubanshe, 1981.

Shao Mingzheng 邵名正 et al. *Zuifan lun* 罪犯論 [On Criminality]. Huairou: Zhongguo Zhengfa Daxue chubanshe, 1989.

Shao Mingzheng 邵名正, ed. *Laogai faxue gailun* 勞改法學概論 [An Outline of Labor Remolding Law]. Beijing: Zhongguo Zhengfa daxue chubanshe, 1990.

Shen Jiali 沈嘉立. "Renda daibiao Zhou Jialiang feifa jujin an zhuiji" 人大代表周家良非法拘禁案追記 [A Retrospective Account of the Case of the People's Congress Deputy Zhou Jialiang's Illegal Retention]. In *Zhonggong sifa heimu*, ed. Xiao Chong, pp. 106–119. Hong Kong: Xiafei'er guoji chuban gongsi, 1998.

Shen Zui 沉醉. *Zhanfan gaizao suo jianwen* 戰犯改造所見聞 [Matters Seen and Heard in the War Criminals' Remolding Facility]. 2 vols. Hong Kong: Baixing wenhua shiye youxian gongsi, 1987.

Shisou ziliaoshi gongfei ziliao 石叟資料室共匪資料 [Materials on the Chinese Communists from the Shisou Archive]. Stanford: Hoover Institution, 1960.

Sima Qian 司馬遷. *Shi ji* 史記 [The Historical Records]. In *Ershiwu shi* 二十五史 [The Twenty-Five Histories]. 2nd ed. Taipei: Kaiming shudian, 1965.

Song Shan 宋珊. *Hong qiang, hui qiang* 紅牆灰牆 [Red Walls, Gray Walls]. Hong Kong: Baijia chubanshe, 1986.

Sun Ping 孫平, Li Honglin 栗紅林, and Hui Xiping 惠西平. *Zhongguo jianyu ren* 中國監獄人 [Chinese Prisoners]. Xi'an: Shaanxi renmin chubanshe, 1989.

Sun Xiaoli 孫曉靂. *Zhongguo laodong gaizao zhidu de lilun yu shijian—lishi yu xianshi* 中國勞動改造制度的理論與實踐－歷史與現實 [Theory and Practice of the Chinese Remolding through Labor System—History and Actuality]. Sanhe: Zhongguo Zhengfa Daxue chubanshe, 1994.

Tang Min 唐敏. *Zou xiang heping—yu zhong shouji* 走向和平－獄中手記 [Heading toward Peace—Prison Jottings]. Urumqi: Xinjiang Daxue chubanshe, 1994.

Wang Anyi 王安憶 and Zong Fuxian 宗福先. "Fengshu ling liu ri: Baimaoling nü laojiao dui caifang jishi" 楓樹嶺六日－白茅嶺女勞教隊采訪紀實 [Six Days on Maple Ridge: A Record of Interviews at the Baimaoling Re-education-through-Labor Brigades for Women]. *Daqiang nei wai* 大牆內外 no. 4 (1988): 3–9.

Wang Fei 王飛, ed. *Shanghai jianyu renquan jilu* 上海監獄人權記錄 [The Human Rights Record of Shanghai's Prisons]. Shanghai: Shanghai renmin chubanshe, 1992.

Wang Ruowang 王若望. "Ji'e sanbuqu" 飢餓三部曲 [Hunger Trilogy]. In *Yanbuzhu de guangmang* 掩不住的光芒 [Glory That Cannot Be Concealed], pp. 78–222. Beijing: Renmin wenxue chubanshe, 1983.

Wang Yitao 王一桃. *Wushige wenyijia zhi si* 五十個文藝家之死 [The Death of Fifty Writers and Artists]. Hong Kong: Ming bao chubanshe, 1989.

Wei Jingsheng 魏京生. *Wei Jingsheng yuzhong shuxin ji* 魏京生獄中書信集 [A Collection of Wei Jingsheng's Letters from Prison]. Taipei: Shibao wenhua, 1997.

Wen Yu 文聿. *Zhongguo zuo huo* 中國左禍 [China's Leftist Calamities]. Hong Kong: Tiandi tushu, 1994.

Wu Hongda 吳弘達. *Zhongguo de Gulage—dalu laogai dui ji nugong chanpin zhenxiang* 中國的古拉格－大陸勞改隊及奴工產品真相 [The Chinese Gulag: The True Story of the Mainland's Remolding-through-Labor Brigades and Slave Labor Products]. Taipei: Shibao wenhua, 1992.

Wu Yanna 吳燕娜 (Yenna Wu). "Bianzheng de xiangxiang: tan *Nanren de yiban shi nüren* zhong xuyi de maodun" 辯證的想像：談男人的一半是女人中蓄意的矛盾 [The Dialectical Imagination: On the Carefully Designed Ambivalence in *Half of Man Is Woman*]. *Zhongwai wenxue* 中外文學 [Chung-wai Literary Monthly, Taipei] 20.1 (1991): 96–105.

———. "*Fusheng liuji* yu *Ganxiao liuji* xushu fengge zhi bijiao" 浮生六記與幹校六記敘述風格之比較 [A Comparison of the Narrative Styles of Shen Fu's (1763–1809?) *Six Chapters from a Floating Life* and Yang Jiang's (1911–) *Six Chapters from Life at a Cadre School*]. *Zhongwai wenxue* 中外文學 19.9 (1991): 79–93.

Wumingshi 無名氏 (pseud. of Bu Naifu 卜乃夫, alias Bu Ning 卜寧). *Hai de chengfa: Xiashaxiang jizhongying shilu* 海的懲罰：下沙鄉集中營實錄 [Punishment of the Sea: A True Account of the Xiashaxiang Concentration Camp]. Taipei: Xinwen tiandi she, 1985.

———. *Hong sha* 紅鯊 [Red Sharks]. Taipei: Liming wenhua shiye, 1989.

———. "Yige dalu qiutu de yishiliu—*Hai de chengfa* xupian, Xiashaxiang jizhongying xinling jingyan" 一個大陸囚徒的意識流－海的懲罰續篇，下沙鄉集中營心靈經驗 [The Stream of Consciousness of a Mainland Prisoner—A Supplement to *Punishment of the Sea,* the Mental Experience of Xiashaxiang Concentration Camp]. In *Hai de chengfa: Xiashaxiang jizhongying shilu,* pp. 113–140. Taipei: Xinwen tiandi she, 1985.

———. *Yuzhong shichao* 獄中詩抄 [Poems Composed in Prison]. Taipei: Liming wenhua shiye, 1984.

———. *Zou xiang Gegeta: yijiu liuba nian shounan jishi* 走向各各他：一九六八年受難紀實 [Heading toward Golgotha: A True Account of My Suffering in 1968]. Taipei: Xinwen tiandi she, 1986.

Xiao Chong 曉沖, ed. *Zhonggong sifa heimu: shijimo de "zhengzhi zhi yan"* 中共司法黑幕－世紀末的政治之癌 [The Dark Side of the Chinese Communist Legal System: A Fin-de-Siècle "Political Cancer"]. Hong Kong: Xiafei'er guoji chuban gongsi (Ha Fai Yi Publishing Ltd.), 1998.

Xue Meiqing 薛梅卿 et al., eds. *Zhongguo jianyushi* 中國監獄史 [A History of Chinese Prisons]. Beijing: Qunzhong chubanshe, 1986.

Yang Diansheng 楊殿升 and Zhang Jinsang 張金桑, eds. *Zhongguo tese jianyu zhidu yanjiu* 中國特色監獄制度研究 [Research on the Prison System with Chinese Characteristics]. Beijing: Falü chubanshe, 1999.

Yang Jiang 楊絳 *Ganxiao liuji* 幹校六記 [Six Chapters from a Cadre School]. Hong Kong: Guangjiaojing chubanshe, 1981.

Yang Wei 楊魏. "Gansu gong'an quda chengzhao xian qu liangming" 甘肅公安屈打成招險取兩命 [The Gansu Public Security Authorities Almost Took Two Lives through Forcing Prisoners to Confess]. In *Zhonggong sifa heimu,* ed. Xiao Chong, pp. 167–177. Hong Kong: Xiafei'er guoji chuban gongsi, 1998.

Zhang Xianliang 張賢亮. "Guanyu shidai yu wenxue de sikao—zhi Cong Weixi" 關於時代與文學的思考—致從維熙 [Thoughts about Literature and Its Epoch—A Letter to Cong Weixi]. In *Zhang Xianliang xuanji* [An Anthology of Zhang Xianliang], vol. 3, pp. 689–695. Tianjin: Baihua wenyi chubanshe, 1986.

———. "Man zhi huangtang yan" 滿紙荒唐言 [Pages Full of Preposterous Words].

In *Zhang Xianliang xuanji*, vol. 1, pp. 187–194. Tianjin: Baihua wenyi chuban-she, 1985.

———. *Wode Putishu* 我的菩提樹 [My Bodhi Tree]. Beijing: Zuojia chubanshe, 1995.

———. *Xie xiaoshuo de bianzhengfa* 寫小説的辯證法 [The Dialectics of Writing Fiction]. Shanghai: Shanghai wenyi chubanshe, 1987.

———. "Xinling he routi de bianhua" 心靈和肉体的變化 [The Transformation of Mind and Body]. In *Zhang Xianliang xuanji* [An Anthology of Zhang Xianliang], vol. 1, pp. 195–201. Tianjin: Baihua wenyi chubanshe, 1985.

———. *Zhang Xianliang xuanji* 張賢亮選集 [An Anthology of Zhang Xianliang]. 3 vols. Tianjin: Baihua wenyi chubanshe, 1985–86.

Zhang Xin 張新. "Yige beipo wangming tianya de Zhonggong faguan de xuelei kongsu" 一個被迫亡命天涯的中共法官的血淚控訴 [The Moving Accusation of a CCP Official in the Judiciary Who Was Forced to Flee for His Life]. In *Zhonggong sifa heimu*, ed. Xiao Chong, pp. 315–322. Hong Kong: Xiafei'er guoji chuban gongsi, 1998.

Zhang Xinxin 張辛欣 and Sang Ye 桑曄. "Zai tong yidu gao qiang houmian" 在同一堵高牆後面 [Behind the Same Prison Walls]. In *Beijing ren: yibaige putong ren de zishu* 北京人：100個普通人的自述 [Beijingese: Personal Accounts of a Hundred Ordinary Persons]. Shanghai: Shanghai wenyi chuban-she, 1986.

Zhang Zhu 張翥. "Shiwan huoji—xingchang ge shen!" 十萬火急一刑場割腎 [Most Urgent! Cutting Out Kidneys at the Execution Grounds]. In *Zhong-gong sifa heimu*, ed. Xiao Chong, pp. 121–128. Hong Kong: Xiafei'er guoji chuban gongsi, 1998.

Zhongwen da cidian 中文大辭典. 10 vols. Taipei: Zhongguo Wenhua Daxue chubanbu, 1982.

Zhu Guanghua 朱光華. *Zhongxing fan: Zhongguo xibu yige daxing laogai nong-chang li de mimi he gushi* 重刑犯：中國西部一個大型勞改農場裡的秘聞和故事 [Long-Term Inmates: Secrets and Stories from a Large-Sized Labor Remolding Farm in Western China]. Chengdu: Sichuan wenyi chubanshe, 1989.

Zuigao renmin fayuan 最高人民法院 et al. "Guanyu liyong sixing zuifan shiti huo shiti qiguan de zhanxing guiding" 關於利用死刑罪犯屍體或屍體器官的暫行規定 [Provisional Regulations Regarding the Use of Executed Criminals' Corpses or Organs within the Corpses]. 9 October 1984.

Fiction in East Asian Languages

Ai Bei 艾蓓. *Nü lao* 女牢 [A Women's Prison]. Taipei: Yuan shen chubanshe, 1990.

"Bai Niangzi yong zhen Leifeng Ta" 白娘子永鎮雷峰塔. In *Jing shi tongyan* 警世通言 [Tales to Warn the World]. Vol. 2, ed. Feng Menglong 馮夢, pp. 420–448. 1624; rpt. Beijing: Renmin wenxue chubanshe, 1981.

Bei Dao 北島 (pseud. of Zhao Zhenkai 趙振開). "Guilai de moshengren" 歸來

的陌生人 [The Homecoming Stranger]. In *Bodong* 波動 [Waves]. Hong Kong: Zhongwen daxue chubanshe, 1985.

Cao Guanlong 曹冠龍. "San'ge jiaoshou" 三個教授 [Three Professors]. *Anhui wenxue* 安徽文學, no. 1 (1980): 17–31.

Chen Yingzhen 陳映真. *Shan lu* 山路 [Mountain Path]. Taipei: Yuanjing chuban shiye, 1984.

Cong Weixi 從維熙. "Baiyun piaoluo tianmu" 白雲飄落天幕 [White Clouds Descend from Heaven]. In *Cong Weixi daibiaozuo* 從維熙代表作 [Representative Works of Cong Weixi], pp. 460–546. Zhengzhou: Huang He wenyi chubanshe, 1987.

———. "Da qiang xia de hong yulan" 大牆下的紅玉蘭 [Reddish Magnolia Blossoms beneath the Prison Wall]. In *Cong Weixi daibiaozuo*, pp. 170–240. Zhengzhou: Huang He wenyi chubanshe, 1987.

———. "Diqige shi yaba" 第七個是啞巴 [The Seventh One Is a Mute]. In *Cong Weixi daibiaozuo*, pp. 80–100. Zhengzhou: Huang He wenyi chubanshe, 1987.

———. *Duan qiao* 斷橋 [The Collapsed Bridge]. Beijing: Zuojia chubanshe, 1986.

———. "Feng lei yan" 風淚眼 [Eyes That Water from a Breeze]. In *Lu hui tou* 鹿回頭 [The Deer Looks Back], pp. 3–171. Beijing: Zhongguo qingnian chubanshe, 1988.

———. "Linjie de chuang" 臨街的窗 [The Window Facing the Street]. In *Cong Weixi daibiaozuo*, pp. 144–169. Zhengzhou: Huang He wenyi chubanshe, 1987.

———. *Lu hui tou* 鹿回頭. Beijing: Zhongguo qingnian chubanshe, 1988.

———. "Meiyou jia'niang de hunli" 沒有嫁娘的婚禮 [A Wedding without the Bride]. In *Ranshao de jiyi* 燃燒的記憶 [Blazing Memories], pp. 475–537. Beijing: Qunzhong chubanshe, 1983.

———. "Ranshao de jiyi" 燃燒的記憶 [Blazing Memories]. In *Ranshao de jiyi*, pp. 82–121. Beijing: Qunzhong chubanshe, 1983.

———. "Xiangei yisheng de meiguihua" 獻給醫生的玫瑰花 [Roses in Dedication to a Doctor]. In *Ranshao de jiyi*, pp. 1–21. Beijing: Qunzhong chubanshe, 1983.

———. "Xue luo Huang He jing wusheng" 雪落黃河靜無聲 [Snow Falls Silently on the Yellow River]. In *Xue luo Huang He jing wusheng* 雪落黃河靜無聲 [Snow Falls Silently on the Yellow River], pp. 1–93. Beijing: Zhongguo wenlian chuban gongsi, 1984.

———. "Yiluo zai haitan de jiaoyin" 遺落在海灘的腳印 [Footprints Left on the Seashore]. In *Cong Weixi daibiaozuo*, pp. 241–363. Zhengzhou: Huang He wenyi chubanshe, 1987.

———. "Yuan qu de bai fan" 遠去的白帆 [White Sails Far Departed]. In *Cong Weixi daibiaozuo*, pp. 364–459. Zhengzhou: Huang He wenyi chubanshe, 1987.

Fu Xuwen 傳緒文. *Yige nüqiu de zibai* 一個女囚的自白 [The Vindication of a Woman Prisoner]. Beijing: Zhongguo qingnian chubanshe, 1989.

Gao Xiaosheng 高曉聲. "Li Shunda zao wu" 李順大造屋 [Li Sunda Builds a House]. In *1979 nian quanguo youxiu duanpian xiaoshuo pingxuan huojiang zuopin ji* 1979年全國優秀短篇小說評選獲獎作品集 [The Anthology of National Prize-Winning Short Stories of 1979], pp. 125–146. Shanghai: Shanghai wenyi chubanshe, 1980.

Gu Hua 古華. *Fanpanzhe* 反叛者 [The Rebel]. Taipei: Yuanliu chuban shiye, 1989.

———. *Furong zhen* 芙蓉鎮 [Hibiscus Town]. Beijing: Renmin wenxue chubanshe, 1981.

"Kai he ji" 開河記 [A Record of Opening Up the Canal]. In *Tang-Song chuanqi ji* 唐宋傳奇集 [A Collection of Tang-Song *chuanqi*]. In *Lu Xun sanshi nian ji* 魯迅三十年集 [The Thirty-Year Collection of Lu Xun], vol. 5. Hong Kong: Xin yi chubanshe, 1967.

Li Baojia 李寶嘉 (Li Boyuan 李伯元). *Huo diyu* 活地獄 [A Living Hell]. 1906; rpt. Taipei: Guangya chuban gongsi, 1984.

Li Bihua 李碧華 (Lillian Lee). *Bawang bie ji* 霸王別姬 [Farewell, My Concubine]. Taipei: Huang guan chubanshe, 1989.

Li Jian 李建. *Nüxing de xue qi* 女性的血旗 [The Females' Bloody Banner]. *Zhuomuniao* 啄木鳥 [Woodpecker] no. 4: 54–74, no. 5: 139–160, no. 6: 128–160 (1989).

Li Yu 李漁. *Lian cheng bi* 連城璧 [Priceless Jade]. Hangzhou: Zhejiang guji chubanshe, 1986.

Liang Peimin 梁沛民. "Xue ji" 血祭 [Blood Sacrifice]. *Zhongguo fazhi wenxue* 中國法制文學 [Chinese Rule-of-Law Literature] 6 (1988): 85–93.

Liu Binyan 劉賓雁. "Diwuge chuan dayi de ren" 第五個穿大衣的人 [The Fifth Person to Wear the Overcoat]. *Beijing wenyi* 北京文藝 11 (1979): 28–35.

Liu E 劉鶚. *Lao Can youji* 老殘遊記 [The Travels of Lao Can]. 1907; rpt. Taipei: Xing Tai wenhua chubanshe, 1980.

Lu Xun 魯迅. *A Q zhengzhuan* 阿Q正傳 [The True Story of Ah Q]. 1921–22; rpt. Hong Kong: Baili shudian, n.d.

———. *Lu Xun xiaoshuoji* 魯迅小說集 [A Collection of Lu Xun's Fiction]. Ed. Yang Ze 楊澤. Taipei: Hongfan shudian youxian gongsi, 1999.

Lü Haiyan 侶海岩. *Bianyi jingcha* 便衣警察 [The Plainclothes Detective]. Beijing: Renmin wenxue, 1985.

Qiu Feng 丘峰. "Zhuibu zhi ye" 追捕之夜 [Night of the Pursuit]. *Dianshi, Dianying, Wenxue* 電視、電影、文學, no. 5 (1990): 61–72.

Shuihu quanzhuan 水滸全傳 [The Complete *Water Margin*]. Attributed to Shi Nai'an 施耐庵 and Luo Guanzhong 羅貫中. Shanghai: Shanghai renmin chubanshe, 1975.

Sui Yangdi yanshi 隋煬帝艷史 [The Merry Adventures of Emperor Yang of the Sui]. 1631 preface. Ed. Wang Yizhao 王以昭. Taipei: Tianyi chubanshe, 1974.

Wang Meng 王蒙. "Maimaiti Chuzhang yishi" 買買提處長軼事 [The Anecdotes of Section Chief Maimaiti]. In Wang Meng, *Wang Meng xiaoshuo baogao wenxue xuan* 王蒙小說報告文學選 [An Anthology of Wang Meng's Fiction and Reportage], pp. 177–191. Beijing: Beijing chubanshe, 1981.

Wang Zifu 王梓夫. *Nü lao ziwei* 女牢滋味 [The Flavor of a Women's Prison]. Beijing: Zuojia chubanshe, 1996.

Xi Zhou Sheng 西周生 (pseud.). *Xingshi yinyuan zhuan* 醒世姻緣傳 [Marriage as Retribution, Awakening the World]. 3 vols. Shanghai: Shanghai guji chubanshe, 1981.

Yang Jiang 楊絳 *Xi zao* 洗澡 [Taking a Bath]. Hong Kong: Sanlian shudian, 1988.

Zhang Xianliang 張賢亮. "Ling yu rou" 靈與肉 [Body and Soul]. In *Zhang Xian-liang xuanji* 張賢亮選集 [An Anthology of Zhang Xianliang], vol. 1, pp. 138–165. Tianjin: Baihua wenyi chubanshe, 1985.

———. *Lü hua shu* 綠化樹 [Mimosa]. In *Zhang Xianliang xuanji* 張賢亮選集, vol. 3, pp. 161–338. Tianjin: Baihua wenyi chubanshe, 1986.

———. *Nanren de yiban shi nüren* 男人的一半是女人 [Half of Man Is Woman]. In *Zhang Xianliang xuanji,* vol. 3, pp. 399–618. Tianjin: Baihua wenyi chuban-she, 1986.

———. *Tu lao qinghua* 土牢情話 [Passionate Words from a Village Prison]. *Zhang Xianliang xuanji,* vol. 2, pp. 3–89. Tianjin: Baihua wenyi chubanshe, 1985.

———. *Tu lao qinghua* 土牢情話 [Passionate Words from a Village Prison]. Trans-lated into Japanese by Ôsato Hiroaki 大里浩秋. Pp. 109–270. Tokyo: Nihon Ajia Bungaku Kyōkai, 1993.

———. *Wode Putishu* 我的菩提樹 [My Bodhi Tree]. Beijing: Zuojia chubanshe, 1995.

———. "Wufa suxing" 無法蘇醒 [Unable to Awaken]. *Xinhua wenzhai* 新華文摘, no. 1 (1996): 75–86.

———. *Xiguan siwang* 習慣死亡 [Getting Used to Dying]. Taipei: Yuan shen chubanshe, 1989.

———. *Zhang Xianliang xuanji* 張賢亮選集. 3 vols. Tianjin: Baihua wenyi chuban-she, 1985–86.

Chinese Character Glossary

Anhui 安徽

Ba Jin 巴金
ba jin chuang 拔筋床
Ba yi 八議
Bai Hua 白樺
Baimaoling 白茅嶺
baizi 稗子
ban 班
bangzhu 幫助
bangzhu hui 幫助會
banzhang 班長
bao chan dao hu 包產到戶
Bao Ruowang 鮑若望
baochou 報仇
baogao banzhang 報告班長
baomi 保密
baowai jiuyi 保外就醫
Beijing 北京
Beijing zhi chun 北京之春
Beiping 北平
Beiyuan 北苑
Bengbu 蚌埠

biaoshi taidu 表示態度
biaotai 表態
bie 憋
bie dalazhe naodai he Lao Er suan zhang 別耷拉著腦袋和老二算帳
bing hao 病號
bu ke xinren fenzi 不可信任份子

Chadian 茶淀
Changcheng 長城
Changchun 長春
Changsha 長沙
changzhang 場長
Chen Kaige 陳凱歌
Chen Ye 陳野
Chen Ziming 陳子明
Cheng 程
cheng 城
chengdan 城旦
Chengdu 成都
chengfa 懲罰
chi hei zao 吃黑棗
chi qing 吃青

221

chi shi fenzi 吃屎份子
Chiang Ching-kuo (Jiang Jingguo)
　蔣經國
Chiang Kai-shek (Jiang Jieshi) 蔣介石
chongjun 充軍
chouchong 臭蟲
chulu 出路
chushen lun 出身論
Cixi 慈禧

da dui 大隊
da gui hui 打鬼會
da hu hui 打虎會
da laogai 大勞改
da lun 大輪
da qiang 大牆
da qiang wenxue 大牆文學
da qiang wenxue zhi fu 大牆文學之父
da qiang wenxue zhi shu 大牆文學
　之叔
Dahuolun 大火輪
dai gong 怠工
Dai Qing 戴晴
daibu zheng 逮捕證
daihao 代號
daijia shizhong 戴枷示眾
dang'an 檔案
Dangdai 當代
Delingha 德令哈
Deng Xiaoping 鄧小平
Deng-Jiang 鄧江
dengji shehui 等級社會
Di Renjie 狄仁傑
diangun 電棍
dianji jinggun 電擊警棍
diao ji zhua 吊雞爪
diqiu xiuli gong 地球修理工
Dong Biwu 董必武

Dongbei 東北
douzheng 鬥爭
Douzheng 鬥爭
Duan Xiaolou 段小樓
dui 隊
duizhang 隊長
dunxia 蹲下

egui 餓鬼
er jin gong 二進宮
er laogai 二勞改
erdeng gongmin 二等公民
Erlitou 二里頭
ermu 耳目

falü de shouxu 法律的手續
Falun Gong 法輪功
fan 犯
fan gaizao jianzi 反改造尖子
Fan Hanru 范漢儒
fan'geming 反革命
fan'geming fenzi 反革命份子
fanren 犯人
fanren de jiaoyu gaizao jiguan 犯人
　的教育改造機關
fansi 反思
fanxing yuan 反省院
fanxinghao 反省號
fapei 發配
faxisi jizhongying 法西斯集中營
fei 匪
fei wo 非我
feibang 匪幫
feiliao 廢料
fen dui 分隊
Feng Xuefeng 馮雪峰
foye 佛爺
fu qiang 富強

fucong lingdao 服從領導

Fujian 福建

Fushun 撫順

fuzhong 浮腫

gaige 改革

gaiguo zixin 改過自新

gaizao 改造

gaizao diyi, shengchan di'er 改造第
　一，生產第二

gaizao fanren 改造犯人

gaizao qingnian zhi sixiang 改造青
　年之思想

gaizao shijie de zeren 改造世界的
　責任

gan nu er bu gan yan 敢怒而不敢言

ganhua 感化

ganhua gun 感化棍

ganqing 感情

Gansu 甘肅

geming rendaozhuyi 革命人道主義

getihu 個體戶

gong nong bing 工農兵

Gong'an bu 公安部

Gong'an ju 公安局

Gongchandang 共產黨

Gongchangling laogai dui 弓長嶺
　勞改隊

gongxing 宮刑

gongzuo danwei 工作單位

Gu Tiancheng 顧天成

guanfan 慣犯

Guangdong 廣東

guangming de weiba 光明的尾巴

Guangzhou 廣州

guanxi 關係

"Guanyu jinyibu jiaqiang jianyu
　guanli he laodong jiaoyang

gongzuo de tongzhi" 關於進一
步加強監獄管理和勞動教養工
作的通知

gunzi 棍子

guojia de zhuren 國家的主人

Guomindang 國民黨

Hai-Lu-Feng 海陸豐

Hainan 海南

Han 漢

Han Dajun 韓大鈞

Han Dongfang 韓東方

Hangzhou 杭州

hao 號

haozi 號子

He Dana 何大拿

He Qixiong 何其雄

Hebei 河北

Heihu 黑虎

Heilongjiang 黑龍江

Hekou 河口

Henan 河南

Hong Xianheng 洪憲衡

Hongse Zhonghua 紅色中華

"Houji" 後記

Hu Jintao 胡錦濤

Hu Yuyin 胡玉音

Hua Guofeng 華國鋒

Huang tudi 黃土地

Huang Xiang 黃翔

Huangpu 黃埔

huichong 蛔蟲

Hunan 湖南

huoche 火車

Ji suo bu yu wu shi yu ren 己所不
　欲勿施于人

jia xing 加刑

jiancha guan 檢察官

jianju 檢舉

Jiang Baochen 姜葆琛

Jiang Jieshi 蔣介石

Jiang Jingguo 蔣經國

Jiang Zemin 江澤民

Jiang Zhenfang 蔣真芳

Jiangxi 江西

jiantao 檢討

jianxing 減刑

jianyu 監獄

jianyu ren 監獄人

jianyu zhidu 監獄制度

jianzheng 見證

jiao pengyou 交朋友

jiao xin 交心

jiaohua 教化

jiaoxun 教訓

jiazhang 家長

jiazu 夾足

jiba 雞巴

ji'e houyizheng 飢餓後遺症

jiefa 揭發

jieji shehui 階級社會

jiji fenzi 積極分子

jiji xingdong 積極行動

jijian 雞姦

Jilin 吉林

jilu 記錄

jin 斤

Jin-Sui bianqu 晉綏邊區

jinbishi 禁閉室

Jingtan fengyun 警壇風雲

jinqu 禁區

jiu er bu wen qi chou 久而不聞其臭

jiuye 就業

jiuye renyuan 就業人員

jizhongying 集中營

juedui fucong 絕對服從

jueshi 絕食

juliu zheng 拘留證

jumin weiyuanhui 居民委員會

junshi fating 軍事法庭

Junzi bu qi 君子不器

kaifang 開放

Kaifeng 開封

Kaiyuan 開原

Kang Sheng 康生

kanshou suo 看守所

kaolong zhengfu 靠攏政府

kong xue 控血

Kulian 苦戀

kugong 苦工

kugong dui 苦工隊

Kuomintang (Guomindang) 國民黨

laji xiang 垃圾箱

Lao Er 老二

lao mao 老帽

lao shi fan 勞釋犯

laocan dui 老殘隊

laocheng ying 勞城營

laodong gaizao 勞動改造

Laodong gaizao fadian 勞動改造法典

laodong gaizao guanjiao shengchan
    dui 勞動改造管教生產隊

laodong gaizao zhidu 勞動改造制度

laodong ganhua 勞動感化

laodong ganhua yuan 勞動感化院

laodong jiaoyang 勞動教養

laodong jiaoyang suo 勞動教養所

laofang 牢房

laogai 勞改

laogai gan jing 勞改幹警

laogai dui 勞改隊

laogai fan 勞改犯

laogai houyizheng 勞改後遺症

Laogai ju 勞改局

laogai shifang fan 勞改釋放犯

laogai ying 勞改營

laohao 老號

laohu deng 老虎凳

laojiao 勞教

laojiao dui 勞教隊

laojiao suo 勞教所

laotou 牢頭

laoyi dui 勞役隊

leifan 累犯

leizi 雷子

li chang 離場

Li Cuicui 李翠翠

li gong 立功

Li Jiulian 李九蓮

Li Wangyang 李旺陽

Li Weihan 李維漢

Li Yuegai 李曰垓

Li Zhiying 李志英

lian wo duan 連窩端

Liang Botai 梁伯台

Liang Qichao 梁啓超

Liaoning 遼寧

Ligong shuzui 立功贖罪

Lin 林

Lin Chong 林沖

lingdao 領導

Lingshou 靈壽

liu 流

Liu Feng 劉風

Liu Jun 劉俊

Liu Lu 劉露

Liu Shaoqi 劉少奇

Liu Shaotang 劉紹棠

liuchang jiuye 留場就業

liufang 流放

liuhao 溜號

liumang 流氓

Lu Buqing 陸步青

Lü dao 綠島

Lü Ying 呂熒

Luo Mai 羅邁

Luo Ruiqing 羅瑞卿

Luo Xinmin 駱新民

mangye 氓爺

mangliu 盲流

Mao 毛

Mao Zedong 毛澤東

mao'er 冒兒

"Meng-Jiang nü" 孟姜女

Miao 苗

Ming 明

mingling 命令

mofan 模範

Nanchang 南昌

nanhao 男號

Nanjing 南京

neibu 內部

Nenjiang 嫩江

Ni lai shun shou 逆來順受

Ningxia 寧夏

nongchang 農場

nongmin 農民

nühao 女號

Pailou 牌樓

Pei Lianzhen 裴連振

peijun 配軍

Peng Pai 彭湃

Peng Zhen 彭真
pidou hui 批鬥會
pingfan 平反
pintie hua 拼貼畫
pipan 批判
pohuai fenzi 破坏份子
Puyi 溥儀

qiang 牆
qiang lao 強勞
qiangjiu yundong 搶救運動
qiangpo 強迫
qiangpo laodong 強迫勞動
qiangzhi laodong 強制勞動
Qianlong 乾隆
Qiao Anping 喬安萍
Qin 秦
Qin Shi Huangdi 秦始皇帝
"Qin Shi Huang benji" 秦始皇本紀
Qin Shutian 秦書田
Qincheng 秦城
Qing 清
Qinghai 青海
Qinghe 清河
Qinghe guan xun dui 清河管訓隊
Qinghe xunlian da dui 清河訓練大隊
qingxing jiao qing 情形較輕

ren zui 認罪
renmin 人民
renmin dang 人民黨
Renmin wuzhuang jingcha 人民武裝
    警察
Ruijin 瑞金

san jin gong 三進宮
sanlei renyuan 三類人員
Sanzhong quanhui 三中全會

sha ji jing hou 殺雞儆猴
Shaan-Gan-Ning 陝甘寧
Shaanxi 陝西
Shang 商
Shang Yang 商鞅
Shangdi 上帝
Shangrao 上饒
Shangyangbao 尚陽堡
shao shuohua 少說話
shehui zhazi 社會渣滓
shehuizhuyi rendaozhuyi 社會主義
    人道主義
shengchan 生產
shenghuo jiantao hui 生活檢討會
Shenyang 瀋陽
Shenzhen 深圳
Shi Zai 石在
shi zhong 示眾
shou zhongshi de 受重視的
shourong jiancha 收容檢查
shourong suo 收容所
Shu jing 書經
shua si gou 耍死狗
shuang laogai 雙勞改
Shuihu zhuan 水滸傳
Shuofang 朔方
si chuai 死揣
Sichuan 四川
Sifa bu 司法部
Sifa ting 司法廳
sige jianchi 四個堅持
silu yitiao 死路一條
sixiang 思想
Song 宋
Song Jiang 宋江
soucha 搜查
su fan 肅反

Sui Yangdi 隋煬帝
Sulian dage 蘇聯大哥
Sun Li 孫犁
Suo Hongyi 索泓一
suqing fan'geming 肅清反革命
Suzhou 蘇州

taidu 態度
Taiping 太平
tanbai cong kuan, kangju cong yan
　坦白從寬抗拒從嚴
Tang 唐
Tang lü 唐律
tangwei 堂威
tanke 坦克
Tao Yingying 陶瑩瑩
taohao 逃號
taopao 逃跑
taopao zhuanjia 逃跑專家
Tian Faqing 田發青
Tiananmen 天安門
Tianjin 天津
"Tiaochu laotao, keyi qiuxin" 跳出
　老套，刻意求新
tie menzi che 鐵悶子車
tie zhuo 鐵鐲
tifa 提法
Tilanqiao 提籃橋
tinghua 聽話
tonghao 同號
tongxue 同學
tongyi zhanxian 統一戰線
tongzhan 統戰
tou ren 頭人
tounao jiandan de qunmeng 頭腦
　簡單的群氓
tu 徒

tu piao 禿瓢
tu xing 土刑
Tuanhe 團河
tuanjie 團結
Tucheng 土城
Tucheng shourong suo 土城收容所
tui tu piao 推禿瓢
tuihua 退化
tuo kuzi ge jiba 脫褲子割雞巴
tuo kuzi ge weiba 脫褲子割尾巴
tuowang shi jiegou 拖网式結構
tuxing 徒刑
tuyi 徒役

waibin zhibu 外賓止步
Wang Fuhai 王富海
Wang Jingwei 汪精衛
Wang Juntao 王軍濤
Wangwu 王武
weiba 尾巴
weida de lingxiu 偉大的領袖
weihai guojia anquan 危害國家
　安全
wenzi yu 文字獄
wotou 窩頭
wu jin qi yong 物盡其用
Wu Song 武松
wu xing 五刑
Wu Zhaoqian 吳兆騫
Wuwei 武威

Xia 夏
Xiamen 廈門
xian pan hou shen 先判後審
xiang gongnongbing xuexi 向工農
　兵學習
Xiang Yu 項羽

xiangyue 鄉約

xiao 孝

xiao dui 小隊

xiao gui 小鬼

Xiao Qian 蕭乾

xiao zu 小組

xiao zuzhang 小組長

xiaohao 小號

xin min 新民

Xing Yixun 邢益勛

Xingkaihu 興凱湖

xing man fanren 刑滿犯人

xingman shifang qiangzhixing
    liuchang jiuye 刑滿釋放強制性
    留場就業

xing man shifang renyuan 刑滿釋
    放人員

xingshi fan 刑事犯

Xingshi yinyuan zhuan 醒世姻緣傳

xinhao 新號

Xinjiang 新疆

Xinjiang shengchan jianshe bingtuan
    新疆生產建設兵團

xinli jianshe 心理建設

xinli xidi 心理洗滌

xinren 新人

xiu diqiu 修地球

xiu er cheng nu 羞而成怒

xiuli diqiu 修理地球

Xu Can 徐燦

Xu Lingjun 許靈均

Xu Xuan 許宣

xuanchuan 宣傳

xuetong lun 血統論

xuexi 學習

xuexi ban 學習班

xuexihao 學習號

xunhua 馴化

Ya'an 雅安

yamen 衙門

yan da 嚴打

Yan'an 延安

Yang Liming 楊黎明

Yang Ya 楊亞

yang ya 佯啞

yangge 秧歌

yanguanhao 嚴管號

yangwei 陽萎

Yangzi 揚子

yaoyi 徭役

Ye Tao 葉濤

yi 役

yi qiong er bai 一窮二白

yiba 尾巴

yiken 移墾

ying 營

Ying Mulan 英木蘭

yinyang ren 陰陽人

yong mu daozi sha ren 用木刀子
    殺人

youyong zhi cai 有用之才

Yu Luoke 遇羅克

yu min zhengce 愚民政策

yuan 元

Yuan Shikai 袁世凱

yuba 獄霸

Yunnan 雲南

Yuzhong shouji 獄中手記

zhai mao youpai 摘帽右派

zhan long 站籠

Zhang Hu 張滬

Zhang Longxi 章龍喜

Zhang Yonglin 章永璘

Zhang Zaixuan 張載軒

Zhang Zhihua 張志華

zhanshu 戰術

Zhao Fugui zixin 趙富貴自新

zhaoxiang 照相

Zheng Guangdi 鄭光第

Zheng Kunshan 鄭昆山

zhengfeng 整風

zhengwei 政委

zhenya fan'geming 鎮壓反革命

zhidaoyuan 指導員

zhiduizhang 支隊長

zhishi fenzi 知識份子

zhong dui 中隊

Zhong Haiyuan 鍾海源

zhong nong 中農

zhongdian renkou 重點人口

Zhongguo gongchandang 中國共產黨

Zhonghua renmin gongheguo jianyu fa 中華人民共和國監獄法

Zhongnanhai 中南海

Zhou 周

Zhou Enlai 周恩來

Zhou Jialiang 周家良

Zhou Zhiming 周志明

Zhu De 朱德

Zhu Xi 朱熹

Zhuang Zi 莊子

zhuang bing 裝病

zhuangjiaren 莊稼人

zhuanzheng 專政

zhuozi 鐲子

zi jiu 自救

zi shang zi can 自傷自殘

ziran zaihai 自然災害

zixin 自新

"Zixu" 自序

zu 組

zuifan 罪犯

zuo feiji 坐飛機

zuo penqi shi 坐噴氣式

zuzhang 組長

Index

Compositor:	Integrated Composition Systems
Text:	10/13 Galliard
Display:	Galliard